A History of Armenia

Vahan M. Kurkjian

Table of Contents

Acknowledgment

I am ever indebted to the Armenian General Benevolent Union for undertaking the publication of this book through a grant from its Golden Jubilee Cultural Program Fund.

I deeply appreciate the generous attitude of Mr. H. Thorossian of Paris, author of "A History of Armenian Literature" in French, who authorized me to use his work as a source for the Chapter on Armenian literature of this work.

I am grateful to Mr. Alvin F. Harlow for his professional services for twenty-five years and for his deep interest in his collaboration.

I owe gratitude to the Oriental Institute of Chicago University for its kind permission to reproduce some of the illustrations from Hans Henning's volume on "Exploration in Hittite Asia Minor."

I also express gratitude to Mr. K. Guiragossian, Executive Director of the Armenian General Benevolent Union, for his scholarly advice and tireless efforts for making possible the publication of my manuscript.

I owe similar pleasant obligation to Mr. Mihrtad Tiryakian, an erudite scholar on history and philology. He rendered me valuable service in editing the manuscript, preparing the index, reading the proofs and placing the illustrations in their proper settings.

I appreciate the kindness of the Bingham Photo-Engraving Company, the Harding Photo-Engraving Company and the Rembrandt Photo-Engraving Company, all of New York, for preparing the engravings in my book free of charge.

I also wish to express my thanks to Mr. M. Sarkisian and much regretted late Ardavazt Koumjian for their efforts in selecting, sorting and preparing the illustrations used in this book.

The Author

Preface

A pioneer American statesman, Patrick Henry, once said: "I know of no means of judging the future but by the past." A nation interested in the past can do much to insure its own preservation. A modern philosopher, Santayana, says, "Those who cannot remember the past are condemned to repeat it;" and as development and change are inevitable in the world as a whole, the lessons drawn from history are a necessity to the perpetuation of national existence.

Armenia, a scion of the Aryan stock, has for four millenniums and more, through two or three revivals and through some of the most devastating misfortunes that ever beset a people, been an advanced post of civilization. It is one of the most ancient of nations. Its leaders — good, bad and indifferent — often made great and shattering mistakes and deplorable bargains with other rulers and oppressors, but the bravery and devotion of its people never faltered. At times it attained a force and splendor rivalling that of the great Eastern empires, at other times it was battered and pushed around by whatever ruthless power had fought its way up to the top of the oriental ferment. In its Urartean age (the name given it by the Assyrians), it fought Assyria and Babylon to a standstill and feared nobody. Then followed a decline, and it became by turns a Persian satrapy, a temporary though unconquered fief of Alexander the Great, a dependency of the Seleucidae, and then once more reached a new peak as an empire under Tigran the Great (95-55 B.C.). And so the story goes.

Written history regarding the beginnings of Armenia is fragmentary and often unreliable. The earliest chronicles were in Greek and Syriac, and were written by Agathangelos, Zenob of Glak and Phaustus Puzant. A part of the history by Mar Apas Katina (one of the sources of Khorenatsi), written originally in Chaldean — not Khaldi — was translated into Greek by order of Alexander the Great. The invention of the Armenian alphabet and the translation of the Bible into Armenian in 432, heralding its Golden Age of literature, produced a legion of historians, who too often, however, accepted legend for history.

Coming down to modern times, a step toward methodical history was taken by the Mekhitarist Fathers of Venice. The three volumes of Armenian history by Fr. Michayel Tchamtchian, whose recital begins with 1784 B.C., are a welcome contribution. To him we owe the identification of a 2107-year line of rulers called "Haigazants," from Haig, legendary founder of the nation, to Vahé, who fell in battle against Alexander the Great. To these he added succeeding dynasties — Arsakhuni, Bagratuni and Roupinian.

A fine Armenian history up to the 11th century is that of Kevork Aslan (1928). As a masterly work on the pre-Christian era, we have the "Critical History of the Cuneiform Period of Armenia," by Astig Katchatrian (1933). Covering 2400 years — 3000 to 600 B.C. — it is rich in geographic and ethnographic data. The History of Armenia from the tenth to the sixth century B.C., by Nicolas Adontz, covers the period of Urartu and Nairi. René Grousset, who wrote its preface, declared that Adontz had established a sound continuity between pre-Armenian Armenia and "Haigian" Armenia. He praised the land as the citadel of a "grand race," the "cradle of an original civilization." Other foreign Armenologists and Orientalists are Layard, Kretschmer, Rawlinson, Maspero, Lehmann-Haupt, Lynch, Sayce, Macler, Gelzer, Marquart, Gutschmid, and Jacques de Morgan. Victor Langlois translated the early chroniclers from Armenian into French. Dulaurier translated the Armenian and other historians of the Crusaders.

Even today, regrettably enough, one dare not tell in detail the whole pitiful story of Armenia's wrongs. Fate has been parsimonious towards the Armenians. The great Christian powers have expressed sympathy for them, but went no further. The Treaty of Sèvres in 1920, which promised them a homeland, in fact, decreed an Armenian state, was ignored by Europe; and three years later, meeting at Lausanne, the great powers admitted, "We can do nothing."

James Viscount Bryce, historian and diplomat, British Ambassador to the United States, said of Armenia in 1916:

> "Those who have learnt what the Armenian race has shown itself capable of doing in the field of art and literature, and who have learnt from history how true it has been to the Christian faith, and how tenacious of its national life, will hope that the time has now at last come when it will be delivered from the load of brutal tyranny that has so long cramped its energies, and allowed to take its place among the free and progressive peoples of the world. It is the only one of the native races of western Asia that is capable of restoring productive industry and assured prosperity to those now-desolated regions that were the earliest homes of civilization."

Lord Bryce's hopes were not to be fulfilled; worse was still in store for Armenia. But it was not crushed. Braced by the never-failing sympathy of its children all over the world, it is maintaining its entity in a part of the homeland. Without attempting to grope for the unpredictable, may I close this preface by a comment from an eminent anthropologist and Orientalist, Professor von Luschan:

> "Homogeneous in language, in religion and physical type, the Armenians may serve as an exemplar. The homogeneity of this people, which is not found in equal or similar degree in any other civilized nation, is interesting as proving that the striking geographical, linguistic and religious isolation of Armenia during its development and florescence has consolidated the type to such an extent that even today, many centuries after the fall of the kingdom it continues almost entirely uniform."

Vahan M. Kurkjian

New York, 1957

Chapter I
The Land

Geography, Generalities

No area on the globe is so fascinating to present-day scholars as the Near East; fascinating because it was the cradle of some of the oldest of civilizations, many of which are now but little more than names to us. In ancient times this part of western Asia, mostly mountainous, with fertile uplands and valleys, was a scene of frequent bloody turmoil in one part and another, being overrun by foreign invaders. Nations, kingdoms rose and fell, sometimes through centuries of struggle. Throughout all this, the most persistent, and longest lived of these nations has been the Armenian.

The story of Armenia is fragmentary and spiced with legend. Up to 500 B.C., it may be divided into the pre-Urartean era, extending roughly from 1500 B.C. to about 858 B.C., and the period of the Urartean Empire, from that date to 518 B.C.

Stone-age remnants found in Armenia prove that the country has been inhabited from a time far back beyond human records. Even in ages so long ago that Mesopotamia was still under water, the Armenian tableland was occupied by people who gradually moved down to such parts of the plain as became habitable with the recession of the waters. The biblical story of the Flood and the spread of mankind to the plains of Shinar is therefore based upon a telescoping of eons of history into a few weeks. True, the Ararat group of mountains was at one time surrounded by water, but it stood that way for ages instead of days, as the old Hebrew legends relate.

It has long been the notion among many Christians that Noah's Ark came to rest as the Flood subsided upon the great peak known as Mount Ararat; this assumption is based upon an erroneous reading of the 4th verse of the VIIIth chapter of Genesis. That verse does not say that the Ark landed upon Mount Ararat, but upon "the mountains of Ararat." Now, Ararat was the Hebrew version of the name, not of the mountain but of the country around it, the old Armenian homeland, whose name at other times and in other tongues appears variously as Erirath, Urartu, etc. The Prophet Jeremiah (LI, 27), writing in 600 B.C., speaks of "the kingdom of Ararat," which kingdom at that time called itself Urartu. Hence the "Mountains of Ararat" may mean any part of the tangled mountain mass of that country. The Armenians never called the colossus of the range, Ararat; to them that mighty double peak was "Massis." Great Ararat or Massis is some 17,000 feet above the sea; Lesser Ararat is 12,840 feet. The great mountain has been chiseled and moulded by earthquakes. As late as July 2, 1840, the old volcano within, long quiescent, stirred again, shook itself, and a great slice of it thundered down in an avalanche, burying a chapel, a convent and a village of 300 families.

The boundaries of Armenia have been frequently altered by conquest and defeat. At times, its people ruled the entire Armenian plateau; at other times they have been compressed within the central part of that tableland. Roughly speaking, historic Armenia — an area of 150,000 square miles — was bounded by Iberia (Georgia) on the north, by Caucasian Albania (present Azerbaijan) on the north-east, by Persia on the east, by Mesopotamian lands on the south, and by Pontus, Cappadocia and Cilicia on the west. Her geographical position made Armenia an economic and political bridge between East and West, over which passed trade caravans from India and Central Asia to the West and vice versa, and which for centuries was an arena for military operations.

The Armenian table-land is very rugged. Its numerous mountain clusters are cleft and separated by gorges and great river valleys. Mount Massis or Ararat, whose snowcapped summit was in ancient times thought to be the abode of terrible genii, even as Olympus was the seat of the Greek gods, is the center of the labyrinth. Extending westward therefrom, the chain divides Armenia into northern and southern sections. Near the center, two great rivers have their sources — the Arax, which flows eastward to the Caspian Sea, and the Aradzani (Murad-tchai), the main branch of the Euphrates, which at first flows westward, then describes a vast loop, almost encircling the watershed of its great sister, the Tigris, before joining it in lower Mesopotamia.

A short distance southwest of Massis lie the Aladagh (Dzaghgantz) Mountains, with one peak rising to 11,500 feet, their slopes covered with pasturage. South of the Armenian plateau is another range, the many-branched Taurus, extending westward and forming the natural frontier between Armenia and northern Mesopotamia. Further southeast, on the southern edge of historic Armenia, lie the Gorduq Mountains, from which flows the western branch (Bohtan-Su) of the Tigris. The main stream and feeders of the western Tigris emerge from the Taurus heights, which divide this watershed from that of the Aradzani.

The mountains of Dévé-Boynu, bordering the Erzerum table-land on the east, lie northeast of the sources of the Arax and south of the mountainous region of Taiq. The Aragadz (Alagöz) and Ara Mountains, looking southward from present-day Soviet Armenia towards Massis and the Arax Valley, border the great Ararat plain, more than 13,000 feet above sea-level, whose Alpine pastures and copious waterage have for centuries fostered extensive cattle-breeding, and whose coolness made it a pleasant summer resort for people from the torrid lower plains. Northeast of Aragadz lie the rich grazing lands of Dzaghgouniatz. The eastern fringes of the Pambak Mountains touch the Lake of Sevan, which is still further enclosed by the mountains of Gunel-dara and Areguni. To the south are the high peaks of Zankezur-Daralagiaz, and still further southeast the mountains of Tchavendour, with forest-covered slopes and upland pastures. Parallel with the Zankezur range, trending north and south, are the mountains of Qarabagh, which slope southward, to the Plain Qarabagh, or steppe of Mil.

Another river, the Jorokh, rising in the Ardaban Mountains near Erzerum, meanders northward to the Black Sea. Skirting far northern Armenia, the Kur River, with many tributaries, flows southeastward to join the Arax just before it enters the Caspian. All Armenian rivers, because of the rough terrain and steep descents, offer unusual opportunities for the development of hydro-electric power.

The three great lakes of historic Armenia, often called seas, are Sevan, Van and Urmia. The freshwater Sevan, known also as Kegham, is more than 6,500 feet above sea level and is 49 miles long. It is fed by some thirty rivers and small streams, and is drained by the cascading River Zanku, which flows into the Arax. Lake Sevan is rich in fish, the trout and ishkhanatzug or prince-fish being especially noted. There is an island in the lake with an ancient church upon it.

The lake of Van is fed by the streams Khoshab, Bergri and Marmet, but has no known outlet. The water is heavy with saltpetre and alkalies, yet there is a fish living in it known as darekh. The lake has four islands, one of which, Aghtamar, is noted for its architectural monuments, including a magnificent church and an ancient "palace."

Largest of the three is the Lake of Urmia or Kaputan Sea, now in Persia, 85 miles long and 4,500 feet above sea-level, and so alkaline that no animal life can exist in it. It has many small islands.

The great plain of Ararat, traversed by the Arax, surrounded by mountains and abundantly watered, has been, since the earliest days of history, the most thickly populated portion of the Armenian table-land. The Sardarabat and Erevan districts are parts of that plain. The mountain ranges bordering the plateau cut off some of the humid winds from the Black and Caspian Seas, and tend to make the atmosphere dry and clear. The abundance of streams flowing from the heights atones for this dryness. The rugged terrain of Armenia and its many levels of altitude cause great diversities of climate in various regions. The famous localities known as the Valley of Alashkert (Bagrevand) and the Plain of Mush (Taron), both watered by the Eastern Euphrates or Aradzani, have played the same economic role in the life of southern Armenia as the Plain of Ararat in the northern central section.

Field Crops and Fruits

In the southern portions, at the lower altitudes, climatic conditions, aided by artificial irrigation, permit the cultivation of semi-tropical crops such as cotton and tobacco. In the same lowland zone grains and rice also thrive, as well as many kinds of fruit. The fine grapes, apricots and peaches of Armenia were famous from very early times. The cultivation of fruit is being extended to the mountain slopes, up to 4,000 feet elevation; some pears and apples are grown at still higher altitudes. Wheat is produced on plateaux, even at altitudes of 4,500 to 7,000 feet. Mutilated and neglected for centuries by war and foreign invasion, the forests of Armenia are sparse and poor, except in the northeastern districts, where they are luxuriant.

Livestock

The natural aspect of the country is favorable to cattle-breeding. In addition to the horned animals, large and small, an important stock is horses, for which Armenia has been particularly distinguished in the past. The mountains and plains abound in game, both furred and feathered; deer, antelope, wild sheep, partridge, ducks, quail, etc. Among wild predatory animals the fox, wolf, bear and hyena are still present.

The mountains are rich in minerals. Since the dawn of history they have been renowned for their copper, tin, iron and varicolored metals. Excavations within the ancient Armenian area have yielded many objects of bronze and iron, dating from remote antiquity. In the modern Gumush-Khana and Alaverdi regions in the northwestern mountains, there were mines of gold, silver and copper. The mining industry has been greatly developed since the establishment of the Soviet regime in Armenia. New mines of valuable metals have been discovered in Zanke-Sur, Meghri and Lori, which, together with the various kinds of marble, granite, tufa, basalt, bemza, etc., are being exploited.

Armenia also has many mineral waters. There are several carbonic acid springs in the watershed of the Hradzan (Zanku) River, among which is the water of Arzni, noted for its curative qualities. Fully as renowned are the hot sulphur springs of Diadin and Jermuk (Isti Su). In the densely wooded dale of Dilijan there are carbonic-alkaline springs. Zanke-Sur and several other localities, also, have similar mineral waters.

Chapter II
Before the Dawn

Palaeolithic Age

The manufacture and use of implements and weapons have vital significance as a measure of the development of primitive man. For hundreds of thousands of years before written history began, these things were made of stone — with some additions of bone and wood in the later periods. This long span of man's existence, whose duration is estimated at anywhere from 500,000 to 1,500,000 years, is known as the Stone Age, and has by various scholars been separated into two or three epochs. An early period of manufacture has been designated by some as the Eolithic, though others include it in the Palaeolithic Age. The Eolithic antedates the Quaternary geological age; the Palaeolithic extends through the whole of the glacial and post-glacial epochs. During this time, man's tools and weapons were fashioned from flint.

Neolithic Age

Following the Palaeolithic era came the Neolithic, when the tools and weapons were more carefully made, sometimes even polished, and when stones other than flint were used, including obsidian or volcanic glass. Bone and wood also came into use, and towards the close of the period, crude carving and fresco, or wall pictures began to be done. Man, who had lived mostly in caves and subsisted on fruit, grain and raw meat, now discovered how to produce fire, a revolutionary milestone of progress in the story of mankind. The arrow and the spear had come into use, and trees began to be felled with axes of sharpened stone, for the construction of boats and huts. Family life was developing, and permanent dwelling places began to be adopted, but as yet there was no private ownership of land. Wild beasts were being domesticated, cattle-breeding and the cultivation of land for agriculture began. Villages came into existence, and the barter of goods took form.

What little we know of these far-away ages has been laboriously worked out through a study of the rarely occasional ruin, village site, human bone, tool, fragment, carving or wall painting discovered beneath the earth or in caves. Findings in various parts of Armenia apparently prove that Neolithic and even Palaeolithic man lived there.

Tools and Implements

The discovery of the production of fire eventually led to the working of the first metals known, copper and tin. The blending of these two produced bronze and ushered in a new area which we call the Bronze Age. As nearly as can be ascertained, the Neolithic Age began in Europe some 10,000 to 15,000 years ago, the Bronze in various parts of Europe from 2000 to 3500 B.C., and the Iron Age, which succeeded it, about 1000 B.C. In western Asia and Egypt, the dates for these eras are earlier.

The increase in the kinds of tools and implements and the appearance of new modes of labor marked a slow differentiation of man's functions from those of woman — though women were doing many things which later came into the province of man; for example, scratching the soil with pointed sticks for the sowing of grain, and aiding in the domestication of beasts — first the dog, then the goat, sheep, hog and cow. Near the close of the Neolithic Era, woman is the central figure in the family, caring for the children and the habitation, gathering fruits, storing foodstuffs, doing such cooking as was done and looking after the domestic animals.

Religious conceptions, the worship of spirits, the disposal of the dead by burning or burying, all these slowly took shape in the same epoch, while the ideas of private or collective ownership of land were still nonexistent. All the characteristics of the Neolithic Era were also those of the primeval inhabitants of the Armenian table-land.

Ancestral Relics in Graves

The first excavations in Armenia, undertaken by Russian savants in 1876, brought to light a burial-ground near Dilijan in which were 76 prehistoric graves. Jacques de Morgan in 1887-89 unearthed 576 graves around Alaverdi and Akhatala, on the Tiflis-Alexandropol railway line. Later on, 300 more were discovered by V. Belck near Elisavetpol (Gandzak), and yet others were excavated by Lalayan (second in importance only to de Morgan's) and Ivanovski. In Turkish Armenia only one tumulus, that of Shamiramalti, near the fort of Van, has been studied so far. But many ancient arms and implements have been discovered, in various places on the plains and slopes, in the Valleys of Lori, on the shores of the Lakes of Sevan and Van, in the salt mines of Koghb (Kulp) and along the Aradzani and upper Tigris Rivers. The oldest Neolithic relics so far found in Soviet Armenia are large stone axes, with grooves which show that the handles were attached by lashings. In Armavir, Vagharshapat and elsewhere, Neolithic weapons, knives, axes, hammers, mortars for grinding grains, saw, makhats (large needles for coarse sewing), awls, made of stone, obsidian or bone, and pottery, some of it with geometrical ornamentation, have been found, as well as traces of human habitations, cremations or other mortuary disposals, fossils of domestic animals, such as sheep, goats and dogs, and remains of wheat and barley.

One human skeleton found on the bank of the river Zanku, with a flint implement beside it, is believed to be that of a man of the Palaeolithic Age. Other excavations of small circular hillocks — at Shresh, near Etchmiadzin and at Eylar, near Erevan — underneath which are graves, usually covered with a slab, have yielded many Neolithic relics. Nearby were cinder beds with objects of stone, funeral urns (proofs of the practice of cremation) and piles of human bones.

Huge stone placements, presumably Neolithic, are numerous in Armenia — dolmens (large unhewn stones resting on two or more smaller ones), menhirs (standing stones), cromlechs (stone circles), and cyclopean walls. The region of Aragadz Mountain is a natural museum of archaeology; and the extensive plains around the towns of Oshakan, Parbi, Amberd and Aghtz, as well as near Shusha and Sisian, are dotted with hundreds of Neolithic monuments.

In megalithic fields on higher levels are found constructions in huge blocks, composed of a number of concentric walls of decreasing heights. Those at Kosh and Aghavnatun, which are the best preserved, might have served either as forts or enclosures of a sanctuary. The wall near Daylakla on a small tributary of the River Arax, is of the same type, though inside were circular or oddly-shaped rooms, walled with smaller stones, which might have been dwelling places roofed with large slabs.

Almost all the excavated graves belong to Metallic eras later than the Neolithic, probably to the later years of the Bronze Age. They are all of similar construction, a sort of box, with four large slabs as partitions and two more as covers, placed together without mortar — a kind of dolmen.

In some tombs the dead are in large jars, usually sitting or squatting, though in some cases two connected jars were used, the limbs being in one, the rest of the skeleton in the other. Objects found with the dead comprised ornaments, tools, broken pottery and weapons such as daggers, swords, lances, axes, bows and arrows. Of 76 daggers found in one cemetery, seven were of iron, the remainder of bronze. A few club-heads of stone were found, one dented ring, which was probably used in boxing, and smaller rings believed to have been parts of a lasso, used either in hunting or domestication of animals.

Ornamental Work

The tools commonly found were knives, straight or curved, the blades of bronze or iron, the handles of bone, wood or metal. There were combs and hones of bronze or gold, adorned with dangling bronze rings. Women's tombs contained iron or bone needles, long and short, as well as bronze tweezers, bronze hooks and forks. As for jewelry, there were earrings of bronze, rarely of silver, sometimes hung with beads of carnelian, glass, porcelain, quartz, agate or alousite. Necklaces usually carried from 40 to 80 pearls. Bracelets, found in large numbers, are of bronze, silver, iron, lead and various beads. They were worn on the upper arm, forearm or ankle, and served not only as jewelry but as currency. Bronze pins sometimes had small heads, some large and heavy, shaped like a bird. Finger-rings, less common than bracelets, were found in the tombs of women, men and even children. There were rich girdles of bronze, bordered with geometric designs, the middle part engraved, often with hunting scenes or mythological pictures. One of these represents a man with an animal's head standing in a chariot drawn by two horses, in front of which an archer pursues a flock of chamois. Another belt shows an archer with a bird's head in a horse-drawn chariot, while over the horses is a scarab (beetle) flying before the arrow of a second archer. Girdle clasps or fasteners were a sort of bow of bronze wire, with a beadle-like pin thrust through an eye. Curiously enough, one such fibula unearthed is similar to that used in Armenia today to tether domestic animals in the manger. Buttons, found in large numbers, served not only to fasten the clothing but as trimmings on the dress or belt.

Ceramics

Ceramics were found in quantity in the tombs. Hand-made pottery is rudimentary. Pitchers for water or wine are spherical, with short necks and flat bottoms. Cooking vessels are also spherical. Cups are in various shapes; in one pattern, a representation of the head of a stag forms the handle. The small, deep dishes which served as oil lamps are still in use in some Armenian villages.

Among other articles discovered are bronze mirrors, chariots, threshing planks, remnants of woolen or flax stuffs, cords, ribbons and leather thongs.

Earliest Metal-Working

The question, When did metal-working begin in Armenia? cannot yet be answered. Jacques de Morgan believes that the iron industry had Armenia as its birthplace before the 20th century B.C. As bronze-working came before iron, and bronze is an alloy of tin and copper, Adontz questions the French scholar's accuracy, pointing out that tin was not found in Armenia or anywhere else in Asia Minor. It was anciently produced in China, in Drangiana (an East Persian province) and the region of the Indus River, from which sources Chaldea and Elam obtained the metal as the alloy for their bronze.

Bronze and Iron Ages

The rise of powerful civilizations took place in Mesopotamia and Egypt during the Bronze Age, and to some extent was based upon the bronze industry. In the Aegean area the Bronze Age had begun in the third millennium B.C. In Chaldea copper appears around 2500 B.C. Bronze is also known as of that time; bronze helmets, the points of lances and other arms, were common. Armenia could not have remained untouched by these cultural developments among her neighbors, and may even have been in the forefront of the movement. The main object of early Assyrian incursions into Armenia was to obtain metals. The iron-working age followed that of bronze everywhere, opening a new epoch of human progress. Its influence is noticeable in Armenia, and the transition period is well marked. Tombs whose metal contents are all of bronze are of an older epoch. In most of the cemeteries explored, both bronze and iron furniture were found, indicating the gradual advance into the Iron Age.

No trace of iron was found in the ruins of Troy. King Tiglatpalasar of Assyria (1117-1080 B.C.) does not list any iron among his Armenian booty. But a later king, Assurnazirpal (884-859), tells of carrying away from Armenia articles of iron, bronze, copper, tin, silver and gold.

The Iron Age appeared in Western Asia after the twelfth century B.C. The contents of the tombs of that era in Armenia are of two classes, some representing a geometric style of art, the others a new naturalistic trend. The bronze belts, displaying human and animal figures, are the first naturalistic experiments. Some resemblance between this style and "Hellenistic" art has been traced, setting the date of such specimens forward to the period of the kingdom of Urartu, beginning in the ninth century B.C. The bronze shields of King Rusa II of Urartu (680-645 B.C.) and of King Rusa III (605-585 B.C.), are excellent samples of this naturalistic style.

Dawn of History

With the Iron Age we enter what we may call the historic period — though the history is still considerably colored with legend, and we must even take with a grain of salt the boasting of kings in their tablets and inscriptions as to their heroic deeds and conquests. The small states of the age of Tiglatpalasar were eventually united to form the Urartuan empire of the ninth, eighth and seventh centuries before the Christian era. No tomb with a date between this and the beginning of our era has been discovered. This may be attributed to the abandonment, under the Mazdeian influence, of the practice of interment. Most of the graves that have been examined were built towards the end of the Bronze Age and have the following characteristics; as the sojourning place of the soul during the transition from earth to the beyond, the grave was a construction of large stones, set together without mortar. There were also underground houses, provided with pottery utensils in a great variety of size, form and color. The cells also contain small spoons and huge jars of black, red or gray-greenish hues. The garments of the deceased were short, bound with a belt, and included baggy, flowing trousers and leggings.

Jewelry and Weapons

Jewelry and other adornments were held in high esteem by both men and women. The body of one woman was literally covered with bijouterie — earrings, finger-rings, necklaces, bracelets on wrists and ankles and a bronze belt with pendants, one in the form of a bell, the other representing a swan. Variously shaped beads and glass trinkets, mirrors of bronze and pendants were necessary to the feminine ensemble. The tiara, a bronze band narrowed as it neared its extremities, was a headdress reserved to princely persons.

The large numbers of weapons found in graves indicate the warlike character of the population. Hunting was a common occupation. Agriculture, cattle-breeding and metallurgy were reaching a high degree of proficiency. No records of the social and political life of these ancient eras have been found, but the people were probably divided into classes and tribes, groups of which, during certain periods, were joined in federations. A lesser unit coming into being was the family.

Objects found in the tombs indicate that the dead were believed to live and to need food after they passed from this life. Huge stone figures testify to the existence of unknown religious cults in remote antiquity.

Enigmatical signs which may be a system of writing, engraved on stones discovered in the region of Garni, on the walls of a cave in the neighborhood of Talin and other places, were sculptured before the rise of the Urartean Empire, and probably contain some interesting bits of history, if they could be deciphered.

Racial Origins

Human skulls discovered in excavations and tombs may shed further light on the question of the racial origin of the people of the land. Most of the 59 skulls collected in a certain area of Russian Armenia between 1887 and 1908 had slowly dried to such a state that they fell into dust at a touch. The ones buried in sandy soil were in a better condition of preservation.

One of the classifications of human beings has to do with the shape of their skulls — the brachycephalic folk being those with most pnearly round heads, while the dolichocephalic have heads much longer than they are wide. Measurements of the discovered skulls prove that the inhabitants of Armenia in those early ages belonged to the latter category. The Italian anthropologist, Sergi, believes that the Mediterranean world had been inhabited by a dolichocephalic race, whilst Asia Minor was peopled by folk more nearly round-headed. The British scientist, W. Ripley, claims, however, that the earliest ethnic stratum in West Asia likewise belonged to the dolichocephalic type, and represented an offshoot of the Mediterranean race. He applied the same theory to the whole of Europe. It is an interesting fact that the domination of the dolichocephalics in Armenia coincides with the Bronze Age, while the succeeding period, that of Iron, is the era of dominance of the brachycephalic peoples, to which those of Nairi and Urartu belonged.

Chapter III
The Neighbors of Armenia

The Sumero-Akkadians

The Chaldeo-Elamite region had, like Egypt, been a seat of prehistoric civilization and of powerful states. Around 3500 B.C., Chaldea appears to have been already divided into two regions, that of the Sumerian race and language and that of the Semitic. The language of the former was spoken in southern Chaldean cities such as Ur, Lagash and others. The race was characterized by a round, brachycephalic skull and an eagle-beaked nose, the face and head being shaven. The Chaldean cuneiform writing may have been created for the Sumerian language. The Akkadian language, spoken in northern Chaldean cities such as Kish, Agade and Babylon, was Semitic. The profiles of the people of that area exhibited a straight nose, somewhat enlarged at its lower extremity. They were long-haired and bearded.

At the dawn of history, the civilization of these sectors was commingling, making it difficult to differentiate the two elements. The Elamites, however, retained their distinctive character. Their capital, Susa (Biblical Shushan), whose origin was far back in prehistory, steadily maintained during the fourth and third millenaries B.C., its conformity with the oldest Sumerian civilization.

Divinities

Every Chaldean city, whether Semitic or Sumerian, had as its prince or Patesi a grand priest of the local deity. Anu was the god of Heaven, Enlil of the destructive elements, Adad of the benevolent elements, Ea of the waters. Sin was the moon-god, Shamash the sun, Marduk the planet Jupiter, Ishtar a goddess of fecundity and of war, and so on. Astrology played a preponderant role in Chaldean society. Temple-observations of massive brick construction, generally pyramidal, in seven tiers or steps, were erected for the study of the course of the stars.

Commercial and Cultural Center

The fertility of the soil of Chaldea explains the wealth of the country. Irrigation canals made Chaldea a great garden, an earthly near-paradise. Agricultural prosperity brought forth industry. No other people was more inventive, especially in the arts of luxury. Their artisans produced stuffs in gorgeous colors, magnificent rugs and furniture, gold and silver articles. Their merchants transported these products by way of the Euphrates and across the desert to Armenia, Cappadocia and Syria, carrying with them also the Chaldean cuneiform writing. From the fourth to the third century B.C., their culture played almost the same role that Hellenism did in the Graeco-Roman period. Correspondence among the Mitanni, Hittite and Egyptian rulers was carried on, as clay tablets testify.

The oldest traces of this civilization, dating from 3200 to 2800 B.C., were discovered in Ur (Tell el Mugayir) by the American-British mission of Hall and Woolley. The objects found consisted of alabaster vases, jewelry (hand ornaments of Queen Shubad), statues (bull's head in gold with beard of lapis lazuli), mosaics (royal banquet with animals in tribute), reliefs on limestone (chariots drawn by asses). A form of heraldic art was established, with figures facing each other, which was transmitted to the Hittites, Assyrians, Persians and other peoples. At Tello (Lagash), cylindrical signets have been unearthed with similar representations, inspired by the Gilgamesh epic. Among them are types of monsters, such as the two-headed eagle, the winged dragon, and the Kherubim, a bull with human head.

The Babylonians

The last Sumerian empire, that of Ur, was overthrown in 235 B.C. by the Elamites from the East and the Amorites from the West. The Elamites founded a dynasty in Southern Chaldea, while the Amorites, a Semitic people from Syria, dominated the North, with Babylon as their center. One of their kings, Hammurabi (2123-2081), put an end to the Elamite dynasty of the South and founded the Babylonian Empire. The Amorites, whatever their racial origin may have been, made Semitism predominant in Chaldea. Hammurabi's reign became a continuation of the dynasty of the ancient Agade — the principal Semite land of Akkad, whose kings, Sharrukin (the ancient Sargon) and Naram-Su, subjugated all Mesopotamia. Hammurabi left to us a famous Code of Laws, engraved on a diorite (granite) stele, now in the Louvre. In the domain of literature, the Amorite period is said to have almost the same importance that the epoch of Pisitratus had for the preservation of Homeric literature. In this epoch appeared the first Semitic revision of the epic of Gilgamesh, a sort of Sumerian Hercules, son of a goddess, but a target for the wrath of another goddess Ishtar, whose love he spurned. To the same epoch also belongs the Chaldean story of the Creation and the Deluge, powerful works which have the tone of the book of Genesis. We are reminded by it of the sorrowful lyricism of the Psalms in the Chaldean litanies and in the Poem of the Suffering Just, so like to the Book of Job. This misery of man before a vengeful God, these pathetic appeals, the moral problem involved in them all, and the images of the ancient theogony, all show the affiliation of the Chaldean to the Biblical genus. Thus, the Chaldean thought, a humanism of the Orient of remotest antiquity, exercised a capital influence on the intellectual evolution of neighboring races. Likewise, Chaldean motifs inspired for many centuries the monumental art of new nations — Hittites, Assyrians, Achaemenid and Sassanid Persians.

The Assyrians

The classical epoch of Assyria is predominantly Semite, despite the fact that ethnically, it comprises other elements also — Sumerian, Mitannian, etc. The

Assyrian became a powerful military race, stronger than its cousin of Babylon. "A thick-set, muscular body, aquiline nose with fleshy nostrils, thick lips, large, bright eyes — this is how the Assyrian looks on their bas-reliefs." Harsh in war, sensual and pompous after victory, cruel to the vanquished, thus do their inscriptions reveal them to us. From the very beginning of their history about the 13th century B.C., they were a permanent military machine. The first kings of Assyria became the grand-priests of two national deities, Assur and Ishtar, the planet Venus. The Assyrian monarchy, however, never did assume a religious character, like that of Egypt. After a short period of eclipse, it conquered Damascus (732) and Babylon (728). Sargon II (722-705 B.C.), who built the palace of Khorsabad, destroyed the kingdoms of Israel and Urartu. The great king Esarhaddon (680-668) subjugated Egypt. After the destruction of Elam in 646, Assyria remained master of the Near East, from Iran to Cappadocia, from Ararat and the Caspian Sea to Egypt and the Persian Gulf. Its capital, Nineveh, became the capital of the world.

Assyrian Cruelty United Opposition

The Assyrians have been severely judged for their cruelty, which, however, unintentionally served the cause of civilization. Through blood and terror, this imperial race eventually united all the East nations under one yoke; through devastation and death it established peace from Ararat to the Nile. The short and frightful *Pax Sargonide*, so it is said, heralded the benevolent *Pax Achaemenide*. The vast political union which the Sargonidae had brought into being was not to disappear entirely. The empire which the Chaldeans, the Achaemenids, the Macedonians, the Sassanids and the Arabs, one after the other, inherited, was destined to preserve until modern times the stamp of the material civilizations of Nineveh and Babylon.

The Chaldeo-Assyrian civilization already contained almost the entire Arabo-Persian civilization in the bud. The Sargonid court, with its gorgeous embellishment, its brutality, its mixture of indolence and ferocious energy, was in itself an epitome of the Orient. The king was an army chief, not a god, as in Egypt. "The King of Legions, the great King, the powerful King, the King of the people of Assur" spent half his life on horseback or in his chariot, hunting or fighting. His people threw the lance and the arrow as their soldiers did, and then, in the hour of *hallali*, with their own hands flayed their prisoners alive, impaled them, gouged out their eyes.

The apotheosis of the Ninevite deities, associated with the Sargonid triumphs, was the apotheosis of the very race itself. Their victory over the gods of Egypt, of Judea and Urartu, became a symbol of Assyrian hegemony in the world. The temple dominated the palace; it was the ziggurat, a square tower of seven stories, each story set back from the preceding one, each one consecrated to a star. On the top of the highest level was the chapel of the divinity, Assur, the eponym of the race or Ishtar, the lady of Arbeles. Here the Sargonid kings, surrounded by their diviners and astrologers, came before their departure for hunting or war, to receive the counsel of the all-powerful gods.

16

High Culture

This ferocious people was, paradoxically enough, also a highly cultivated one. Well versed in Babylonian literature, they gathered from it and transmitted to us its priceless heritage. Assurbanipal (669-626 B.C.), their last king, collected in Nineveh an enormous library, thousands of tablets of which have been recovered and placed in the British Museum. Through it, the scientific and literary knowledge of those days, the Chaldean legends and the royal Assyrian inscriptions have reached us. The recital of the achievements of Assur-Nazir-Apal II is an impressive example. "I killed one in every two," says he. "I erected a wall in front of the great gate of the city. I flayed the chiefs and covered this wall with their skins. Some of them were walled in alive in the masonry; others were impaled along the wall. I flayed a great number of them in my presence, and I clothed the wall with their skins. I collected their heads in the form of crowns, and their corpses I pierced in the shape of garlands. . . . My figure blooms on the ruins; in the glutting of my rage I find my content."

Assyrian art illustrates these texts. The painted bas-reliefs of Nineveh and Khorsabad may be regarded as a royal record, told through stone fresco paintings. Furthermore, Chaldean and Assyrian art was also derived from the Hittite. The Hittites imparted to the Assyrians the idea of decorating the plinth — the square base of their columns — with mythological or historical cavalcades.

Hunting scenes and those of war are parts of such decorations. In the representation of the lion, the Assyrians are considered supreme. Multifarious other pictures represent winged bulls, eagles, and aquiform monsters. Old themes like those of the Sumero-Akkadian cylinders, developed by the Hittites, were recovered by the Assyrians and transmitted to Iran. Assyrian civilization penetrated also into Urartu and to other "Alarodian" peoples in the direction of the Caucasus. It was a seed which gradually germinated in Transcaucasia, in southern Russia and the Altaic regions.

Chapter IV
Ancestral Stocks

Early Migrations

Who came first to the plateau of Ararat — the Armens or the Urarteans? Both peoples had migrated there from somewhere and later moved again westward. Some scholars see in Urartean art, architecture, language and general culture traces of kinship to the Etruscans of the Italian peninsula. It appears likely that the ancestors of the Urarteans reached the tableland first. Some theorists assert, however, that centuries before the Urartean appearance, there lived in the land an original stratum of Hay-Armens.[1] Kevork Aslan declares that the Armens, peacefully penetrating into these highlands, found there a population akin to themselves in speech and customs. Possibly this refers to the inhabitants of the land of Hayasa.

It seems evident that the two principal ancestral stocks were the Hay and the Armens. National tradition represents the Armenians as descendants of Japheth, Noah's third son, and as coming to the plateau in later centuries from Babylon. They are connected with the Torgom-Togarmah and Ashkenaz of the Old Testament. Tilgarimma (Gurin), a fortress in Melitine (Malatia), is identified with the name Togarmah. Gamir or Gomer, father of Togarmah, is identified with the name of the people called Cimmers or Gimmers, the Gimirri of Assyrian inscriptions. The Ashkanazians, another appellation assumed by the Armenians, are the Azguza of the inscriptions (Ezekiel XXVII, 44; XXXVIII, 6; Jeremiah, LI, 27). According to Khorenatsi (Moses of Khoren), Armenian historiana — whose source is the Syrian Mar Abas — Haig or Haik, was the son of Togarmah.

The Accepted Theory

There are thousands of inscriptions in Armenia still undeciphered. But with the available Greek records, cuneiform inscriptions, Armenian traditions and philological studies, we are led to certain conclusions as to the origin and development of the Armenian people.

As to the history of the people, the accepted theory is that many centuries before our era, their ancestors lived in Europe together with the ancestors of the Greeks, perhaps in Thrace or Thessaly. J. Marquart has pointed to the similarity between the Thessalian words manu and sibyna (or sivyna) and the Armenian words manr (small) and souin (bayonet). The "Geography" ascribed to Khorenatsi has this significant phrase, "Great Thessaly, from which Armenians —" Professor N. Marr draws attention to the identity of the Armenian Astuadz (God) with the Phrygian Sabatius (chief god). In some Armenian communities, God was appealed to or

---

[1] The name Hay (Armenian), to be pronounced as "high."

18

referred to recently as Asbadz. Katholikos John, the historian, mentions Thiras, the ancestor of Haik, as also the ancestor of the Thracians.

Herodotus (484-425 B.C.) wrote that the Armens, crossing the Hellespont from Europe, had passed through Asia Minor to reach their ultimate homeland. In company with certain Balkan and Grecian tribes, the Armens crossed from Europe into Asia around the beginning of the twelfth century B.C., destroyed the kingdom of the Hatti and settled in Asia Minor for a stay of 600 years. During this long period, the racial, cultural and linguistic traits of the Armenians, even their anthropological type, showed the influence of their neighbors. They seem to have been particularly affected by Nessit-Khets, by non-Indo-European proto-Khets (Hatti) and by the Subarians (Khurri or Kharri).

Armens in the Iliad?

Marquart believed that he had found references to the Armens in the *Iliad*. He thinks that the "Arims" from Cappadocia settlements mentioned in that epic as composing a part of the Greek naval forces may have been Armenians. The Vulcan of the Greek legends is now being identified with the Argaeus (Erjyas) Mountain in Cappadocia. Here the Armens lived for some time in the proximity of Phrygian settlers. Some ancient historians claimed that the Armens were of Phrygian origin, though Father Joseph Sandalgian believed that they were the ancestors, not the descendants of the Phryges.

The first eastward movement of the Armens is thought to have been through the valleys of the Gelkit (Gail-ket or Lupus)[2] River, south of the Black Sea, thence to the upper Euphrates and Ararat. Recent writers, however, incline to the view that the march had been effected towards the southwest of the Armenian plateau, to the provinces of Alzi (Aghtzniq), thence to Taron (Mush) and the upper valleys of the Arzanias River (Eastern Euphrates) and the plain of Ararat. The northern districts, those of Terjan and Erzerum, were conquered later by Artashes-Artaxias I.

Circilius of Pharsalia and Medius of Larissa, fellow-travelers of Alexander the Great, have left an account, according to which the Armens must have moved by two routes, one along the Euphrates towards Akilisene (Erzinga), the other towards the plain of Kharberd (Harpoot) and the mountain valleys of the Tigris River. These settlements were of strategic and commercial value, which indicates that the Armens had been recognized as the military allies of the Medians. Furthermore, the itinerary described almost agrees with the statements of Khorenatsi; Haik the hero, he says, advanced from south of the Lake of Van northward to the lands of Taron and Hark, and thence to Ararat.

---

[2] Gel or Kail in Armenian means wolf; ket means river.

Several authorities agree that the incoming Armens were culturally inferior to the native elements, the Hay and others, by whom they were deeply influenced in manners, mode of life, agriculture and crafts, in traders and religious worship. The legends of Haik, Bel, Arama, Ara, Shamiram, Anggh and Torq, which Khorenatsi quoted from the Syrian Mar-Abas, should therefore be traced to pre-Armen origins.

According to Marquart, the name Armen was a compound of the root Arm and the Urartean suffix ini — as in Chaldini and Muskini. He thinks it probable that the Urmeni people of the inscription of Menuas (810-778 B.C.) at Malatia, were the same as the Arim-Armens who lived in those areas about the time of the completion of the *Iliad*. This theory, concurred in by Lehmann-Haupt, is further supported in Marquart's opinion, by an Armenian variant of the combat between Zeus and Typhon. Khorenatsi describes the heroic encounter of Aram with the titanic Payapis, in the vicinity of Argaeus Mountain. Khorenatsi's account may have been an echo of ancient stories about King Aramé of Urartu. Such conclusions are open to criticism, but the Armens spoke an Indo-European language, and there is no doubt, says Professor Manandian, that they were closely related to the Thraco-Phrygians.

The Melting Pot

Professor K. Patkanian believes that of the two component races, the Hay dwelt in the basin of the Lake of Van, the Armens in the valley of the Arax. Another element of considerable importance was the incorporation of the Hittites with the Armens, according to Leo, an Armenian scholar. Professor N. Marr believes that from the natives (of the Hay stock) the Armenians learned industry, agriculture, commerce and religious worship. The classic Armenian tongue, the Grabar, was the expression of that high culture whose origin and blossoming took place in the western and northern parts of the basin of the Lake of Van. Another distinguished scholar, M. Caracashian, thinks the Hay speech dominated that of the Armen, and became the common or royal dialect during the Arsacid (Arshakuni) dynasty.

"It is impossible to contemplate," says he, "without amazement the literary quality of the remnants of that language. The richness, purity, choice, poetic adornment, taste and philosophy found in the style of their exquisite relics, all indicate a high degree of national political and intellectual culture.... The Armenian literary language of the first half of the fifth century (A.D.), which our translators ... did not create, but did learn ... is a marvelous work, if not a miracle itself, and the only mark of its past greatness left by the Armenian kingdom."

Starting Point

According to the best authorities, the Scythians, emerging from Chinese frontiers in the interior of Asia in the beginning of the ninth century B.C., had, after long wandering, settled in the southwestern portions of Russia, adjacent to the shores

20

of the Black Sea. Some years afterward, they began to spread to right and left, some of them towards the Caucasus and Armenia, others towards Thrace and Asia Minor. Cimmerians or Gamirs, who had preceded them into Cappadocia, and from whom that country had received another of its names, Gamirk, were now pushed eastward, to thrust, in their turn, the Armen settlers of the region towards Armenia. The Scythians, also known as the Ashcusa, Ashkanazian or Sace, have left as their memorial in Armenia, the district of Shacasen, in the province of Uti.

According to one theory, the Armenians, under this pressure from the west, receded eastward, crossed the Euphrates, and becoming divided into three groups, they penetrated into Akilisene, Taron and Atiapene, on the Assyrian frontier, and finally into the valley of the Arax. Here, about the end of the fifth century B.C., the Alarodians lived, occupying a distinct area with the Mitannians. It was during this period, the eighth and seventh centuries B.C., when human hordes were rolling like tidal waves hither and yon, uprooting populations and revolutionizing the political and social life of Asia Minor, that the Armenians were finally settled in what came to be their national home.

Aborigines Absorbed Urarteans

Despite the migrational cataclysms, large groups of the aborigines remained intact in many places, especially in mountain retreats; and these were from time to time welded into the Armenian people. From their first settlements in the southwestern portions of the Armenian highlands and plains — where they were known as Arminiya by the old Persians, and Arminioi by the Greeks — they spread northward into the valley of the Kur, absorbing various tribes. "Under political divisions suggesting the existence of various kings," says François Lenormant, "a study of the names of cities, provinces and regions, also of personalities and deities, demonstrates a great racial and linguistic unity among the inhabitants of that vast country, and a religious system closely binding together the numerous independent kingdoms." However, more than a dozen alien tribes or races are found to have been ingredients in the Armenian melting pot. Professor H. Manandian enumerates the following — Mards, Khalds, Garduchs, Aramaeans, Alarods (Urarteans), Madiens, Saspirs, Outis, Miks and Paskirs.

Lenormant pictures the early Armenians as "a vigorous, hardy and warlike people, accustomed to the rigors of an ice-cold climate, attached to its homeland, but ready to sacrifice possession, even life, for liberty." The "ice-cold climate" is of course a slight exaggeration; winters are severe in the higher mountain areas, but on the whole, the climate is temperate. Jacques de Morgan remarks; "in the course of the events which upset Asia, the Armenians stood fast in their newly-conquered land and valiantly retained their nationality, language and mores down to our day.... Their brothers the Phrygians, are now only a vague memory. The Hellenes, the Italiots and the Gallians alone from among their contemporaries survive at present.... Titles of nobility in this race are more than

21

3000 years old, older than those of the majority of the European nations. (Even) India and China can hardly claim such antiquity of origin."

Just how close the connection was between the Armenians and the Urartean monarchy is not clear. Some are inclined to find in the Armenian historical writings of Khorenatsi traces of royal and princely names of the Khaldi-Urartean state — Aram from Aramé, Manavaz from Menuas, Armenak-Armaniek from Ermina, Anushavan from Inuspuas. Father Der Sahakian, the Mekhitarist, lists 40 of the 256 Armenian clans as of Urartean descent.

Sandalgian gives an instance proving the recognition even by the rulers of Urartu of the widespread use of the Armenian tongue. King Aram, after conquering Cappadocia, "ordered the inhabitants of the land to learn and speak the Armenian language." This historian also tells us that garrisons of 10,000 men each were stationed by King Valarces (Vagharshak) for the defense of the frontiers, while exarchs were appointed in the East, "along the borders of Armenian speech."

Urartu, after three centuries as a "world power," making conquests and fighting toe to toe with the mightiest of ancient empires, Assyria, finally fell before the might of Darius I, King of Persia in 518 B.C. The names Biaina (Van) and Thuspa (Tosp) were thereupon changed to Armenia, and an Armenian kingdom began to rise on the ruins of Urartu.

Opposition to Persia, then Alliance

The Armenian element had long since become conspicuous in the Persian armies under Xerxes and Darius. An Armenian prince, Tigran Erouandian, at the head of an Armenian contingent of 20,000 infantry and 4,000 cavalry, accompanied Cyrus when he took the Lydian capital, Sardice, in 546 B.C. and captured King Croesus. It had not been easy for Darius I to subdue Armenia. "I, King Daraya-ush," says he, "sent to Armenia my servant Dadarsis, an Armenian, and bade him Go! and chastise that rebel people which does not obey me." But despite the supposed support of the god Ormizd, the Persian army suffered three defeats within thirty-one days. Its general was thereupon dismissed, and victory finally won by another Persian commander. An Armenian prince named Arakha, by impersonating Nabuchodonosor, the son of Nabonidas, was even able to hold the Babylonian throne for a short time. Armenia or Arminya as Darius knew it ("Harminayap" in Susian inscriptions) was the eighteenth of the twenty-four satrapies of the empire. Of the eight armies of Persia, one was under the command of an Armenian, presumably Tigran Erouandian, mentioned above.

Cyrus the Great (ca. 559-529 B.C.) and the Persian kings who followed him respected the cultural and social identity of all nations within their domains. The Armenian language, though as yet unwritten, was the medium of general intercourse on both banks of the Arax and Euphrates Rivers. The Armenians also had their own distinctive temples of worship, customs, dress and weapons. With the advent of the Persian Achaemenid rule, Armenia, together with the Mari

(Medians) and other nations, was subjected to Persia from 519 to 486 B.C.; later, in 330 B.C. to the Macedonians, and finally, to the Seleucidae until 189 B.C. Although under foreign rule, they were, during these centuries, developing their own kingdom and became, culturally, economically and ethnographically, the conquerors of the plateau which came to bear their name.[3]

---

[3] Father Leonce Alishan, writing about a century ago, contributed a curious bit of lore when he listed a number of European peoples who represented or believed themselves to be originally emigrants from Armenia. Among them were the Pelasgians, Pannonians, Bavarians, Irish, Etruscans, Dalmatians, Sapinians, Tuscans, Czechs, Saxons and others. This Mekhitarist erudite scholar then chides those modern Armenians who "ignore the seniority, the centrality of their own nation, its traditions and testimonials, and the wonderful formation and richness of its national language."

Chapter V
The Hittite Empire

First Appearance

The Hittites first appeared in history in the twentieth century B.C., as inhabitants of the Anatolian plateau with the city of Hattushash — the modern village of Boghaz-Keuy in Turkey — as their capital. The Hittites were a composite people, fundamentally of Asian origin, but dominated by Indo-European aristocratic elements from the neighborhood of the Bosporus. Their culture, a mixture of indigenous elements, has been enriched by borrowings from the Chaldean. Parts of the Hittite texts, especially the rock inscriptions, were written in a peculiar hieroglyphic script not yet completely deciphered. But at the same time the Hittites also used the Chaldean cuneiform letters. Archaeological expeditions have discovered in Hattushash entire sets of royal archives in cuneiform tablets, written either in the Semite Babylonian, the diplomatic language of the time, or in the various dialects of the Hittite confederation.

The Hittites worshipped Teshub, the great god of mountain summits and of the thunder — whose symbolic emblems were the hatchet and the bull — and the great goddess, prototype of the Greek Kybele. After settling in Asia Minor and occupying Cappadocia, Phrygia, Lydia, Pontus and parts of Armenia and Cilicia, the Hittites began, in the twentieth century B.C., to make forays also into northern Syria and Mesopotamia. In 1925 B.C., they invaded and plundered Babylon and destroyed the dynasty of Hammurabi. More than five centuries later, in 1375, they subdued the powerful kingdom of the Mitanni, southwest of Armenia, at the great bend of the Euphrates River.

The Hittite empire then stretched from the Black Sea and Lydia to the frontiers of Assyria. In the south, it established its suzerainty over North Syria in 1350 B.C. In 1295 it was defeated by Rameses II at Qadesh (the modern Tel-Nebi-Mend) near Homs, yet the Egyptians were forced to yield the northern half of Syria to the Hittites. A treaty of alliance between the two nations was concluded in 1279. From 1229 to 1192 B.C. the Hittite Empire suffered periodic invasions by the maritime Aegean hordes. Then simultaneously came the disastrous attacks by the Thraco-Phrygians from the northeast and the Assyrians from the Southeast. The latter became the master of parts of Syria and Mesopotamia; then in 1110 they subjugated the dwindling Hittite kingdom of Carchemish (modern Jerablus, on the west bank of the Euphrates). In 1060 the Hittites regained this stronghold and held it until 715, when they were finally absorbed into the Assyrian Empire.

Successors of the Chaldeans

In the fourteenth and thirteenth centuries B.C., the Hittites played a dominant role in the politics of western Asia, becoming, in partnership with the Egyptians, successors to the ancient Chaldean Empire. For a while, when the Babylon of the Kassite kings was dormant, they became the link between the ancient civilization of Chaldea and the subsequent Assyrian civilization.

Thanks to the labors of German, French and Czechoslovak scientists, Hittite art has now been identified, through excavations at Boghaz-Keuy and Yazili-Kaya (Cappadocia), at Ibriz (Lycaonia), Malatia (lesser Armenia), Carchemish and Zenjirli on the Syro-Cilician frontier. Although inspired by the ancient Chaldean art and by certain modes of the Egyptian — even by Mycenean Greek architecture — Hittite art has been proved to have had a stamp of real originality.

Architectural Designs

By studying the divine procession of the rock temple of Yazili-Kaya, or the splendid relievo of the Sun-god on the calcareous block of Boghaz-Keuy, one discovers a branch of Mesopotamian art as effective as the Chaldean, omitting however, the episodical detail of the Assyrian.

Carchemish

The second archaeological group is that of Carchemish (14th to 9th centuries, B.C.). Some of the relief carvings of these groups disclose more affinity with the ancient Sumero-Akkadian art than with the Assyrian. On more recent reliefs, scenes of royal and civilian life take precedence over religious subjects.

Zenjirli

The Zenjirli group (14th to 8th century B.C.) displays beautiful bases of columns, formed by two conjugated sphinxes in the Mesopotamian manner; in the same style, a number of lions guarding the gates, with bodies in relief. The lion and sphinx seem to have inspired the lion and cherub-guardians of the gates of the palace of Sargon.

In addition to the hunting scenes in Zenjirli and Carchemish, there are representations of the god Teshub, armed with thunder, and fine types of Hittite warriors in their national costume — tiara-bonnet, a twisted braid of hair striking the nape, and long-tipped belt fringes falling to the thigh, shoes with recurved toes. To the north of Zenjirli, at Malatia, there has been preserved a beautiful bas-relief (now in Paris), representing a prince riding his chariot in chase of the stag. This work, executed about 1000 B.C., has been regarded as a prototype of hunting scenes of the Assyrian bas-reliefs.

Hittite Influence

The Hurri-Mitanni kingdom of Armenia kept close contact with its western neighbor, Hittite or Hatti land. Masses of population were often transplanted from one country to the other. The Manda — warriors of the Mitanni — had been living in Hatti as a privileged class. For two and a half centuries, the Hurri-Mitanni ruled over the Hatti. In Katmuch, the "rebellious" Hatti troops and the Moschi were united against Tiglat-Pileser II in 1130 B.C. Later on, Hatti warriors fled before the Phrygian-Moski and crossed to the eastern side of the Euphrates. Urartean kings took over from the Hatti the lower area of the Arzanias (Murad Su) — the eastern branch of the Euphrates, which includes the cities of Palu, Harpout (Harberd) and Malatia (Melitine). Argistis I of Urartu transferred 6,600 persons from Hatti land to his own country. Rusas II successfully warred against the Hittites in the seventh century B.C. Even in the second century B.C., the Armens under Arataxias and Zariadres (Artashes and Zareh) took the region of Ekelisine (Ekeghiatz-Erzinjan) from the Kataons, that is, from the Khita or Hittites.

This age-long relationship, sometimes friendly, at other times hostile, brought about mixtures in language and blood, creating the "Hittite" type among the Armenians, and a store of words common to the two peoples; also a similarity in architecture, sculpture and the crafts.

Sea-Peoples

Another storm, coming from the West and through the straits, burst upon Asia Minor in 1200 B.C. This cataclysm is known as the Thracian-Phrygian or "Sea-People's" invasion. The only known evidences of this catastrophe are found in the ruins of Troy, in the sudden interruption of the Hittite inscriptions, and a short record from the Pharaoh Rameses III (1200-1168 B.C.), which reads, "People dwelling in the islands came forth . . . spread immediately. No nation whatsoever could resist their soldiers. All were devastated. They were marching towards Egypt, the flames of torches preceding them. . . ."

These invaders must have clashed with Assyria, whose military and commercial outposts at that period reached to the Euphrates. Recently discovered Assyrian inscriptions refer to certain tribes of the conquering army, among which were the Mosks or Musks. In 1170 B.C. the Muskayas captured from Assyria the countries known as Alze (Aghtznik) and Purukkuzi, to the east of the Euphrates. These were the Mosches of the Greeks, a people in the Pontus Mountains lands, scattered through eastern Asia Minor, after the fall of the Hatti empire. This revolution in the political world was the result of a famine in southern Russia during the time of Assurdan I of Assyria (1192-1157 B.C.), which compelled some of the population to emigrate to the southern side of the Black Sea; others were deported.

By the incursion of the Sea-Peoples, the frontier of Hither Asia was pushed from the Aegean and Adriatic Seas back to the Euphrates and the Tigris Rivers. The

Mushki state, one of those created east of Hatti after the latter's fall, with its center in Cappadocia, had, in the half century following 1075 B.C. or thereabouts, expanded its rule as far as the land of Alshe (Alze) and beyond, to the Lake of Van. The terror they spread was still reechoing in man's memories in the days of the priest-prophet Ezekiel. He was one of the 8,000 Jews taken to Babylonia in the first exile, 597 B.C. In his Lamentations for Tyre, Ezekiel cites the Meshek (Mushki), together with other neighboring or related peoples.

Later on, Sargon of Assyria (722-705) tells in his inscriptions of victories over several nations, among which were the Moschi, under King Mita; "I gave my daughter to Ambaris (Ampalis?), King of Khilakku (Cilicia). He was unfaithful to me and allied himself with Ursana of Urartu and Mida of Mushki. They (Kusas?) captured my towns and districts in Tabal land ... Mida sent me tributes. ... He acknowledged the power of the great god Ashur."

The central location of the Mushki is identified by Forrer as Phrygia. Within its approximate frontiers were Kummuch (Comagene), Millita (Melitene), Tilgarium (Gurin), also Divrik, Akn and Arapkir, all west of the Euphrates. Tabal was west of Kummuch. Northwest of Tabal was Khilikku, which at that time included Mozacca-Mazhac (Caesarea). Phrygia was still farther west.

The Mushki were ethnically related to the Tabal, Gamer, Mada, Thorgoma and Ashkenaz (Tabal, Gimmerians, Mitanni, Togarma and Ashkuza-Scythians), all Indo-Europeans. The Armens claim to be the issue of Gamer, Torgom and Ashkenaz. The Mushki therefore had been in southwestern Armenia since the twelfth century B.C.; first as invaders, and then as an important part of the population, finally being absorbed in the Christian nation.

The same people or some of its tribes seem to have settled in other parts of Armenia or near by. The oldest record of a clash between Tiglat-Pileser I (1300 B.C.) and the Mushki was in southern Armenia. Rusas II of Urartu fought against the Mushki-ni on the west (although allied with them later against Assyria). Then, after some centuries, the Roman historian Pliny (23-79 A.D.) mentions the "Moscheni" on the southern border of Armenia, which designation properly fits into the name of the population of the southern province of Moks or Mokq, on the river Bohtan — Bit Moksaye in the Assyrian, Moxene in Latin. Marquart locates the ancient land of Moschi as bordering on the Iberian (Georgian) district of Moshket. The last habitat of the Moschi-Mosches was in Goukarq, one of the northern provinces of Armenia.

As to their origin; Moschi is just another name for the Phrygs, who infiltrated Armenia as Phryg-Armens. It was against them that Rusas II of Urartu (685-675), waged a war of defence which soon had to be directed against the Gimmers, too. King Mita of the Moschi, and Midas, the founder of the Phrygian kingdom, were one and the same person. In the East these people were called Muski, in the West they were known as Phrygs.

The Biblical story points to a close relationship between them and the Togarmah, Gamer and Ashkenaz. The Armenians have assumed the titles of the "House of Torgom" and the "Ashkenazi Nation." The traditional ancestor of the Armenians, Haik, was a son of Gomer, one of the six sons of Japheth. Ashkenaz, Riphath and Togarmah were the sons of Gomer.

Chapter VI
The Country of Hayasa-Khayasha

A Federation in Future Armenia

Hittite inscriptions deciphered by E. Forrer testify to the existence of a mountain country, the Hayasa, lying around the Lake of Van. According to P. Kretschmer, Hayasa or Khayasa, identified with Haik, Hayk or Hark, was inhabited before the coming of Armens. The suffix sa of Hayasa corresponds to the stan (habitat) derivative of Hayastan (Armenia). The name of that pre-Armen people may be found in the writings of Greek historians, Choi, Chai or Chaoi, the ch being sounded like the Greek letter X. The identity of the names Hayk and Hayasa had been asserted by Karl Rot, long before Kretschmer. As to the form Hayasa-Azzi in the inscriptions, A. Goetze thinks the name Azzi represents the Alzi or Alzini of the Assyrian and Urartean inscriptions.

Golden bowl of early bronze age (Kirovakan)

The cuneiform tablets of Boghaz Keuy have preserved the names of four successive kings who ruled the "Quasi-republican organization" — as Professor Eugene Cavaignac calls it — of Hayasa. They were Karannish, Mariyash, Hukkanash, and Anniyash, the four covering a period of 55 years, from 1390 to 1335 B.C. The first-named of these kings made incursions into the Hatti or Hittite empire, which were checked by the Emperor Dudhaliyash and his successor, Subbiluliuma. Mariyash, the next king of Hayasa, who had married a Hittite princess, was punished with death because of his breach of matrimonial contract. Hukkanash, the third in the line, also married a Hittite princess, the sister of the Emperor Subbiluliuma.

Palace Ethics

The marriage treaty of this couple contained some interesting stipulations peculiar to the time. "My sister, whom I gave you in marriage," says the Hatti ruler, "has sisters; through your marriage, they now become your relatives. Well, there is a law in the land of the Hatti. Do not approach sisters, your sisters-in-law or your cousins; that is not permitted. In Hatti Land, whosoever commits such an act does not live; he dies. . . . In your country, you do not hesitate to marry your own sister, sister-in-law or cousin, because you are not civilized. Such an act cannot be permitted in Hatti."

Despite these restrictions imposed upon Hukkanash, he was no meek and submissive brother-in-law in political and military affairs. As a condition for the release of the thousands of Hittite prisoners held in his domain, he demanded first the return home of the Hayasan prisoners confined at Hatti. The Hittite Empire had been subject to constant harassment by its eastern neighbors, from the basin of the upper Euphrates to Aravanna (Erevan of today) and Tebruzzi (Tabriz). One of the most important of these enemies crouched on its eastern border was the kingdom of Hayasa-Azzi.

Hittite-Hayasa Wars

"Mursil, the Hittite Emperor," says Cavaignac, speaking of that period, "was busy in the wars waged against Azzi or Hayasa, which were as bitter as those waged against Arzava (Western Cilicia). About the beginning of Subbiluliuma's reign, that country (Hayasa-Azzi) was subject to Hittite influence, but won its freedom later on. Annyash, the King of Hayasa, had sacked several districts and refused to release the prisoners taken. He had created a political union of the tribes of Armenia, and organized a kingdom which extended from the River Iris (Yeshil-Irmak) to the Lake of Van."

Hayasa's good fortune did not continue long, however. The Hittite Mursil[4] II, having consulted the oracles, invaded Hayasa in 1340 B.C. In the following spring he crossed the Euphrates and re-organized his army at Ingalova — Angegh, Angl — which, about ten centuries later, was to become the treasure-house and burial-place of the Armenian kings of the Arshakuni-Arsacid dynasty. One of the captured fortresses lay on the west side of the Lake of Van.

The Annals of Mursil thus describe these campaigns:—

> "The people of Nahasse arose and besieged" *(name indecipherable).*
> "Other enemies and the people of Hayasa likewise. . . . They plundered
> Institina, blockaded Ganuvara . . . with troops and chariots. And because
> I had left Nuvanzas, the chief cup-bearer, and all the heads of the camp

---

[4] The late Professor H. Adjarian, of the University of Armenia, identifies the names of Mursil-Murshel and the Armenian Mushegh-Mushel.

and troops and chariots in the High Country, I wrote to Nuvanzas as follows; 'See the people of Hayasa ... have devastated Institina, and blockaded the city of Ganuvara.'... And Nuvanza led troops and chariots for aid and marched to Ganuvara.... And then he sent to me a messenger and wrote to me; 'Will you not go to consult for me the augur and the foreteller? Could not a decision be made for me by the birds and the flesh of the expiatory victims?'

"And I sent to Nuvanza this letter: 'See, I consulted for you birds and flesh, and they commanded, Go! because these people of Hayasa, the God U, has already delivered to you; strike them!'

"And as I was returning from Astatan to Carchemish, the royal prince Nana-Lu came to meet me on the road and said, 'The Hayasan enemy having besieged Ganuvara, Nuvanza marched against him and met him under the walls of Ganuvara. Ten thousand men and seven hundred chariots were drawn up in battle against him, and Nuvanza defeated them. There are many dead and many prisoners.' "

"And when I arrived in Tiggaramma, the chief cup-bearer Nuvanza and all the noblemen came to meet me at Tiggaramma. I should have marched to Hayasa still, but the chiefs said to me, 'The season is now far advanced, Sire, Lord! Do not go to Hayasa.' And I did not go to Hayasa. . . ."

Decline of Hayasa

Hayasa as a fighting power was practically eliminated by the expedition of Mursil II in 1340 B.C. But after Mursil's premature death in 1320 B.C., the Hatti empire suffered a series of shocks. His elder brother Arvandas (Erouand) had also died young. A natural phenomenon, the eclipse of the sun, had terrified the people. A dreadful epidemic of some sort took a vast number of lives, including that of the Queen. The population of the capital was decimated to such a degree as to require the forced immigration of new inhabitants from adjoining countries. Taking advantage of the ensuing debacle, Mursil's nephew, Arma-u-as (Aramais?), contested against the heir-apparent for the succession to the crown. Still more serious was the menace of the external enemies of the land, especially those of the North and East, who devastated the country in revenge for Mursil's conquests. A record exists of the incursion of the Kaskas or Kaskians, who crossed the Halys River with 800 chariots and advanced as far as the capital, which they plundered. The King was compelled to remove the idols and the paraphernalia for the worship of the dead to a safer place.

Bronze caldron from Hayasa

The Kaskas — whose home J. Garstang places in Armenia — attacked by way of Amasia. Leonard King describes them as an "unruly people" living between the Euphrates and the Lake of Van, and a constant menace to the Hatti. "No Hatti King," says he, "was able to establish his power there permanently." It may therefore be safely assumed that Hayasa still exerted its influence. In any case, however, the days of the Hattite hegemony were numbered. The Assyrians forged ahead and gradually spread their domination over southern and western Armenia.

The origin of the Hay element is still a mystery, but the existence of the land and people of Hayasa-Azzi as a factor in relation to the Hatti covers a long period, beginning "before the expansion of the Hittite empire towards Syria," according to Professor A. Goetze. Several prominent authorities agree in placing Azzi to the north of Isuva. Others see Hayasa and Azzi as identical.

Fall of Hittite Empire

The Hittite or Hatti Empire was overthrown 140 years after Mursil's campaign in Hayasa. In 1180 B.C., Indo-European tribes, crossing the Dardanelles and the Bosporus, overran Asia Minor, destroying a number of States and cities, among which was Hattushash, the Hittite capital. One of the three greatest tribes of the invasion was that known as the Armens. In the words of Fr. Hrozny, "the Hittite Empire fell under the attack of the 'sea peoples,' and also of the Thracians, Phrygians and Armens." Other scholars coincide in Hrozny's opinion that the "Phrygians and Armens became the heirs of the powerful Hittite Empire."

Chapter VII
The Kingdom of Urartu

A Redoubtable Foe

One of the great chapters in the history of Armenia is or should be the epic of the monarchy which the Assyrians called Urartu, but which was known to the Hebrews as Ararat. Herodotus called its people Alarodians. Urartu is regarded by history today as one of the earlier incarnations of Armenia. In Urartu was manifest not only the indomitable fighting spirit of the later Armenians, but also the same tendency towards development of a higher culture. As a noted authority, H. A. B. Lynch, remarks, Urartu was "no obscure dynasty which slept secure behind the mountains, but a splendid monarchy which for more than two centuries rivalled the claims of Assyria to the dominion of the ancient world."[5]

Its Peak Years

As a nation, it lived through many more centuries than that, but it was only between 860 and 585 B.C. that it actually disputed with Assyria the right to dominate western Asia. Its beginnings are lost in the mists of pre-history. Its people must have migrated from somewhere to the west into the Armenian plateau, then for the most part known as Nairi. They called themselves Khaldians[6] or children of the god Khaldis, just as the name of the Assyrians reflects the name of their god Assur. The cuneiform characters of their inscriptions were for centuries Assyrian; but later on the language changed to or was absorbed in the local one. The Assyrian was a Semitic language, while Urartean was neither Semitic nor Indo-European. Urartean culture is believed to have been similar to the Hittite and Assyro-Babylonian, blended with native characteristics. The later Urartean monuments still hold a mystery for us as to their affinity with the Armenian language, witness of a glorious past. It has not yet been possible to decipher these inscriptions with any aid from the Armenian language. N. Marr, Nikolsky, Lehmann-Haupt and earlier scientists have classified them as in the Japhetic speech-group, and the Armenian experts, A. Calantar and G. Ghapantsian, agree in this finding. Professor Nikolsky has found hundreds of words, both nouns and verbs, showing affinity between the Urartean and the modern Utean.[7] As early as 1879 H. Hübschmann pointed out in the Urartean inscriptions several words and suffixes — such as ili, ini, and uni

---

[5] H. A. B. Lynch, "Armenia, Travels and Studies." 2 vols., London, 1901. Vol. II, p56.

[6] Not to be confused with the people of Chaldea.

[7] Eight villages of the Uti district still retain the ancient language. Of their 230,000 population two centuries ago, only 10,000 have retained their Christianity. The majority have been forced into Islam. Shamkhor and Ganzak townships included in the district, northeast of Armenia.

— borrowed from Caucasian idioms, especially Georgian and Aghouanian (Albanian).

Mystery of Origin

Where did these people come from? From Asia Minor, declares Lehmann-Haupt, seeking proof for his assertion in their metallurgy, architecture and folkways. Professor Shestokov, a Caucasian author, wrote in 1939 that "The oldest states of the Soviet Union were founded 3,000 years ago to the south of Transcaucasia. The oldest among them, that in the Ararat area, by the Lake of Van, was called Urartu. Its kings ruled over Georgian tribes." Here is another theory as to the origin of the people once dwelling in Nairi, which comprised the entire Armenian plateau. Even when the greater part of that tableland became Urartu, the regions on two flanks of it, from Amit (Diarbekr) to Anzitene (Harpout), together with Habushkia in Zab Valley, and Paddira, south of Musasir, were still called Nairi. The name Nairi-Urartu reveals kinship with Hurri, Namri, Kirruri and other names with the suffix ri, having no connection with Semitic idioms.

Professor Edward Schultz was one of the first to obtain original information on Urartu, when he visited Armenia in 1827. He was murdered there by a Kurd, but his papers, containing 42 inscriptions found at Van and in its neighborhood, were saved. The later discoveries of Burnouf, Lassen and Rawlinson stimulated interest in Oriental antiquities. Layard visited Van in 1850 and took new copies of the inscriptions. Of special interest were one tablet on the rock of Van, and an inscription on a stone in a ruined wall. The first contains the name of Xerxes, son of Darius, in the same characters as those of Behistun and Persepolis. The second resembles Assyrian writings. All others are of a language peculiar to Van. Another mysterious text was read by Hincks in 1847, and following these Professor A. H. Sayce added "a new language and a new people to the museum of the ancient Oriental world." Thereafter the known Vannic texts were doubled in extent by the German archaeologists, Lehmann and Belck, who, in the words of Lynch, called up "a vanished civilization from the grave." But even so, alas, they could evoke only a broken and fragmentary body; so much has been lost by the ravages of war and vandalism and time.

Van-Tosp

The seat of this theocratic monarchy was Thuspa, capital of the territory of Biaina, corrupted into the form Van. The Armenian national historian, Moses of Khoren (Khorenatsi), mentions Van as "in the province of Tosp." In some of the ancient inscriptions, one finds, "King of Biaina, inhabiting the city of Thuspas." Going back into history we find Tiglat-Pileser I, King of Assyria, asserting that he conquered twenty-three kings of Nairi in 1114 B.C. These "kingdoms" must have been very small, indeed; and when we find that this same Tiglat claimed to have slain with his own hand ten elephants and 920 lions, we are inclined to receive his statements with reserve. In an inscription of the Assyrian Assurbelkala (1077-1060 B.C.), first appears the name Uruatru. A Shalmanaser of Assyria (1028-1017 B.C.), claimed the conquest of "the entire country of Uruatru" in three days. In inscriptions of Ashurnasirpal (885-859 B.C.) the name appears as Urardhu or Urarthu. The succeeding king Shalmaneser, now called by most historians the Second (859-825 B.C.) sent an army against a king of Urartu named Aramé,[8] whose capital was Arzasku or Arzaskun, identified with the modern Melazgerd, north of Lake Van. Aramé, who, according to Adontz, was the first organizer of the Urartean Empire, was defeated and his capital taken by Shalmanaser in 857 B.C.

Aramé

To say that he was the "organizer" of the Empire, means that he combined the "Nairi countries" into a confederation under the aegis of the god Khaldis, supplanting an earlier Biaina confederation. Some authorities believe that not Aramé but Sardur I (844-828) was the organizer of the confederation. Sardur was the son of Lutipris, who succeeded Aramé. He left an inscription in the Assyrian language, calling himself King of Sura, which, according to Professor Albrecht Goetze, is the same as Subaru. If this is so, the Urartean kings' claim of Hurrite descent entitled them to domination in Subari, or Upper Mesopotamia. Sardur's other titles were "Great King," and "Ruler of Four Regions," *i.e.*, Shar-Kishatti, according to Babylonian and Assyrian inscriptions.

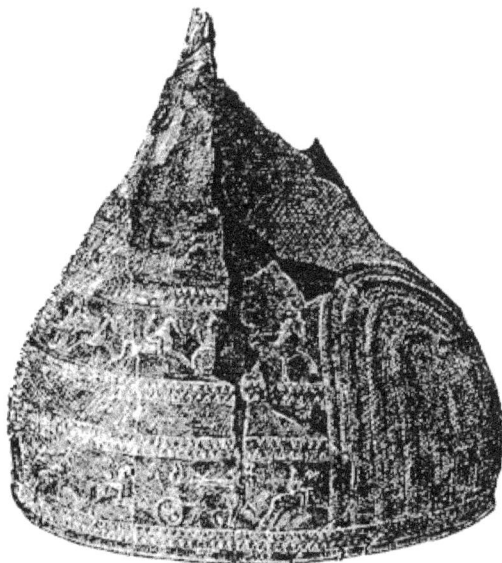

Bronze helmet with inscription of King Sardour
(Found at Karmir Blour — "Red Hill")

---

[8] Aramé is the form favored by Lynch. Joseph Sandalgian writes it Aramis, while Lehmann-Haupt calls it Aram, the name of the legendary conqueror pictured by Khorenatsi.

35

Sardur I

Sardur built a fortress of huge stones west of the Rock of Van, and Ispuinis, his son and successor, chose that rock as his residence and as the holy seat of the god Khaldis. Ispuinis was a contemporary of Adadnirari IV of Assyria, son of Shalmanaser and husband of Queen Shammuramat (Semiramis). Ispuinis fought and defeated his powerful rival, and was thus enabled to found a Khaldian colony at Musasir, west of the Pass of Kelishinin, where he erected a commemorative stone with inscriptions in Khaldian and Assyrian. Ispuinis and his son Menuas brought the empire to its peak. Under them it extended from the Zagros Mountains in the East to Palu in the North and Malatia in the West.

During their reigns great works were constructed around Van, including the aqueduct of Shamiram-Su, 45 miles in length, completed by Menuas, which brought the pure water of the Khoshab River to the eastern shores of Lake Van (whose water is undrinkable), enabling the King to found there a "Menuas city." This canal irrigates the plain of Van even to the present time.

Ispuinis and Menuas

Officials were appointed to inspect the canals, to keep their channels clean, to distribute the water according to regulations and to plan effective measures against overflowing. Menuas planted a garden, dedicated to the memory of the wife of Ispuinis; he repaired and embellished the temple of Khaldi in Van, and he strengthened the great fortification of Melazkert. No better location for a fortress against a power operating from the southern lowlands could have been chosen by the builders of an empire on the Armenian plains. Made more secure by a fleet on the lake, and by the fortification of the passes of Mount Varag, the place became of first-rate military importance only when the centers of hostile force lay in Mesopotamia. These facts explain the comparative immunity and rapid development of the empire of the successors of Sardur I, at a time when Assyria was ruled by warlike monarchs. The period of Ispuinis and Menuas is perhaps the most brilliant in Urartean history.

Argistis I

The political ascendancy of Urartu was enhanced further by the weakness of Assyria under Shalmaneser III (782-772). Under Argistis I (785-755), son of Menuas, the Vannic Empire was still at the zenith of its power. The future city of Armavir rose on the bank of the Arax River in honor of Khaldis. The whole Armenian tableland was subject to Urartu, and its inscriptions recording conquests are found from Lake Urmiah to the Euphrates River at Malatia. Thus having become an unrivalled power in Hither Asia, it imposed its suzerainty in 775 B.C. upon the kingdoms of Kummuch (Diarbekir), Tabal (west of Malatia) and several other kingdoms and principalities. Later on, in 758, after crushing the revolt of the Hatti king of Milidu (Malatia), Sardur III, successor of Argistis I, moved southward, put the Great King of Carchemish (Jarablus) under tribute, and captured the whole territory as far as Halpa (Aleppo). The empire of Assyria was then encircled, says the Turkish scholar, Professor Shemseddin, as if "in an iron hoop."

Sardur III

Argistis left a record of fourteen years of his reign on the walls of chambers hewn in the Rock of Van, while Sardur III's victories are inscribed on a monument erected on a spot called "the Treasury Gate" in the fortress of Van. The Urarteans, then in close contact with the Hittites in the west, had in the east as neighbors the Minni or Manni, in the southerly portion of the Urmiah basin. Records of victories are also found inscribed farther north, on the shores of Lake Sevan, at Alexandropol (now Leninakan), at Hasankala (Erzerum), etc.

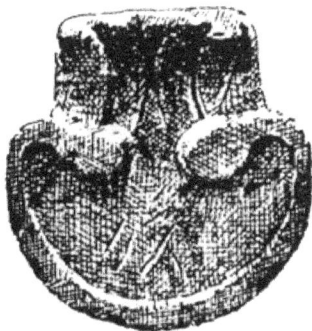

Mold for casting bronze ax (Leninakan)   Bronze ax

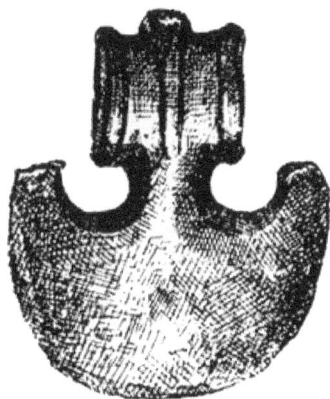

This brilliant era of Urartu did not last long. Sardur III's Assyrian contemporaries, Assurnirari (755-745) and Tiglat-Pileser III (745-727), waged war upon him, and the latter dealt him a telling blow, routing him, together with his allies, the kings of New Hatti (in Malatia), of Gurgum (Marash) and a score of others. The Menuas-city was destroyed in 735 and the conqueror claimed to have taken 73,000 prisoners.[9] Hatti princes thereupon recognized the king of Assyria as their suzerain lord, instead of the Urartean potentate. Sardur fled deep into his mountains with a broken spirit and health, and sank into a physical decline, of which he died in 734 B.C.

Rusas I

Rusas I (733-714 B.C.), a vigorous and sagacious prince, reorganized the army, suppressed domestic turbulences and revived the morale of the people. From Thuspa he transferred his seat to a hill later known by the Turkish name Toprak-

---

[9] Among the allied rulers, more than twenty in number, who fought against the Assyrians was one Aramu, son of Agusi, King of Arpad, modern Tel-Rfad, north of Aleppo.

kaleh (the earthen fort). This Rusas-city was supplied with water from an artificial lake in the side of the Varag Mountain. All this he recorded on a stele which in 1898-9 was taken to the Museum of Berlin.

Part of an Urartean throne (bronze)

However, he was given little opportunity to rebuild Urartu's old eminence. Sargon II (722-705), the most terrifying figure among the occupants of the Assyrian throne, darkened the political horizon of all the Near-Eastern lands. Tusas organized a coalition of the states of Western Asia and strengthened the position of Urzana, King of Musasir, his vassal and ally. But in a sanguinary battle described in an inscription found near the shore of Lake Sevan, the Khaldian army, though resisting stubbornly, was defeated by Sargon, who also overwhelmed Musasir and plundered its temple. In the vast quantity of spoil carried to Nineveh were many idols belonging to the Urartean kings.

Even after this terrible loss of men and material, Rusas did not yield to despair. Whilst neighboring nations were trembling with fear of the Assyrian scourge, Rusas replenished the reservoirs of his strength and for the time being, saved his kingdom from destruction. But another black chapter was in the making for him. Cimmerian hordes from the North, sweeping through the mountain defiles, down into the regions of the Urmiah and Vannic lakes, surprised Urartu and wrought great destruction. According to one version of the outcome, the army of Rusas, unable to offer adequate resistance, melted away, and Rusas committed suicide in 714. But T. A. Olmstead, in his *History of Assyria,* questioning the reliability of the Assyrian royal scribes regards this as a mere spectacular raid, without enduring results. One inscription, speaking of the fate of Rusas, says "With his own iron dagger, he pierced his heart as he would to a pig and ended his life." Olmstead compares this with a slightly later Assyrian inscription in which the defeated king is pictured as being ill, though there is not a word about suicide. It may well be that this malady caused his death.

Argistis II

Argistis II (714-680), son and successor of Rusas, rid himself of the Cimmerian hordes by deflecting their trend to westward, into Cappadocia. As to his relationship with Assyria, the latter's reports are silent, the explanation undoubtedly being that Sargon was not victorious at the time, but had been forced into a defensive attitude. Argistis II, however, was engaged in secret activities, the center of which was the province of Harda or Kharda, the modern Kharberd or Harpout. The canton of Inzit, the Hantzit of the geography of Armenia, was then a part of the province of Alzi or Aghtzniq.

Sargon, once so boastful of his devastation in Urartu, now sent envoys to Argistis, professing great friendship. The Urartean king, however, did not alter his plans; he continued his preparations, and increased his pressure upon Assyria in the Eastern Tigris basin. Sargon's son, Sennacherib, then a provincial governor, urged his father to send more troops to that area, informing him of Argistis's order to his prefects to "seize the governors of the Assyrian king in Kumai and drag them before me."

Sennacherib was assassinated in 681 — by two of his sons, Adramelech and Sharazer, according to the Bible.[10] Professor N. Adontz ascribes this crime to the second son only, Ardi or Arad-Ninlil, who, allied with Adramelos Nebusaresur, the governor of Maraski, fought against his own brother Esarhaddon. Defeated at Carchemish, the two fled into Armenia.

Efforts have been made to decipher the cuneiform inscriptions of Armenia through the present-day Armenian language. The failure of these attempts has led some to believe that the inscriptions in question must be in some unknown, alien tongue, neither Indo-European nor Semitic.

Linguistic Connections

One investigator, P. Jensen, finds a certain similarity between the Urartean language and that in which the letter of King Tushratta of Mitanni (found at Tel-el-Amarna, Egypt) was written. For example, the name of the god Tesub of the Mitanni closely resembles that of the god Teisbas of Urartu. Another scholar thinks that ancient Armenia or Urartu had a cultural connection with Asia Minor and Syria — citing the Hurri-Mitanni or Subarean remains in upper Mesopotamia and Syria as having points of resemblance to the characters of the Khaldian inscriptions.

---

[10] "And it came to pass, as he was worshipping in the house of Nisroch his god, that Adramelech and Sharezer his sons smote him with the sword; and they escaped into the land of Armenia *(Ararat in the original Hebrew)*, and Esarhaddon his son reigned in his stead." (Isaiah XXXVII, 38)

There appears to have been a pre-Indo-European substratum of speech which strongly influenced the Indo-European-Armenian. Professor N. Marr, a Khaldist authority, suspects that the language of the Vannic cuneiforms is of the type of several modern Caucasian dialects of the Japhetic class. however, the Aryo-European must have exerted great influence upon the Urartean, even long before the times of the Vannic Empire.

Urartean horsemen and war chariot, appearing on the bronze quiver that bears Sardour's name.

On the other hand, E. Meyer cites names of royal princes many centuries before Christ in the Taurus area and Palestine, and later in Commagene; names such as Arta-tama, Arta-skana and Artamana, all more Iranian in character than Indian, and all bearing the Arta prefix which persists in Armenian names to this day. But there were names such as Kundaspie and Kustaspie, which were originally Indian, their forms then being Vindaspa and Vistaspa. Other significant links are found in the Hatti-Mitanni treaty (1387-1367 B.C.), which contained the names of other than gods, and in the Sanskrit numerals, yeka (one), tria (three) and panja (five), as found in the treatise upon horse-training by Kikkuli of Mitanni (1400 B.C.).

The Subarean (Asianic-Hurri-Japhetic) language is the basic stratum of the various above-mentioned tongues; it was topped and strongly affected by the

Aryan-Mitanni language, from which mixture the Urartean sprang up, it being related in turn to the old Hatti-Asianic, the new Caucasian and through Indo-European elements, to the Aryan languages. On this Indo-European-Armenian foundation was superimposed the Urartean speech, which was forced upon the conquered natives, from whose dialects also an additional stock of words was assimilated in the course of time. Traces of anthropological types of culture, religion and social customs are being discovered from time to time under the Armen stratum. The same may be said of the linguistic heritage of the past.

In his analysis of the known Iso-Urartean root-words, Professor Ghapantsian of Erevan University identifies one-fourth as of Hittite character. Many other root words and grammatical forms of non-Indo-European types have been found, but belonging to an Asia Minor group. All non-Indo-European elements, the Urartean and others, descend from the Subarean common origin. The same applies to the anthropological strata of the population of Armenia, whose chronology is stated by Professor A. Hatch as follows:

Subarean basic stratum	dating from 3000 B.C.
Harri-Mitanni-Aryan stratum	dating from 2000 B.C.
Mosch-Muski-Aryan-Phryge stratum	dating from 1176 B.C.
Hatti major infiltration into Armenia	1200 B.C.
Khald-Urartean rule in Armenia	9th century B.C.
Phryge-Armen rule in Armenia beginning	650 B.C.

Urartean bronze statue-goddess   Ornamental objects in gold (found at Douin)

Chapter VIII
The Beginnings of Armenia

Period of Legend

The Armenians have their full share of legends regarding their origin; legends in which spirits, gods and superhuman heroes, the forces and phenomena of nature, play dominant parts. In such myths may be traced occasional historical facts. The impossible thing is to disentangle the fact from the fiction. The most pervasive figure in this national folklore which has come down to us through songs and ballads is that of Haik.

The Hero-Ancestor

Haik, the wonderful archer, long ago became established in the national legend as the ancestor of the Armenians, bequeathing to them the patronymic Hay, the name which the Armenians apply to themselves. This legend takes us back to that prehistoric epoch when the first Armenians arrived in the land of Urartu, under the leadership of a great commander. Haik, according to the story, revolted against a tyrant, Bel of Babylon, and departed for the North with his family and followers. Bel, at the head of a large army, pursued and came upon him. Haik engaged Bel in battle, killed him with an arrow, dispersed his rabble of warriors and freed the land which is known as Hark[11] — *i.e.*, the country of the Hai people.

The names of the places mentioned in the myths — Hark, Haikashen, Hayotz-tzor, are found around the Lake of Van, the region where the Armenians settled. Haik, the nahapet (tribal chief), whose household included 300 men, waged his successful battle in the "land of Ararat." After his victory over Bel, the chieftain proceeded towards the northwest, whose inhabitants voluntarily submitted to his authority.

This legend is reminiscent of the invasion of the Armenians from the west. The bringing of Haik from the south in the narrative may be traced to the wish of the Christian historians of Armenia — Khorenatsi and others — to connect the story of Haik and Bel with the Biblical narrative of the construction of the Tower of Babel.

An historical character?

Father S. Der Movsessian believes that Haik was "an historical person." He was later deified and worshipped as "Deus Armenicus," the man who led a Hittite

---

[11] The terminal letter k changes the word from singular to plural.

colony into Armenia in 580 B.C. and vanquished the last Urartean king, Menuas II, whom tradition has transformed into the tyrant Bel. Gradually the name Haik, derived from Hay, became an adjective or adverb, synonymous with heroic valor, prowess and beauty. This view has been endorsed by another savant, Father S. Matikian, a Mekhitarist of Vienna, who connects Haik with Hai or Hay, the old name of the Armenian people, and offers in support of his argument the names of Assyria, Athens and Rome, each named in honor of its particular deity-hero. Haik, says he, that titan of popular legend, was one of the greatest of gods, equal to the Indra of India, the Assur of Assyria, the Hattu of the Hittites and the Khaldi of the Khaldian-Urarteans. The Haik of Khorenatsi reminds us of Marduk, mentioned in the Bible, a Babylonian divinity (represented in our skies by the planet Mercury) whose arrow slew Bel because of his rebellion against the gods. In a similar manner, the dragon Verethra had been destroyed by Indra, the enemies of Athens by Athene, and the enemies of Germany by Odin. Just as Haik fled from Babylon because of Bel, whom he eventually killed, so Zeus had escaped to the mountains of the Caucasus, later to return to Sicily and hurl fatal arrows into the bodies of his titanic foes.

Haik linked with Orion

Ancient legendary heroes and demigods were often, in popular imagination, transfigured into stars — as in the case of Marduk and Mercury — so that the people would have nightly evidence of their celestial existence. In the old popular sense, Haik means a giant, and in some manner he became connected with the Orion of Greek legend — perhaps because Orion, too, was a hero of fine stature and features. The latter was accidentally slain by Diana, who was in love with him, and in her remorse she turned him into a brilliant constellation. Other mythological cults saw Orion as the god of the wind and storm; the "thunderous Orion" of the Babylonian conception drove away evil spirits. And so it came to pass that this constellation mentioned twice in the Bible (Job IX, 9; XXXVIII, 31) and called Orion in the Greek text, was, in the Armenian translation, turned into Haik.[12]

The linguistic relation between the names of Haik and Hai or Hay is not entirely clear. The prototype of Hay or Khay has been traced by some scholars to the name of the great god Khaldi. Father L. Alishan believes that the name Hay was derived from Haik, and that the national patronymic was originally Ha. Ha-os was the name under which the nation was mentioned by the Georgian historians, the ending os being a Greek usage. The appellation Ha still existed in certain Armenian localities until 1915; also in the plural form Haik or Hek, Khaik or Khek, as in Khekotz-Vank, the monastery of the Armenians.

---

[12] Which maketh Arcturus, Orion, and Pleiads, and the chambers of the south. (Job IX, 9). Canst thou bind the sweet influences of Pleiades or loose the bands of Orion? (Job XXXVIII, 31).

Tel-el-Amarna tablets

All the above conjectures concerning the name Hai or Hay were supplemented by discoveries during excavations in Tel-el-Amarna, Egypt, in 1887. There 350 clay tablets were found, the archives of the Pharaohs Amenophis III and Amenophis IV (1350-1335 B.C.). The deciphering of these led to the discovery of Hattushash, the capital of the forgotten Hittite empire, at the site of the modern Turkish village of Boghaz-Keuy, near Yozgat, Asia Minor. The cuneiform inscriptions on the Hattushash tablets, deciphered in 1925 by Hugo Winckler and Bedrick Hrozny, disclosed a hitherto unknown state, Hayasa, located in what came to be known as Armenia, northeast of the Hittite empire. "The similarity of the words Hayasa and Hayastan," says Prof. A. Hatch, "is so obvious that I am tempted to declare that the oldest name of Armenia has already been discovered." The form Haystan, however, is of a later date, formed from Hay and Stan. The Persian suffix stan — sthana in Sanskrit — indicates "the place, the home."

Origin of the name "Hay"

The etymology of the word Hay still remains a controversial problem. Some authorities derive it from Pet, of an Indo-European language root, meaning ruler. It is said that the Armens who invaded Armenia were called by the subjugated natives Pet. Strange as it may seem, comparative philology has certain formulae of linguistic evolution which make it possible for Pet to become in the course of ages, Hay. For the word peter or pater (father) the Armenian has hayr (pronounced *hire*), while the word for mother is mayr (pronounced *mire*).

But other scholars find the origin of Hay in Khald or Hald, the name of the national god Khaldis, worshipped by the early inhabitants of Armenia. Kh here is pronounced like the guttural X of the Greek alphabet or the German ch. The ancient Urartean Empire, of which the city of Van was the capital, is known to some scholars also as the Vannic, but more generally as the Khaldean or Haldian empire. By a process of phonetic evolution, Khald becomes Khayd, and then sloughing off the final d, we have Khay. In fact, places still in existence around the Lake of Van were, before the Armenian deportation in the First World-War, called Khaik or Khek, meaning Armenians. In many districts, villages spoke of themselves as Khay, and still thought of the country as Khayastan.

There are yet other theories. P. Jensen, who claimed that the Armenians are the descendants of the Hittites, derived Hay from Hatio-Hatti, another word for Hittite. Father Joseph Sandalgian found in the Vannic inscriptions the word Uas or Huas, the name of the god of wind, whose worshippers were called Huas, a name which, he believed, was gradually metamorphosed into Hay.

Armenia as a Median Ally

Cyaxares, King of Media, aided by Babylonia, destroyed the Assyrian kingdom in 605 B.C. and captured its western refuge, Carchemish on the Euphrates.

44

Nineveh, its capital, had already been razed. The Medians put an end, likewise, to the Urartean kingdom, and advancing further west, by 590 were attempting the domination of Asia Minor. The battle, waged between the Medes and the Lydians on the banks of the Halys River on May 28th, 585, was interrupted by a solar eclipse, and peace was concluded, fixing the river as the frontier between the two empires. Media was then a confederation of states, each one maintaining its own religion, language and laws. By that time, Armens had settled in Armenia, living in neighborly relations with Khaldean-Urarteans and as subjects and allies of the Median kingdom; so states Xenophon in his Cyropedia.

In 550 B.C., Cyrus (Kuros) the Persian monarch, waged war on Astyages (Azhdahag) of Media, and seized his power. The Medes thereupon entered into alliance with the Persians, with the state of Armenia as another member of the federation. The Armenian king, who had two sons, Tigran and Sabaris (Shavarsh), had been defeated by Astyages and compelled to pay annual tribute. The Armenian army was then composed of 40,000 infantrymen and 8,000 cavalry. The king's assets were some 3,000 talents, or about $30,000,000. Upon the outbreak of hostilities between Media and Babylonia he had renounced his treaty obligations to the Medes. Cyrus, then commander of the army of Cyaxares, captured the Armenian king and his family, but soon released them through the intercession of Tigran, the king's son, who was a friend and hunting companion of Cyrus.

It may be adduced from Xenophon's story that the Armens who had crossed the Euphrates in the early sixth century B.C. accepted the Median king as their suzerain, in addition to their own chief, whom Xenophon also calls "king" (Basileus). The Armens who occupied and cultivated the plains of their new home, also needed grazing lands for their cattle, and for that reason continued their feud with the Khalds, the inhabitants of the mountain-sides. This friction, which had facilitated the Median predominance in the country, came to an end by reason of the reconciliation — and eventual intermixture of the two main elements — the incoming Armens and the older stock, the Urarteans.

Early Armen kingdom

A folklore poem dealing with Tigran Erouandian, contemporary of Astyages and Cyrus, has caused Khorenatsi to confuse the Tigran of the sixth century B.C. with the Tigran the Great of the first century B.C. However, Xenophon's account, evidently based upon popular songs and stories, confirms the existence of an Armen kingdom immediately after the fall of the Urartean. Savaris (Shavarsh), Vahagn, Nerseh, Zareh, etc., the successors of Tigran Erouandian, were Armens by race, despite their Median or Persian names. The adoption of Iranian names and customs was the result of intimate relations established between the two peoples. Witness Khorenatsi's narrative of the marriage of Tigran's sister Tigranuhi with Astyages, King of the Medes, whom Tigran was finally forced to slay in battle.

Achaemenid-Persian rule

Armenia had become a dependency of Persia after the fall of the Median empire in 550 B.C. The Armenian contingents, cavalry and infantry, had taken part in Cyrus's conquest of Lydia in 546 and of Babylonia in 539. A rebellion of ten subject nations — one of them Armenia — broke out against Persia during the reign of Darius I (522-486). The Armenians were compelled to acknowledge defeat after five battles, one of them fought on Assyrian territory. "Arakha, an Armen, the son of Haldita," pretender to the throne of Babylonia, was also defeated and executed. Armenia became thereafter the thirteenth of the twenty provinces of the Empire, ruled by satraps — "khshatrapa" in Persian. Native grandees, however, were permitted to exercise a certain measure of authority under the satraps.

The forced union accomplished among the powerful states of the East — Assyria, Babylonia, Lydia and Egypt — contributed greatly towards the known world's commercial and financial development. Land and sea communication with India was established during the Achaemenid period. Darius I reopened the canal connecting the River Nile with the Red Sea, which had been dug during the period of the Pharaohs. Darius I also introduced an improved monetary system, and safer and quicker means of travel and transportation. In conjunction with several peoples of the Euxine Sea coast, the Armenian satrapy paid to the Imperial treasury 400 talents, equivalent to $400,000. Armenia also supplied the King's stable with 20,000 foals for every annual festival of Mithra. Armenian military forces had been joining the Persian army from the earliest times. Those who served under Xerxes in the invasion of Greece in 480 B.C., says Herodotus, "were armed like the Phrygians, and together with these, they were commanded by Artomex II, son-in-law of Darius." Their weapons and equipment were all alike. At that time the Armens had occupied only southwestern parts of Armenia, while the Saspeirs and the Urarteans or Alarodians lived in the plains of Ararat. The Persian "royal" highway, connecting Sardice (Lydia) and Susa (Persia) passed across the modern Malatia-Harpout-Diarbekir-Jezireh areas.

Chapter IX
Armenia as Xenophon Saw It

Retreat of the Ten Thousand

Greek mercenary soldiers, ten thousand in number, who had been aiding the younger Cyrus of Persia against his brother Artaxerxes, returned home in 401 B.C., after the defeat and death of Cyrus at Cunaxa. On their way back, they passed through Armenia, and the *Anabasis* (going up), written by Xenophon, their leader, contains some valuable information about that country. Their precise itinerary has not been definitely traced, but according to the generally accepted theory, they crossed the Centrites (Kentrides) River, the modern Bohtan-Su, north of Til, reached the Teleboas River, the modern Kara-Su, in the plain of Mush, and then the Euphrates near Manazkert, fording it where it was only knee-deep. Thence they marched to Olti, the country of the Taochci (the Armenian province of Taiq), south of Kars. From the "great rich and populous city" of Cumnias, in the Scythian country (the more modern Cumri, still later Alexandropol and now Leninakan), they proceeded through the area of Zarishat and south of Ardahan, and finally through the mountains of the Macroni and Kolchi tribes to the Black Sea port of Trebizond.

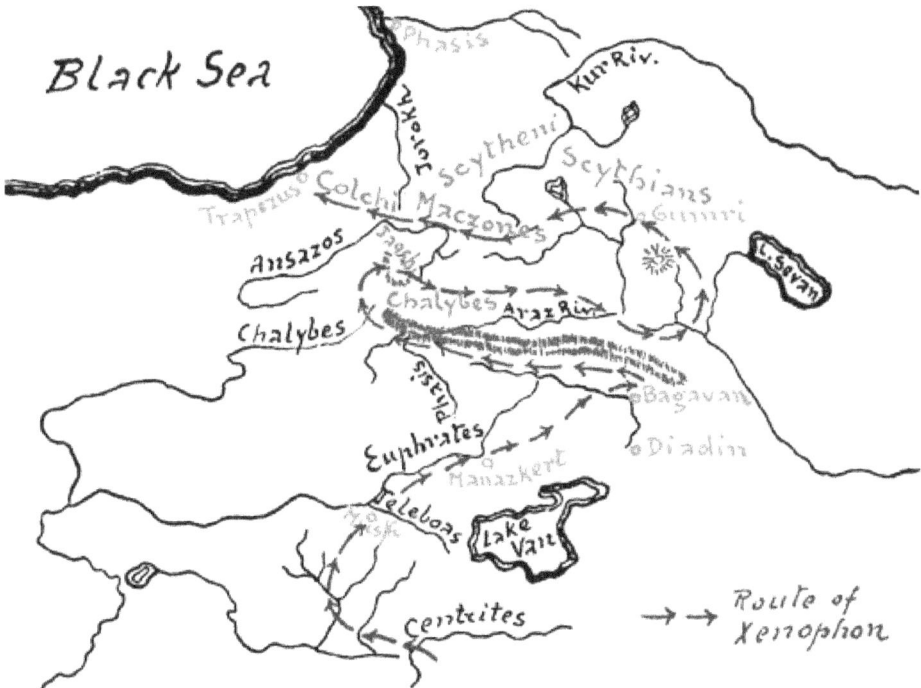

Route of Xenophon and the Ten Thousand (401 B.C.)

Armenia is described by Xenophon as a vast and rich country, with Orondas (Erouand) ruling as satrap and Tiribaz as uparkos or vice-governor. In Xenophon's time the Armens had not yet occupied the plain of Ararat, which was then inhabited by Saspeirs, Alarodians (Urarteans) and the oldest native tribes. The Kartuchi (Korduq of the Armenian geography), living in the south of the Centries, were a warlike people, not subjects of the Persians. They and the Armens were in almost continuous conflict, which, says Xenophon, explains why there were no villages in existence on the right bank of the Centrides, in the vicinity of modern Serd.

Armen Kinship with Khald-Urarteans

The Kartuchi were a sedentary people, with a comparatively high degree of civilization. Their dwellings were described by the Greek soldiers as elegant and furnished with many copper utensils. They had plenty of provisions and wine kept in cemented cisterns. According to Strabo, they were skilled architects, experts in the tactics of besieging fortresses. Their arms consisted of bows and slings. The bows were one and a half yards long, and the arrows more than a yard. This mode of life does not harmonize with cattle-growing nomadic people, such as the Kurds. The Armens therefore, thinks Marquart, must have been kindred of the Khald-Urarteans. The army of Orondas, says Xenophon, besides Armens, included Mards and Khaldian mercenaries. The latter were a doughty people, noted for their long shields and spears. The Khaldian soldiers of Orondas are considered to have been the inhabitants of Sassoun and the Khoyt Mountains, who maintained their independence until their assimilation with the Armens. As to the mercenary Mards, they were, according to Herodotus, an Iranian nomadic tribe, to be identified, in Marquart's opinion, with the modern Kurds. The tenth century Arabian historian Masoudi states that the Kurds acknowledged as their ancestor the chieftain Kurd, the son of Mard. In Armenian history the Kurds have been known as the "Mar people."

The district of Mardistan, in historic Armenia, corresponds to Artaz, west of the modern Maku, Iranian Azerbaijan. The district of Mardali (Mardaghi) must have been located to the south of Erzerum, north of the Bingöl sources. The Mards of this section of the country were evidently immigrants from the South, says Adontz. The bulk of the tribe occupied one of the southern areas of Vaspurakan (Van), near the upper course of the Centrides River. Xenophon mentioned particularly the extremely fierce and hardy Chalyb tribe, called Chaldaioi by Strabo, living in the Pontic Mountains, and mostly engaged in iron mining and forging. (The Greek marchers covered the distance through this coastal area — 50 parasangs or 150 miles — in seven days.) Several authors classify this people as being of the same stock as the Khaldi-Urarteans. The Taochi and the Phasian tribes, neighbors of the Chalybs, who likewise offered stiff resistance to the Greeks, are represented in the Taiq and Pasian districts of Armenia.

The above-mentioned tribes and several others, including the Kimmerian-Scythian settlers from southern Russia, dating from the eighth century B.C., were all independent of Persia. Scythian tribes, the Saspeirs of Herodotus, had occupied considerable areas extending from Colchis to Media — around modern Nakhjavan and as far as Kars, Leninakan and the plain of Ararat. Alongside the Kimmerians and Scythians should be listed the Sarmatian tribe, which includes the Siraqs and the Gogs, after whom the Armenian provinces of Shirak and Gougarq seem to have been named. The Mesoch-Mushkians, the Outians and the Pactians were also among the inhabitants of the Armenian plateau, each having its own language or dialect, and particular kind of social life and culture. They were all eventually assimilated with the Armens, adding their numbers to the larger elements from the Khaldi and the Hittites.

Armen Economics and Commerce

Despite the agreement entered into between Tiribaz and the Greek chieftains, some of their soldiers "insolently" burned some of the villages where they were to stop. They even had the audacity to capture the tent of Tiribaz — who, relying on the treaty, seems to have been unprepared — and carried away his silver-footed bedstead and his cups, as well as his bakers and cup-bearers (Xenophon).

Finding the villages evacuated, the Greeks spent seven days in sumptuous eating and drinking. "The tables everywhere were loaded with the meats of lamb, goat, pig, veal and chicken, as well as bread of barley and wheat. They drank beer from a great jar, sucking it through a tube." The horses of Armenia, says Xenophon, were smaller than those of Persia, but livelier. Being told that horses were sacrificed to the sun, Xenophon gave his old horse, in exchange for a foal, to a village chief, to be sacrificed, after being fattened.

Land of Plenty

Besides plenty of wheat, barley and cereals, the Armen villages had in store raisins, perfumed wine, sesame, fragrant oil of almonds and turpentine. The people were both cattle-breeders and agriculturists. They exported many horses. Herodotus calls the Armens polyprobatoi, "rich in animals." Distinction should be made, however, between the civilization in the different parts of the country. Stately houses with towers on the banks of the Centrides River were in striking contrast to the underground dwellings near the sources of the Euphrates. The rural life of the Armens was indicative of a patriarchal or family character. A group of villages was surrounded with barricades and was governed by a village chief or Komarch (archon tes komes) representing the satrap. Payment of taxes to the Persian king was made collectively. The absence of cities was noticeable. Various clans, settled in villages under local chiefs, supplied a specified number of soldiers to the army of the nearest petty king. A general of Darius was one of these kings. By the large numbers of the Armenian army serving under the Great Persian monarch — recruited from one section of the Armenian plateau — we are led to believe that all of the comparatively small number of new settlers were soldiers. The same was true in the Georgian and Albanian lands of the Caucasus, as pointed out by the Georgian historian, J. Tchavakhishvili. The word eri in the ancient Iberian (Georgian) language meant both people and soldiers. The Medes, after subduing the kingdom of Urartu, utilized the Armens in keeping that turbulent people under subjection. Marquart notes that the settling of the warlike Armen colonists in the strategic places in the Armenian highlands was because of their military capacity. From all this, Manandian reaches the conclusion that, as the ancient Slavons, so the ancient Armens were in the period of "warring democracy." The same may be said of the Medes and the Persians of old, whose democratic organization and public assemblies point to their having a soldier population.

Hence the destruction in the ancient East, even as in the medieval West, of the cultural great powers, had been mainly achieved by the so-called "barbarian" new peoples, such as the Medes, Persians and Armens. Applying the principle to the Armens, Prof. Marr has remarked, "And now there succeeded, one after the other, warlike Aryan peoples, just as in later times came inrushing masses of Turks. These Aryan races who, at that time, were certainly savages by comparison with the natives, were nevertheless strong in their military organization, and subdued the culturally higher races, intermixed with them and created a new world."

Attention is called by Manandian to the fact that the commercial intercourse between Babylon and Armenia was carried on for the most part by the Assyrians. Business transactions, limited in Armenia in those days, were principally in the hands of the Semitic peoples, while the Armenians were essentially farmers and cattle-breeders.

Chapter X
Alexander the Great and his Successors

Persian Decadence

The centralized government of Darius I began to disintegrate in the fourth century B.C. The provincial satraps were striving for independence, and the Greeks were looking with covetous eyes upon the wealth of the East. Philip of Macedonia, after unifying all Greece under his sway, was ready to embark upon an expedition against the Persians when he was assassinated. His son Alexander (336-323 B.C.), overthrew the Persian Empire in three great battles, and at Babylon in 331, proclaimed himself sole ruler of the united Macedonian-Persian Empire. But only eight years later, Alexander, after expanding his conquest to the borders of India, died at the age of thirty-three. Three of his generals thereupon divided his new empire among themselves, one centering his rule in Macedonia, another in Egypt, while the third had has capital at Antioch, Syria, which was founded by the general Seleucus Nicator (the Conqueror).

Greek Culture

Alexander, a pupil of Aristotle, had pursued an ideal, the welding of Asia and Europe by the introduction of Greek culture into the East. He had exchanged groups of inhabitants between the two continents, had built new cities in the East and populated them with Greek colonists. He encouraged intermarriage between the two racial elements, himself taking as his bride a Bactrian princess, Roxana. It was thus that Hellenic culture — literature, science and philosophy — was diffused through Asia. This intellectual intercourse, with its accompaniment of extended commercial connections, gave impetus to the development of crafts and productivity. Cities sprang up and quickly attained opulence. Colossal amounts of gold and silver, captured from the treasury of the Persian kings by Alexander, now came into business circulation.

Tetradrachma of Alexander the Great

A New Era for the Armens

Through the Macedonian conquests and the subsequent Seleucid domination in Hither Asia, there opened for the Armens a new era of political and economic advancement, which lasted 140 years — from 330 to 190 B.C., at which latter date the kingdoms of Artaxias (Artashes) and Zariadres (Zareh) were founded. The events of this period are not clearly recorded by national and foreign historians, but the study of Greek and Roman chronicles is helping to solve many problems and to correct erroneous assumptions hitherto adopted by many authors. The occupation of Armenia by Alexander's forces, for example, as related by Strabo and others, should be confined to Armenia Minor, whose government had been entrusted by Alexander to the Persian satrap Mithrines (Mihran). As to Armenia proper, it had by that time its own governor, Orondes-Erouand, who led the Armen army against the Macedonians in the battle of Arbela (331 B.C.), which was the death-blow to the Persian Empire.

The kingdom of Cappadocia had been reduced by the Macedonian commander Eumenes. "But Ariarat, the son of the slain king," says Diodorus, "escaped to Armenia in company with a few men, and later on, procuring soldiers from Ardoates, King of the Armens, fought and killed the Macedonian general, Amuntas, quickly expelled the Macedonians from the country and regained his father's kingdom." Reinach and other Armenists have proposed to read the above name Ardoates as Artavazdes. Marquart and Manandian prefer the reading Artoandas (Orontes, Erouand). The date of the founding of the Cappadocian kingdom through the aid of the Armen king must have been about 270 B.C.

Tetradrachma of Seleucus I Nicator

Under the Seleucidae

The Seleucid Empire stretched from the Hellespont to India. Armenia Major, Armenia Minor and Sophene maintained at that time their autonomous identity by paying money tribute to the suzerain and giving him military aid when called upon. Armenia Major then included a part of the Armenian plateau — only four of the fifteen provinces of later date, namely, Fourth Armenia, Aghtzniq, Tourouberan and Airarat. In the third century B.C., the city of Armavir, in Aiaratat, was the capital of the Erouandian dynasty, known to Khorenatsi as the Haikazants, Haikazian or Araratian. Greek annals tell us of the existence under the Seleucids of native "kings" of Armenia Minor and Sophene. One of them, whose name is unknown, had, according to Memnon of Heraclea, tendered shelter and aid to Ziaelas, son of the King of Bithynia, and enabled him to occupy his father's throne, which he did from 250 to 228.

Another Greek author, Polianus, says that the Seleucian Antiochus Hierax, in revolt against his brother, King Kallinikos, entered Armenia through Mesopotamia and took refuge at the court of Arsabes, the King, in 230 B.C. This monarch may be identified with Arsham, King of Sophene, who founded the city of Arshamashat, in the so-called Beautiful Plain, between the Euphrates and Tigris. The defeat suffered by Antiochus III in 190 B.C. was a signal for uprising in all nations subject to or threatened by the Seleucid regime. The Armenian lands, though not included in the Seleucid Empire, had been subjected to Hellenistic influence. The coins minted in the Armenian area during that period bear inscriptions in Greek. The province of Sophene, particularly that part adjacent to the northern border of Mesopotamia, near the international trade route, had all the advantages necessary to make it a great center. The fortress of Damissa, on the western bank of the Euphrates, was a halting station for caravans moving to or from Persia.

As another emporium in Sophene, its capital city, Gargatiokert, has been mentioned by Pliny and Strabo. Marquart proposes that the name be corrected by Argatiokerta, assuming that its founder was Argatias, son of King Zariadres of Sophene. The site of the city, according to Marquart, may be found in the ruins of the fort of Anggh, near the modern Egil or Arghana Su, one of the sources of the Tigris River.

Chapter XI
Artashesian and Zarehian Kingdoms of Armenia

Decline and fall of Seleucid Empire

Possessions in India were lost to the Seleucid Empire in 305. Fifty years later Diodorus, governor of Bactria and Sogdiana, rebelled and founded a separate kingdom. Cappadocia, Pontus, Armenia and Atrpatakan (Azerbaijan) had already secured semi-independence. Thereafter, in the third and second centuries B.C., the Seleucids were confronted with two mighty rivals — the Parthian Arsacids (Arshakists) and the Romans.

Arsaces-Arshak I founded the Parthian kingdom in 249 B.C. His brother and successor, Trdat-Arshak II, won a victory over Seleucus II, consolidated his rule in Parthia and subdued Hyrcania, modern Asdrapat, on the southeastern border of the Caspian Sea. In the meantime Rome extended its rule over the eastern countries of the Mediterranean (218-201 B.C.) and through the Battle of Magnesia, was solidly established in Asia Minor. Rome at first made a pretense of acting as the protector of oppressed nations, but in reality its policy tended towards domination and exploitation of them all.

Artaxias-Artashes and Zariadres-Zareh, the governors of Armenia, appointed by Seleucus the Great, sided with the Romans and declared the independence of two new kingdoms created by themselves. That of Artashes was the larger. According to Strabo, it included the Caspian area — Phaitakaran, Vaspurakan[13] (province of Van), Phaunitis (corrected by Hübschmann to Sunitis-Sewniq), Taiq, Xorsene (Ardahan), Gogarene (Gougarq), Karenitis (Erzerum), Derzene (Derjan) and Tamoritis (Timoriq). In the invasion of Armenia by Seleucus in 165 B.C., Artashes suffered defeat, but he soon recovered his rights.

Armenia Flourishes under Artashes

The great achievements of Artashes supplied material for many songs and folklore of ancient Armenia, some of which Khorenatsi has fortunately preserved for us. A song about the city of Artashat begins as follows: "Artashat went to the spot where the waters of Arax and Medzamor intermingle, and being pleased with the hill, he there constructed a city, calling it Arashat, after his own name. The Arax River aided him with the timber of forests;[14] he therefore carried out the construction easily and quickly, and erected therein a temple."

---

[13] Hübschmann considers the inclusion of this district doubtful.
[14] Meaning that timber was brought down the river by rafting.

Here Khorenatsi had the legendary Armenian world-conqueror, Artashes II, in mind.

The advent of Artashes I is described by Straboa as follows: "Armenia was first ruled over by the Persians and the Macedonians, and then by the Seleucians, who had conquered Syria and Media. The last ruler, Orontes, was an issue of Hyrcanis, one of the seven Persians. The country was thereafter divided into two nations by Artaxias and Zariadres. . . . They governed by the recommendation of the King (Antiochus the Great), but after his defeat, they reigned separately, and were declared as kings."

Tetradrachmae of Antiochus the Great Thayer Note: the legends read ΒΑΣΙΛΕΩΣ ΑΝΤΙΟΧΟΥ = "OF KING ANTIOCHUS".

The Orontes mentioned above is the Erouand of Khorenatsi's History — though he is confused as to the exact time, place and connections. His account of the construction by Erouand of the city of Erouandashat is worth quoting:

Building of Erouandashat

"In his time, the court was transferred from the hill called Armavir, because the Arax River had changed its course, and during the long winter, when cold north winds blew, the stream froze entirely, so that there was not enough water for the royal residence. Thus discomfited and likewise in search of a stronger location, Erouand transferred the palace to the West, upon a rocky hill, almost surrounded by the Arax, with the Akhurian flowing in front. He encircled the hill with fortifications, and in many places within the wall, he cut the rock as low as the base of the hill at the river's level, so as to permit water to run into the cisterns for the drinking supply."

It may be deduced from the above statement that the city of Erouandashat was built about the beginning of the second century B.C., or even earlier, by Orantas-Erouand, the predecessor of Artashes I.

Frontier-Markers

Two inscriptions of Aramaean characters discovered on the shore of Sevan Lake bear the name of Artashes I, according to Prof. A. Barisov of the Leningrad Ermitage. These tower-like square pillars were probably frontier-stones, mentioned by Khorenatsi in these words:

"After all the virtuous deeds and meritorious acts he (King Artashes) gave orders to fix the limits of villages and farms, because he had increased the population of the land of Armenia by bringing in many people from abroad and settling them in mountains, valleys and plains. And for the boundaries, he established such landmarks as these; he ordered square stones hewn, and buried in the soil, with sockets cut in them and square pillars erected thereon, a little higher than the ground. Artashir, the son of Sassan, jealous because of this, ordered the same to be done in the land of the Persians, and that it be called after his own name, so that the name of Artashes would no longer be remembered. But it is said that no uncultivated land, either on the heights or on the plains, had been left in Armenia at the time of Artashes, because the country had become prosperous."[15]

The discovery of stone landmarks with inscriptions in Aramaean letters is exceedingly important, for it proves the existence of a written literature in Armenia even before the invention of the Mesropian alphabet. This very fact, besides placing Artashes I among the great figures of history, explains the phenomenal blossoming within so short a time, of the Golden Era of Armenian literature, in the fifth century A.D.

Parthians Halted by Tigran

During the reigns of the successors of Artashes I, the Parthians under Mithridates I invaded many Seleucian possessions in the East. Their conquests were expanded by the succeeding king, Mithridates II (123-88 B.C.), who had waged war also on Artavazd, the son of Artashes I, and carried away as hostage the young Tigranes (Tigran II), the king's nephew. "The Parthians," says Strabo, "conquered the countries of the Medes and Babylonians, but not Armenia. Invasions were repeated again and again, but the country was not subdued by force. On the contrary, the Parthians were vigorously resisted and vanquished by Tigran," Artavazd's brother and successor.

---

[15] According to Prof. A. Dupont-Sommer of Paris, the two inscriptions commemorate a royal fishing, that of King Artashes on the shore of Lake Sevan.

Chapter XII
The Armenian Kingdom
Up to the Advent of the Arshakunis (Arsacids)
(190-95 B.C.)

Armenia in the Roman period

Artashes, Founder of Armenian Independence

The establishment of Roman supremacy in Asia Minor also brought about the independence of the two Armenian princes. With the Roman Senate's approval, both Artashes and Zareh assumed the title of king, and gradually extended their respective domains, at the expense of various neighboring peoples. "The Armenian language," says Strabo, "was then spoken in that entire region." As to the wars of conquest waged during this period, we have only the somewhat unreliable narrative of Khorenatsi. He tells us how Artashes captured from Erouand, the usurper, the stronghold of Erouandakert and the district of Shirak; how later on he reduced Armeno-Media, east of Ararat, taking it from Argam, a dynast of the powerful family of the Maratzis (or Mouratsans), descendants of the Median king, Astyages-Azhtahag.

Many acts attributed to Artashes II and his son Artavazd by Khorenatsi fit better into the known picture of the historic Artashes. Even the legend related to the capture and marriage of Satenik, the daughter of the King of Alans, should be placed in the reign of the founder of the Armenian kingdom.[16]

The newly-born Armenian kingdom had to face internal difficulties. Local princes, lords of vast domains, showed a tendency to contravene the royal authority in the provinces. But the new kings knew how to win the loyalty of these nobles of the conquered countries by respecting their prerogatives and by honoring many of them with positions, high-sounding sinecures at court.

New Capital, Artashat

It was decided that a new capital must be created to replace Armavir, which the River Arax, by changing its course, had left dry and indefensible. The new capital, Artashat (Artaxata or Artaxhsata) named in honor of its royal founder, was also built beside the Arax, but in a strong position on an eminence laved on three sides by the river. There is a tradition that the fallen leader, Hannibal of Carthage, a refugee in Armenia after his defeat by the Romans, selected the site and planned the city. It was located near the point where the rivulet Medzamor empties into the Arax. Its ruins may be seen about fifteen miles south of Erevan.

King Zareh also possessed many strongholds. One of these, Domisa on the Euphrates, had a position of both strategic and commercial importance, being on the caravan route connecting the Halys River with the valley of the Tigris.

Troubles with the Seleucidae

The claims of the Armenian kings to independence did not long remain unchallenged. Antiochus Epiphanes, of the Seleucid dynasty of Syria, after waging successful wars in that country and in Egypt, coveted new extensions of his authority and turned his eyes towards the East. Artaxias suffered defeat at his hands in 165 B.C., but soon recovered his losses, taking advantage of internal troubles in Syria, which compelled Antiochus to return home. Artashes was thus enabled to retain his throne, and Zareh, too, was saved from peril. The former

---

[16] This episode was the one of which the minstrels sang, — in the following strain: "The valiant King Artashes, mounted on a beautiful black steed, swinging a thong of red leather, decorated with golden rings, quick as an eagle which cleaves the air, crossed the river, hurled the red leathern thong with golden links around the waist of the lady, dame of the Alans, inflicting much pain on the waist of the frail young princess, and roughly brought her to his camp."

Another song had it that "A rain of gold fell during the marriage of Artashes; pearls rained at the wedding of Satenik." Artavazd — according to legends, dedicated to the demons — had been captured by the Azats (powerful spirits) and concealed in the darkness of a cave of Ararat. He never ceased in his effort to break the iron fetters, so that he might regain his liberty.

died in 160. His son and successor, Artavazd, according to legend, was subject to spells of dementia, and committed suicide while on a hunting expedition. His younger brother is said to have abandoned the government to a court dignitary, he himself preferring to live in obscurity in Akilisene.

Armenization of Asia Minor

The region lying west of this province, towards the Halys and Lycus Rivers (Kizil-Irmak and Kelkit) was colonized by Armenians, settled amidst the remnants of older populations of Cappadocia, such as the Tibarens, the Chalybes and the Cataons. This was Armenia Minor,[17] which had its national rulers, often in alliance with those of Armenia Major, but sometimes acting independently. Armenia Minor for a time fell under the domination of Pharnac, King of Pontus (190-156 B.C.), the most powerful prince in Asia Minor at that time. The Euphratean Armenia of Sophene escaped a similar fate, thanks to the help of the King of Cappadocia, who had guaranteed its independence in return for the cession of the fortress of Domissa. The Kingdom of Pontus, already engaged in war with the Romans, was unable to retard the expansion of Armenia, which was soon to shine with glory under Tigran the Great.

Provinces of Greater Armenia

---

[17] Armenia Minor, together with Pontus, became later a sort of Roman province, with the city of Cabira (Sebast-Sivas) as its metropolis. In Nicopolis on the frontier of Armenia, a Roman legion was stationed. Ancient Melitine, where the Armenian element was preponderant, was later — from the second to the fourth centuries — known as Armenia. By another administrative division, the Romans created a third Armenia, adding to it parts of Pontus and Cappadocia, so that Armenia Minor comprised, about the beginning of the fifth century, the following provinces — Armenia I, with Sebaste as its chief city; Armenia II, chief city Meletine; and Armenia III with Caesarea (Kayserieh) as its metropolis.

The Rise of Parthia

But now a new colossus had arisen in the East. The Parthians, emerging from Bactriana, had subjugated Media, Persia, Babylonia and Mesopotamia as far as the Euphrates. Their monarchs had assumed the title of Arshak, and one of them, Tirdat I, had defeated Seleucus II and taken him prisoner. The brilliant campaign of Antiochus the Great had not arrested their surge, and the Parthians finally dominated all western Asia. Mithridates II, the Great (114-86 B.C.) otherwise known as Arshak IX, after having assured his eastern frontiers by a great victory over the Scythians, turned his arms against Artavazd II, King of Araxian Armenia. The latter had taken from Media and Iberia many districts, the restoration of which Mithridates demanded.

Checked by Armenia

But the stubborn resistance which the Parthian King met in Armenia forced him to conclude peace, his only compensation being the taking as a hostage the heir apparent, who later became Tigran the Great. Mithridates failed in his attempt to reconstitute the ancient Persian Empire, while Armenia survived her fiery ordeal and preserved her independence. But this denouement unhappily led Armenia into tempting fortune. She expanded her territory until it extended from the Caucasus to Mesopotamia and Syria, without being disturbed, either by the Parthians, occupied by internal dissensions, or by the Romans, with Mithridates of Pontus kept in check.

The kingdom of Armenia was then bordered on the north by Iberia (Georgia), inhabited by Caucasian tribes dwelling since the remotest antiquity in the valleys of the Kur and its tributaries descending from the Caucasus. The Iberians, living in the plain, had adopted the costumes and manners of the Armenians and Medes. They cultivated the land, but those living in the mountains, bellicose by nature, were devoted mostly to military activities. Artaxias and his successors had contested their possession of the portions of the Gogarene, where the Armenian element was in the ascendency. Later on, however, these two peoples became more friendly. The Armenians and Iberians, as well as the Albans (Aghuanq) were compelled to accept the supremacy of the powers which had arisen to east and west of them; but they maintained a measure of autonomy and their own royal dynasties.

Neighboring Principalities

The region of Mesopotamia adjoining Armenia was divided among several independent principalities, such as Atiapene, Commagene and Osrhoene. The last-named, inhabited by Syrians and Greek colonists planted there at the time of Alexander the Great's conquest, had Ourha or Edessa as its capital. The existence of Osrhoene dates from the time of Antiochus (136 B.C.). Its kings, all bearing the surname of Abgar, were of various origins — Syrian, Mede, Persian and Armenian. They recognized the supremacy of Rome and maintained friendly relations with Armenia.

The invasion of the Arshak, Mithridates II, had not altered the aspect of affairs in this part of Asia. But according to Khorenatsi, sixty years after Alexander's death in 323, Arshak the Brave ruled over the Parthians in the land of the Kushans, and his grandson, Arshak the Great, conquering the entire East, bestowed the throne of Armenia upon his brother Vagharshak (Valarsaces), who thus became the founder of the Arshakuni dynasty of Armenia. This story has its elements of fact. One Vagharsh did become the first Armenian Arshakuni king, but his accession actually took place later, towards the end of the second century B.C.

Chapter XIII
Tigran the Great

Bargain with Parthians

Tigran II, younger brother of Artavazd II and ruler of Armenia from 95 to 54 B.C., obtained the throne by ceding to the Parthians the districts which their predecessors had wrested from the Medes and Iberians, a seizure which supplied the excuse for the expedition of Mithridates II of Parthia.[18] A quarrel arose between him and King Ardan (or Vardan) of Sophene, and Tigran attacked the latter, vanquished him and took over his domain. When Euphratean Armenia was thus suppressed, Tigran's kingdom then extended from the valley of the Kur to Melitine and Cappadocia. Mithridates VI of Pontus, who aspired to the annexation of Cappadocia, sought an alliance with Tigran by marrying one of his daughters to him. So by the treaty which followed the marriage, Cleopatra, a girl of courage as well as high education, became the Queen of Armenia.

Tetradrachma of Tigran II the Great

---

[18] The reader should notice the distinction between Mithridates II of Parthia (114-86 B.C.) and Mithridates VI, Eupator, of Pontus (123-68).

Tetradrachma of Mithridates the Great

Rome Drawn Into Imbroglio

The ensuing invasion of Cappadocia in 93 B.C. compelled Ariobarzan, its king, to yield and hurry to Rome for aid. His appeal won a ready response. The great Roman general Sulla came to Asia Minor, reinstated Ariobarzan on his throne and forced the Armenian army to retreat to the east bank of the Euphrates. The Eastern allies did not, however, admit defeat. The civil war which raged in Rome in 90 B.C. gave them the opportunity of regaining their advantage on the field of battle, and once more Ariobarzan was put to flight.

Tigran Gains Supremacy

Tigran's star was now in the ascendency. When Parthia's great king, Mithridates II, died in 86, Tigran felt himself equal to the task of proving his supremacy over the Parthians. He recaptured the lands which had been ceded to them, and marched still further to seize Atropene, Gordiene and a part of Mesopotamia, thus once more subjugating the territory of old Nairi-Urartu. To this were soon added the domains of Adiabene, Mygdonia and Osrhoene. The Armenian armies penetrated further into Greater Media and reduced its capital, Ecbatana, in whose royal palace Tigran had once been held as a hostage. It of course followed that he had now become the "King of Kings," a title which he inscribed on his coins. So the supremacy of Asia, which had belonged to Parthia under the Achaemenids and Seleucidae, was in this triumphant moment transferred to Armenia.

Tigran's glory attained its apogee when he was invited to Antioch in 83 B.C., and offered the crown of the Seleucid dynasty. Syria, which had long been torn by internal strife, under Tigran's rule enjoyed full peace for eighteen years. His power reached even beyond the confines of Syria proper, to include Palestine on

63

the south and Cilicia on the west. But like most Oriental monarchies, his kingdom was only an assembling of uncongenial peoples, with no cohesion.

Building of a New Capital

The expansion of his domain to the south and west made necessary the creation of a new and more centrally located capital. Artashat (Artaxata), the old capital, isolated in a remote province, lay too far to the north. Tigran therefore built in the southern part of Armenia the new city of Tigranocerta (Tigranakert), named in his honor. It was probably northwest of Nissibin, at the foot of the spurs of the Taurus chain.[19] As one enthusiastic writer says, the city seemed to spring from the earth as if by enchantment. In the splendor of its palaces, gardens and parks, in the richness of its ornaments and stored treasure, it is thought by some to have rivalled Nineveh and Babylon. Its walls were fifty "brasses" or fathoms (300 feet) high, and stables for the horses were built into their lower parts. The royal palace was in the suburbs, surrounded by a park, in which were many dens for wild game and ponds for fish. Tigran also constructed a strong fort near the palace.

By royal order, the grandees of Armenia were compelled to transfer their residence to the new city. Thousands of Greek families were deported from Asia Minor, as were others from Adiabene, Assyria, Gordiene and Arabian Mesopotamia, to build up the population of the new capital, which at once took on a cosmopolitan character.

Oriental Pomp

Tigran's public appearances were spectacular. He displayed all the pomp and magnificence becoming to a successor of Darius or Xerxes. Theoretically an equal of the gods, he clothed himself in a tunic striped in white and purple, and a mantle entirely purple. He always wore everywhere (even when hunting) a tiara of precious stones. Four of his vassal kings stood about his throne, and when he rode forth on horseback, they ran on foot before and beside him. When he received persons upon affairs of state, these kinglets stood around him, "with crossed hands."

Greek Culture

As polygamy was the rule in the East, great numbers of concubines were kept in a gynaecium, where Cleopatra ruled as Queen. Although the entire region was oriental in all traditions, under the influence of the scholarly Queen, Greek manners and culture were to a certain degree introduced into the kingdom. The

---

[19] According to classical writers, whose information is far from precise, Tigranocerta must be placed north of Nissibin, at the foot of the hills of Tur-Abdin, near Mardin. A more modern writer identifies it with the fortress of Tigra, mentioned by Darius I. Sachau, the German orientalist, believed it to have been on the hill now called Tel-Armen. Kiepert places it north of the Tigris River in the Arzanan. Belck and Lehmann propose the site of Miyafarkin (Martyropolis), near the Batman-Tchai River.

royal princes were taught the Greek language and sciences. Tigran himself, called upon to occupy the throne of the Seleucidae, could not have been a stranger to Greek art and letters. A theater was built in Tigranocerta, and the King invited Greek actors there to give performances in their own language. According to historians the plays performed were of the Bacchic or sensual type. Metrodorus, the Greek writer, a native of Scepsis, in Troy, once a minister of Mithridates, spent several years in the palace, writing the life and achievements of Tigran. Unfortunately, his history has not been discovered. Another famous Greek, Amphicrates, the rhetorician, was among those invited to Tigranocerta. Artavazd, the King's son, wrote dramas and histories in Greek. Remains of his works survived as late as the first century A.D.

Tigran was forty-seven years of age when he married Cleopatra. By her he had three sons, two of whom were slain by his own hand; one of them during a rebellion, when the son took up arms against his father. On another occasion, while hunting, Tigran fell from his horse, and a second son, instead of rushing to his aid, picked up his father's crown and placed it on his own head; whereupon the infuriated King struck him dead. The third of these sons, also named Tigran, having expressed profound regret and sympathy for his father at the time of this accident, was given a crown by Tigran, but later on he too revolted against his father. The son, Artavazd, who succeeded Tigran, was not the child of Cleopatra.

Despite some objectionable aspects of his social, domestic and public life, Tigran deserves honor as a torch-bearer of Hellenistic culture. "The two great kings of Pontus and Armenia," says Jacques de Morgan, "were the last ones capable of reproducing in their states the beautiful civilization of Hellas."

Contradicting Mommsen's assertion that the Armenian and Pontian struggles were reactionary movements, Professor Manandian claims that Tigran's progressive measures met strong opposition in Armenia from the old partisans of Oriental ways of life. He further declares — and is supported by other scholars — that the conquests and achievements, as well as the wealth and prosperity attributed by Khorenatsi to Tigran I, should be credited to Tigran II, the Great. Khorenatsi, misled by ancient popular songs and traditions, ascribed even the building of Tigranocerta to Tigran I, who lived 560 years before "the Great."

His Empire Short-Lived

However, great though Tigran II was in ability, the empire created by him was doomed to be short-lived and a mere flash of lightning in history because of Roman ruthlessness and the mad audacity of his father-in-law Mithridates. The verbal treaty made between Sulla and Mithridates in 84 B.C., was only an armistice. Murena, the Roman governor of Asia, arbitrarily and without the approval of the Roman Senate, renewed hostilities, but his attacks were repulsed. Mithridates appealed to Rome for peace, but in vain; the internal politics of Rome required brilliant victories abroad. Lucullus came to Asia with a powerful army and navy, and Mithridates, forsaken by his own officers, was badly beaten, even his son seeking favor with the invaders. There was nothing left for him but to take refuge in Armenia. Tigran alone hesitatingly promised him aid, though it meant fighting not only the Romans but also the Parthians, who (according to Gutschmid) held a bitter grudge against him and were already formally at war with him. Plutarch, always ready to besmirch Tigran, attributes to him a cold and unconcerned attitude towards his father-in-law. Other historians give us a different picture of Tigran, who in answering a demand by Lucullus for the surrender of Mithridates, replied: "The whole world and my own conscience would condemn me if I should surrender the father of my wife to the enemy."

Oppressions of Lucullus

The outcome was inevitable. The entire territory of Pontus was seized by the Romans and pillaged. The large and flourishing cities of Heraclea (modern Eregli) and Amisus (modern Samsun) were ruthlessly sacked and destroyed. Not content with enormous sums of money demanded as war indemnity from the impoverished population, all private property — lands, houses, personal adornments of women — were subjected to heavy taxes. The people, reduced to bankruptcy by the rapacious conqueror, had, in the space of only fourteen years, acquired a debt of 2,000 talents, about $20,000,000.

Lucullus had been secretly planning a sudden assault on Armenia, without a declaration of war. Immediately after the rejection of his peremptory demand for the person of Mithridates, the Romans marched upon Tigranocerta. Upon his return from a Phoenician expedition, Tigran had refused to believe the news of the appearance of Romans on Armenian soil; but now, facing the cold reality, he issued orders for resistance, at least to the extent of retarding the movements of the enemy. But it was now too late. One of his generals, Mihrbarzan, at the head of an infantry division and 3,000 cavalry, was defeated and slain in an engagement with the vanguard of the Roman army under Sextellus. The Armenian troops were dispersed Tigran, upon hearing of this disaster, fled to the northern part of his country, leaving his treasure and wives in Tigranocerta. Another Roman force under Murena pursued him hotly and seized his baggage. Meanwhile, Sextellus invested the new capital and captured the suburbs and the palaces situated outside the walls.

Allies in Tigran's Army

Tigran still possessed enormous resources in the form of territory, money, soldiers and munitions. Encamped on a plateau on the northern slope of the Armenian Taurus, he reinforced and reorganized his army. In response to his appeal, the Kings of Adiabene, Atropatenes, Iberia and Albania came to his aid, as well as some Arabian chiefs. Having thus collected an army, whose numbers some estimate as high as 100,000, and learning that Lucullus had laid siege to his capital with a comparatively small force, Tigran disregarded the advice of Mithridates to surround the enemy and cut off its supplies, and instead, thought only of rescuing his treasures. A corps of 6,000 of his cavalry succeeded in piercing the enemy lines by night and bringing off the women and a part of the valuables.

Now emboldened by this achievement, Tigran sallied forth with his main army, in the hope of scattering the besiegers. When he reached a height from which Tigranocerta was visible in the distance, Lucullus left Murena with 6,000 cavalry to watch the city and prevent a sortie, and himself marched with 10,000 infantry and some horsemen to meet the King. "If they are coming as emissaries," Plutarch represents Tigran as saying, as he looked down in some perplexity upon the small advancing force, "they are too many; if as antagonists, they are very few." The story that he made such a remark is derided by Manandian, in view of the inaccuracy of the quoted strength of the two armies. Plutarch gives 14,000 to 15,000 as the number of Lucullus's troops; Ammianus and Mommsen accept this estimate and place the strength of Tigran's host at 300,000. This great disparity of 1 to 20 has been questioned by several scholars, who propose 70,000 to 80,000 as the number of the Armenian army, and add to the Roman forces the number of their Anatolian allies, another 15,000, thus reducing the ratio 1 against 2, or thereabouts.

Armenian Disaster

It was an autumn day, October 6th, 69 B.C. when this milestone in Armenian history was reached. Lucullus began the attack by leading two cohorts up a hill which Tigran had neglected to occupy. From there the Romans dashed down upon the cavalrymen, who recoiling from the shock, fell back upon the infantry, throwing the latter into disorder. Within a short time the army of Tigran was defeated and scattered, and the King in flight lost his tiara and diadem.

Tigran and Mithridates could not avoid the fact that their situation was critical. All the provinces lying south of Taurus were lost. Greek troops entrusted with the defense of Tigranocerta mutinied, and despite the efforts of Mancius, the commander of the place, these mercenaries surrendered to the Romans the portions of the city they were supposed to defend. So with the promise of the Romans that the wives and property of the alien citizens be spared and they be repatriated to their respective homelands, Tigranocerta fell. The city was then given up to plunder. The booty was enormous; the treasury alone contained 8,000 talents in gold coin, not to mention other riches hoarded there. Each Roman soldier received 800 drachmas as his share of the spoil. In the still uncompleted theatre, the victory honoring Lucullus was celebrated.

Lucullus spent the winter (69-68 B.C.) in Gordiene, seeking alliances among the petty kings of the neighborhood, who were ready to shake off the yoke of Tigran. The Roman labored to win the friendship of Phraates, who had succeeded old Sanatruk on the throne of Persia. Phraates, however, held aloof, for he had received messages from Tigran and Mithridates which informed him that the Romans were casting greedy eyes upon his empire, too. Lucullus had in fact been contemplating an attack upon the Parthians, but his army was not just then in condition to undertake a campaign. He broke camp around the end of spring, to cross the mountains separating the valley of the Tigris from the plain of Mush, and arrived in Armenia at the right season, when the wheat was not yet ripened.

Tigran's army, reinforced by Mithridates, had taken strong positions on hills, while the cavalry, commanded by the King himself, endeavored to cut the Roman's supply line. Lucullus, at the head of his legions, ascending the valley of Arzania, marched towards Artashat (Artaxata). This ancient capital of Armenia contained much wealth, including the remainder of King Tigran's treasury.

Indecisive Battle

Tigran, maneuvering to draw the Romans away, marched along the opposite bank of the river, menacing the enemy's rear. The armies met in battle in September, 68. The Median cavalry and Iberian lancers at first seemed invincible, but when Roman infantry forded the river and attacked them, they took to flight. While these fugitives were being pursued by the Roman horsemen, Tigran attacked the legions, and Mithridates harassed them from the rear. For a moment the Romans were in real peril, but Lucullus, plunging desperately with his cavalry into Tigran's own regiment, threw Mithridates into confusion. The armies drew apart after both had suffered heavy losses, but the result was indecisive, and the allies were able to execute an orderly retreat and occupy new positions in force.

Lucullus Retires from Armenia

Artashat was still far out of reach of the Romans, and the Armenian summer was near its end. After the Roman army had marched a few stages, its advance was halted by a sudden cold wave and heavy snowfall. This, climaxing his failure to crush Tigran during several months of campaigning, discouraged Lucullus. He abandoned the project of reducing Artashat, and moved back towards the South, consoling himself with the capture of the city of Nissibin, in Mygdonia, whose governor was Guras, Tigran's brother. During the eight years of this campaign, with no decisive victory, the Roman army appeared to have become a mere convoy for the loot which Lucullus took from cities, temples and palaces for his own private gain, and which made him a wealthy man and a noted gourmand for the rest of his days.

As Lucullus withdrew into Mesopotamia, Tigran and Mithridates returned to their countries. The King of Pontus even fought an engagement against a lieutenant of Lucullus and killed 7,000 of his troops. The allies took the offensive soon after this, again invading Cappadocia and driving the Romans out of Pontus. Tigran eventually became the master of all the provinces north of the Tigris River. So the Romans lost all the gains of recent years; the great victories of Lucullus vanished like a dream.

Tigran in his old age had the misfortune of seeing his home broken up by domestic dissensions. Although the children which Cleopatra gave him were impatient to reign, none of them did. Zareh, who was the first to revolt, together with several other malcontents, lost his life in battle.

Enemy Aided by Tigran's Son

Rome could maintain her Asiatic possessions only by continuing the mortal struggle to crush Tigran and Mithridates. Pompey, who succeeded Lucullus in 66 B.C., was now at the head of considerable forces in Cilicia. After spending the winter in that country, he marched against Mithridates. The King of Pontus had been struggling hard to win an alliance with the Parthians, but the emissaries of Pompey forestalled him and succeeded in concluding a pact with Phraates. As for the younger Tigran, Pompey offered to Phraates, his father-in-law, aid in undertaking a powerful diversion in his favor in Armenia. While Pompey, at the very first encounter, put Mithridates to flight, Phraates and young Tigran penetrated into Armenia, compelling the old king to retire to the mountains; but they lost much time and drained their strength in a siege of Artashat, which offered a stiff resistance. Phraates, lest a longer absence augment domestic troubles, finally returned to his country. The younger Tigran was defeated by his father and fled to the Roman camp.

Tigran II Surrenders

Pompey set out towards Artashat with his army, but was still fifteen miles away when the heralds of old Tigran appeared, followed by the King himself. He had come humbly to ask for peace. At the gate of the camp, a lictor helped him to alight from his horse. When he saw Pompey, he removed his diadem, and was about to prostrate himself before the Roman general, but the latter prevented him, made him sit by his side, and consented to a peace, on condition that Tigran renounce his acquisitions in Syria and Asia Minor, and pay 6,000 talents indemnity and recognize young Tigran as the King of Sophene.

The aged, weary monarch accepted these terms, promising to the Roman troops a gratuity of fifty drachmas per soldier, one thousand per centurion, and one talent to each tribune. But his son, who had hoped to occupy the throne of Armenia, could not conceal his discontent. He carried on secret intrigues with the Parthians which were presently discovered, and he was put in chains by Pompey. This was a violation of such international law as prevailed then, and was a humiliation inflicted upon the King of the Parthians. Phraates sought the liberation of his son-in-law but in vain; young Tigran, his wife and children were sent to Rome to be paraded in the triumph of Pompey. The peace granted by Pompey obliterated all the conquests of Tigran the Great, and reduced Armenia's terrain once more to her ancient borders.

There were a number of reasons for Armenia's greatness being so short-lived. She was surrounded by an agglomeration of peoples whom she could not assimilate until she could overcome the powerful Roman and Parthian influences upon them. Also, Armenia herself was disrupted by internal strifes, the result of her feudal form of government. This explains to some degree why the attempt of Tigran the Great had been unique in his country's history, and why he, notwithstanding his mistakes and defeats, represents a brilliant page in the story of Armenia.

Chapter XIV
Artavazd — The Last Tigrans

Roman Rule Supreme in Western Asia

The struggle with Rome had been long and exhausting. It began with the first skirmishes of Mithridates against the Romans, and extended over many years; but Pompey triumphed at last, and assured the Roman domination of the Asiatic continent. Since Mithridates and Tigran were thoroughly beaten, there remained no other obstacle from the Pontus-Euxine to Egypt and the banks of the Tigris. Armenia had fallen and counted only as a sort of barrier against the Parthians. Pontus, Cilicia and Syria were reduced to the status of Roman provinces, and Antioch, the capital of the Seleucidae, became the Roman metropolis of western Asia. Cappadocia's kings had long since become loyal subjects of Rome. In Mesopotamia the Abgars had also acknowledged allegiance to Rome, as had Antiochus, the Seleucid king, who had fallen to the rank of a simple governor of Commagene. The face of the Eastern world had been completely changed since the arrival of Pompey; the states which Alexander's conquests had brought to life had, by 64 B.C., all disappeared.

Artavazd Threatened by Crassus

Artavazd II (from a coin)

The only remaining people in western Asia unconquered by the Romans were now the Parthians; and the Roman military chiefs vied with each other for the honor of making war on these Easterners, each general hoping to win renown like that of Caesar and Pompey. Crassus, member of the famous Triumvirate with Caesar and Pompey, won the coveted command and hastened to Syria. It was the misfortune of Armenia to serve often as a battleground for the antagonists; while in the interior, the great ones, some favoring Rome, others Parthia, fomented civil war by calling to the throne no less than ten kings in fifty years. Old Tigran was still living, but since the year 54 he had associated his son Artavazd with him in the government. A prince of irresolute nature, though of cultivated mind,[20] Artavazd could not escape the misfortunes which were destined eventually to bring him to a tragic end. In fear of both Romans and Parthians, he sought to evade the dangers by taking the side of whichever antagonist seemed to prevail at the moment — a fatal vacillation.

Defeat and Death of Crassus

Crassus hastened to cross the Euphrates, dispersing a number of opposing forces, and rushing his conquest in order that he might proclaim himself Imperator. When he resumed campaign in the following year, 53, Artavazd presented himself as a Roman ally, offering to put 6,000 cavalrymen at the disposal of Crassus and to give him passage through Armenia, where the Roman army would find provisions, a favorable terrain and the assistance of 30,000 horse soldiers. The Imperator refused these propositions, preferring to take the route through Mesopotamia. This proved to be a fatal error. His army was soon surrounded by the Parthian cavalry under Surena, and the Roman rout became a disaster. Cherished Roman eagle standards were captured, Crassus himself was slain, and only a few remnants of his army succeeded in reaching the Euphrates. Artavazd, who had been charged with the duty of blocking the Parthians, promptly abandoned the Roman cause. He made advances to Orodes, the Parthian king and sought his alliance, which was accepted and consecrated by the marriage of Artavazd's sister with Pecoras, the son of Orodes.

Since the Roman army had been crushed, it was now easy for the Parthians to invade Syria, and in 51 they besieged Antioch. Rome, then torn by civil wars, could give no thought to the deliverance of Syria, which was thereupon occupied by the Parthians and Armenians for fifteen years.

It was not until the powerful duumvirate of Octavius and Mark Antony arose in Rome that the Romans recovered Syria, Antony being given the government of the East as his portion. His lieutenants everywhere repulsed the Parthian-Armenian allies. Syria was evacuated by them by the time of Antony's arrival in Asia. Artavazd now executed another volte-face by placing auxiliary troops at the disposal of the Romans. Antony accepted the offer, and in accordance with the Armenian king's advice, avoided the arid plains of Mesopotamia, so fatal to

---

[20] We owe this information to Plutarch. Khorenatsi is in error in representing Artavazd as an ignorant King, devoted to hunting and gluttony.

Crassus, and took the route via Armenia to march on Ecbatana and Ctesiphon, with the intention of striking at the heart of the Parthian Empire.

Antony's disaster and Revenge

But again a colossal disaster befell the Romans (36 B.C.), and Antony, in battle and retreat, lost 80,000 men before reaching the borders of Armenia. This the duumvir believed to be due to the treachery of Artavazd, and he began planning revenge. Two years later he paid a visit to Armenia, where, by way of cozening Artavazd, he solicited the hand of one of the King's daughters for a son of Antony and Cleopatra, the Egyptian Queen. Soon after this, Antony arrived in Nicopolis, in Armenia Minor, and invited the king to meet him there for a consultation. Artavazd feared treachery, but reluctantly accepted the invitation. He walked directly into a trap. He was seized, together with his wife and children, bound with golden chains, and taken to Alexandria, where he was offered to Cleopatra, to be exhibited in a triumphal parade.

Denarius of Mark Antony and Cleopatra
"Armenia Devicta"

Artavazd's Rragic End

The dethroned monarch became a nuisance, indeed, a menace to Cleopatra, whose desire it was to bestow the throne of Armenia upon her son Alexander. She finally rid herself of Artavazd by having him beheaded after the Battle of Actium in 31 B.C. This son of Tigran the Great, who lacked the strength of character to maintain a real neutrality, paid for the mistakes of his life in a manner of which even the so-called barbarians disapproved.

Upon his death, the Armenian nobles placed upon the throne Artashes II (Artaxias), the eldest son of Artavazd, who had found refuge among the Parthians. The young Alexander, whom Antony and Cleopatra had intended to be king of Armenia, could not take over the throne because of Parthian opposition.

72

Antony, then in the final months of his struggle with his former partner, Octavius, was unable to aid his son. But Artashes's accession to the throne was repugnant to the ideas of Rome. When Octavius (now rechristened Augustus) came to the East in 29 B.C., the Roman partisans gained sufficient strength to drive out Artashes. Once more Armenia fell under Roman influence; but Augustus found it advisable to endow the country with an autonomous government under its native King. He gave his great general, Tiberius, the task of putting the affairs of Armenia in order and enthroning Tigran III (brother of Artashes), who had been transferred from Alexandria to Rome. Tiberius accomplished this program more easily because Artashes had died before the general arrived in the East. He insured Roman predominance in Armenia, and the princes who succeeded one another on the throne rendered homage to Rome for the next quarter of a century. These princes, issue of the family of Tigran the Great, still claimed the title of "King of Kings."[21]

The reign of Tigran III did not last long, nor did that of his son, Tigran IV and of his daughter, Erato, the two latter married to each other in accordance with Oriental custom. (They were only half-brother and sister, having different mothers.)

Tigran IV was dispossessed by Augustus because of suspected treachery, and Tiberius came again to Armenia to replace him with Artavazd, a cousin of Tigran's. This arbitrary act led to discontent and finally to civil war, partly instigated by Tigran, whom Phraates, King of Parthia, was secretly backing. Matters having reached the stage of rebellion against Roman authority, Augustus sent his godson, Caius Caesar, to bring about an appeasement, but before his arrival, Tigran IV was killed in a riot, while his associate, Erato, took to flight. As the Parthian King had renounced his activities to avoid provoking Rome, Caius Caesar suppressed the revolt, and in the year 1 A.D., the Armenian throne was bestowed upon Ariobarzan, a Mede by origin, who was accepted because of his eminent qualities.

End of Artasheshian Dynasty

But Ariobarzan very shortly was killed by accident, and Augustus nominated Artavazd, his son, as his successor. This Median dynasty, however, could not be maintained. The national opposition to foreign rule soon found expression in the assassination of the King. Augustus thereupon abandoned his ill-conceived policy and sent Tigran V, a descendant of the national dynasty, to occupy the throne. But the nation's tranquility, apparently restored by this concession, was soon disturbed. The nobles recalled Queen Erato, but her reign was short, and her overthrow marked the end of the dynasty of Artashes and Tigran. The Armenians

---

[21] Armenian coins in silver and bronze, from that epoch, with the effigy of the sovereign and the inscription, "King of Kings," still exist.

73

were unable to agree on the choice of a King until 16 A.D., after which they had to accept any prince imposed upon them by the Parthians or the Romans.[22]

Owing to the lack of historical documents, we are not sufficiently informed as to all the causes of the fall of this national dynasty, though it may in general be attributed to the incessant strife of the aristocratic families with the royal authority.[23]

---

[22] Moses Khorenatsi, supported by Syriac traditions and Eusebius, creates a successor of Tigran the Great and Artavazd, one Arsham, making him a nephew of Tigran and the father of Abgar of Osrhoene. According to this tissue of fables, Tigran's first successor ruled in Edessa and in Nissibin until the accession of Artashes. The national historians have copied him, lacking any knowledge of the events which took place in Armenia before her conversion to Christianity. Carrière, the French scholar, was the first to demonstrate that the name Arsham or Arschama, borrowed from Laboubna (Lerupnia), is a nickname (Oukhama) given to Abgar, meaning "the Black," "the negro" and not "the father of Abgar."

[23] This view has been questioned by certain modern Armenian scholars, chiefly by N. Adontz.

Chapter XV
Rivalry between Parthia and Rome

Roman Suzerainty

The Emperor Augustus, instead of reducing Armenia to the status of a province, kept her under a sort of vassalage. In accordance with the wishes of the nobles of the country, he had maintained the succession to the throne in the royal family of Tigran. But after the extinction of the national dynasty, the Parthians and the Romans each tried to hand Armenia over to such princes as would be the more devoted to their respective causes. None of these so-called rulers, however, could secure the succession to his own family.

The historians who describe the military operations of the Romans in the East give no space to these kings of Armenia whose tenure depended on this or that foreign power. As for the Armenian chroniclers, they ignore the very existence of such rulers. At one time during this period, Vonon, the son of Phraates IV of Parthia, came to Armenia, offering himself as a candidate. The release of this Vonon, long held as a hostage in Rome, had been demanded of the Romans by the Parthian nobles after the assassination of Orodes II; he was crowned, but was soon dethroned by Artaban III, king of Parthia. The occidental manners which he had acquired in Rome being disliked in his home country, he fled to Syria.

Zeno a Popular King

About this time Germanicus was sent from Rome with the mission to stop the encroachments of the Parthians in Armenia. The two opposing elements in the country finally agreed upon Zeno as occupant of the throne. He was a son of Queen Pitidoris of Pontus, whose husband, Polemon, was a loyal vassal of Rome. From his early youth Zeno had practiced Oriental manners. His love for hunting and feasts made him popular in Armenia. Germanicus, upon arriving in Artashat, placed the royal circlet on his head in the presence of a great multitude, and the nation offered homage to the new monarch, acclaiming him by the name "Artashes" (18 A.D.). This was a clever choice, and won Germanicus a sort of triumph.

Parthia Seizes the Throne

Peace prevailed in Armenia during the sixteen years of Zeno's reign, but upon his death in the year 34, Artaban, the King of Parthia, placed upon the Armenian throne his eldest son, Arshak (Arsaces). He furthermore claimed all the treasures hoarded by Vonon in Syria and Cilicia and everything else to which he, as an alleged successor of Darius and Alexander, was theoretically entitled. The answer of the Emperor Tiberius to such demands was the concentration of more Roman forces in the East. Once again, Armenia was to become for twenty-five years the theater of bitter warfare between the two greatest powers of the known world. The alternate triumphs and reverses of each of the opponents in rapid succession subjected the native population to cruel oppressions for alleged sympathy with the side temporarily in eclipse. Mention may be made of the devastation inflicted upon Armenia in 44 A.D. by King Mithridates of Caucasian Iberia, a satellite of Rome, who ruled in Artashat for several years.[24]

King Trdat the Pahlavid

Statue of Trdat I King of Armenia
(Marble, Louvre Museum)

Parthian supremacy in Armenia was asserted upon the advent of Valarses I (Vagharsh) of the Pahlavid family (50-90 A.D.), who bestowed the throne upon his youngest brother Tiridat or Trdat I. The new king drove the Iberian usurper away, but when he retired to Parthia for the winter season, Rhadamist reappeared and committed many brutal acts of vengeance. Exasperated by such excesses, the people of the capital revolted while Trdat, the King, was on his way back. Rhadamist fled towards the Caucasus, and was saved only by the speed of his horse.[25]

---

[24] This tyrant was himself suffocated under bed-cushions by his own nephew, Rhadamist, who had seized the throne of Armenia. He had taken oath not to kill his uncle by either fire, steel or poison.

[25] His wife, Zenobia, who rode with him, was, so says tradition, pregnant at the time. In order not to retard her husband's flight, she threw herself into the Arax River. Shepherds rescued her and carried her to the palace, where Trdat treated her in a manner due to a royal lady.

Romans Destroy Artashat

Again Roman intervention was called into play. The Emperor Nero sent in 58 A.D. Domitius Corbulo to check Trdat's incursions within the eastern borders of the Roman dominions. Corbulo's legions soon reached the suburbs of Artashat and forded the river avoiding the bridge in order to execute a flanking movement. But Trdat had already evacuated the city. Corbulo set fire to it and reduced it to utter ruin. He then proceeded southward to capture Tigranocerta. By that time the King of Kings himself had assumed the high command, and was threatening a Roman force stationed on the banks of the Arzanias River. Corbulo changed his course and hastened to the aid of the endangered legions, but in the end he accomplished nothing more than a successful retreat to the west of the Euphrates, which Valarses consider as the frontier of the Roman Empire.

Rome was celebrating an imagined triumph over the enemy when messengers arrived from the victorious Parthians, bringing evidence that the Roman legions had been forced to evacuate Armenia. The Emperor ordered a continuation of the war, but was willing to discuss terms of peace. Corbulo, after some negotiating, finally agreed to recognize Trdat I as King, on condition that he receive the crown of Armenia from the Roman Emperor. Trdat consented to this compromise, and also to a preliminary curious sham ceremony.

Pretended Crowning by Nero

The Romans erected in the camp near Artashat a rostrum surmounted with a curule chair,[26] upon which was placed an image supposed to represent Nero. Then from a distance Trdat appeared at the head of a magnificent parade of military and civilian dignitaries. The Parthian and Armenian cavalry were arrayed along one side of the platform in gorgeous national trappings. On the opposite side were ranged the Roman legions, with their brilliant display of eagles and ensigns, and with statues of divinities between the lines, as if they were in a temple. Sacrificial animals were first slaughtered. Then Trdat marched forward, took his own diadem from his head and humbly deposited it at the foot of Nero's statue. The spectacle is said to have stirred the legionaries with a deep and intense emotion. Trdat next replaced the crown on his own head, and the pompous ceremony was followed by many gestures of courtesy and by feasts spread by Corbulo.

Trdat's Journey to Rome

But Trdat must next go to Rome to be crowned by the Emperor himself. Before setting out on this excursion, he paid visits to his mother and brothers in Media and Parthia. He then began the long journey, accompanied by his family and an imposing retinue, comprising many feudal lords and 3,000 horsemen, Armenia, Parthia all being represented in the cavalcade. Trdat himself being a chief Magian

---

[26] A chair in which the higher Roman magistrates had a right to sit (chariot).

of the Zoroastrian religion, avoided the sea route and traveled by land, Mazdeism prohibited spitting in the water or desecrating it with any other refuse of the human body. Their route therefore lay across Thrace, through Illyria, on the eastern shores of the Adriatic, and Picenum, in northeastern Italy, the journey taking nine months. Trdat, a handsome and noble figure, rode on horseback, having his children and the Queen at his side. Throughout the entire time his wife must have her face screened from the public gaze, according to Oriental custom; but instead of using a veil, she wore a golden helmet whose visor, when lowered, completely covered her countenance.

Trdat and Nero, 66 A.D.

Nero awaited Trdat at Neapolis (Naples), sending a state chariot to carry the visitor over the last few miles. No one was supposed to approach the Emperor armed, but Trdat maintained his dignity by refusing to remove his sword as he approached the ruler of the world, though as a compromise, he agreed to its being firmly fastened in the sheath, so that it could not be drawn. At Puteolis, the modern Pozzuoli, near Naples, Nero ordered athletic games to be staged in honor of his guest. The Armenian King himself had opportunity to display his ability as a marksman by shooting one arrow through the bodies of two buffaloes.

Pageantry in Rome

The climax of the ceremonies was of course reserved for the world's capital. Rome was profusely decorated with flags and bunting, and gorgeously illuminated at night. On the day after their arrival, Nero came to the forum, clothed in triumphal vestments and surrounded by dignitaries and soldiers, all resplendent in gay attire and glittering armor. While he sat on the imperial throne, Trdat and his retinue advanced between two lines of soldiers. Arriving in front of the dais, the Eastern King knelt, with hands clasped on his breast. When the thundering shouts and acclamations excited by this spectacle had subsided, Trdat thus addressed the Emperor:

"My Lord, I am a descendant of Arshak and the brother of the Kings Valarses and Pacoras. I have come to you who are my god; I have worshipped you as the Mithra; I shall be whatever you would order me to be, because you are my destiny and fortune."

To which Nero replied in these words:

"You have done well by coming here to enjoy my presence in person. What your father has not left to you and what your brothers did not preserve for you, I do accord to you, and I make you King of Armenia, so that you, as well as they, may know that I have the power to take away and to grant kingdoms."

After this reply, Trdat mounted the steps of the platform and knelt, while Nero placed the royal diadem on his head. When the young King was about to kneel a second time, Nero lifted him by his right hand after kissing him, made him sit by his side on a chair a little lower than his own. Meanwhile, the populace gave tumultuous ovations to both rulers. A Praetor (judge), speaking to the audience, interpreted and explained the words of Trdat.

"Golden Day" of Festivity

Great public entertainments continued for some time after the coronation ceremony. The interior of the Theatre of Pompey and every piece of its furniture were entirely gilded for the occasion; for which reason Rome ever afterwards recalled that date as "the Golden Day." Daytime festivities were on a scale no less lavish than those of the night. Royal purple awnings stretched as protection against the heat of the sun. Nero, clad in green and wearing a chariot driver's headdress, took part in the chariot race. At the evening banquets, in gold-embroidered vestments, he sang and played on the lyre. In memory of these events, the Senate honored Nero with the laurel wreath and the title of Imperator, or commander-in-chief of the armies.

Munificence of Nero

Fragments of ornamental carvings from the temple of Garni

No reception comparable to this in magnitude and splendor is recorded in the history of Rome. Besides the enormous sum spent in festivities, the Roman Government bore the entire cost of the journey of Trdat and his retinue from and to their homeland. Nero also made a gift to Trdat of 50,000,000 sesterces, equivalent to about $2,000,000. Amazed by the extravagance of the Emperor,

Trdat is said to have expressed to Corbulo his surprise at his serving such a master. On the other hand, he remarked to Nero, "Sire, you have a wonderful servant in the person of Corbulo."

World Peace

Peace prevailed at this time throughout the Roman Empire. Nero therefore closed the gates of the Temple of Janus, which were never shut save in times of universal peace.

When Trdat returned to Armenia, he took with him a great number of skilled artisans for the reconstruction of Artashat. He renamed the capital Neronia, in honor of the Emperor; he embellished the royal residence of Garni, near by, with colonnades and monuments of dazzling richness.

Greek inscription of Trdat I relative to the reconstruction of the fortress of Garni

Armenia Assailed by Barbarians

Rome now counted upon Armenia as a loyal ally, even after Nero's death and through the entire duration of Vespasian's rule in the East. Armenia also enjoyed peace until a new invasion came to trouble her. The Alans,[27] together with other Caucasian tribes, fell first upon Media and then, in 72 A.D., upon Armenia. Trdat valiantly attacked the barbarians, and had a hairbreadth escape from being caught with the leather noose or lasso which the Alans used to capture enemies. The invaders were repulsed, though carrying with them considerable plunder in their retreat, and alternate sorties went on for some time before peace was concluded.

---

[27] Alans, by the Armenian historians and by H. G. Wells; Alains by R. Grousset.

Trdat's Death

A major problem remained, however, blocking the way to any improvement of international relations. Trdat died in 75 A.D., leaving no issue to succeed him, and Rome's choice fell upon an alien, non-Arsakhid prince. Khosrov II (Chosroes) the Parthian King, wasted little time in dethroning this puppet and replacing him with his own nephew. Trajan, the Roman Emperor from 98 to 117, in his zeal to enhance the glory of his reign, came to Armenia in person in 115 and camped before the walls of Karenitis, the modern Erzerum. The Parthian incumbent, failing in his attempts to cajole and placate Trajan, sought to take flight, but was killed by Roman guards.

Armenia Chooses Own King

The victory thus won by Trajan proved abortive, and Rome, under Hadrian (117-138), once more found it advisable to adopt the wiser policy of Pompey, Antony and Augustus, and permit the Armenian nobles to choose their own ruler. The political horizon was thus somewhat cleared in the East, despite some depredations committed by the King of Iberia, a protégé of Rome. The accession in 138 of Antoninus Pius, a strong and upright Emperor, assured a period of tranquillity, which continued until the appointment by Rome of Sohemus, a prince of Syrian origin, as King of Armenia.[28] The Parthian army now entered Armenia and routed the Roman legions in Akilisene, whereupon Sohemus fled. The Romans then came in full force under Priscus, and after capturing Artashat, marched upon the Parthian capital, Ctesiphon, which they overthrew and subjected to devastation. Sohemus was reinstalled on the throne of Armenia in 163, and Roman influence in the country became well-nigh supreme.

On the death of Sohemus in 185, the Armenian throne was bestowed upon Sanatrouk, the son of a nephew of one of the Abgars of Osrhoene. He ruled in peace for twenty-seven years, during which time he constructed the city of Mdzur (or Mdzurq) in Sophene.[29]

Although a loyal ally of Rome, he remained neutral in the war which raged between the two Roman Emperors, Niger and Septimius Severus, in 195.

---

[28] Son of an Arshakid mother and Achaemenid father.

[29] This name was until recent times confused with that of Nissibin-Mdzbin. One copyist seems to have changed the name. Khorenatsi represented Mdzbin as a center of learning, where he allegedly found the Armenian history, written by one Mar Apas. The location of Mdzbin is far to the south, and outside the Armenian frontiers, while the city built by Sanatrouk was near the center of Armenia Major. Its site has been identified with some ruins at the confluence of the Aradzani and one tributary of the Euphrates Rivers, west of the extensive plain of Mush, which in turn lies west of the Lake of Van. The positions of the fortress and the town had great strategic and commercial value. The German archaeologist Tomasheck identifies the site of Mdzur with that of Oghakan, the stronghold of the famous Armenian warrior, Mushegh Mamikonian. Phaustus, historian of the fifth century A.D., mentions the fort of Mdzur as in ruins. According to Sebeos, the ruins of the royal palace, with its marble columns, were still in evidence in the seventh century.

Artaban, the King of Parthia, who was supporting the cause of Niger, fomented a disturbance in Armenia which cost Sanatrouk his life.[30]

---

[30] According to Khorenatsi, Sanatrouk became a precursor of the Christian faith in his own country, but later renounced it and condemned to martyrdom the apostle Thaddeus and his own daughter Sandukht, who had also become a convert. He is further said to have massacred all the children of Abgar, in order to eliminate all pretenders to the throne. Notwithstanding the confusion of names and dates, it is certain that Christianity had penetrated into Armenia as early as the reign of Sanatrouk, 166 to 193.

Chapter XVI
Persian Civilization

Mitanni Were Indo-Iranian

The Persians, the Medes and most of the other peoples of ancient Iran belonged to the Iranian race of "Aryan" (Indo-European) origin; which, in other words, means that it was a branch of the Indo-European group. The time of their settlement in Iran is not known, but there is ample evidence to show that the region northwest of Mesopotamia had been inhabited in the fourteenth century B.C. by the Mitannian people, whose kings had Indo-Iranian names, and who worshipped Indo-Iranian gods.

The primitive Iranian language was closely connected with Sanskrit. It has two dialects; first, the "ancient Persian" — the speech of Fars or Persian proper — which is the language of Achaemenid inscriptions; second, the Zend, representing a speech of Media, which was the language of the Mazdean Bible, the Avesta. A more recent form of the Iranian was Pehlevi, the language of the Parthians and Sassanians.

Emergence of Medes and Persians

The first Iranians emerging in history were the Medes, inhabiting the present Iraq-al-Ajami. In 612 B.C. their king Cyaxares (625-584) took Nineveh and destroyed the Assyrian Empire, which was divided between the Medes and their allies, the Babylonian-Chaldeans and the Syrians. In 550 B.C. the Median Empire was overthrown by the other great Iranian people, the Persians, whose King, Cyrus (Kuros), thereupon annexed all Media, Asia Minor, eastern Iran as far as the Indus River, and finally, the Babylonian Empire, including Syria. His dynasty, the Hakhemenish (Achaemenid), ruled until 330 B.C. One of its kings, Cambys, also conquered Egypt in 525. Shortly after this, the throne was occupied by Darius I (Darayavush) (521-486 B.C.), of a collateral branch of the Achaemenids. This monarch and his son, Xerxes I, vainly attempted to conquer Greece. Their successors were forced to satisfy themselves only with meddling in the brawls among Greek cities, until the day when Persia's last king, Darius III, was defeated by Alexander the Great in 330 B.C., and his empire lost forever.

The ancient Persians have always been regarded as one of the nobler peoples of the East — loyal, chivalrous and humane. "Young Persians," said Herodotus, "are taught three things — to ride a horse, to shoot with the bow, and always to tell the truth."

Indo-Iranian Religions

Before the separation of the Iranians from the Indians, the Indo-Iranian tribes worshipped two groups of divinities; the Deva — "Celestials" — and the Asura or Ahura — "Lords" or "Masters." After their separation, Iranians and Indians treated these two categories differently. The people of India deified the Deva, reducing the Ahura to the status of mere titanic enemies of the gods, presently becoming demoniacal. The Iranians, on the contrary, made demons (dev) of the Deva, recognizing the Ahura as the only true gods. According to the inscriptions of Darius I, the Iranians of the Achaemenid period had gone even further; one of the Ahura, worshipped under the name of "the Wise Lord," Ahura-Mazda, was recognized as the "greatest of the gods," if not indeed the Supreme Being of the Universe. The Achaemenid kings appealed to Ahura-Mazda alone, thus approaching monotheism. An essential feature of this religion was the lighting of fire upon an open-air altar. Many sculptures on Achaemenid tombs picture the sovereign in front of the lighted altar, with Ahura-Mazda appearing above as a winged genie. Mithra, once a social god, was then assimilated with a solar deity. Along with this dynastic religion, there existed the sacerdotal caste of the Magi (Magu).

Zoroastrianism

Scholars place Zoroaster's epoch in the seventh century B.C. Born in Media, he retired into seclusion at the age of twenty, began to preach at thirty and converted to his new faith Vishtaspa, the King of Bactria, who had thrown him into prison. At 77 he was slain by Turanian invaders. The *Gatha*, the first texts of the Avesta, seem to belong to the founder's epoch. This religion is based upon a sort of dualism — the principle of light and the good, Ahura-Mazda, the only god, as opposed to the principle of Darkness and evil, Angra Manyu, the Mazdeian Satan. The first created all good things, the second all bad things in existence. Some hypostasis appearing as angels in Christianity as affiliated with Ahura-Mazda; the six "immortal Saints," or the Amesha-Spenta, personified as Vohu-Mano, "the Good Thought;" Asha-Vahishta, "the Best Virtue," etc. Below these genii are the Yazata, in the front rank of which we meet Atar, "the fire," "the son of Ahura-Mazda;" also Apo, the water; Hvare, the Sun; servant of the Benevolent god Mithra; the Fravashi (hreshtak in Armenian), guardian angels as well as the divine substance of the soul; Verethragna (Bahram, the Vahagn of Armenia), the angel of victory, etc.

Opposing this army of the good was the army of the bad, created by Angra-Manyu, in which are the daeva (dev in Armenian) and other figures of the Indian pantheon — the demons, the druj or ghouls, and the pairika (peris) or fairies. World history is that of the endless duel of the Good and the Bad. The Mazdeians believed in the immortality of the soul. After death, one must, according to one's conduct in life, cross the Bridge of Judgment, either to the Abode of the Blessed or to Hell. This ensemble of dogmas has an optimistic finale. At the end of time there will appear a sort of Messiah, Saoshyant, the son of Zoroaster, who will preside at the resurrection of the dead. A deluge of molten metal will overwhelm the world and bring about the Last Judgment. All wicked beings will be destroyed and all the good preserved. While the Achaemenid kings buried their dead, orthodox Mazdeists exposed theirs, lest the touch of the corpses defile the holy principle of the fire, of the earth or of water.

Achaemenid Liberalism

No monarchy could have been more liberal than the Achaemenid, the administrative organization of which was the work of Darius I. He divided his enormous domain into twenty provinces, each headed by three royal functionaries — the satrap, the secretary or chancellor, and the commander of the forces. Envoys were sent periodically to inspect the provinces. The centralization thus attained did not do away with nationalistic groups; the Persians permitted all existing cultures to continue. Their tolerance towards the religions of subject peoples was remarkable by contrast with the intolerance of other conquerors. The Assyrians, as it were, waged war against foreign deities, taking into captivity, along with the worshippers of each, *Yahveh* of Israel, *Bal* of Tyre, *Marduk* of Babylon, *Sushinah* of Susa, *Amon* of Thebes and *Khaldis* of Urartu. The later Mazdeian fanaticism of the Sassanid epoch was unthought of in the time of the Achaemenids, Cyrus became almost a national hero for them, and Esther, a Jewess, sat on the throne beside a legendary King Ahasuerus, 519-465 B.C.

A regulated system of taxes replaced the arbitrary ransoms imposed by the Assyrians upon their subject peoples. A network of main highways, with couriers speeding over them put all quarters of the empire in close touch with each other. Wars between races, peoples and cities ceased. Peace, the "Achaemenid Peace," similar to the Pax Romana of a later date, was established for about two centuries, in all the East; the Caucasus — from the Bosporus and Cyrenaica to the Jaxartes and the Indus Rivers.

That the Persians did not attain the military and cultural high level of the Greeks does not justify their being regarded as specimens of Asiatic "barbarism." On the contrary, they eminently represented Aryanism in the Oriental world. They and the Romans were the only ancient peoples able to maintain for very long a great empire — a task in which the Greeks, despite their brilliant qualities, failed.

In a literary way, the cuneiform script was quickly adopted by the Achaemenids, with simplifications which brought the number of symbols to thirty-six. All their inscriptions are written in the cuneiform, whether edited in the old Persian or in texts engraved in trilingual form — ancient Persian, Elamite-Anzanite, and Chaldean. As to material civilization, the Achaemenids became the heirs of the old monarchies of the Tigris and Euphrates. It may be said that the capture of Nineveh by the Medes and of Babylon by the Persians resembles the conquest of Iran by the old nucleus of the Chaldeo-Assyrian civilization.

Achaemenid Art and Architecture

The Achaemenids made innovations in the entire artistic domain, beginning with architecture. Instead of the Assyrian brick basement with stone facing to receive the bas-reliefs, they founded their palaces on strong stone sub-structures still visible today. They borrowed from Egypt the stone column as well as the idea of rock sepulchres. The Mazdeian religion did not require temples. The two Achaemenid architectural ensembles, Susa and Persepolis, are therefore only palace groups. In sculpture, the Persians had Assyria as their teacher, although they soared high in the reproduction of details in the sphere of pure thought and abstract speculation. The Assyrian garb was sumptuous and heavy. Among the Iranians, dress was simpler. The Mazdeian theology inspires representations of divinity, but instead of the multiple gods of Chaldeo-Assyrian sculpture, only the image of Ahura-Mazda (or of the royal Fravashi) is found in Persepolis. This image, a new representation of the Master of Wisdom, really fits into a spiritualism more refined than that of the Hebraic, and as transcendent as that of Plato. Only under the Sassanids did Mazdeism, instead of this winged figure, prefer an equestrian Ahura-Mazda, a copy of the image of the Great King himself.

Reminding us of the Sargonids, the Achaemenid king appears in various attitudes: in adoration before a fire-altar, in the pose of a conqueror, with his enemies in chains, and in the act of striking down a monster. In all these scenes the Achaemenid king, like Ahura-Mazda, wears on his head a tiara with a sort of bonnet, partly of cloth, rising from it, larger at the top than at the bottom. He wears the wide "Median robe, with long, slowing sleeves reaching to his feet.

The royal throne was supported by a throng of subject peoples, each one in its own peculiar type and costume. The enameled bricks found by the Morgan expedition in Susa, show the development in beauty of this art, originally Assyrian. The archers were armed with bows, quiver and spear, garbed like the kings in a loose, long, wide-sleeved tunic, wearing on their heads a sort of *calotte* (skull-cap) held by a cord.

Chapter XVII
The Arsacids (Arshakunis) of Armenia

Parthian Attempts on Armenia

Since the middle of the first century A.D., the Parthians had been endeavoring by every means to attach the Armenian Crown to their dynasty; and the accession of Trdat I marked the culmination of the efforts of Ardaban III and Valarsh I. But the Romans had so far frustrated all these attempts. The Emperor Hadrian had permitted the accession of a new Arsacid, and Antoninus Pius, Hadrian's successor, foiled the Parthian designs by naming a Syrian prince to the throne. However, an occasion soon came to weaken Armenia's Roman protection. The Parthian Valarsh or Ardaban IV, profiting by the civil war raging among four contenders for the Roman throne, found himself in a position to follow the line of his predecessors. He took the side of the locally dominant pretender Niger against Septimius Severus, and this enabled him to send his nephew Valarsh to Armenia in 193. His partisans later assassinated Sanatruk, the Roman protege.

Coin of Emperor Antoninus Pius showing him crowning the King of Armenia

As a representative of the royal house of the Arsacids, the young Valarsh was given a hearty welcome by the Armenian nation. His family, which had ruled several Touranian peoples in the Central East, was known under the name of Pahlavi, which means Parthian. It reigned in Bahl Zariaspa after the fall of the Greek kingdom of Bactriana in 126 B.C. The Kingdom of the Pahlavi continued to exist at Bahl until the middle of the sixth century, when it was overthrown by Khosrov I, the Sassanid. The Pahlavi Arsacids were considered by the Orientals as having more rigid morals and beliefs than the earlier Arsacids, who were accused of practicing Occidental customs.

Since the fall of the dynasty of Artashes, the throne of Armenia had been occupied by monarchs, none of whom could leave the succession to his descendants. They were for the most part elected. The descendants of Valarsh were maintained upon the throne until the first quarter of the fifth century because it suited the Romans better to protect these Arsacids, as political enemies of the Sassanids. These kings called themselves Arshak, which means monarch; hence their dynasty is known under the generic designation of Arshakuni-Arsacid.[31]

Activities of Valarsh

Valarsh adhered to the policy which best served Armenian interests, that of cultivating the friendship of Rome. When the Emperor Septimius Severus was marching on Ctesiphon in 197, Valarsh went to meet him and promised to aid him with auxiliary troops. For the third time within the space of a century, the Romans entered the royal city of Parthia.[32]

After the death of Septimius Severus, his son Caracalla renewed the campaign at a moment when the Parthians were weakened by internal dissension. The city of Edessa, the capital of the kingdom of Osrhoene, was the center of defense of upper Mesopotamia. To enable him to announce a victory, Caracalla suppressed this tributary state, threw Abgar, its King, into prison, and reduced the capital city to the status of a Roman colony.

Caracalla's Inept Policy

Since 197 Armenia had maintained a scrupulously correct attitude towards Rome. Now Caracalla, greedy and sadistic, invited Valarsh and his sons, then in rebellion against their father, to appear before him, pretending that he would arbitrate the quarrel. But upon their arrival at his headquarters, they all suffered the same treatment as had the King of Osrhoene. This odious trick brought about a revolt of the Armenians. Caracalla hurled a formidable force against them, but the infuriated Armenians repelled it.

Valarsh Dies in Prison

Valarsh, once a sincere ally of Rome, despite his blood relationship with the Parthians, died in prison in 216. In times of peace he had done much towards the improvement and enrichment of his country. The portion of Hazarapet, or

---

[31] Armenian historians, such as Phaustus, Agathangelos and Khorenatsi, extend the designation of Arshakuni to anterior Armenian kings, such as Sanatrouk and Tigran the Great. Arshak is the generic title of the Parthian kings, as was Pharaoh in Egypt and Shah in Persia. The ending uni or ouni has been borrowed from the idiom of the Urartean inscriptions, and is still used by the Armenians in the same sense as the actual termination *ian*.

[32] This great city, (Tisbon) of which only majestic ruins remain, was on the east bank of the Tigris, opposite Seleucia, about 20 miles below Baghdad.

superintendent of the fields and products of the soil, was one of his creations. He also introduced the use of the solar year of the Persians, together with the Feast of Navasard or New Year, which became one of the great solemnities of paganism, and which was celebrated in pomp at Bagavan, a metropolis of pagan worship. Valarsh had conferred upon the noblemen of Armenia commissions at the royal court. He constructed many towns and buildings, among them the castle of Valarshakert, on the upper Arzanias River, the eastern branch of the Euphrates, and the city of Valarshapat,[33] which became the capital of the Arsacids. His many acts promoting the welfare of his country place Valarsh in a high rank among the Kings of Armenia.

Trdat II (Khosrov I) 185-216

The Emperor Macrinus, who reigned in 217-218, concluded a peace with the Parthians which involved the payment by them of a huge indemnity. He won the Armenians by recognizing Trdat II, the son of Valarsh, and setting at liberty the Queen Mother, whom Caracalla had imprisoned. He also restored the lands owned by the Armenian Kings in Cappadocia. Trdat was thus enabled to rule in tranquillity for the time being. During his reign many illustrious families of Bactriana in Central Asia, the cradle of the Armenian Arsacid dynasty, emigrated to Armenia. Among these were the Kamsarakans and the Mamikonians, the first-named related to the royal house and the second composed of bold warriors. Trdat received them hospitably and gave them freeholds. Unfortunately, a strange uncertainty overhangs the story of Trdat II and his brother Khosrov, who succeeded him. The earlier Armenian historians completely ignore Trdat and attribute the events of his reign to that of his brother Khosrov I. Hence the dates of their reigns are in dispute.

Rise of Artashir

The truth was that the great Parthian Empire was nearing its end. The Arsacids had not been able to establish a homogeneous administration or a permanent army, nor had they a regular law of heredity. After the death of a king, the nobility simply made a selection from among the claimants or pretenders to the throne, membership in the Arsacid family being a prerequisite. The Great King could act only with the consent of a council composed of his leading vassals. The greatest hereditary officer, next to the King, was the commander of the army. Compelled to depend upon such an organization, Artaban V could not put down the insurrection stirred up by Artashir the Sassanid, son of Papak, a great Persian feudatory. Artashir won the Parthian army to his support, killed Artaban in battle in 224 and assumed the title of "King of Kings." He seized the whole of Persia, Media and a part of Iran. He strengthened Mazdeism, the Zoroastrian orthodoxy, restored the Magians to their former power, and thus brought about a renewed persecution of Christians.

---

[33] apat and kert are Persian endings, meaning "built" or "founded."

89

Coin of Artavan V, the last of the Arsacid Kings of Persia

The accession of the Sassanids is a major fact, a milestone in the history of Armenia as well as Persia. The friendship long existing between Parthians and Armenians, because of the relationship between the ruling families and the similarities of customs and religious ideas, was now broken and replaced by an implacable and enduring enmity.

The Sassanid dynasty was no mere tribe of nomads; it was highly civilized. Artashir, in order to insure unity in the teaching of the national religion, chose a mobed of noted sanctity who was given an opiate, under the influence of which he slept for seven days, and upon awakening, dictated the entire creed of Ahura-Mazda or Ormuzd. Under the Sassanid dynasty — which endured for more than four centuries — ecclesiastical interest was very powerful. Holding the natural elements as sacred, they charged that Christians defiled the earth by their burials, defiled water by washing in it and ignored the sacredness of fire.

Drachma of Artashir I, founder of the Sassanid Dynasty of Persia

Artashir Moves Against Armenia

The Armenians, embittered not only by the Sassanid overthrow of the Armenian Pahlavid dynasty but by their insistence upon imposing their religion upon their old allies, gave sanctuary to the children of the deposed King Artaban. Artashir, greeted in 227 as the restorer of the ancient religion and language of the Persians and given the title of *The Mazdeian, Issue of the Blood of Gods, King of Kings of Iran and Aniran* (such was the legend on his coins), moved against Armenia in 229. Trdat (Khosrov II) resisted, and aided by the Medes and some Caucasian tribes,[34] repulsed the assailants. But this defeat did not balk the hopes of Artashir, who now raised anew the claims of the Achaemenids to all Asia, and demanded that the Roman Empire surrender to him the ancient territories of Darius. He invaded those areas, laid siege to Nissibin in 231, and sent scouts even into Cappadocia.

Alexander Severus Saves Armenia

Rome was thus forced to reopen a struggle destined to drag through four centuries. The young Emperor Alexander Severus (222-235), taking the field in 232, sent a great army to the East, which was joined by the Armenians and some of the northern tribes. The center of this invading host marched on Mesopotamia, the right towards Chaldea and the left through Armenia towards Atropatene. But the center was stopped by an overpowering mass of the Persian army, commanded by the King himself; the left wing, including Trdat's Armenians and the northern tribesmen, though it obtained considerable booty, was pressed back from Media to Armenia. The right wing also met stiff resistance, but withstood it, though Artashir might have won a victory had he been able to hold his discontented troops together. It was a stalemate. Alexander celebrated a somewhat illusory triumph in Rome, but the fact remained that he had saved Armenia. In exchange for this protection, Armenian auxiliaries were sent to Maximinus — who succeeded Severus in 235 — to serve in the war against the German tribes.

But in 238 Artashir reopened the struggle and captured Nissibin. Shahpur I, son and successor of Artashir, continued the warfare; the Persians advanced as far as Antioch and compelled the Emperor Gordianus to embark upon another expedition to the East. Timisthe, the Emperor's father-in-law, repulsed Shahpur and was advancing towards Seleucia, northeast of Babylon, when the Roman Soldier Philippicus assassinated Gordianus, seized the Imperial throne, and concluded a peace with Shahpur, surrendering to him Armenia and a part of Mesopotamia.

---

[34] Agathangelos lists these tribes as the Aghouans (of Caucasian Albania), Georgians, Huns, Lepins, Jeghbs, Casps, etc.

Drachma of the Sassanid King Shahpur I

Fall of Artashat

Hostilities were resumed in 252, and the Persians laid waste the Roman territories of Mesopotamia and Syria. The Armenian King had troubles of his own at home, especially with turbulent and rebellious vassals, among them Selkuni, lord of the district of Taronitide (the modern Mush), whom Shahpur had won to his cause. In 253 the Persians captured Artashat, the Armenian capital, together with the family of its King, he having taken refuge in Roman territory. The Armenian throne was then bestowed by Shahpur upon Artavazd, with an order to introduce fire-worship into the country.

Shahpur I defeated by Palmyra

The woes of the Armenians under this domination were made heavier when the Roman Emperor Valerianus was taken prisoner in 260 by the Persians, who then invaded Syria and Asia Minor. But the fortunes of war took a sharp turn in the following year when the army of Shahpur suffered a staggering defeat at the hands of Odenathus, King of Palmyra, whose subjugation had been sought by the King of Kings. Odenathus advanced as far as the gates of Ctesiphon, after capturing the treasures and wives of Shahpur, but he did not demand the release of the captive Roman Emperor. Thus reduced almost to impotence, Shahpur's hold on Armenia was weakened, and the partisans of Rome in Armenia began trying to shake off the Persian yoke. Even Artavazd, the Armenian King, advised Shahpur, his sponsor, to set the old Roman Emperor at liberty; and when this was not done, he quitted his throne in 261.

Uncertain Period

The turmoil of almost constantly recurring wars, with their destruction of cities and memorials, the absence of written records and the inevitable partisanship of such reports as we have, have left the Armenian history of this period fragmentary and vague. The King who succeeded to the Armenian throne in 261 is by several writers called Khosrov, though he could scarcely have been the one who was the younger brother of Trdat II. But his reign was broken into, at the time when Persia — and once, so some reports say, Palmyra — took over his country briefly. For one short period there seems even to have been a state of anarchy.

With the whole Orient in agitation, it was impossible for the Armenian King to enjoy a stable authority. But he clung to his throne with a tenacity which induced the Persians to plot his assassination. This was finally accomplished by an emissary named Anak, sent by Shahpur. The monarch left an infant son named Trdat who, according to tradition, was spirited into Roman territory.

Romans Destroy Palmyra

In addition to this major objective, the Persians sought to take advantage of the internal conflicts then raging in Rome. But their situation became precarious in 273 when the powerful Emperor Aurelius, suppressing the civil strife, marched upon Palmyra with intent to subdue its Queen, Zenobia, widow of Odenathus. She claimed the Persians and the Armenians as her allies; but Persia, disturbed by domestic dissensions, made no move to aid her, while the Armenians preferred the friendship of Rome. Aurelian overthrew Palmyra, and the unfortunate Queen was compelled to walk in his triumphal procession through the Roman streets.

Persians Crippled

The Emperor Carus, at the head of a formidable army, entered Ctesiphon in 283. The Persians were only partly relieved by his sudden death in the field — reputedly by lightning. They had to withdraw from Armenian affairs and cease all aggression against Rome for a decade. But the restoration of a national monarchy in Persia was a fact of the highest importance in Oriental politics. The Sassanid sovereigns never sincerely abandoned their claims to the possessions once comprised within the Achaemenid frontiers; and the new dynasty, founding its claim on a religious basis, reestablished the political affairs of the Persians, which had fallen into grave disorders under the latter Arsacid kings.

Chapter XVIII
Trdat III and St. Grigor (Gregory)

Rise of Christianity

While Ahura-Mazda was recovering power in Iran, the creed of Jesus Christ was making great progress throughout the Roman Empire. To the opposing political interests of the two rival Empires there was to be added within a few years the most implacable of all hostilities, that engendered by religious convictions.

For centuries before the restoration of Mazdeism, the Iranians, Armenians and Romans gave little thought to any religious differences among themselves. The gods of the Parthians, as well as those of Armavir, Artashat and Ani (Kamakh) were tolerated under the prevailing Roman lenity. Moreover, the Eastern relations, tinged with Hellenism, had many common links with those of the West, and the ingenious assimilation of the Romans averted the danger of religious conflicts among the various peoples paying tribute to the Empire. This wise tolerance, carefully maintained during the course of three centuries, was fated soon to crumble. In the era now opening, the national cult would dominate the political scene, even as Assyria had once dominated Asia in the name of the god Assour. The religion of Christ must struggle, at first against Mazdeism, later against Islam.

Legend of Abgar

Shortly after the death of Christ, his creed made its appearance in Armenia. With the growth of the Church, legends began to accumulate. One had it that King Abgar V of Edessa, known as Oushama, suffering from a chronic disease, invited Jesus to come to his capital and heal him, and even to reside there. Moses Khorenatsi gives an alleged copy of the letter. Christ was unable to go to Edessa, so the story goes, but the Apostle Thaddeus visited Abgar later, cured him and baptized him.[35]

First Missionaries

The Armenians had not then acquired the art of writing, hence no contemporary documents of the first three centuries after Christ have come down to us, and we have only traditions regarding the earlier years of that period. The belief persisted that the Apostles Thaddeus and Bartholomew — and sometimes also another is named — first preached the Gospel in the land of Ararat; but when? We do not know whether these men were of Christ's own Twelve or of the Seventy sent out later. Some authors assert that 'Thaddeus" was really one Adda, or Adde, a court

---

[35] Pertaining to Loussavoritch (Illuminator).

94

official who became Bishop of Edessa, and was one of the martyrs of 166 A.D. The legend continues, however, that Thaddeus from Edessa passed over to Artaz in Armenia, established a church there and converted many persons, including the Princess Sandoukht, daughter of King Sanatruk, who then ruled over Adiabene and a part of Armenia, and that the King condemned his own daughter to death for her apostasy. As for Bartholomew, another source reports his evangelizing in Elam, Persia and India, his return to Armenia late in Sanatruk's reign and his martyrdom at Van. Thus the Armenian Church Fathers claim apostolic origin for their Church, and the Armenian Patriarchate as a direct successor of the first bishops consecrated by the two apostles.

National chroniclers testify to the existence in the third century of two Christian Churches in Armenia, the one at Artaz and another in the province of Sewniq. Denis of Alexandria mentions one Merouzhan as Bishop of Armenia in that century. But Christianity battled its way upward only against strong opposition from Persia and later from the Emperor Diocletian (284-305).

Mazdean Infiltration

No archaeological monument of the Sassanid period has yet been discovered in Armenia; but some rare coins minted by the Princes of Iberia (Georgia) prove that Persian influence extended as far as the foot of the great chain of the Caucasus Mountains, and therefore over a part of Armenia. Attempts of the Court of Ctesiphon to bring Armenia into the Persian orbit by conversion to Mazdeism were continued for centuries under the Sassanid dynasty. Wherever military or governmental units went, they were accompanied by Mazdian priests; churches were demolished, ceremonies other than Mazdean were forbidden, all sacred vessels and ornaments were seized, and customs abhorrent to the Armenians were decreed.

Legends of Prince Trdat

The infant Prince Trdat, who had been smuggled out of Armenia at the time of the murder of his father, grew up in Roman territory of Asia Minor, thoroughly imbued with its language, literature, customs and religion. Of imposing stature and handsome features, his athletic dexterity and personal prowess made him a popular hero both in the circus and on the battlefield. Fantastic stories were told of his Herculean strength. "His breathing," says Agathangelos, "crumbled the banks of the rivers and stopped the eddies of the rivers." In a chariot race — where he usually excelled — he once stopped a rival's chariot just by seizing the spokes of the wheel in his hands. When rebellious Roman soldiers in force attacked the palace of his friend, Caius Flavius Licinius, with intent to slay him, Trdat is said to have stood alone at the gate and beat them off. Agathangelos asserts that he was highly gifted intellectually, well read in Greek literature and the philosophical sciences of his time.

Accession of Trdat III

It was by this eminent Roman Licinius — later Emperor — that Trdat was brought to the attention of Diocletian, who had ascended the throne in 285. Two years later he authorized Trdat to assume the Armenian crown, and sent him under heavy escort to his kingdom. Upon his arrival at the frontier, Trdat III, then twenty years of age, was recognized as the heir to the Pahlevid dynasty and welcomed to the throne. But the tranquillity seemingly guaranteed by his Roman backing did not continue long. Narseh, the successor of Shahpur, attacked the country in 294 and forced Trdat to take refuge in Roman territory. Narseh then proceeded to overrun the Roman possessions in Mesopotamia and Syria.

Roman-Persian War

Diocletian ordered the Army of Syria, under Galerius, into action. But this commander handled his legions badly on the dangerous plains of Mesopotamia, where he suffered a disastrous defeat. Trdat, who was fighting with his archers and cataphracti or mailed men, in the Roman ranks, barely escaped capture by swimming across the Euphrates, though encumbered with his armor. Fortunately for the Armenians, Galerius, following the strategy set by Diocletian, was able to reverse the tide. With Trdat reconnoitring, he led a new army through Armenia, while Diocletian himself held the passage of the Euphrates. On this occasion, the story was different; Narseh was wounded and he and his army put to flight, leaving his tent and family at the mercy of the conquerors.

Peace and Prosperity

Under the terms of a treaty signed immediately afterward, Narseh was obliged to yield the five provinces of Armenia which Shahpur had seized, namely, Arzanene, Moxuene, Zabdiene, Rhimmene and Gordiene (297 A.D.). Trdat was now firmly established in his kingdom, and a period of peace was assured, lasting until the reign of Constantine. Diocletian's guarantee of the autonomy of Armenia kept Trdat free from Sassanid plotting, and the incursions of Caucasian tribes ceased when he married the Princess Ashkhen, daughter of Ashkatar, King of the Alans.

Trdat in the early years of his reign held the views of his Roman mentors towards the Christians, who were looked upon as disturbers of the social order. Wedded to paganism, the King was very hostile to the new religion, and was particularly vexed by a preacher named Grigor (Gregory), who was winning many converts. He ordered Gregory seized and confined in a dungeon of the citadel of Artashat, where he was treated with great cruelty.

Grigor the Illuminator

Here we meet the great evangelist of Armenian history, whom some chroniclers also call Grigor Partev. "Gregory the Parthian" was born about 257, of royal Arshakid stock. His father, Prince Anak, coming to Armenia ostensibly as a fugitive from Sassanid tyranny, had assassinated Trdat III's father during a hunt at the instigation of the King of Persia, to whom the power of this sovereign, as an ally of the Romans, seemed a menace. The fatally wounded King, on his death-bed, ordered the extermination of Anak and all his family, which sentence was carried out with one exception. One small boy, Gregory, was saved and taken to Caesarea in Cappadocia, where the brother of his foster-mother, a Christian, sheltered him and reared him in the evangelical faith.

Some other ancient writers have represented Gregory as a native of Cappadocia and a scion of the noble family of Souren of Bactria, but the version given here is the one most commonly accepted. As he neared manhood, his whereabouts were evidently not kept secret, for on coming of age he married a daughter of an Armenian Prince who was a Christian. Of this union two children were born; then the couple separated from each other, in order that Gregory might take up a monastic life. He went to Armenia in the hope of atoning for the crime of his father by evangelizing his homeland.

Diocletian Persecutes Christians

Here again we must quote tradition. Diocletian in 303 ordered a general persecution of Christians throughout the Empire, and thirty-eight women who had been converted in Rome, notably two heroines named Hripsimeh and Gayaneh, who had assisted Gregory in his missionary work, had escaped from Roman territory into Armenia and secluded themselves near the city of Vagharshapat. King Trdat, according to legend, heard of their presence and of Hripsimeh's exquisite beauty, and had her brought to his palace. He proposed marriage to her; she refused him, however, escaped somehow, but was captured, and with all her women companions, suffered death by the executioner's sword.

Trdat is Forced to Summon Gregory

In punishment for this crime, Trdat was stricken by a loathsome disease, which forced him to retire from appearance in public.[36] In this extremity, a vision came to the monarch's sister, the Princess Khosrovidukhd, hinting of the power that might lie in the prayers of the holy man languishing in the castle dungeon. One detail, which might very well be true, is to the effect that the King was aware that Gregory was the son of his father's assassin. He was therefore reluctant to yield to his sister's entreaties; but he had tried all the most reputable physicians of his time and appealed to all his ancestral divinities for relief, in vain. So at last he yielded, had the emaciated Gregory brought forth from his cell and besought his help. The apostle readily offered his prayers, and the King was speedily healed. Touched by gratitude and the unshakable faith of the preacher, and awed by the power of his prayers, the King accepted Christianity, as did all his court.

---

[36] One variation of the legend has him turned into the semblance of a wild boar.

Armenia Becomes Christian

Gregory, still a plain monk, then went to Caesarea, where the Exarchus Leontius gave him the double sacerdotal and episcopal consecration. His two sons, Vardan and Aristaces, their names Grecianized into Vrthanes and Aristakes, had studied in Caesarea, and become Christian clergymen. On his way back into Armenia, Gregory overthrew the Temple of Ashtishat; then proceeding to Bagavan, he was welcomed by the King and his retinue, as well as a group of clergy from Cappadocia and northern Syria. He baptized a great number of converts, among whom was the King, and then began the official evangelization of his country. This was in the year 303 — though some chroniclers give it as 301. In either case, it was some time before the Emperor Constantine the Great allegedly saw the flaming Cross in the sky with the words In hoc signo vinces — "In this sign shalt thou conquer" — on the morning of a battle, and thereupon decreed that the Roman Empire should be Christian. Armenia, therefore, claims to have been the first among the nations to adopt Christianity.[37]

Pagan Priests Resist Christianization

The conversion of the nation was not accomplished without great difficulty; the pagan priests, possessors of vast fortunes, were politically and economically powerful. They had since the earliest times wrung profit from the people by every possible act and circumstance. Gregory, backed by Trdat, found little trouble in converting some districts whose inhabitants yielded peacefully to the change. But in others which were more recalcitrant, the bishop, accompanied by the principal nakharars and their soldier-serfs, used force, destroying idols, demolishing the pagan temples and slaying priests who opposed the mission with arms. According to the ancient historian, Zenob of Glak, the resistance was violent in the district of Taron and the territory of Palouniq. In the great burgh of Kissaneh, a real battle took place between the army of the pagan priests and that of the State. Gregory "gave order to pull down the idol of Kissaneh, which was of copper and twelve arms'-lengths in height." The pagan priests fought fanatically, crying, "Let us die before the great Kissaneh be destroyed." "This spot," says Zenob, "was the gate of demons, whose number was as large at Kissaneh as in the depths of hell," and who cried out, "Even if you should drive us away from here, there shall never be rest for those who wish to domicile here."

Nakharars Gather Pagan Treasure

But while Gregory was aiming at the conversion of the people and the annihilation of paganism, the nakharars were thinking of the riches accumulated in the temples. "The following day" (after the fight at the temple of Kissaneh), says Zenob, "a pagan priest was brought to the Prince of Sewniq" (one of Gregory's noble escorts). "He was pressed to reveal the place where the treasures

---

[37] This assertion of the Armenian historians has been corroborated by Eusebius of Caesarea (260-340), "the Father of Ecclesiastical History." He has the reputation of being second only to Origen in learning among the Church Fathers.

were hidden; he refused and died on the gibbet in torture. It has been impossible to discover the treasures since."

As to the lands belonging to the pagan sanctuaries, each of the new churches received a share of them. "After having laid the foundation of the church," says Zenob, "and deposited therein the relics, St. Gregory erected the wooden sign of the Cross of the Lord at the very gate, on the site of the idol Kissaneh, and left Anthony and Gronites to manage the church. He appointed Epiphanes as the superior of the monastery, giving him forty-three monks and assigning him twelve villages for the support of the establishment."

In all, the villages assigned to the new clergy contained 12,298 houses and could muster an army of 5,470 cavalry and 3,807 infantry. All these villages had long been appropriated to the service of the idols. Armenian chroniclers, themselves zealous champions of the new religion, attribute to Trdat and Gregory many acts of violence during the establishment of Christianity, and maltreatment of the pagan priests and their adherents, deepening the bitterness of feeling between the two factions.

Christianization Completed

The official conversion of the Armenian State to Christianity was completed in 305, soon after the abdication of Diocletian and his co-Emperor Maximian. In that year Gregory was duly elected as the supreme head of the new Church, and went in great pomp to Caesarea, to receive the investiture from Leontius, the metropolitan of that city. Caesarea was famous at that time as the greatest center of Christian faith in the East, and the jurisdiction of its bishop extended over a major part of Asia Minor. From that date, Grigor (Gregory) Loussavoritch became the Katholikos, the great Bishop of Armenia.

Greek Church Claims Authority

The ordination of Gregory and three of his successors by the Metropolitan of Caesarea has been the ground for the Greek Church's claim for authority over that of Armenia. A similar claim has been made by the See of Byzantium, overshadowing that of Caesarea; also by the See of Antioch, which pretended to hold a pre-eminent jurisdiction over all the churches of Asia, from the Mediterranean Sea to India. All these claims have been confuted by factual proofs found in history. Furthermore, no credence is given by modern European scholars to an alleged pact, said to have been entered into by Trdat and Gregory during a visit to Rome to greet the Emperor Constantine after his conversion, and, it is said, to render an act of submission to the incumbent Bishop of Rome, Sylvester I (314-335), whose office, later known as Pope, was claiming headship over all Christianity.

Only a short time before this, even in Constantine's early years, some of the most violent objections to the religious revolution, for such it really was, had been coming from the Roman Caesars. An expedition under Maximinus Daia, then

Governor of Syria and Egypt, was launched in 310 with the object of reinstating paganism in Armenia, but met, as Eusebius tells us, with strong military resistance and was not successful. The conversion of Constantine changed all that.

Etchmiadzin, Holy City of Armenia

The King aided Gregory in building the city of Etchmiadzin on the site of ancient Vagarshapat; it became the holy city, as well as the intellectual center of the Armenian nation.[38] Gregory continued his evangelism for a number of years, always a target for attack by his enemies, and finally retired to the mountains of Akilisene, in Upper Armenia, to end his days as an ascetic. He entrusted the administration of church affairs to his son Aristakes, who had been his suffragan since 318. As such, Aristakes attended the famous Council of Nicaea, called by the Emperor Constantine in 325 to settle doctrinal troubles, and in particular to condemn the heresy known as Arianism, which doubted the divinity of Christ. There bishops from all over the Empire shaped a creed which is accepted as ecumenical by the Eastern and Roman communions.

Death of St. Gregory

St. Gregory died in his cave on Mount Sepouh in 325, one of the highest among the Armenian saints. He is also a saint in the Roman Catholic calendar. The adherents of the national Church founded by him are often designated by Loussavortchakan,[39] to differentiate them from the Armenian Catholics or Protestants. Aristakes succeeded his father in the patriarchal See, and was eventually assassinated in Sophene by Archelaus, a Roman functionary. A great-great-grandson of Gregory, Nerses, later served as patriarch.

But little less glorious than Gregory's was the part played in the progressive movement by King Trdat III, the most illustrious figure in his dynasty. It must be admitted that the conversion of the country was as much a political as a religious move. By giving Armenia a national religion, Trdat set her free from alien influences. Rome then and for several years afterward had remained pagan, while Persia had restored its Zoroastrian cult. "Changing the state religion was therefore to assert the Armenian nationality, to give to the Haikian people an

---

[38] Etchmiadzin, whose name means "the place where the only begotten Son descended," counts a succession of 161 Katholikoses or patriarchs, extending from Gregory (305-325) to Vazken I (1955-). In Christendom this high office is comparable to the Papacy. The Katholikos of Etchmiadzin has on many occasions been compelled by circumstances to play the role of sovereign in relation to the Armenian people. The See has not always remained in Etchmiadzin; at one time and another, it has been found necessary to remove it to Douin, Ani, Aghthamar, Sis and other places; but in each and every location, it maintained the same spiritual role.

[39] Pertaining to Loussavoritch (Illuminator).

additional personal character, capable of contributing to the preservation of the race, and hence, to its independence."[40]

Persia Plots Assassination

However, the conversion of Trdat and his people, presently followed by that of the Roman Empire, filled the Persians with fears for the future; they saw visions of an alliance of Christ-worshipping princes against Mazdeian Iran. In an effort to forestall this danger, they won over, through secret agents, a number of Armenian princes and dignitaries, concocting a plot to restore paganism in the land of Ararat. Even the King's own chamberlain became a traitor. Relying on assurances of safety given by this man and other feudal lords, Trdat visited the province of Alkilissene (modern Erzinjan). There the plotters followed him and wounded him during a hunting party. The chamberlain completed the crime by poisoning him.

National Mourning

Far from furthering the cause of Zoroastrianism, the murder of Trdat had the opposite effect. He was regarded as a martyr, and placed in the calendar of Armenian saints.

---

[40] Jacques de Morgan, "Histoire du Peuple Arménien," 1928.

Chapter XIX
Successors of Trdat — Partition of Armenia

Character of Khosrov II

Khosrov II (330-339), known as Kotak (the Little or Short), who was placed on the throne by the Christian party, lacked the moral and physical vigor of his father, yet under his rule, Armenia enjoyed a period of prosperity. He was tactful and diplomatic, and backed by Vrthanes, the new Katholikos and by the Generalissimo, Vatcheh Mamikonian, he showed a certain mettle whenever internal troubles arose.

Troubles of his Reign

The most serious of these was an attempt to assassinate the Katholikos at Taron (Mush district), a plot hatched by pagan priests, and encouraged by the Queen. Next came the turmoil caused by the Manavazian and Ordouni families, who had been waging a bloody vendetta with each other. They refused to heed any counsel, even the intercession of the Katholikos, and at length, both houses were destroyed by the royal army under the Generalissimo Vatcheh.

Scarcely had the country returned to quietude when it was again harassed by a new incursion of its Caucasian neighbors, the Alans and other mountain tribes, who committed depredations in the Arax Valley and in Karinid (the modern Erzerum district). King Khosrov barely escaped capture at their hands. Once more the Generalissimo took the field, and aided by the Bagratids and the Kamsarakans, put the marauders to flight.

In 337 Khosrov gave his attention to the construction of the city of Douin. Emperor Constantine the Great died in that year, leaving his Empire divided among his three sons, Constantine II, Constans and Constantius. Shahpur II of Persia now reopened hostilities, but again the eminent general Vatcheh, performed marvels of military skill, repulsing the Persians and inflicting heavy punishment upon certain Armenian lords and princes for their treasonable conduct. But Vatcheh fell at last in battle, and King Khosrov's death followed soon after.

King Tiran

Khosrov was succeeded by his son Tiran (339-350). Though endorsed by the Christian party, the new King was a disappointment, intellectually and morally. He soon antagonized the clergy and the great Mamikonian family, which had been the mainstay of the throne. On the death of the Katholikos, the patriarchal See was entrusted to his son Houssik, the King's son-in-law, who was held in high esteem for his attainments as well as his descent from St. Gregory. But Tiran, incensed by the young Patriarch's criticism of his public and private conduct, ordered him to be beaten to death, the immediate reason being the denial of admittance of the King to a church in Sophene on a feast day in 346.

Tiran committed other acts of like barbarity, among them being the massacre of the Ardzruni and Reshtuni families, who were accused of having secret relations with the Persians. But the attempts to crush the power of the feudal lords, including the Mamikonian family, were doomed to failure.

Shahpur's War on Rome

Shahpur II launched a new war on Rome in 338, accompanying it with a bloody persecution of the Christians of Persia and Mesopotamia. This war, which continued for 25 years, dealt a severe blow to Roman prestige in the East. Shahpur's main object was the capture of the basin of the upper Tigris, where lay the route to Ctesiphon. The banks of the river were taken and lost by turns, but the fortress of Nissibin resisted the Persian assaults for eight years.

Tiran Blinded

For some time Shahpur left Armenia unmolested; but at length he lured the Armenian King and his family into a trap. Tiran was brought to the Persian capital, and upon an accusation of collusion with Rome, was thrown into prison and blinded. Infuriated by this brutality, the people of Armenia took up arms and expelled all Persians and their partisans from the land. Shahpur, daunted by the uprising, set Tiran and his family free, and in 350 consented to recognize Arshak II, the blind King's son, as the successor to the horse.

Arshak's Reign

During the seventeen years of Arshak's reign, Armenia became the scene of competitive disputes between the two empires and of domestic quarrels. Constans II, the Roman Emperor, contrived the marriage of Arshak to Olympia, a Roman princess, daughter of a prefect.[41] He also ordered the remission of the taxes on the lands which the Kings of Armenia owned in Asia Minor. The Persian King likewise offered Arshak many tokens of favor, in an effort to win his neutrality. In fact, Arshak remained a bystander during the wars between Rome and Persia until the accession of Julian, the so-called Apostate, to the Roman throne in 361.

---

[41] In a letter addressed to the Anchorites, the Patriarch Athanas of Byzantium reproaches Constans for having given to a barbarian (foreigner) the hand of a princess who had been promised to Constantius.

Nerses Made Patriarch

The patriarchal authority had been conferred in 352 upon Nerses, the Court Secretary, a grandson of the Katholikos Houssik. (Paren and Shahak, who had occupied the position from 347 to 351, did not belong to the House of Gregory.) Nerses was 27 years of age when he was made Bishop and sent to Caesarea to receive the investiture. He became one of the most eminent patriarchs in Armenian history, not only because of his reforms in ecclesiastical, social and charitable spheres, but also because of his great influence in international affairs.

After an abortive assault upon the Roman stronghold of Nissibin in 350, Shahpur hastened home to ward off the attacks of Eastern enemies. About ten years later he reappeared in Mesopotamia, ruined the city of Amida (Diarbekir), and put its defenders to the sword. Among the soldiers of the Roman legions who perished there were a great number of Armenians.[42]

Shahpur Claims Armenia

Shahpur thereupon dispatched envoys to the Emperor Constantius II, claiming Mesopotamia and Armenia. King Arshak, aware of the imminent danger threatening his family, retired to the mountains. The people of the country, seemingly thus left to their fate, were divided into two parties; one took the side of the Persians, while the others, who favored the West, were forced to take refuge in Roman territory. Constantius rejected the Persian demands and went to the East to lead his army in person. Arshak met the Emperor in Caesarea, and aided and encouraged by him, returned to his capital. All those who had been exiled to the Roman territories came home also.

But the war was scarcely begun when Constantius died in Cilicia in 361, and Julian, already proclaimed Emperor by some of the soldiers, succeeded him. Julian prepared to strike a decisive blow against Persia. Arshak sent ambassadors to him, expressing loyalty, and received instructions to join him in Antioch with his forces. But ensuing developments were disastrous for the Romans. Julian was mortally wounded in battle in 363, and the army proclaimed Jovianus, captain of Julian's life guards, Emperor. Under his command, the army reached the Tigris, but found the river too strongly defended to cross. Shahpur proposed as terms of peace the surrender of the Roman conquests west of the Tigris, together with the fortress of Nissibin and other strongholds in Mesopotamia; also the cessation of Roman aid to Armenia, with whom Persia was again at war. Jovianus yielded to the terms of this humiliating treaty in 364.[43]

---

[42] The famous Roman historian, Ammianus Marcellinus, who was then in Amida, barely escaped with his life. In his attitude towards the non-Roman peoples of the Empire, this writer, by the way, is far more just and liberal than Livy or Tacitus.

[43] Upon his arrival at Antioch, the new Emperor proclaimed himself a Christian, upheld the Nicene creed and rescinded the edicts of Julian against the Christians.

Armenians Fight Alone

The Armenians, though abandoned by Rome, fought stubbornly for four years against Persian encroachments. An embassy headed by the Katholikos Nerses was sent to Constantinople to solicit the aid of Valens, Emperor there since 364; for the Roman Empire was now functioning in two parts, with the respective capitals at Rome and at Byzantium or Constantinople. This appeal met with no success, mainly because Valens himself supported the Arian party during the religious quarrels which at that time raged over the whole Eastern Empire. According to Khorenatsi's story, the Katholikos Nerses, professing the orthodox view, was even confined in seclusion on an island (Toulis) by order of Valens. In any case, when military affairs on the eastern frontier assumed a threatening aspect, the Romans were disinclined any longer to interfere with the designs of the Persians on Armenia, and concluded a discreditable treaty with them in 376.

King Arshak Escapes

The story of the struggle carried on during this critical period contains many episodes of Armenian valor. Vassak Mamikonian, the military leader, again and again repulsed the attacks of the Persians, who had been joined by several Armenian lords, such as Meroujan Ardzruni and Vahan Mamikonian. On one occasion they devastated the districts of Sophene and Akilisene and violated the graves of the Arshakid kings at the castle of Ani-Kamakh. The King barely escaped to Asia Minor, and Vassak was forced to maintain alone the defense of the province of Ararat. The situation having reached a dangerous stage, and the pleadings of the Katholikos Nerses being without avail, King Arshak went directly to Shahpur, who through letters and emissaries had been promising him sincere friendship. Arshak was at first accorded a royal welcome, but he was presently seized during a feast and sent in chains to the fortress of Oblivion (Anhoush berd) where he was executed or committed suicide in 367. The Generalissimo Vassak, his companion in exile, was flayed alive and his body suspended at the prison gate.

Arshak did not lack the intelligence, courage and will power required of a sovereign whose destiny it was to offer stiff resistance to foreign invasion, and to try vainly to unify and solidify a feudal kingdom, some of whose nakharars showed a tendency to undermine the central authority. But he committed many mistakes and cruelties which overshadowed his virtues and contributed to his tragic end. He ordered the assassination of his own nephews, Gnel and Tirid — whom he suspected of designs on the throne — and married Parantzem, the beautiful widow of Gnel. To him is ascribed the destruction of the house of Kamsarakans, his own relatives. The death of Olympia, his Roman wife, has been attributed to poison, allegedly administered to her in the Holy Sacrament by a priest acting at the instigation of the King, though this story should be taken with reservations.

Queen Murdered, Pap Crowned

Arshak's widow, Queen Parantzem, had taken refuge with her son Pap in the fort of Artakers. After a long resistance to the Persian army, she contrived during the siege to send Pap away to Neocaesarea (modern Niksar) in the Roman territory. The fort was finally taken and the Queen brutally slain. But the country was not yet completely reduced. Mountain sections continued to fight stubbornly, in hope of receiving aid from Byzantium. The Emperor Valens had promised an Armenian delegation headed by Mushegh Mamikonian that he would defend Armenia. Prince Pap, then 22 years old, was escorted by an Imperial legion back to Armenia and crowned in 368. The Jovianus treaty, which had abandoned Armenia to the mercy of Persia, was revoked by Valens.

Battle of Bagrevand

The ensuing Battle of Bagrevand (371) was a decisive victory for the Roman-Armenian army. The Mamikonians, the Kamsarakans and the Bagratids were especially conspicuous in the fray. Merouzhan, the leader of the Armenian renegades, and many of his followers perished. King Pap, who accompanied by the Katholikos had been watching the fight from the hill of Npat, recovered the throne of the Arshakuni dynasty. The military command of the country was entrusted to Mushegh Mamikonian, to whom Trajan, the Roman commander in the East, lent full support. Mushegh succeeded in curbing the turbulent Armenian nobles.

Although now firmly established in his heritage, the young king still had many difficulties to overcome. He was under Roman suzerainty, and yet he had to appease the Persian monarch, and meanwhile, to combat insubordinate tendencies within his own kingdom, a particularly thorny problem being the friction between Church and State. In holding the ecclesiastics in check, Pap had provoked their antagonism, and the death of the Katholikos in 373 was attributed by later clerical historians to wine poisoned at a banquet by the King's order. Contemporary chroniclers, however, testify that Pap was deeply grieved by the loss of his saintly mentor, and gave him a stately funeral.

Assassination of Pap

A tragic fate was reserved for Pap himself. The Emperor Valens was led to suspect his loyalty, and while visiting the city of Tarsus in Cilicia, he invited Pap to meet him for a conference. The latter came unsuspectingly, but being warned of impending peril, he escaped and returned safely to his own country, eluding pursuit by Roman horsemen. The Emperor believed that he had been warned by the Magians, whose destruction Valens had vowed. The Roman commander Trajan presently set another snare, a banquet which Pap was induced to attend. While music and songs resounded in the hall and cups passed from hand to hand, a burly barbarian sprang forth at a sign from Trajan and stabbed the young King to death (374). Nothing could justify this dastardly act, for Pap had always remained loyal to the Emperor, and had rejected all of Shahpur's advances and threats.

The pro-Roman party in Armenia, though shocked by the assassination of their King, restrained their indignation. The Emperor, realizing that brute force had gone too far, and desirous of appeasing the country, sent Varazdat, a nephew of Pap, a young man highly reputed for his mental and physical gifts, to occupy the Armenian throne.

Flees From Civil Strife

Shahpur, having failed on the battlefield, now proposed to Valens in 375 that Armenia be divided between the two powers. The Emperor rejected the proposal, but sent Victor Magistrianus to the Persian King to discuss the question. This emissary was cozened into exceeding the bounds of his authority and agreeing to the Persian proposal. In the meantime, the internal condition of Armenia was imperilled through friction between King Varazdat and the grandees, culminating in the assassination of Mushegh Mamikonian, the leader of the latters' party. Manuel, the son of Mushegh, took up arms against the King and compelled him to flee from Armenia in 378, after four years of reign.

Varazdat's life was saved, but the country was thrown into confusion. The Persians took advantage of the turmoil and invaded Armenia; but their occupation was a short-lived one. Shahpur II died in 379, and the Persians evacuated in haste. Manuel, the dynamic Mamikonian, had rallied a formidable national force for action.

Dual Reign of Pap's Sons

In the hope of putting an end to the anarchy in the land, the pro-Roman party placed upon the throne the two sons of Pap, Arshak and Valarshak, incidentally wedding them, the first to the daughter of Manuel and the second to the daughter of Sahak, the Bagratid. Unfortunately, this measure did not bring about the hoped-for peace and order. Discontent and rivalry between the great feudal houses led to new domestic embroilments. Matters were further complicated in the same year by the death of Varshak to whom had been given the administration of the province of Ararat and some neighboring districts.

Armenia Partitioned

Theodosius the Great, Roman Emperor since 379, concluded a treaty with Shahpur III in 384, under which the partition of Armenia became a fact. The greater part of the country was then constituted a vassal state under Persian suzerainty. The smaller part, comprising the Karenitid, the Sophene and a section of the Taronitid, formed a Roman province.[44] Persian Armenia was ruled by princes of her own Arsacid dynasty for forty years longer, or until its annexation to the Persian Empire.

Subsequent events demonstrated Rome's unwisdom, in betraying Armenia. The Empire was now an immediate neighbor and open target for Persian attack, and the later irruption of the Arabs.

Khosrov's Brief Reign

Shahpur III appointed Khosrov, a descendant of the Arsacid house, as King of Armenia (385-391), and gave him a sister in marriage. It was not long, however, until Khosrov was dethroned and placed in confinement at Ctesiphon, apparently for too great assertiveness of his royal authority. He had bestowed the Patriarchal power upon Sahak, son of Nerses and well known for his sympathy with the West. He had also restored many feudal lords to their former status of nobility. Vramshapouh,[45] brother of Khosrov, to whom Shahpur now entrusted the rule of Armenia, was not honored with the title of King until ten years later, when Yazdegert I sat upon the throne at Ctesiphon.

Vramshapouh a Good King

Vramshapouh succeeded in winning the confidence of the Persian monarch, as well as of the pro-Roman party of his country. The election of Sahak to the patriarchate was ratified by Yazdegert; the Patriarch's son-in-law, Hamazasp Mamikonian, was given the high office of Generalissimo, a heritage as it were, which had for a long time been withheld. These appointments were among the King's prerogatives, as were those of the Mardpet, the guardian of the harem, who was also the administrator of the Royal domain, and the Apset, who placed the crown upon the King's head at his coronation.

Mesrop-Mashtotz

The wise and beneficent reign of Vramshapouh was made particularly illustrious through the agency of a man of exceptional ability and merit named Mesrop-Mashtotz. A native of the rural community of Taron, Mesrop had studied in one of the schools established by the Katholikos Nerses, acquiring among other things, a mastery of the Greek, Syrian and Persian languages. After several years' service in the army, he was appointed royal secretary. But he was not satisfied in

---

[44] Noeldeke gives the date of this partition as 390, during the reign of Bahram IV. Notwithstanding this impolitic act of Theodosius, he is ranked among the saints of the Armenian church, because of his religious orthodoxy!

[45] The name Vram-Shapouh (Bahram-Shahpur) had been assumed by the Armenian prince in compliment to his Persian overlord; likewise, his son Artashes called himself Artashir upon his elevation to the throne.

this routine position; his soul was stirred by ideas. He resigned his post and entered into the service of the Church.

But in assuming clerical garb, Mashtotz could not be content with passive virtues. Intellectual pursuits in those days centered in the Church. Since Rome under Constantine had adopted Christianity, science, literature, benevolence and lawmaking had all come into the field of the clergy. Enthusiastic, yet serene and serious, Mesrop had chosen such a career — to preach, to serve, to enlighten, to educate. He was forty years old in 394 when he took over his first field in Goghten, modern Agoulis, in the province of Ararat, where he began teaching and preaching with several associates. Thereafter, he moved to other areas, finding spiritual darkness in the mountain districts in the north and east of the country, where paganism had numerous followers.

Katholikos Sees Need for Alphabet

After the adoption of Christianity by Armenia in apostolic days, its spread was slow, because Church and community remained far apart. Readings, prayers and chants were conducted in Syriac or Greek. Clergymen were mostly aliens who were not acquainted with the Armenian language. Occasional translations did not avail. Congregations could not memorize "anything, not half," exclaims Phaustus Buzandatsi, "not even a trifling trace nor gleam." By a happy coincidence, the Patriarchal See at this time was occupied by Sahak Partev, a scholarly and zealous leader. To him Mesrop confided his concern, and found that the mind of the Katholikos had long been occupied by the same problem. What was the remedy? They agreed that sermons, prayers and chants should be heard in the people's vernacular; yes, and more than that, a translation of the Scriptures. But there could be no written word, because Armenians had no alphabet with which to write it. The old cuneiform or hieroglyphic, once used in temples and in courts, had been discarded and replaced by Persian or Greek or Syriac. An alphabet was necessary.

Work on Alphabet Begun

Another happy coincidence was that so wise a King as Vramshapouh sat upon the throne. He became interested in the project at once, and was its great patron, materially and morally. He told Mesrop that he had heard of an ancient set of Armenian characters in the library of a Syrian bishop named Daniel, in Edessa, and Mesrop, in company with several younger men, hurried to that place to obtain the precious treasure. It was brought to Armenia, but after two years of experiment, proved defective and inadequate. Other clues were followed by Mesrop's young men, all devoted to research — noble pilgrimages, not for commercial or military purposes. There were two centers, Samosat, on the Euphrates in Byzantine territory, and Edessa (Urfa), Syrian under Persian rule, between which the young students were divided, some in each. One of Mesrop's disciples, Korioun, his biographer, tells us how tirelessly his master worked, day and night, how eagerly he traveled everywhere in the hope of obtaining some advice or new idea, how feverishly he toiled and worried and prayed.

109

Alphabet and Grammar Completed, 405

At last, in the year 405, his efforts were crowned with success. According to some ancient Armenian chroniclers, by the addition of twelve letters to those of Daniel — seven vowels and five consonants — Mesrop had created what became the present Armenian alphabet [46] (the letters "o" and "f" were added in the twelfth century). A Greek expert in penmanship, Rhupanus, arranged the letters, 36 in all, after the Greek order. The alphabet answers perfectly the phonetic requirements of the mother tongue, and through its use, one can give the exact sound of almost every word in any other language. Mesrop also produced a grammar. The Armenian language had of course always had its fixed grammatical forms, unwritten rules, and Mesrop now reduced these to writing.

Legend of Miraculous Origin

The tradition that the alphabet was a miraculous creation was permitted to spread in order to pacify the Greek ecclesiastics and the Emperor Theodosius II, who saw in it a new weapon by which the national spirit might be strengthened. And yet it was indeed a miracle! The invention of the alphabet which has assured to this day the preservation of the nation, despite centuries of tribulation and the vicissitudes of fortune, was little short of wonderful in that critical period of Armenia.

Translations

Let us consider the factors which helped the miracle to take form. Two objectives prompted Mesrop — the diffusion of the Christian faith in his country and the emancipation of the Armenians from the influence of foreign preachers. He and Sahak had perceived the ominous signs of an oncoming torrent, and hastened to construct a bulwark against it. The saintly Katholikos busied himself in translating the Old and New Testaments into Armenian, and encouraged the younger clerics to translate the works of the early Church fathers — the writings of Ephrem the Syrian, the Hexameron (six days of creation) of Basil of Caesarea, the homilies of John Chrysostom, the Ecclesiastic History of Eusebius, History of the Conversion of Edessa, the (apocryphal) correspondence of Jesus with Abgar by the Syrian Laboubna, the Syriac Liturgy and that of St. Basil. There are hymns attributed to Mesrop and Sahak.

Mesrop Spreads Knowledge

Mesrop, the first apostle of Armenian education, now traveled through the country from province to province, from Vagharshapat to Goghten and thence to Vaspurakan, Sewniq, Artsakh, Kartman and even to remote mountain recesses

---

[46] The eminent linguist H. Ajarian rejects this view and believes that Mesrop after discarding altogether the so-called Danielian characters, invented himself the entire Armenian alphabet.

inhabited by the most backward groups, whom Korioun describes as "beastly in habits, barbarians and monstrously inclined." Mesrop preached to these almost forgotten folk in their own dialects, instructed them and opened schools for them. The results were little short of phenomenal. A whole population began to feel the thirst for knowledge and was able to satisfy it. The country boy was taught, together with the offspring of nobility, the grandson of the pagan priest in company with the scion of the Illuminator's house. As time went on, men began to write originally in Armenian — Korioun, Eznik, Agathangelos, Phaustus. "Thus," writes Korioun, "the happy and most desirable country of Armenia became an object of admiration, indeed."

Armenia Closer Knit by Reading

So swiftly did the Armenian language grow, blossom and flourish that the intellectual success achieved in so short a space of time is one of the most inspiring chapters in the history of civilization. The Armenian mind longingly turned towards the light of knowledge. No longer did it need the services of self-seeking alien tutors. The various clans, separated from each other by physical and social barriers — mountains, rivers, dialects and traditions — were now being linked together by the spiritual tie of the written and spoken word. The Church therefore, enriched by its own letters, became a moral light, as well as a stronghold for national consolidation. It was the champion of the new spirit amidst brute selfishness and under the oppressive Asiatic atmosphere, spreading the gospel of love and charity, brotherhood and equality.

Oppression Checked by the Emperor

But the intellectual dawn was soon to be darkened by gloomy political clouds. These first appeared on the western horizon, where the Greek Governor of Western Armenia forbade the teaching of Armenian letters. A deputation composed of Mesrop and Vardan was dispatched to Constantinople to protest this ruling, and was successful. Emperor Theodosius II and his joint ruler Pulcheria not only granted permission for the teaching of Armenian, but even provided appropriations from the civil list to finance the instruction. Finally, Mesrop was honored with the title "Akumit," ("a man of high learning") while Vardan was created a "Stratelat" or General.

United Nation

Here was a triumph! The nation, long politically divided, was now united, spiritually and intellectually under the aegis of the Church. A band of bright young men, some sixty in number, formerly students in Greek and Syrian, became interpreters, instructors and preachers. To that group were subsequently added forty graduates from Sahak-Masrop Armenian schools. Prominent among these were Hovsep, Hovhan, Ghevond, Gute, Mandakuni, Yeznik, Korioun and Mambreh.

The alphabet had enriched Armenians mentally, spiritually and in moral courage. In 450, at the great Council of Artashat, their leaders, lay and clerical, rejected the demand of the Persian King that they renounce Christianity. They did not give up the fight, but persisted until the Persian monarchy granted religious and political autonomy in 480.

On the death of Vramshapouh in 419, the Katholikos visited the Persian court and obtained Yazdegert's consent to the release of Khosrov from his long imprisonment in the fortress of "Oblivion," and his reinstallation upon the Armenian throne.

Tolerance Turned to Enmity

For several years after his accession Yazdegert I had been tolerant towards Christians and harsh against Persian magnates and Magian priests.[47] The churches of Assyria, as well as those of Armenia, Iberia and Albania, had their autonomous governments, with an official supreme head, the Katholikos. But when in 418 a fanatical Assyrian bishop, Abda, set fire to a Mazdeian temple in Susa, capital of Elam, the King turned against the Christians and persecuted them. In sharp contrast with his former friendly attitude, he now seemed resolved to stamp out Christianity, and with the idea of accomplishing this end in Armenia, he appointed his own son, Shahpur, as governor of the country in 419. When Yazdegert's reign was ended soon thereafter by assassination, Shahpur returned home to claim the throne; but he too quickly fell a victim to the partisans of opposition.

The Hundred-Years' Treaty

With the beginning in 420 of the nineteen-year reign of Bahram V over Persia, hostilities against the Roman Empire and persecution of Christians were intensified. His first expedition into Armenia under Mihr-Nerseh, an able general and astute diplomat, met with defeat in Arzanen. After some indecisive engagements, operations were suspended in 422, and the Hundred Years' Peace treaty was signed, under the terms of which the Persians accorded full religious liberty to Christians, while Romans promised the same rights to the devotees of Zoroaster.

Intrigues against Artashir

In the spirit of this treaty, Bahram sought to placate the Armenians by agreeing to the nomination of Artashir, the seventeen-year-old son of Vramshapouh, as their King. But the leading members of the nobility soon resumed their intrigues, under pretense of disgust at the youthful King's vices. The old besetting political weakness of the Nation, feudalism, which the monarchy could never quite crush, rose again to plague Armenia. The King was recognized by the nobles as their

---

[47] Hazkert is the Armenian form of Yazdegert or Yadzgard or Iazdegert.

supreme head, at whose call they must assemble their forces in emergencies; they were his vassals, even when Armenia was entirely in vassalage to one empire or another. When the ruling monarch was powerful enough, his will was the law, and the life of the grandees was in his hands; an insurgent lord might be punished by death or by the loss of all or a part of his possessions.

Kingdom Abolished

But Artashir was too young and too weak to cope with this perverse and intractable aristocracy. Taking no heed of the sage argument of the Katholikos Sahak that "a sickly lamb is preferable to a robust wolf," the grandees appealed to the Persian Crown, asking for their ruler's dethronement. Artashir and Sahak were thereupon summoned to Ctesiphon, where Sahak's arguments were of no avail. The King was deprived of his royal title and power in 428, and from that date Armenia was reduced to the status of a Persian province. This was the end of the Armenian-Arshakid dynasty after 376 years of existence.

The Armenian court had been a brilliant one at times, resembling in vestments and table service those of the Medes and the Persian Kings — the flowing, gorgeously colored robes of royalty and aristocracy, heavily embroidered in gold and silver and studded with gems, the ceremony highly formal. But all that, through the recalcitrance of the Armenian peerage, had now come to an end.

Deposition of Sahak

Sahak was detained in Ctesiphon, on the charge of being the leader of the Grecophile party in Armenia. He was also informed that he had been deprived of his office as supreme head of the Armenian church. Thus both Arshakid and Pahlavid families vanished from the historical scene. Sahak was so admired in the Persian court for his wisdom, fearlessness and eloquence that he was permitted to return home at the end of six years. He lived six years longer, dying at the age of ninety in 439. Six months later, Mesrop followed him to the grave, having lived to be eighty-five.

Armenian Kings, Patriarchs and Persian Kings

The Arshakid Kings

Trdat III	287-294 and 297-330
Khosrov III	331-339
Tiran	340-350
Arshak II	350-367
Pap	367-374
Varazdat	374-378
Arshak III-Vagharshak	378-389
Khosrov IV	385-387

Vramshapuh	387-414
Khosrov IV (restored)	415
Shahpur	416-420
Interregnum, Persian rule	420-423
Artashes (Artashir)	423-428

The Patriarchs

The Conversion	305
Grigor	305-325
Aristakes	325-332
Vardanes	332-339
Houssik	339-347
Paren	347-351
Nerses	352-373
Shahak	
Zaven	373-386
Aspourakes	
Sahak	387-439

The Sassanid Kings

Narseh	293-303
Hormuzd II	303-310
Shahpur II	310-379
Artashir II	379-383
Shahpur III	383-389
Bahram IV	389-399
Yezdegert I	399-420
Bahram V	420-439

Chapter XX
Period of the Marzbans — Battle of Avarair

Marzban Government

For two hundred years after the fall of the Arshakuni dynasty of Armenia in 428, the country was governed by Marzbans (Governors-general of the boundaries), nominated by the Persian King. Of the thirty-five Marzbans who ruled in succession, six were Armenians. Western or Byzantine Armenia was at that time ruled by Curopalates (Governors), almost all Armenians by race, but with limited prerogatives.

The Marzban was invested with supreme power, even to the imposing of death sentences; but he could not interfere with the age-long privileges of the Armenian nakharars. The country as a whole, enjoyed a considerable autonomy. The office of Hazarapet, corresponding to that of a Minister of the Interior and Public Works, was entrusted to an Armenian, as was also the post of military Commander-in-chief. Each nakharar had his own army, according to the extent of his domain. The "National cavalry" or "Royal force" was under the Commander-in-chief. The tax collectors were all Armenians. The courts of justice and the schools were directed by the Armenian clergy.

Three times during the Marzbanic period, Persian kings launched persecutions against Christianity in Armenia. The Persians had tolerated the invention of the Armenian alphabet and the founding of schools, thinking those would promote the spiritual severance of Armenia from the Byzantine Greeks; but on the contrary, the new cultural movement among the Armenians actually proved to be conducive to a closer relation with the Greeks.

Intolerance Under Yazdegert II

The internal policy of Sassanid Persia had now taken on an intolerant attitude in the matter of religion. All the races living within the Iranian Empire henceforth must, in conformity with Mazdeian tenets, worship the sun and fire. King Yazdegert II (438-457), was a mixture of contrasting emotions. In the words of Yeghisheh, "One day a ferocious bull" or "an enraged lion" or "a furious tempest," on another day a man of "sweet disposition . . . who would humble himself from a haughty arrogance." He considered himself the first servant of Ormuzd (Ahura-Mazda), through whose grace he would crush the Graeco-Roman power, revive the empire of Cyrus and place all Asia under the influence of Iran. Repudiating the Hundred Years' Treaty of 420, Yazdegert invaded the Byzantine territories of Mesopotamia, destroyed cities, burned churches and seized captives. The Emperor Theodosius II, unable to take the field, concluded a humiliating peace in 441, which, among other terms, stipulated that those Persian Christians who had taken refuge in the Byzantine domain must be surrendered.

The triumphant Iranian then turned his attention to Central Asia, marching against the Kushans or Hephtalites, a hardy people of Medean origin, ruled by Arshakid princes, descendants of Darius the Great. Their country embraced modern Bukhara and Pahl, and they had fought successfully against Persia. After seven years of hostilities (442-448), Yazdegert, at the head of a formidable army, inflicted a severe defeat on the Kushans, at Marvroud, near the River Murghab, where the Armenian cavalry became noted for its valor.

Derbend Gates

The reconstruction of the Derbend Gates had already been accomplished before the Kushan War. The road is between the Caucasian Mountains and the Caspian Sea, in flat country, which offered an easy way for incursions into northern Persia by the Mazkouts or Black Huns, a nomadic tribe ruled by princes and claimed Arshakid descent. Acting under the suspicion that the Armenians might, in an attempt to revolt against him, get assistance from the Mazkouts, Yazdegert rebuilt a great wall called the Jora Bahag or Gate of Jor-Derbend by the Armenians.

Yazdegert's Persecutions

He then unleashed a religious persecution. In his opinion, a model king, who adhered to the true faith and laws of Zradasht (Zoroaster), must devote his life to the glory of Mazdeism, by abolishing false creeds and bringing their followers into the true path of God. Speaking to the Armenian nakharars, whom he had summoned to Ctesiphon, he said, "I look upon you as herds of animals scattered through a wilderness. It gives me deep grief to think that God may be angered at me and be revengeful on your account." He of course did not admit that he was prompted also by political considerations. His vast empire was inhabited by many peoples with different religions and languages. Some of them were of Aryan stock, others non-Aryan or Touranian. Several of these peoples, such as the Armenians and Caucasians, were looking to the Emperor of Byzantium for aid at the opportune time for revolt.

Mihr-Nerseh Advises Moderation

In his desire to achieve his political purposes, Yazdegert called in Mihr-Nerseh, an elderly retired official, a military, diplomatic and administrative genius. He advised peaceful means rather than force in the effort to absorb Armenia. "You know," said he to his King, "how extensive and valuable Armenia is. But that country is also a neighbor of the Roman Caesar, whose tenets and worship she has adopted. If we succeed in bringing her people to our own laws, then they will love you and the Aryan world. And when the Armenians come nearer to us, we shall certainly win the Georgians and the Aghouans (Caspio-Albanians), too."

The Role of Vassak

The rapprochement policy seems to have found a supreme Armenian advocate in the person of Vassak, the Marzban, the powerful nakharar of Sewniq, the mountainous province bordering on the Persian frontier. While a youth of fifteen, he had been sent, in accordance with the Oriental custom, to the Persian capital as a hostage. After his coming of age and returning home to inherit his father's realm, he evinced brilliant qualities. The bishop-historian Koriun speaks of him as "the brave Sissakan, sagacious, ingenious and foresighted through God-given grace." This worthy grandson of the fearless nakharar Andok had effectively sponsored Mesrop's educational efforts. But his later conduct marred his early reputation. Upon the downfall of the Arshakuni dynasty, Vassak developed a burning aspiration for royal distinction, through the restoration of the kingdom. In the early stages of the politico-religious crisis, he artfully worked in harmony with the nationalist group; but when the hour of final test arrived, he became the head of the pro-Persian party, in opposition to the pro-Roman element. This party included chiefs of prominent aristocratic families, such as the Mamikonian brothers — Vardan, Hmayak and Hamazasp; Arshavir Kamsarakan, the Lord of the Arsharuni and Shirak districts; Ardak the great Ishkhan (prince) of the province of Moks, Vahan Amatuni; Nershapuh Ardzruni; Tatoul Vanandatsi; Arsen Endzayetsi. Among the motives of the chiefs in league with Vassak — "the renegades," as they are called by the historians, Parbets and Yeghisheh — was their grudge against the clergy who had been preaching the gospel of human brotherhood and the protection of the peasant and laborer against exploitation by the feudal masters of the land.

Restrictions Tighten

Den-Shapuh, the Persian High Commissioner, concealed the iron hand in the velvet glove. His lavish entertainment of the aristocratic families and cultivation of social relations between them and the Persian residents, with a view to implanting in the country such alluring customs and ways of life as were prohibited by the Christian church, contrast sharply with his political and economic repression of the people. After completing a census and land registry of the country, he imposed oppressive taxes on property and persons. He then replaced Vahan Amatuni, the "nation's father" and Hazarapet, with a Persian, and conferred upon a Mazdeian magian (priest) the post and dignity of chief justice.

These measures did not bring results quickly enough, so Mihr-Narseh, "Grand Vizier and Commander-in-Chief of Eran and An-Eran," promulgated an edict, enjoining upon the Armenians the advisability of "giving up the erroneous and foolish ways of the Romans, thus depriving themselves of the benefits of the Persian perfect religion." He exhorted the Armenians to remain no longer astray, deaf and blind, but to study and adopt the doctrines of Zardusht.

117

Council of Artashat

A general assembly was held in Artashat in 449, to discuss this edict and ponder an answer. The meeting was presided over by the Katholikos Hovsep, and attended by seventeen bishops, eighteen major nakharars of both parties, many noblemen, chor-episcoposes (suffragans), monks of high rank and noblemen priests, whose spokesman was Ghevond Yeretz (Priest).

Courageous Answer

The answer of the Council to the Vizier, though respectful in tone, was a categorical refusal. The lengthy missive, as quoted by Yeghisheh, may not be a verbatim copy, but it throws much light on the sentiment and temper of the leaders of the nation at that critical moment. The following lines epitomize their carefully reasoned decision:

> "From this belief no one can move us, neither angels nor men; neither fire nor sword, nor water, nor any other horrid tortures. All our goods and our possessions, are in your hands, our bodies are before you; dispose of them as you will.

> "If you leave us to our belief, we will here, on earth choose no other lord in your place, and in heaven choose no other God in place of Jesus Christ, for there is no other God but him. But should you require anything beyond this great testimony, here we are; our bodies are in your hands, do with them as you please. Tortures from you, submission from us; the sword is yours, and here are our necks.

> "We are no better than our forefathers, who, for the sake of this faith surrendered their goods, their possessions and their bodies. Were we even immortal, it would become us to die for the love of Christ. . . . We should die as mortals, that He may accept our death as that of immortals."

Yazdegert Summons Nobles

The King of Kings, when informed of this rejection, flew into a rage and sent an order for the chief dignitaries to appear before him in Ctesiphon. They came, fifteen in number, headed by Vassak Sewny and Vardan Mamikonian. Their arrival was not heralded with military honors, as was the usual custom. Before receiving them in audience, Yazdegert had sworn "by the great Sun God, that if tomorrow morning, at the rise of the magnificent one (the sun), the nakharars would not kneel before it with him, and acknowledge it as god, they would be imprisoned and chained, their wives and children exiled into distant lands, and the imperial troops and herds of elephants would be sent to Armenia to demolish their churches and shrines."

Nakharars' Submission

The nakharars, after their dismissal from the awesome presence of the great monarch, spent the whole night in discussing their dilemma, and finally agreed among themselves to make a pretence of yielding, for the sake of their homes and families. So on the next day, escorting the King of Kings, they went to the "House of Ashes"[48] and knelt as in adoration of the rising sun, in accordance with the Mazdean rites. Yazdegert, in great joy, heaped honors and gifts upon them and called them "his beloved ones and friends."

The Magian Propagandists

In pompous array, the nakharars were sent off to Armenia accompanied by 700 Magi, who, within twelve months from the Armenian New Year's Day in Navassard (August) were to convert the entire country to Mazdeism. They were required, so Yeghisheh, to lock and seal the doors of the holy churches; to deliver to the imperial treasury all the sacred symbols, vessels and ornaments; to prohibit teaching by Christian priests; to educate in public the wives of nakharars and the sons and daughters of noblemen and people in accordance with the Magian doctrine; to force the monks and nuns to wear lay costume; to suppress marriage laws and establish polygamy, to let daughters marry their fathers, sisters their brothers, grandchildren their grandparents; to have edible animals slaughtered after being sacrificed to the gods; to keep rubbish and cow-dung away from fire; to forbid the killing of certain animals but to destroy reptiles and vermin; to wash their hands with cow's urine, so that water might not be defiled.

Peasants Drive off Magians

Fantastic laws and indecent practices such as these above were to be forced upon a people which had inherited and developed a civilization of its own, and for 150 years or more had officially adopted Christianity. But the Persian experiment proved unworkable. Scarcely had the strange cavalcade crossed the frontier at the village of Anghel (Anggh), 120 parasangsa east of Douin, in July, 449, when a horde of peasants, armed with clubs and slings and led by a fiery priest, Ghevond, assailed and put the trespassers to feeling — an ominous rumble of a coming storm.

Vardan Mamikonian

The great nakharars, most of them ashamed of their sham apostasy, avoided appearance in public, and stole away to their respective homes. The few among them who, for selfish considerations or in honest conviction, were still in favor of compromise with Persia feared to speak out. Even Vassak was in perplexity. Despite his being the wealthiest man and holding the highest position in Armenia, he was suffering from intense mental agony. His two sons were

---

[48] So called in secret satire by the Armenians.

hostages at the court of Ctesiphon; his son-in-law, Varazvaghan, an open renegade, ever busy in intrigues against his father-in-law, had fled to the Persian capital. Moreover, Vassak realized that his promises to the King of Kings were doomed to failure. He had been warned by the chief Magi himself that "Though our gods themselves were to come to our assistance, it would still be impossible for Magian doctrines to gain a footing in Armenia. Who can withstand men like these, who are neither afraid of chains, nor frightened by tortures, nor allured by wealth?"

Armenians Gird for Action

This pronouncement of a foreign functionary of deep learning and eminent position was truth, indeed. The Bible and the works of the Church Fathers, translated into Armenian between 422 and 432, followed by the teachings and preachings of two groups of young men, one hundred strong, almost all graduates from foreign seats of learning, had permeated the soul of the nation with a fervent zeal for Christianity. Men and even women, "armed and helmeted, sword in belt and shield in hand," were ready to accept the challenge, to fight and die for freedom of faith and conscience. The had implicit confidence in Vardan, too, who was destined to be their leader. He was the son of Sparapet (General) Hamazasp Mamikonian, and of Sahakanoush, the daughter of the Katholikos Sahak Partev, a descendant of Gregory the Illuminator. It was the tradition of the House of Mamikonian "to serve the Godly Homeland and to die for it." Theodosius II, the Byzantine Emperor, and Vram, the Persian King, had conferred the rank of General upon Vardan. He had visited Constantinople on diplomatic missions. As a soldier, with a record of service in forty engagements, he had led the Armenian contingents of the Iranian army and won laurels in campaign of Khorassan (modern Turkestan).

Vardan Departs

Upon his return from Ctesiphon, the disunity among his countrymen threw him into such deep despair that he set out with the members of his family for Byzantine Armenia, where he hoped to live unmolested by the missionaries of Mazdeism. The Nationalist party, however, hurriedly sent a delegation to entreat him to reconsider his resolve. Even his political opponents, including Vassak, joined in the appeal, and the pressure became so strong that he yielded and returned. At the General Assembly which thereupon convened, he exhorted the leaders to cease dissimulation and stand bravely for Church and Country. All present came under the spell of his personality.

Vassak, who was in friendly contact with Persian headquarters, was now surrounded by a Nationalist force and declared himself on oath as a defender of the Faith. Posthaste, messengers soliciting aid had been dispatched to the great satraps of the border provinces, to the Byzantine Governor-General, and to the new Emperor.

Vardan's Early Successes

Alarmed by news of these appeals and preparations, the Persian high command had rushed an army to Trans-Caucasia. The Armenian army was thereupon divided into three parts. The first one, under Nershapuh, was sent to oppose the invaders from the North; the second, under Vassak, was stationed in Sewniq for flanking movements, while the third, under Vardan, undertook the defense of Caucasian Albania. The campaign was crowned with brilliant success. After scattering the forces of the common enemy, Vardan hurled his cavalry still farther north and razed Yazdegert's boasted barrier, the Gate of Jor. An alliance between the Armenians and the larger Caucasian tribes was then concluded.

No Help from the Empire

But this bright course of victory did not continue long. The Armenian pdelegation to the Byzantine Court met bitter disappointment in its hope of aid. Attila, King of the Huns, one of the barbaric tribes who overthrew ancient civilizations in the early centuries A.D., then ruled over a conquered territory stretching from the Caspian Sea to the Rhine, and even threatened Constantinople, where the Emperor drained his meager treasury to purchase peace of the barbarian. Not until Attila's sudden death in 453 was the pressure relieved. But as long as "the Scourge of God" menaced the very gates of his Capital, no Byzantine Emperor dared irritate that other great enemy, the King of Persia.

Vassak's Treachery

Nor was there any effective aid in sight for Armenia from other quarters. Finding the situation precarious and taking advantage of the absence of two Nationalist armies, Vassak and his followers threw off their pretense of patriotism, and openly stood against the uprising. A state of civil war ensued, in which Vassak seized key positions in the Ararat province and committed many acts of vengeance, including the destruction of churches, imprisonment of priests and arrest of boys from the Mamikonian and Kamsarakan nobility, to be sent to the Persian capital as hostages.

In the autumn of 450 Vardan hurried home, traveling more than 400 miles in thirty days, an almost incredible speed in that era. The renegade armed forces had fled into the well-nigh inaccessible heights of the Sewniq Mountains, which Vardan soon blockaded. Hoping to avoid further bloodshed, however, he sent a last appeal to the Persian King, assuring him of Armenian loyalty, if only religious freedom remained untouched. Yazdegert, who had just returned from a disastrous expedition against the Kushans, responded favorably, declaring a general amnesty for political offenders, and religious freedom for his Armenian subjects. The renegade party was loud in its expressions of joy and gratitude to the King, but the Nationalists still doubted the sincerity of the Crown, the Marzban and his Persian advisers. Hostilities inevitably broke out soon; in the spring of 451 the enemy forces under the Grand Vizier Mihr-Nerseh crossed the

Arax River, and pushing northward to the Caucasus defiles, held the gates through which the tribal allies of the Armenians were expected to hasten in aid.

Armenian Crisis

Isolated, deprived of any assistance from outside, even divided among themselves, the Armenians now faced the greatest crisis they had yet encountered. The Persian King had been assured of the absolute neutrality of the Byzantine government, while Vassak was not only acting as an adviser to the Persian commander, but was in correspondence with the allied nations of the Caucasus and the powerful princes of border provinces, subtly trying to discredit the Nationalist movement. Vardan and his colleagues fully realized the gravity of the situation; but with the very existence of the Armenian nation at stake, they accepted the challenge for a cause which they held as sacred.

On Easter Day, April 13th, 451, the Persian army arrived in Her and Zarevand (modern Khoy and Salmasd, Persia), and laid out a camp, defended with bastions, moats and towers. After a review of his army in the plain of Ararat, Vardan sent out a detachment of 2,000 cavalrymen to reconnoiter the enemy's position and forces. These scouts fell into a brush with the Persian rear guard, annihilated it and returned exultant to their own camp. Resolved to meet the foe on the frontier, so that the fertile fields and valleys of the country might be saved from devastation, Vardan near the end of April rushed his army 120 miles in five days, to the vicinity of Artaz.

The Armies Confront Each Other

The Armenian forces were camped in a vast plain between Artaz and the districts of Her and Zaravand, known also as Shavarshakan plain (the modern Maku, Persia), near the village of Avarair. The rivulet Deghmoud, a tributary of the Arax, separated the two opposing hosts. The Armenian army, comprising 66,000 cavalry and infantry, recruited from among the standing forces of the nakharars, plus civilian volunteers, was accompanied by a considerable number of the clergy, who conducted services and encouraged the soldiers. The army was divided into four wings. The first, the right, was entrusted to Khoren, Prince of the Khorkhuruni clan, aided by Arsen Endzayetsi and Nerseh Qatchberuni. The center was given to the command of Nershapuh Ardzruni, aided by Mirhshapuh the Mardpet and by Prince Artak of Moks; the left wing was under the Generalissimo himself, aided by his brother-in-law, Arshavir Kamsarakan, Papak Araveghian, Tatoul Vanandatsi and Tajat Gnduni. A fourth division, the reserves, was under the command of Hamazaspian, brother of Vardan. The army included archers, spearmen and swordsmen, all on foot, but its main strength was in its light and heavy cavalry, all armor-clad. Vardan, who had organized and drilled them, also supplied equipment to all who needed it.

The Persian Army

The Persian army numbered 300,000 men, 40,000 of whom were Armenians — the regiments of Vassak and his followers. In addition to the Persian elements, the enemy force included contingents from various Caucasian, Caspian and central Asian territories. The center was held by the division of the Madyan or "Immortals" — 10,000 horsemen under Mushkan Nusalavurd, the Commander-in-chief. A herd of trained elephants, each carrying an iron tower full of bowmen, was another menace. The rear guard was reinforced by a column of elephants, on one of which, in a barbed tower, the Commandant sat, viewing the entire battlefield and directing movements.

On May 26th,[49] 451, the Aryan division of Mushkan Nusalavurd and the Armenians of Vardan Mamikonian faced each other in battle array. The Eve of the Feast of Pentecost, according to Yeghisheh, assumed the aspect of the religious rally. On one side of the battle line the Persian Commander-in-chief reminded the apostate Armenian princes of the precious marks of honor to be given by the King of Kings to all those who would bravely face the errant Armenians, "whose valor they knew." On the other side, Vardan, who from childhood had been well versed in the Holy Scriptures, now read aloud the deeds of the Maccabees, who successfully fought against Antiochus in defense of their faith. Then Ghevond, the priest, delivered a discourse, after which all the catechumens in the army were baptized and received the Holy Eucharist. The whole army rejoiced, crying out, "May God look down in mercy upon our voluntary self-offering, and may he not deliver the church into the hands of the heathens!"

The Battle of Avarair

To quote Yeghisheh,

> "Both sides being thus prepared and seized with a mighty rage and burnt with a wild fury, rushed against each other. The loud cry on both sides sounded like the clash of clouds, and the thundering sound of the noises rocked the caverns of the mountains.

> "The countless helmets and the shining armor of the warriors glowed like the rays of the sun. The flashing thousands of swords and the swaying of innumerable spears seemed like an awful fire being poured down from heaven.

> "But who can describe the tremendous tumult caused by these frightful noises — the clangor of the shields and the snapping of the bow strings — which deafened everyone alike?

---

[49] The date accepted by the Patriarch Ormanian, an authority on the Church calendar.

"One should have seen the turmoil of the great crisis and the immeasurable confusion on both sides, as they clashed with each other in reckless fury. The dull-minded became frenzied; the cowards deserted the field; the brave dashed forward courageously, and the valiant roared. In a solid mass the great multitude held the river; and the Persian troops sensing the danger, became restless in their places; but the Armenian cavalry crossed the river and fell upon them with a mighty force. They attacked each other fiercely and many on both sides fell wounded on the field, rolling in agony.

"Amid this great confusion the brave Vardan looked around to observe that a group of courageous and select Persian warriors had forced the left wing of the Armenian division to retreat. He immediately attacked with great vehemence, battered the right wing of the Persian army, and pushed the enemy back towards their beasts. Then he surrounded and slaughtered them. Thus he created such a great disorder that the troops of the Madyan Corps were dislodged from their prepared position and were put to flight without actually being defeated."

Vardan's Martyrdom

"The Persian general Mushkan," continues Yeghisheh, "observing some scattered Armenians who had remained behind in the mountain vales, shouted encouragement to the soldiers of the Aryan army around him, who were holding a position against Vardan's troops. There on the battlefield consciousness of defeat came to both sides, because the piles of the fallen bodies were so thick that they looked like craggy masses of stone.

"Mushkan, seeing this, ordered Ardashir, who was seated on the wild beasts as if atop a lofty watch-tower or in a fortified city, to incite his troops with the loud sound of huge trumpets and he himself surrounded him (Vardan), with his vanguard. But the valiant Vardan with his brave warriors played no lesser havoc in that place, where he himself was found worthy of martyrdom.

"As the battle continued, the day drew to its close and the fighting ceased towards evening; many were in death's agony; and the bodies of the slain were so thickly heaped together that they looked like fallen trees in the forest. Broken spears and shattered bows were strewn all over and because of that the sacred bodies of the blessed could not be fully identified; and there was a terrible panic and confusion over those who had fallen on both sides. The survivors were scattered over the hilltops and in more protected valleys; and whenever foe met foe they slew each other. The work of destruction continued without pause until sunset.

"And because the great Sparapet (General) of the Armenians had fallen in the battle there was no longer any chief around whom the remainder of the troops could rally. They became dispersed and threw themselves into strongholds of the country and occupied by force many regions and fortresses which no one could capture.

"And these are the names of the heroes who perished on that battlefield; the brave Vardan, the valiant Khoren Khorkhoruni; the daring Artak Baluni; the amazing Tajat Gntuni; the wise Hmayak Dimaksian; the wonderful Nerseh Qatchberuni; the youthful Vahan Gnuni; the just Arsen Endzayetsi; the progressive Garegin Servantsian.

"These 287 heroes and the nine distinguished nakharars perished there. Besides these 287 warriors, 740 others of the royal house, the house of Ardzruni and other nakharars inscribed their names in Book of Life on the day of that great battle. They numbered 1,036 altogether."

General Amnesty

On the side of the Persians, 3544 died, among whom were nine very distinguished men, by whose loss Mushkan was greatly disturbed. While he was thus sadly meditating, Vassak, who had hidden among the elephants, came to him and showed him stratagems whereby he might take the fortified castles. On the order of the King and on his own testimony and on that of the priests who were with him, Mushkan swore an oath, and sent forth messengers who announced that with the ceasing of the insurrection, the King had granted permission for the building of churches and for establishing all things as they were formerly. But though the King's order was in this instance truly followed, yet the people's confidence was not immediately restored, as the forces of both parties were broken, and the Armenians, through many former deceptions, had long been familiar with the treacherous nature of Vassak.

Chapter XXI
Vahan Mamikonian and the Patriotic Uprisings

Guerrilla Warfare

The Armenian army was beaten in 451, but far from being destroyed. Guerrilla wars flared around strongholds and along impregnable heights. Mushkan's columns penetrated into the central regions of the country, but failed to crush the heart of the people. The blood of the great leader, Vardan "the Red," had cemented together the revolutionists and those who had hitherto been unconscious of the national peril. "Thereupon," says Yeghisheh, "they quitted their homes, their cities and boroughs; the bride left her couch and the bridegroom his chamber; old folk gave up their chairs and infants their mother's breasts; youths, maidens, all men and women arose and fled to remote fastnesses. Without murmuring, they lived upon herbs and forgot their accustomed meats. The caves they considered as the apartments of their lofty dwellings, and subterranean abodes were as frescoed halls. The songs they sang were psalms, and they read the Scriptures with a holy joy. Each was to himself a church, each a priest; their bodies served them for the sacred altars, and their souls were the offering. No one mourned despairingly for those who had fallen by the sword, and nor were any greatly troubled for their nearest friends. With peace of soul they suffered the loss of all their goods. Patiently they endured all fatigues, although they looked forward with no joyful hope, for the greater number of their most distinguished princes, their brothers, sons, daughters and many of their friends were scattered in various places of hiding."

Persians encounter resistance

The chief centers of resistance were in the north-western parts of Armenia, the dense forests of the "gloomy land of the Khaltiq;" the thickly wooded province of Artazakh on the east, in the South the impregnable recesses of Tmoriq, the southeastern regions of Korduq, the castles of the province of Ararat, the strong forts of the Kapouyt (Blue) Mountain. The Persian forces attempting to reduce these last two spots had been wiped out. The Persians suffered a crushing defeat at a remote village in the province of Taiq, on the frontiers of Khaltiq, where a large number of Armenian nobles, together with their families and fighting liegemen, had been collected. This battle cost the life of another patriot leader, Hmayak Mamikonian, brother of the martyred Vardan, but it had a decisive effect, for it put an end to Persian military operations in Armenia. The Commander-in-chief, Mushkan Nussalavurd, reported to his imperial master that repressive measures would only result in the desolation of the country, in contravention of the Mazdean tenets, and that Vassak should be held responsible for all this bloodshed and misery.

Trial of Vassak

The Armenian leaders of the uprising, having lodged complaint with the royal court against the deceit and intrigues of Vassak, they were all summoned to Ctesiphon, the winter capital, in the early part of 452. Vassak, who must also appear, reached the city even before the great caravan, and was endeavoring to win the good graces of the courtiers. Because of their being brought in chains, it required eighty days for the priests to arrive. The court was held under the presidency of Mihr-Nerseh, and the inquiry continued for several days. During his alliance with his nationalist fellow-countrymen, Vassak had written to the Byzantine Emperor and to his general in Anatolia, to the rulers of Georgia and Albania, and to the princes of Andzevatsiq, Hashdeniq, Dzopq and Anghel-town, asking assistance in the struggle against Persia. His letters, all stamped with his own seal, were introduced, and together with other evidence, made clear his duplicity. Mushkan himself charged Vassak with treachery, declaring that even after the battle, he had betrayed many by false oaths and lured them from their strongholds, (of which he then took possession), executing or imprisoning not a few of them. It was also proved that he had been guilty of peculation with regard to state tributes.

Condemned to Death

On hearing the sentence passed by the tribunal on these and other charges, the King announced that he would deliberate before deciding what to do with this great malefactor. Twelve days later, he commanded the assembling of all dignitaries. Vassak, also summoned, appeared in the full dignity and insignia of his high office as Marzban. He wore a golden tiara and a massive chain of gold, embellished with pearls and other rare ornaments, earrings, a collar around his neck, a robe of sables and all other marks of his rank. The Armenian princes who had of their own accord come from their homeland, as also the priests who were already there, were herded together in chains before the royal gate. Vassak entered and seated himself in the hall where public judgment was pronounced on the highest personages. A chamberlain of the court now appeared and questioned him, saying, "I come from the King to ask you: from whom and for what worthy service did you receive all these distinguished honors?" And he reminded him of all that had been said at the tribunal where he was condemned.

The jailor now led him to prison, stripped him of his robes and clothed him with the garb of death. So rigidly did the royal officers claim the return of misappropriated tribute from his family that, although he brought in compensation all the goods of his parents and all those of the women, the State claim could not be liquidated. And after all, the sentence of death seems to have been commuted. Yeghisheh says that Vassak fell violently ill in prison; melancholy bore him down, his body shrivelled, and finally "a secret death smote him." "The King commanded," he adds, "that because of his offenses against Armenia, the place of his burial should not be made known. His name is not listed among the faithful, and he is unmentioned at the holy altar of the Church."

Martyrdom of the Ghevondians

The troubles in Armenia had given the Kushans an opportunity to make incursions into Persia, and Yazdegert II for the third time led a punitive expedition against them, but suffered a humiliating reverse. The disaster was for the most part due to sedition in the army, but the Magi attributed it to the insults which the Armenian priests had put upon the gods, by destroying the fire-altars and quenching the sacred fire, thus committing unforgivable offenses. The monarch, furious over his defeat and fearful of incurring the enmity of the Magi, proceeded to take vengeance upon the Armenian priests, who had been exiled to Nushapur Castle, in far-off Hyrcania (Mazandaran). Den-Shapuh, the Imperial High Commissioner, was accordingly sent to accomplish their punishment, after "due process of law." In cold blood, he ordered the execution of the Katholikos Hovsep and the Priest Ghevond, then the Bishop Sahak of Reshtuniq and the remainder of the dauntless champions of the Christian faith. The Church has dedicated a feast day to the memory of the Ghevondians, as well as of the Vardanians.

Effects of the Persecution

The persecutions spelled material and physical ruin for Armenia. She lost on the battlefields or in captivity the major part of her younger generation, of her scholarly clergy, her wealth and industry. On the other hand, however, her losses fanned the spirit of resistance in defense of inalienable human rights. The results were not less detrimental to the suzerain power, depriving it of the valor of the Armenian warriors and of an abundant flow of revenue from that country. Yazdegert bitterly regretted the failure of the whole enterprise, the loss of Vardan and the destruction of the Jor Gate. In the hope of regaining the good will of his subjects, he now curtailed taxes and declared national faiths free. In a final decree, he ordered all those who had unwillingly accepted Mazdeism to turn back to Christianity. The execution of this edict he entrusted to the new Marzban, Adr-Ormizd-Arshakan.

Repatriation of Armenian Nakharars

Thirty-five nakharars of Armenia, all in chains, were sent in 452 to Hyrcania, south of the Caspian Sea. Later, they were transferred eastward, to the castle of Nushapur, in Khorassan. In 460 King Peroz (Firuz) son of Yazdegert II, sent them still further east, to Hrev (modern Herat) in Afghanistan, to join the Aryan cavalry force, then engaged in fighting against the Kushans of Bactria. And at last, in 463, they were liberated and returned home after twelve years of exile.

Policy of Peroz

As fanatical a Mazdean as was his father, Peroz cherished the design of bringing the Armenians into the fold of the state religion; but instead of taking oppressive measures, he resorted to gentle persuasion, through gifts and promotions. This policy led to a spiritual decadence. Religious enthusiasm and patriotic zeal, once characteristics of the sturdy highlanders, now seemed to yield place to ignoble allurements, to a scramble for power and gain. "Virtue and wisdom vanished from Armenia," says Ghazar Parbetsi (Lazarus of Parbi). "Valor was dead, Christianity in hiding. The famous Armenian cavalry which — always under renowned and victorious commanders — had constituted the real strength of the Persian army, had now become an object of scorn and derision for all."

Rival Parties

The pro-Persian party's ascendancy seemingly procured through corruption, could not long remain unchallenged. Once more, party lines asserted themselves. The "Loyals," or "Faithful," as Lazarus distinguished the Pro-Romans from the "Apostates," acknowledged the Katholikos Gute as their leader, supported by the Mamikonians and Kamsarakans. The rival party was headed by Cadisho Khorkhoruni, patronized by the Marzban himself, Adr-Vshnasp, a Persian, whose mission was the peaceful penetration into Armenia of the worship of sun and fire.

Dethronement of the Katholikos

In the hope of averting the fatal effects of this bloodless penetration, the Katholikos secretly sent messengers to the Byzantine Emperor, Leo I, soliciting military aid. This appeal unfortunately placed the Katholikos in a perilous position. Spied upon and betrayed by Cadisho, he was summoned to Ctesiphon. He was able to confute a charge of treasonable acts but was divested of his patriarchal authority (475).[50]

Vahan Mamikonian

At this point, the simmering discontent of the Armenian masses almost reached the boiling point. A revival of the nationalist spirit was in evidence. The vast majority of the peasants, townsmen and aristocrats were interested only in the liberation of the homeland. They were unanimous in the selection of their new leader — Vahan Mamikonian, son of the great Vardan's brother Hmayak and of the Lady Tzwik, a daughter of the prince of Vassak Ardzruni. In boyhood Vahan and his younger brother had been kidnapped by Vassak, the Marzban, and sent as hostages to Ctesiphon. A grand-uncle of the children, Ashousha, the powerful Bdeshkh (Viceroy) of Georgia, succeeded in obtaining the release of the young hostages in 455 and restoring them to their mother, who was then residing in the province of Goukarq, as a guest in the mansion of her sister, Anoush-Vram, wife of Ashousha. Lazarus speaks of Tzwik as "far excelling in virtue and wisdom all other women of the Armenian homeland."

The martyred General Vardan Mamikonian and his wife Dstrik had left two daughters, Shoushan Vardeni and Vardanoush. The first died unhappily, because

---

[50] Released from Ctesiphon, he retired to his native village, Othmus, where he died in 478.

129

of the cruelty of her apostate husband, Vazken, the son of Prince Ashousha. The second became the bride of the valiant Arshavir Kamsarakan. Vahan inherited his uncle Vardan's rights and title as the head of the Mamikonian house, Vardan having left no male issue.

Persian King Distrusts Vahan

To the brilliant family traditions, to an excellent education under his mother's care and to a thorough training in the military science, Vahan added the natural gifts of sagacity, sound judgment, energy and calmness. King Peroz, well aware of Vahan's high qualifications, wished to entrust an exalted position to him, but always hesitated to do so, because of the fervent nationalism of the Mamikonians. The king's caution was well grounded, and served the purpose of the villainous Cadisho, who, not satisfied with the Loyalist defeat in the fall of the Katholikos, had been plotting against Vahan. He repeatedly reminded the Persian government of the Mamikonians' leading role in previous revolutionary movements. "It would be impossible," he frequently declared, "for Vahan to remain in Armenia without instigating a rebellion."

Vahan's Politic Compromise

Deeply grieved by such vile attacks, and unable to endure the calumnies any longer, Vahan set out for the Persian capital, where, heeding his high-ranking friends' advice, he subjected himself to soul-torture, and in the words of the historian Lazarus, "faltered in faith;" which merely means that he attended the Mazdean ritual service. Such a demonstration appeared to be the only way for him to baffle his enemies and return home in triumph. Soon after this, he was rewarded with an enviable appointment — the post of Inspector of the Gold Mines. The promotion of their dreaded rival fanned the jealousy in the breasts of the pro-Persian leaders into a raging flame. An accomplice, Vriv by name, son of an Assyrian who held a position in the office of the mines, was dispatched to Ctesiphon to report that Vahan had been secretly hoarding large quantities of gold, with intent to organize an armed force from among the Greeks and the Huns. Vahan, hearing of this, promptly hastened to the capital to lay at the feet of the sovereign so large a quantity of the precious metal that the court was amazed. He invited investigation, called attention to the simplicity of his life and convinced the King that his course had been entirely upright.

The falsity of Cadisho's testimony having thus been exposed, Vahan returned to his home with fresh laurels of distinction. Yet he was suffering, day and night, because of the stain of apostasy which he yearned to wipe away. Fortunately, the opportune moment was not long in presenting itself. A formidable revolt against Persia broke out under King Vakhtank in Iberia (Georgia), thrilling the Christian population of the Caucasus and Armenia with the hope of gaining some advantage.The Armenian nakharars approached Vahan and urged him to take the lead in immediate action. "Vakhtank is powerful," they say. "By joining our forces to his own, we can withstand the Persians."

Vahan's reply, as quoted by Lazarus, is characteristic of the man. "You may be right," said he, "and reflecting on the uncertainty of life, I dread quitting this world with the name (apostate) fastened upon me. I wish my mother had never given me life. Still, I cannot take part in your project. I well know the power and arrogance of the Ariq (Persians), as well as the indolence and deceitfulness of the Horoms (Romano-Greeks). As to the Georgians and the Huns, the former are weak, having only a few horsemen, while the latter are not yet in sight; their coming is uncertain. But above all, you should distrust your own selves, because you are a false and unreliable people."

The nakharars, undaunted by this plain speaking, met the chief's argument with the following retort; "We place our confidence neither in the alliance of the Horoms nor in the cooperation of the Huns; but first of all, in the mercy of God, in the intercession of St. Gregory, in the death of our ancestors, and finally, in our own deaths. For we all prefer to perish at the same time, rather than witness, day after day, the humiliation of the Church and the desertion of the faithful."

Vahan Joins Rebellion

Impressed by these resolute utterances, Vahan gave his assent to their proposal, and was seconded by his brother Vassak, who was among the group. With their hands upon the Gospel, they all took a solemn oath in the presence of the priest Athik of Betchni. The meeting had been held in secret, but rumors of the proceeding leaked out that same night. The Persian Marzban fled precipitately. The Armenians pursued him, but succeeded only in overtaking his treasure-laden mules and in catching the arch-traitor Cadisho.

Armenian Government Set Up

An Armenian government was set up in 481. The possible of Marzban was entrusted to Sahak Bagratuni; the army was put under the command of Vahan Mamikonian. The marvelous deeds of valor achieved by the troops of Vahan during the following four years remind us of the heroic era of ancient Rome. Many a time they skilfully retired from battle-fronts or escaped through blockade lines; thrice they seized the city of Douin, and four times they won battles against greatly superior forces. The first victory, that of an Armenian squadron of only 300 rebels against 7,000 regulars, took place in front of Agori, a village on the slope of Massis. The Persian Marzban, Adrvshnasp, was slain in that engagement. The second victory was gained near Nersehapat, a village in the very plain of historic Avarair, where Vardan Mamikonian had fallen, thirty-one years before. The third triumph was that of a handful of men at the village of Erez, district of Arsharuniq, the modern Vartov; and the fourth and most brilliant of all was a defense by a mere forty daredevils against 4,000 assailants in the village of Shdev, where Cdihon, the renegade Prince of Sewniq, a giant in stature, perished.

Guerrilla warfare was still being carried on by Armenian bands under Vahan in the mountain fastnesses of Taiq, and by the Georgian rebels under King Vakhtank, in the forests of Aphkhazia, when a fortunate occurrence brought them relief. King Peroz having been slain in his war against the Hephtalites in 484, his brother and successor Vagharsh (Valash) decided to settle the Armenian question in a peaceful manner. He sent a high commissioner, Nikhor-Vshnasp, to Armenia for negotiations. When he reached frontier, Nikhor informed Vahan through envoys, of the object of his mission. After listening to the deputation, Vahan sent messengers to Nikhor with these proposals as a basis for negotiation:—

I. Religious worship in accordance with Christian doctrines and rites to be declared free. No Armenian to be appointed as a Magian officer. No public position to be given as a reward for conversion to Mazdeism. Fire altars to be removed from Armenia.

II. The rights and privileges of the nakharars (the satrapal houses) to be restored.

III. The King himself to direct the investigation and render judgment, whenever an Armenian nakharar shall have been charged with some offense.

Treaty of Nuvarsak

Agreeing to these proposals, Nikhor extended an invitation to Vahan to visit him. Vahan set out for the Persian headquarters of Nuvarsak, after having eight Persian noblemen delivered to the Armenian camp as hostages. When Vahan approached Nikhor's tent, he ordered his men to sound the trumpet. Persian officials objected that the Aryan Commander-in-chief alone had the right to be announced by trumpet. Vahan replied that he would act according to the Aryan regulations only when he had entered the Aryan King's service. His interview with Nikhor was cordial. The Commissioner conveyed to Vahan his master's greetings, commended his courage and wisdom and exculpated him for his acts.

Nikhor's Commendation

"For a brave man," said he, "it is much better to die after demonstrating his merit, even for one day, than to live long by enduring continuous blows. You and your companions did not fear death, but performed valorous deeds. For the blood of those from among you who died because of the foolish pride of Peroz, the gods will demand retribution. As for you who have survived, you are not guilty, and shall remain unharmed." After the exchange of more such words of courtesy — as quoted by Lazarus — and mutual agreement on the basic points of peace, a banquet was set in honor of Vahan and his party. On the following day Vahan promised, at Nikhor's request, to send a cavalry regiment to Persia, to fight the enemies of Valash.

Vahan Appointed Marzban

Vahan's crowning success was still ahead. He now journeyed to the Persian capital, and was granted the favors requested by him, among them restoration of the Mamikonians and Kamsarakans to their feudal ranks and rights. Vahan's elevation to the Marzbanic dignity took place soon after his return to Armenia. These happy events were celebrated in the cathedral of Douin, under the presidency of the Katholikos Hovhan Mandakuni. The service was one of thanksgiving and joyous festivity. "The church was crowd to its capacity," says Lazarus, "with every class of people — nakharars, azats (freemen), ostaniks (nobility) and plebeians, male and female, old and young, even the newly-wed brides, who for joy had for a moment forgotten their bridal shyness." The multitude packed the streets and all near-by open spaces.

In his sermon, the Katholikos stressed the beauty and necessity of charity, harmony, reconciliation and forgiveness. Having the leaders of the pro-Persian party in mind, the venerable prelate desired to urge a gracious moderation upon the winning side.

Armenia Regains Autonomy

The treaty of Nuvarsak was a compromise between the court of Ctesiphon on the one side, and the Armenian clergy and nobility on the other. Armenia, through the successful resistance of the Vahanian band, had regained her autonomy and freedom of National church and culture. The treaty afforded, also, opportunity for progress in the economic growth, intellectual development and feudal stabilization of the country.

"Vardan and Vahan," says Kevork Aslan, "whose memory as symbols of liberty and bravery has been kept bright by posterity, occupy a distinct place in the history of the Armenian people. Their passionate love of freedom, their fearlessness in danger, their inflexible will power, impressed upon the minds of the great ones as well as the masses the ideas of nationalism and independence. Their patriotic zeal saved Christianity in Armenia, which Persian persecutions had threatened with total destruction."

Vahan's Benign Rule

Vahan ruled for twenty years — 485 to 505. He was succeeded by his youngest brother Vard, who, suspected of pro-Greek tendencies, ruled only four years. However, during the rule of Vahan and almost all of the following marzbans, Armenia enjoyed peace and economic progress. The Persian government during that time was absorbed in the problems of internal unrest and in armed conflict against Byzantium, mostly waged outside the Armenian frontiers.

Chapter XXII
Armenia in the Fifth and Sixth Centuries

Divisions of Armenia

By the treaty of 387, the western part of Armenia, along the line of Karin (Erzerum), Niphrkert-Mdzpin (Nissibin), had been turned over to the Byzantine Empire and administratively divided into northern and southern sections. The northern part, with the city of Karin as its center, was known as Inner Armenia, and had been annexed to the Empire after the death of Arshak III the Arsacid, in 391. The southern part comprised the five satrapies, or autonomous feudal states.

Armenia Minor (Pokr Haik) was already under Byzantine domination before the division of Armenia, and consisted of two parts — First Armenia, with Sebastia (Sivas) as its center, and Second Armenia, with Melitine (Malatia) as the capital. The internal status of Western Armenia had remained almost unchanged, with its native social order and laws prevailing. But it submitted to some change under the Emperor Zeno (474-491), when Armenian princes had joined the forces revolting against him. Zeno suppressed the hereditary feudal prerogatives of the Armenian princely houses in the southern provinces. The nomination of the head of the house became the Emperor's vested right. Other radical changes were decreed by Justinian in the sixth century.

Justinian Reorganizes Western Armenia

During the Persian-Byzantine wars in the first quarter of the sixth century, the divided feudal units of western Armenia had been unable effectively to defend the eastern borders of the Empire. Western Armenia was therefore subjected to military reorganization in 528 by Justinian, whose name is most familiar to the modern world as a legislator and codifier of the law. First, Second and Inner Armenia and Pontus were all combined to form a general military zone. The Armenian satrapal regiments were made parts of the Imperial divisions. Through this rearrangement, the military functions of both Greek governors and Armenian nakharars were abolished.

After the conclusion of the peace treaty with Persia in 532, Justinian set to work on the administrative, judicial and legislative reorganization of Western Armenia, with intent to make that region finally a province of the Empire. Accordingly, all its territorial areas and the ancient Armenia Minor formed one grand unit, composed of four administrative regions, under the names of First, Second, Third and Fourth Armenia.

Legislative edicts promulgated by Justinian in 536 ended some ancient laws and customs in Western Armenia. By the same edict, women were entitled to inherit dominion rights. The main object of this legislation was to parcel out the inherited estates of the Armenian princes. The same laws aimed also at putting an end to hereditary rights within private domains; in other words, to unite and absorb Western Armenia into the Byzantine hegemony.

Insurrections in Western Armenia

The restriction of the authority of the nakharars, and even more definitely an increase in taxes, stirred popular discontent and uprisings. In the Karin district at that time there lived the last remaining issue of the House of Arshakuni, among whom Hovhan and his son Artavan were prominent. They had as neighbors the Bagratunis of Sper and the Mamikonians of Taiq. These all combined their forces to foment insurrections (537-539). The movement started in the northern portion of Western Armenia, as the immediate result of the assassination of Prince Hamazasp of Sper by a Byzantine proconsul. The rebels massacred the Imperial troops and swept all Byzantines out of Western Armenia; but in turn a Greek army in great force was rushed to the scene and checked the revolt. Many Armenian nakharars were executed or exiled to distant parts. The Emperor's severity dealt such a blow to the military efficacy of the Armenians that their leaders never again regained their martial power in those parts of their homeland. That which Sassanid Persia had failed to accomplish in eastern Armenia through centuries of struggles, Byzantium succeeded in bringing about in Western Armenia at one stroke.

Persian Oppression in Armenia

In the second half of the sixth century, the Persian Government resumed its oppressive policy in Armenia. It imposed heavier taxes, demanding payment in cash, treated the nakharars with suspicion and restricted their economic and political exemptions. Complaints against these provocations were intensified by the tyranny of the Persian Marzban Souren. His attitude towards the clergy and the nobility was insolent, and he provoked the indignation of the masses by attempting to erect a Mazdean temple in Douin.

Armenian Rebellion

The Byzantine government took advantage of the ill-feeling brewing against the Persians in the Caucasus. In 570 the Armenian chiefs concluded a secret agreement with Byzantium, under which the latter guaranteed the liberation of Eastern Armenia and recognition of it as an independent state. The discontented Armenian princes having made some remarks against the Marzban, Manuel Mamikonian was killed in retaliation. His brother, Vardan Mamikonian, rose in rebellion in 571 and captured the city of Douin. Souren the Marzban was slain in turn, and Persian officials and soldiers fled. For two years the rebels continued their resistance against the Persian armies, but the failure of the Byzantines to send promised aid at last compelled them to lay down their arms. Hovhan II

Capeghian, the Katholikos and Vardan the general repaired to Constantinople in the hope of obtaining imperial assistance in recovering their homeland, and circumstances sustained their hopes. Persia, whose eastern frontiers were again menaced by Hunnish hordes, would suffer greater embarrassment from an accelerated Armenian rebellion. Acting upon such a theory, Byzantium declared war against Persia in 572.

Second Partition of Armenia

But the imperial edict did not prosper; several successive defeats forced the Emperor to ask for peace in 579. A treaty was signed, but its terms did not satisfy Ormuzd IV, successor of Khosrov I (Chosroes).[51] He renewed hostilities, and now the Byzantines were more fortunate, for they had a new and able Emperor, Maurice (Morik) of Armenian origin. He pushed forward, even into Persia itself, and brought the war to a successful conclusion by supporting the claim of Khosrov II against his rivals and restoring him to the throne in 591. In return for his aid, Maurice received from the new King the major part of Armenia, extending from the western shore of the Lake of Sevan and the valley of the Azat River to the Arax, thence by a straight line across the Lake of Van to Nissibin.

Maurice for Crushing Armenia

But the Armenians paid a price for Byzantine aid. Bishop Sebeos relates that the Emperor Maurice sent to Chosroes II the following letter:

> "We have among us an unruly nation which foments disorder. See, let me collect the Armenian chiefs from my side and concentrate them in Thrace, and you collect the Armenian chiefs of your side and order them to be sent to the East to fight your enemies. If they kill, your enemies shall have been destroyed; but if the enemies kill, they will have destroyed our mutual foes. Then we may live in peace, because if they remain in their country, we shall enjoy no rest."

Khosrov agreed to this proposal, and the Armenian soldiers were all transferred to foreign lands; those of the Byzantine area to distant parts of the Empire, and those of the Persian section to the East. This policy of the two dominating powers created bitter resentment in Armenia and brought about seditions under Sahak Mamikonian and Sembat Bagratuni.

Maurice Assassinated

The strict military discipline imposed by Maurice provoked the Imperial army to mutiny. The revolt of the popular factions in Constantinople followed in 602, culminating in the assassination of Maurice by the usurper Phocas. The Persian

---

[51] Peace prevailed for a long period, under Khosrov I, called Nushirevan (531-579), the most tolerant among Sassanid Kings.

leaders, who had been seeking a pretext to denounce the treaty of 591, now assembled their army as if to defend the rights of the heirs of Maurice, but in reality to recapture the territories ceded to Byzantium. The Imperial internal crisis gave them an opportunity for successes in the field. In 616 they occupied Syria and Egypt, and even encamped before Constantinople. But fortune eventually favored the Christian Empire. Heraclius unseated the usurper Phocas in 610, seized the throne, developed into an able general and took the field against the mighty foe in the East. His first attempt in 622 to get a foothold in Armenia was unsuccessful; but in his second campaign, in 624-626, he swept the Persian army before him across the Armenian highlands to the Tigris, where he won a decisive victory. Two years later, he advanced to the environs of Ctesiphon, recovered the True Cross from the Persians and brought it back to Constantinople.

Khosrov Assassinated

The Persian reverses brought about grave disorders in their capital, which reached a climax in the assassination of Khosrov II. His son Kavad concluded a new treaty with the Byzantine, or as it was beginning to be called, the Greek Empire, by which the greater part of Armenia again passed into Western hands. The administration of the Persian area of Eastern Armenia was now handed over to an Armenian Marzban, Varaztirotz Bagratuni, while that of the Byzantine section was entrusted to an Armenian governor, Mezhezh (Mjej or Mezezius) Gnouni.

Feudaries under the Marzbans

Marzbanic Armenia was a typical feudal country. By comparison with the Arshakuni period, its economic status was more advanced. However, Peasantry and Aristocracy were still the two basic classes of the nation. After the fall of the Arshakuni kingdom, the monarch of Sassanid Persia, the common suzerain of the Armenian feudatories, determined ranks among the Armenian nakharars, as judged by their situation, landed holdings and military force. The most powerful ones among them under the Arshakuni kings — the Sewnis, Bagratunis, Ardzrunis, mamikonians and Kamsarakans — retained their respective positions during the Marzbanic period. About the end of the sixth century, the Saharuni and Reshtuni houses appear to have risen high in power. The situation was different in Western Armenia, where Armenian satrapal houses came to an end in 535 A.D.

New Law of Land Ownership

The law of land ownership was definitely changed under the Marzbans. During the Arshakuni regime, the satrapal lands were considered indivisible, each of them forming a unit, under the rule and jurisdiction of the chief of the house or clan. In the Marzbanic period, there came a change; the Sepouhs, the junior members of the satrapal line, received authority to take possession of their share, and to be known as new landlords. The share of the Sepouhs was called sepouhakan or sebhakan. Armenia in the Marzbanic era was covered with a network of feudal estates. The clergy were feudaries, too, and they also increased in number under the Marzbans. There were four episcopates or dioceses in the fourth century, rising to fifteen in the first half of the fifth century. Through purchase, donation and otherwise, they acquired extensive landed properties.

Rural Class

The peasants, the second basic element of the population, became subject to double exploitation under the Marzbans — by the old, native land-owners on the one hand, and by the Persian and Byzantine powers on the other. Upon the division of a property or a change in ownership by sale or donation or otherwise, the people living on the land were likewise handed over to its new lord. The peasants had to give to the land-owner one portion of their products, and to the Church one-tenth portion, known as bdugh (fruit).

The peasant belonged to the Anazat (unfree) class. Offenses committed by Azats and Anazats were not subject to the same degree of penalty. The blood-wite, the fine levied for the murder of an Azat, was higher than that for an Anazat. An Anazat offender was sentenced by the court to corporal punishment and condemned to hard labour; as for the Azas, they were usually sentenced to pay various amounts of cash. The peasants were heavily taxed also by the Persian and Byzantine governments. The former had imposed a land tax (Hass in Armenian) and personal tribute (Sak), also custom-house duties (Baj) on merchants. All objects subject to taxation were registered in the book called "Divan." For the classification of the taxes, a census of men was taken and surveys made of every productive item. Tax-gatherers added to the burden of the people by arbitrary exactions.

Peasants Suffer

The condition of the rural population grew worse during the second half of the sixth century, when the land taxes became payable in cash. As a result, the peasants often fell into the hands of usurers. Men between 20 and 50 were subject to payment of a poll tax and land products were taxed at various rates — one-third, one-quarter, one-fifth and one-sixth, according to the quantity of the yield, the method of irrigation and the kind of product. Serf labour was to some extent still in force in Armenia until the last quarter of the nineteenth century; that is, common people were drafted for labor on public works — for the construction of roads, bridges, canals and dams, and for the excavation of mine shafts.

Growth of Trade

The economic life of the country showed a gradual improvement during the Marzbanic period, parallel to the growth of cities and the bettering of relations among the crafts and trades. As to civil life, its improvement was enhanced by the economic developments in Hither Asia and Byzantium. One of the international commercial transit routes from Oriental countries crossed through Douin on its way to the West, to the ports of the Black and Mediterranean Seas. On that route were the ancient mercantile cities of Armenia — Artashat, Erouandashat and Theodosiopolis-Karin (Erzerum). Over it Armenian, Jewish, Arab and Syrian merchants exchanged raw silk, spices, drugs, precious stones and other goods. Many of the business men moved their residences into such centers. The long periods of peace between Persia and Byzantium during the fifth century contributed much to the expansion of trade connections between East and West. In Douin the traders of India, Persia and Georgia transacted business and exchanged wares and commodities with the merchants of Byzantium. "Douin is an excellent place," remarks Procopius, Greek historian of the sixth century. "It has a healthy climate and abundance of good water. Its distance from Theodosiopolis is eight days journey. In that region there are plains suitable for riding. Populous villages are situated not far apart, and numerous merchants conduct their business in them. For from India and the near-by Iberia, and from all the nations of Persia, and some of those under Roman sway they bring in goods and carry on their dealings with each other there."

Besides being a transit medium, Armenia was also a center of production. It exported horses, mules, wine, dyes, grain, oil, metals, rugs, textiles, etc. The system of cash payment of personal tribute aided in the encouragement of trade. It compelled the peasant to bring a part of his products into the market, in order to obtain currency. At the same time usury flourished. A document surviving from those days tells us that: "Money is lent for profit, interest being demanded thereon. Shamelessly, poor people's flesh is devoured and their blood drunk. Cash is given in certain amounts, but demanded in double. They (the usurers) reap without sowing the seed; they collect output and hoard their iniquitous earnings."

Artisans Numerous

Among the inhabitants of a city, the artisans outnumbered all other classes. Their products, together with those of the peasants, constituted the major part of the goods offered for sale in the inner market. Many handicrafts, such as pottery, tanning, wood and iron working, wine-making, weaving and the goldsmith's art, were in an advanced stage of development. It was the custom for an artisan to keep the methods of his craft secret, revealing them only to his heirs. Socially, merchants and artisans had a higher status than the peasants.

Feudalism Chief Weakness

The Kings of Armenia could never quite crush feudalism, which was the chief political weakness of the Nation. Nevertheless, the King was recognized by the nobles as their supreme head; they were his vassals, even when Armenia in turn was entirely in vassalage to one empire or another. At the time when the ruling monarch was powerful enough, his will was the supreme law, and the life of the grandee was in his hands. An insurgent lord might be punished by death, or by

139

the loss of all or a part of his lands. In wartime the vassal nobles must assemble their forces at the call of the king, to be put at the disposal of the commander-in-chief.

Few large cities existed in Armenia, but many castles and forts were surrounded by villages. In the mountain areas, because of the severity of their climate, the peasants' dwellings were half buried in the earth. They were warm enough during the winter, and were stocked with provisions for the family and domestic animals. Until the invention of the Armenian alphabet, the masses lived in ignorance, their only fragments of intellectual culture being found in temple chants or minstrel songs.

Armenian Mores

The morals, manners and customs of the Armenians for many centuries were similar to those of the Medes. The family head had full authority over his children, their wives and his grandchildren. The father gave his daughter to a suitor in marriage for a gift commensurate with the possessions of the latter. Among the common people domestic life seems to have been smooth and harmonious. The wife's fate depended upon her husband's will; she might, if such was his whim, be summarily repudiated. Polygamy was the rule among the nobility. The organization and administration of justice were irrational, all being at the mercy of the King and the nakharars. Criminals were thrown into underground dungeons, and punishment often included bodily torture, in accordance with Persian practice. Political convicts were frequently deprived of their eyesight by branding or laceration, a procedure prevalent in the Byzantine Empire. Such inhuman customs were more or less abated or suppressed after the conversion of the nation to Christianity; then trials were held and sentences pronounced by the high clergy in accordance with canonical laws.

Chapter XXIII
The Arab Khalifate

Emergence of the Arab Nationality

Since the earliest ages, numerous and varied tribes had been scattered over the vast area of the Arabian Peninsula, breeding their own camels and wandering from place to place. Only a small number of the Arab tribesmen had settled permanently on the western edge of the peninsula and engaged in agriculture and trade.

From the fourth century A.D., the city of Mecca had been a center of commerce. Foodstuffs and manufactured goods were imported there from the Byzantine and Persian domains, while precious stones, gold, odoriferous oils, tropical fruits and frankincense, all Arabian products, were exported, particularly from Yemen. Arabian cities and villages which had suffered much from the irruption of Persian and Abyssinian hordes also felt the destructive effects of the wars between Persia and Byzantium in the early centuries of the Christian Era.

In the seventh century the opportunity came for the wealthy Arab chieftains to correct this situation by uniting their forces. The element that gave the victim cohesion was the religion of Islam which had just been founded by Mohammed. Born in Mecca about 570, Mohammed's life was undistinguished until he reached forty. He then, as the result of an alleged vision, launched his cult, which he called the True Religion, epitomized in one sentence, "There is no God but God, and Mohammed is his Prophet." Despite some vicissitudes, his following steadily increased. Eventually he headed an army and conquered southwestern Arabia, including Mecca, which he entered in triumph in 630, and made it thereafter the holy city of Islam. He sent messages to the monarchs of Byzantium and Persia, demanding their recognition of his religion and suzerainty.

Death of Mohammed
Rise of the Khalifate

Mohammed died in 632 and was succeeded by Abubekr, with the title Khalifa, *i.e.*, "Successor or Vicar of the Prophet." He soon declared a "Holy War," wild horsemen being charged not only to spread the true religion, but to conquer and loot rich nations and cities for the aggrandizement of Islam. Within ten years the Arabs became masters of Syria, Palestine, Phoenicia, Mesopotamia and Egypt. Then they surged eastward across Afghanistan, Turkestan and Baluchistan to the very borders of India. Even the mighty Persian Empire succumbed to their fury. In three wars the armies of Yazdegert III were dispersed, Ctesiphon was sacked (in 637) and the books of the Royal Library were thrown into the Tigris. To the west the Arabs subdued all North Africa — Tripoli, Tunisia, Algeria, Morocco and

Barbary — and even crossed the Mediterranean to take over Spain[52] in 713. By the middle of the eighth century, they had conquered an empire as large as that of Rome had once been, stretching from India to the Atlantic Ocean. The great Khalifa might have swept his gaze over it and boasted, like Augustus Caesar, that he ruled the universe.

Armenia under Persian and Imperial Rule

Since that ancient era when the Armenians had first taken possession of the land of Ararat, existence for them had often been precarious. However, this people, destined to an endless struggle for independence, was for a thousand years completely subjugated only for comparatively short periods, because both Persians and Romans followed a shrewd course of according to it a considerable measure of liberty under the rule of governors who frequently were chosen from among the nation's own princes. The Armenians were therefore in some degree the allies, rather than the subjects, now of the Roman Emperors, now of the Persian Kings!

Arabs Bring a Gloomy Era

With the entrance of the Arabs upon the stage, a darker chapter in the history of Armenia began. The Moslems regarded the Christian peoples of the conquered countries as their property, and resorted to every sort of persecution to force upon them the faith of Islam. Yet the Armenians clung tenaciously to their own religion, the last shield for the protection of their nationality. Their martyrdom began when the Arabs first appeared in the country of Van. They spread all over Western Asia in the first half of the seventh century. After having defeated the army of Yazdegert III at Kadesiya, they completed in Nehavend (641) the ruin of the already exhausted Sassanid monarchy.

Thus they brought the East under subjection, but in the North and West they encountered more serious obstacles. The Byzantine Empire, powerful not only militarily but in prestige and the superiority of its culture, although kept busy on the Danube and in Thrace by the incursions of Northern barbarians, offered considerable resistance to the Mohammedan invaders. The Emperor Heraclius (610-641) in a series of campaigns in 622-628 had crippled Persian power and consolidated Byzantine authority over the entire Transcaucasian region. His coins circulated there, along with the Sassanid daric. The Moslems dared not attack Constantinople, but the Empire's eastern provinces being more vulnerable, they overran Armenia.

---

[52] Where they were known as Moors, and from which they were not finally driven for nearly eight centuries. Specimens of their architecture are among the glories of Spain to this day.

First Arab Invasion

Towards 639, under the leadership of Abd-er-Rahman, 18,000 Arabs penetrated the district of Taron and the region of the Lake of Van and put the country to fire and sword. Now for the first time on the battlefield the Armenians met these warriors — poor, ill-called, ill-armed, but recklessly brave and inflamed with an intense fanaticism until then unknown among ancient peoples. Persians and Romans had something to gain by tactful treatment of the Armenians, alternately their subjects and their allies. But these children of the desert knew no political expediency, nothing to curb their severity in dealing with "infidels."

Bishop Sebeos, an eye-witness and the only historian to record the story of the Arab conquest, writes with bitter lamentation (in his *History of Heraclius*) of the sad fate of his country. On January 6th, 642, the Arabs stormed and took the city of Douin, slaughtered 12,000 of its inhabitants and carried 35,000 into slavery.

Horrors of the Conquest

"Who can tell," says the Bishop, "the horrors of the invasion of the Ishmaelite, who set both the land and the sea ablaze? ... The blessed Daniel foresaw and foretold like misfortunes.... In the following year (643), the Ishmaelite army crossed to Atrpatakan (Azerbaijan) and was divided into three corps. One moved towards Ararat; another into the territory of Sephakan Gound, the third into the land of Alans. Those who invaded the domain of the Sephakan Gound spread over it, destroying, plundering and taking prisoners. Thence they marched together to Erevan, where they attacked the fortress, but were unable to capture it."

Constans II, then Emperor in Constantinople, sent occasional reinforcements to Armenia, but they were inadequate. The commander of the city of Douin, Sembat, confronted by the unpleasant fact that he could no longer hold out against the Ishmaelite horde, submitted to the Khalifa Omar, consenting to pay him tribute. Sembat was soon replaced by the Mohammedan Othman (644).

"The Arabian army which was in Ararat," continues Sebeos, "penetrated into the territories of Taiq, Georgia and Albania, seizing captives and booty. Thence it marched to Nakhjavan ... but could not reduce the city. However, it took the fort of Khram, slaughtered the garrison and carried the women and children into captivity."

Emperor Compels Armenian Loyalty

The first Arab governor of Tiflis was installed in 646. The Byzantine government dared not permit the Arabs to establish themselves as a threat on the plateau of Erzerum. But Constans II, incensed against the Armenians, resolved to recapture their country by force and compel them to accept the Greek brand of Christianity, fatuously hoping thus to bind them more tightly to the Empire. He did not succeed in his doctrinal objective, but the new Armenian prefect, Hamazasp, who regarded the taxes imposed by the Moslems as too heavy, yielded to the Emperor. Khalifa Othman, in retaliation, ordered the massacre of 1,775 Armenian hostages then in his hands, and was about to march against the Armenian rebels when he was assassinated by his own soldiers in 656.

His second successor, Moawiyah, Khalifa of Baghdad (661-680), resumed Othman's projects, devastated Armenia and retook it from the Emperor, who called upon the unfortunate Armenian people to yield him obedience again.

Armenian Retort to Emperor

"How many times," retorted the Armenians, "while submitting to the government of the Greeks, we have received only trifling aid from it, even during our worst calamities! On the contrary, our submission has often been rewarded only with insults! To take the oath of loyalty to you means to expose ourselves to destruction and death. Leave us, therefore, under the domination of our present masters, who accord us their protection."

This answer naturally did not please the Basileus. He dispatched an army which ravaged Armenia, carried away what little wealth the Arab conquerors had overlooked and took away 8,000 Armenian families to be sold as slaves far from their homeland.

Armenia Ravaged by Greeks and Arabs

The Arabs suspecting that the Armenians were restive under their rule, once more overran and laid waste the Ararat province, razed many cities, spread death and desolation, and demolishing the island fortress of the Lake of Sevan, condemned its defenders to slavery. Justinian II, on the other hand, relentlessly continued his endeavors to force the Armenians to accept the Orthodox creed, and in pursuance of this missionary work, ordered his troops to ravage Upper Armenia, Iberia and Albania, which had been compelled to yield to the power of the Khalifas. Thus the Armenians were persecuted by the Moslems because of their Christianity and by the Byzantine Greeks because of mere differences in creed.

Byzantine Intolerance

"The Byzantine court at that time, says Jacques de Morgan, "exhibited the spectacle of a most ferocious religious intolerance; a fierce hatred stirred the Greeks against those peoples who did not have the same beliefs as they did. . . . These passions and the futile wrangling resulting therefrom weakened the Empire; but the Emperors, like the people, had been blinded by the subtleties of casuistry, of sophistical reasoning, while menacing armies pressed hard upon all the frontiers."

Armenian and Greek bilingual inscription (seventh century A.D.)

But the Greek domination in Armenia did not continue long. The Basileus, after five years of odious exactions, called his legions home, and Abd-el-Melek, the Omayyad Khalifa, again overran the country, occupied the city of Douin, ousted the Greek prefect and appointed as Governor one Abd-Allah, a cruel master who sent the most prominent Armenians in captivity to Damascus. Among them were the Katholikos Sahak and Prince Sembat. The latter, having succeeded in escaping, was appointed to the leadership of Armenia by Leontius, the new Byzantine Emperor in 695.

Reign of Terror

In 702 the Emir Mohammed bin Merwan, the Governor of Mesopotamia, Assyria and Azerbaijan, had been driven away by the Greek legions. But soon after the withdrawal of the latter, the Emir regained his authority and tightened his grip by terrorizing the inhabitants. In Nakhjevan, Armenia, he locked up many prominent persons in the church, and setting fire to the edifice, burned them alive. Meanwhile, Byzantine statesmen were debating questions of dogma with the Armenian clergy! Synodic meetings were being held to decide whether or not it would be proper to mix water with wine in the celebration of the mass, or to add to the trisagion the words, "who has been crucified."

Theology was not, of course, the only preoccupation of Armenians. The higher clergy, with the Katholikos at their head, also meddled in politics. They sought to appease their Moslem masters by demonstrating their ritual divergence from the Greeks.

The struggle between the Greeks and the Arabs had increased Mohammedan power, and therefore their contempt for all other peoples who did not adopt their faith. Bishop Sebeos has left to us the Armenian translation of a letter which "the King of the Ishmaelites" sent to "the Emperor of the Greeks." The Moslem monarch wrote:—

145

Contemptuous Letter to the Emperor

"If you wish to live in peace, renounce your vain religion. . . . Abjure this Jesus and turn to the great God whom I serve, the God of our Father Abraham. Disband the multitude of your troops and dismiss them to their countries, and I will make you a great chief in those lands. I will send Osticans (military governors) to your city. I will search for all treasures and divide them into four parts; three for me, one you. Also, I will give you soldiers, as many as you may want, and levy on you such tribute as you can pay. Otherwise, how could that Jesus, whom you call Christ, who was unable to save himself from the Jews, deliver you from my hands?"

A bitter insult, indeed, to the ancient Empire, where no longer did any sense of national honor seem to stir the souls of the people. Bishop Sebeos further reveals the Emperor's fear that there was little he could do about the situation. He says that the Emperor entered into the House of God, prostrated himself with his face to the ground and prayed abjectly aid and for confusion and destruction to the Moslem enemies. He doffed his purple and his crown, put on sackcloth, sat on ashes and ordered the proclamation of a fast in Constantinople.

The Arabs had first penetrated into southern Armenia in 639. Their earlier efforts were not attended with great success, but they soon overran most of the country, and the Armenians were compelled to recognize the authority of the Khalifa in 652. Thirty years later the Greek Emperor Justinian II made war on the Moslems, but his enterprise was short-lived, and Armenia was again abandoned to the Khalifas.

Christianity Uprooted in Transcaucasia

After conquering Armenia proper, the Arabs held Georgia and occupied Tiflis. The Armenian provinces of Taiq, Gougarq, and the basin of the Phasis River were under Byzantine rule, as were the northern part of Asia Minor, Lazistan and the littoral of Euxine-Pontus (Black Sea). The capital of Georgia became thenceforth the government seat of the northern provinces of the Khalifas, and the people of these regions, unable to resist, were for the most part "converted" to Islamism. Among them were Armenian and Georgian princes, clinging to their domains. Thus Christianity almost disappeared in Transcaucasia, excepting in the mountains and inaccessible places. Churches and monasteries were demolished, mosques and minarets erected in all the cities and towns.

However, some Armenians and Caucasians, taking refuge in natural citadels and on mountains in the vicinity of the Rion River, clung to their Christian faith and hoped for a counter-offensive. They made frequent sorties upon the Arabs, with occasional successes, but their descendants had to wait long before they could reconquer their land. In the mountainous regions extending from the north side of the Arax River towards Ispir, Kars and Artwin, many castles of Armenian

146

seigniors were perched like eagles' nests on well-nigh inaccessible summits, offering shelter to the rural population of the neighborhood in times of trouble. These fastnesses could be reached only over mere goat-trails, and could have held out for months, even for years, against entire armies. So, while Moslem chants and prayers resounded in the plains and valleys, church bells high above, often hidden in the clouds, could be heard ringing calls to the faithful.

Arabs Stimulate Commerce

From the economic viewpoint, the Arabian conquests, though they profoundly upset the general situation in the East, gave commerce a new impetus. At first, gold currency was minted almost entirely by Roman Emperors; Oriental princes issued coins only in small amounts. The Arabs put into circulation a large quantity of dinars, and so forced Byzantium to raise the weight and standard of the coin. Furthermore, the vast extent of their empire enabled the Moslems to spread their commercial relations throughout the Eastern world. Maritime routes were opened between the Persian Gulf, the Red Sea and the coasts of India, Africa, Malaya and China. The Greeks, too, became to a certain extent tributaries of their rivals. Continental highways still functioned through Iran, Armenia and Mesopotamia over well-worn roads which were known to the Phoenicians of old, and which Moslem Semites followed to reach Tibet, central China and India.

Moslems Overreach Themselves

After the conquest of Anterior Asia, the Arabs did some colonizing in these regions, but in Persia, Transcaucasia, Armenia and Asia Minor, the ancient races continued to occupy the soil, the Arabs reserving to themselves the collection of taxes and the government. The very extent of the Arab empire, however, compelled the Moslems to divide and weaken their forces. They had invaded all the Mediterranean coasts of Africa and Spain, and seemed to be on the point of conquering Europe when, in 732, they were checked by Charles Martel in the great battle at Poitiers, in France, in what has been called not of the seven most decisive battles in history. The weakening of the garrisons of Armenia by reason of these far-off expeditions permitted the Armenian princes to attempt, from the middle of the ninth century, a reaction which was crowned by success in 885. On the other hand, the fear inspired by the Moslem invasion of the south of France was to bring about, two centuries later, the grandiose idea of the Crusades.

The withdrawal of Arab troops from the Caucasus and Armenia encouraged the mountain folk to come down from their eyries to their ancestral domains. The Armenians and Caucasians later on crossed the frontiers of the Arab empire, stirring revolt and founding little kingdoms in many places. Byzantine Emperors gave countenance to these movements and aided them, in the hope of bringing all these peoples under their own rule. In Constantinople the statesmen refused to believe that Moslem power could last; they did not perceive the vast difference between the political and military organization of the Arabs, based upon religious fanaticism, and that of the various barbarian peoples against whom the Roman world had been struggling for centuries.

Civil War

It should be noted that even among these devastating Arabs there were occasional upright leaders who disbelieved in oppression. One of these, the Ostican Merwan, adopted in 744 a policy of moderation in Armenia, and upon his elevation to the Khalifate, he nominated Ashot, a Bagratid, as governor of the country. This excited the jealousy of the rival family, the Mamikonians, who, under the pretense of opposing foreign domination, began a civil strife which presently became a senseless rebellion against the Khalifa. In the heat of it, the Armenians even imprisoned Ashot, their fellow countryman. The revolt was literally drowned in blood. Sembat, son of Ashot, was killed and other chiefs dispersed.

Revolt of Moushegh (Mushil)

Three tyrannical Arab governors, Suleiman (766), Bekir (769) and Hassan (778), delivered thousands of Armenians over to the cruelty of the soldiers. These oppressions resulted in another uprising. Moushegh, the Mamikonian, at the head of 5,000 men, attacked the troops of Hassan, who were then devastating the district of Taron. The Armenians won a brilliant victory, but greatly outnumbered, they failed in their final objective. Moushegh fell on the battlefield, and his son Ashot drove the Arabs out of several provinces and fortified the city of Ani, a natural stronghold in the district of Shirak, on the cliffs above the Akhurian River (the Arpa-tchai).

Ani, New Capital of Armenia

Here the plateau falls away on all sides in high cliffs — on the east and south to the Akhurian, on the west to the Dzaghgotza-tzor (valley of flowers) or Alaja-tchai, which joins the Akhurian south of the city, causing the city's site to end in a sharp, towering point. On the north-eastern boundary, the base of this wedge-shaped site, there was another protection in the form of two deep ravines, one draining towards the Akhurian, the other towards the Alaja-tchai. Across the neck between them, a double rampart was constructed, dotted with towers and dominated by a massive donjon which overlooked the great gate of the city. The citadel stood on a high point near the southern extremity of this fortress-city, whose total area was about 185 acres. The construction of the ramparts was not completed until the time of Sembat II (977-990).

In Europe there are several cities still encircled by their medieval fortifications. In the East, ruins of this sort are numerous; "but no ruin," says De Morgan, "can be compared to that of Ani, in the profound impression it leaves on the visitor to this dead city, lost in an immense solitude and still bearing scars of the deep wounds inflicted at the time of its death-agony."

Under the Bagratids, Ani was the home of a large and prosperous population. It had numerous churches and a palace or two, some of whose beautiful walls, of

Ruins of the Castle of Ani.

multicolored volcanic stone, were often as light in weight as pumice. The cathedral and the sanctuaries consecrated to apostles were the principal religious edifices; the chapels were so numerous that a popular oath was "by the Thousand and One Churches of Ani." The ruins of those devastated monuments of antiquity still stand, whilst private buildings have disappeared in rubble. No traces of streets, of public places or markets are to be seen; brushwood and brambles cover them all.

Other Bagratid princes and many Armenians besides Ashot contributed to the embellishment of this capital through the two centuries from 885 to 1077. Older generations had seen Artaxata, Tigranakert, Douin and many other flourishing Armenian cities disappear, one after another. Through Ashot's enterprising vision, Ani became a great center of commercial, political and spiritual activity, and because of its impregnable situation, seemed destined to endure.

Harun Al-Rashid (786-809)

The great Harun al-Rashid, fifth of the Abbasid Khalifas, was more humane than his predecessors who ruled in Baghdad. While maintaining his Arab governors in Armenia, he enjoined his lieutenants, Yezid II and Khuzima, to treat the Armenians with less rigor. Notwithstanding this order, the Christians were mercilessly subjected to the fanaticism and cupidity of these masters. In the district of Bagrevand, the deputy of Yezid caused one of his slaves to be strangled and the body thrown into a ravine near Etchmiadzin. Then, charging the monks of that place with the crime, he plundered the sanctuaries and put forty-two priests to death. Fortunately for Armenia, some of the ostikans (governors) sent later from Baghdad were more humane. Special mention should be made in this connection of Hol (818-835), appointed by the Khalifa Al-Mamoun. But among the Arabs themselves bitter competitions often prevailed, with sinister reactions upon the subject peoples. One Sevada, a Moslem chief, concocted a plot against Hol, and the Armenians foolishly took sides with the rival. The movement was soon crushed and the Armenians suffered in consequence.

149

Another Reign of Terror

Later on, however, Bagarat the Armenian, whom the Khalifa Motassim had appointed as governor of the Ararat provinces, effectively aided the Arab authorities in the suppression of the revolt of Babek, a Persian leader. Despite Bagarat's loyalty, Khalifa Motawakkil replaced him with a Moslem governor, Abou-Seth (Abou-Saïd), and then by the latter's son, Youssouf, whose extortions goaded the Armenians into another uprising; this in turn affording another pretext to those in power in Baghdad to inaugurate a new reign of terror in the unhappy country. Churches, villages and cities were burned, nobles were exterminated, the people reduced to slavery and entire communities put to death for refusing conversion to the Moslem religion.

Bagarat was sent as a prisoner to Baghdad, and a little later his successor, Sembat Bagratid, was likewise seized, taken to the Arab capital and tortured. But all this bloody persecution, continuing under several governors, among whom Bogha, of Turkish origin, surpassed the others by his atrocities, did not break the Armenian spirit. At this juncture the Byzantine Empire complicated the Arabs' problem by invading Mesopotamia and Syria. Encouraged by this, the Armenians once more arose in revolt under Ashot, son of Sembat. Finding himself thus confronted by two doughty enemies, the Khalifa Motawakkil decided to get rid of one of them in the easiest way, and gave the Armenians their autonomy in 859, appointing Ashot as the governor of his own country and bestowing into him the title of "Prince of Princes" of Armenia.

Ashot, Prince of Princes

Ashot was worthy of the title. He revived the country, reorganized the army and entrusted its high command to his brother Abbas, who was soon put to the test. Jahab, the Arabian, a son of the rebellious Savada, invaded Armenia at the head of 80,000 troops. The Armenian army under Abbas, though much inferior in numbers, dealt a crushing blow to this enemy on the banks of the Arax River. The scene of conflict has been spoken of as the Field of the Forties, because 40,000 men there destroyed a force of double their number. This menace having been eliminated, Ashot now devoted all his energy to the welfare of his people. He built new towns, encouraged architecture, and constructed highways to facilitate commercial intercourse. Meanwhile, the concurrent change of policy towards Armenia in Baghdad manifested itself even more openly. Threatened by revival of Byzantine power, the Khalifa Mutamid (870-892), sought still further appeasement by sending to Ashot the insignia of sovereignty. The Emperor Basil I (867-886), who, though born in Macedonia was Armenian by ancestry, likewise agreed to recognize Armenian autonomy, and in 885 conveyed similar honors to Ashot, who, in the following year hastened to Constantinople to greet the new Emperor, Leo VI. Nevertheless, the Empire continued to cherish a longing for the assimilation of the country. Ashot was troubled by the recalcitrance of certain powerful feudatories, but on the whole his reign was one of peace and prosperity, due as much to the counterbalancing antagonism of the two great neighboring powers as to the patriotism and virility of the Armenian people and their loyalty to their religion.

Chapter XXIV
The Bagratid Dynasty — The Bagratuni

Tradition

Armenian chroniclers, almost all of them clerics, have labored to connect the beginnings of their nation with Biblical tradition, and thus have altered ancient legends in order to prove the descent of the family of Haik from Abraham. In accordance with this thesis, the Bagratids are represented as being of Jewish origin. Their great ancestor Sembat or Shambat is alleged to have been brought from Judea to Armenia by King Nebuchadnezzar as a captive. They represent Bagarat, a descendant of Sembat, five centuries later, as being honored by Vagharshak I, the first of the Arsacid Kings of Armenia, with the title of Aspet or Commander of the Cavalry, with the special privilege of placing the crown on the head of the kings on their accession to the throne. The incumbent of this function was called Tagadir (Crowner).

According to modern authorities, Bagarat must have been of pure Armenian stock, an issue of chieftains who had accompanied Haik in his march towards the Land of Ararat. The district of Sber (Ispir) on the upper Jorokh River, was the ancestral domain of the family, which was greatly enriched in the course of time through conquests or alliances with other princely houses. The high valley of Jorokh, protected by almost inaccessible mountain masses, long remained immune from attack. There was a time when the Bagratid territory comprised a great number of important centers of Armenia, such as the Gougark, the Tourouberan, Tariunq (Bayazid), Bagaran, Shiravakan, Ani, Kars, Artwin and Mush.

Ashot Becomes King

One of the Bagratid princes having married the heiress to the throne of Georgia, bequeathed that Kingdom to his family. The succession continued to the middle of the eighteenth century. It is due to the high repute of the Bagratids that Kevork (George) II — the Patriarch of Armenia in 878-880 — and the nobility appealed to Constantinople and Baghdad for a kingly title for Ashot the Bagratid, who had justified all the hopes placed in him.

The harmony manifested among the chiefs of Armenia in their choice of a king did not last long. Personal ambitions were kindled, and Ashot himself was compelled to take up arms against pretenders to the throne. One of these rivals who defied the royal authority was his own son-in-law, Grigor Ardzruni, Prince of Vaspurakan (Van); but this man was at the same time involved in a conflict with the Moslem emirs of Khoy and Salmas, and was killed during an encounter. After quelling other uprisings and establishing peace and a sort of security, Ashot went to Constantinople to pay a visit to Emperor Leo VI (886-911), "the Philosopher," who had Armenian blood in his veins. This visit implies a closer political relationship between the two nations and a hope on the part of Armenia of emancipation from the continuing threat of oppressions. The power of Baghdad had been markedly diminished in the northern parts of its domain, and yet the governors of Azerbaijan and Kurdistan were constant menaces to the peace and safety of the Armenian people.

According to Armenian historians, Ashot was welcomed in the Greek capital by a magnificent reception. He and the Emperor signed two treaties; one political, the other commercial. Leo promised to send legions for the defense of Armenia, but Ashot in turn was to supply the imperial army with Armenian contingents. Indeed, he had already taken such steps towards this end that the troops under the command of Prince Meghrik arrived while he was still sojourning in the Constantinople, and were sent northward to fight the Bulgars.

Ashot did not live to enjoy the benefits of his diplomatic success. He died while on his journey back home by the way of Trebizond. His remains were buried in Bagaran, the ancient city of the idols, on the Akhurian.

Sembat the Confessor (890-914)

Sembat I, the only son and heir of Ashot, was proclaimed king by the Katholikos George II and the nobles. Unfortunately, the young king's uncle, the ambitious Abbas, held the high command of the army, and he forthwith marched towards Ani with intent to overthrow his nephew. The Katholikos succeeded in persuading him to stop at Kars, where he captured Adrnerseh the Bagratid, the Armenian governor of the Georgian territories, who had placed the crown on the head of Sembat. The young king, however, proved to be worthy and equal to his new responsibility. He hastened to organize an army, besieged Kars, and forced his uncle to release Adrnerseh and recognize his own authority as king.

Byzantium and Baghdad Recognize Sembat

The Khalifa Motadid-Billah (892-902) and the Emperor Leo sent royal insignia to Sembat. He was able not only to restore peace to his kingdom, but to extend its frontiers on the north as far as the Colchids and the passes of Darial, and on the southwest as far as the city of Karin.

Van and all the southern part of the old Armenian territory were then under the direct rule of the Arabs, and Afshin, the Emir of Azerbaijan, who had recognized Sembat in behalf of the Khalifa, was suspiciously watching the southward expansion of the young king. The renewal of the alliance with the Greek Emperor excited his anger, and he entertained a design to bring Armenia again under Arab rule through his own enthronement at Ani. Although there was a disinclination in Baghdad to incur new difficulties with Constantinople over Armenia, yet no opposition was offered to the Emir's conquest of that country.

Afshin Defeated

Sembat, advised of troop movements towards Nakhitchévan, began to mobilize his forces. But in an effort to avoid armed conflict, he sent the Katholikos George to the headquarters of the Emir for negotiation. Afshin showed a pretended readiness for friendly settlement of differences, but proposed that the king come in person for discussion. Sembat, scenting a trap, declined the invitation, and the Katholikos was thereupon placed in detention. The Emir now dropped his mask, and hostilities began. The Azerbaijan army advanced as far as the center of the Armenian kingdom, and an engagement took place at the foot of Mount Aragadz (Alagöz), the enemy force being defeated and put to flight.

Afshin Triumphs

Afshin, however, was not yet crushed. On the news of the incursions in the Armenian district of Taron by Ahmed, the Governor of Mesopotamia, he re-entered Armenia and besieged Kars, forcing it to capitulate. The Queen, the wife of the heir-apparent and other Armenian princesses were carried as hostages to Douin. In order to obtain their deliverance, Sembat was compelled to surrender to Afshin his own son Ashot, and his nephew Sembat, and to give his niece to Afshin in marriage.[53]

Despite all sacrifices, Sembat failed to maintain his country's tranquillity. He quarrelled constantly with the Christian rulers, who were his neighbors. For political reasons, he had put the royal crown of Georgia upon the head of Prince Adrnerseh. Many Armenian princes, stirred by jealousy, appealed to Afshin in 898 to take action. The Emir was busy with preparations for another invasion of Armenia when death took him unawares. He had become enraged at his chief eunuch, who, won by the liberality of Sembat, had returned to him the captive Armenian princesses. The eunuch would have suffered the consequences of Afshin's wrath had not death intervened. Afshin's brother and successor Youssouf inherited his grudge as well as his position in Azerbaijan.

Sembat Enrages Youssouf

It had been the Armenian king's custom to send to the Khalifa his annual tribute through the hands of the Emir of Azerbaijan. Sembat, feeling it intolerable to continue this procedure, and suspecting that the sum would be considerably less if he paid it directly to Baghdad, submitted his proposition in writing to the new Khalifa, Moktafi (902-908), who accepted his offer and sent him a golden crown in token of good will. This modification of the long-standing custom — which meant a reduction in his income — naturally enraged Youssouf, so he managed to induce the Khalifa to double the annual tribute imposed upon the Armenians.

---

[53] Although banned by their churches, marriages of Christian ladies to Moslem chiefs became a frequent means of appeasement. Several centuries later, a Comnenus, Emperor of Trebizond, gave his daughter in marriage to the Khan of Tartary, in the hope of enlisting his aid against Mohammed II, the conqueror of Constantinople.

This drastic measure in turn compelled Sembat to increase the taxes of the lords within the orbit of his authority. These men, resenting the additional burden, thereupon revolted against their sovereign.

Sembat saved the situation by seizing the rebel chiefs and having the eyes of several of them burned out, after the fashion of the times.

Youssouf, taking advantage of these dissensions, again invaded the central province of Ararat and dealt a telling blow at the prestige of Sembat by proclaiming, in the name of the Khalifa, Moktadir, Sembat's traitorous nephew, Gagik, as King of Vaspurakan. Not satisfied with this political coup, Youssouf renewed his devastating invasions, and conquered a considerable area of Armenian territory. During one of the engagements in 911, several princes, including Sembat's son and nephew, were captured by Youssouf and put to death. The Katholikos, Johannes VI, the historian, also one of the captives, was liberated after a year's detention, on payment of a heavy ransom.

Gagik's Remorse

The new King of Vaspurakan, tormented in conscience at the sight of the horrors caused by his own nefarious conduct, asked Sembat's forgiveness and offered him an alliance. But that unfortunate monarch did not feel strong enough to continue resistance to the Moslem foe, and retired to the fort of Kapouyt (the Blue Castle), situated on the rocky heights east of Mount Massis. The Emir blockaded the place in 913. After a long siege, Sembat surrendered, on promise of safe conduct. In the meantime Gagik, still remorseful and repentant of his evil deeds, again offered Sembat his cooperation. Informed of this change of attitude on the part of Gagik, Youssouf treacherously seized Sembat and cast him into a dungeon at Douin. But that was not the last of the sufferings of the unhappy monarch. Youssouf laid siege to the fortress of Erentchak, in the province of Sewniq, and in order to compel its inhabitants to surrender, he ordered Sembat to be dragged in chains before the walls of the fort and subjected to torture. Sembat could have won his liberty had he renounced his Christian faith, but this he positively refused to do. The Emir finally condemned him to death. He was beheaded and the body taken to Douin and exhibited on a cross at the public center of the city (914).

The twenty-two years' reign of this second ruler of the Bagratid dynasty covered one of the worst periods of horror and butchery in the history of Armenia. The nation's life was further embittered by the internal conflicts which raged among the local chiefs.

Ashot II (914-929)

Ashot II, the son of Sembat, succeeded to his father's tottering throne, striving to rule a country whose key positions were garrisoned by Arabs, and whose native grandees were loath to recognize the authority of a single sovereign sitting at Ani. Despite these difficulties, Ashot II succeeded in driving the enemy troops from his dominion. His bravery won for him the title of Yergat, "of Iron," but his strength was not equal to the tremendous task undertaken by him. The emir, infuriated by the victories of Ashot, launched ferocious counter-attacks, bringing general misery and anarchy to Armenia. The country was drenched with the blood of martyrs; cities and towns were depopulated, agriculture almost disappeared. Revolting atrocities and outrages were committed, with no regard to age, sex or condition. Thousands of women and girls were distributed among the troops. The only hope of saving one's life or honor lay in apostasy. And to these horrors were added the inevitable scourge, a widespread famine, lasting several years. In the words of the Katholikos, historian Johannes, even "The hands of upright women cooked their own children, and they became their food."

The desperate plight of Armenia at last stirred the Emperor of Byzantium to whom Ashot appealed for assistance. At the invitation of Constantine VII (Porphyrogenitus), an Arsacid descendant, the Armenian ruler went to Byzantium where he was received by the Emperor with royal honors. Ashot returned to Armenia with a contingent of Greek troops which enabled him to reduce several cities and to clear the enemy and rival forces from the plain of Erevan. Among the places taken was the rebel town of Koghp, situated at the confluence of the Akhurian and Arax, belonging to Ashot the Generalissimo, the King's cousin. This Ashot, feeling that he had been humiliated by his sovereign, took up arms against him in 921. Youssouf, in order to inflame the struggle between the members of the dynasty, proclaimed the other Ashot as King of Armenia in Douin. Despite the decisive defeat suffered by the false King Ashot, and a reconciliation between himself and the real king, thrice achieved through the mediation of the Katholikos, the pretender insisted in maintaining the royal title until his death in 936.

Ashot Abdicates

Ashot II had to face and overcome many other emergencies. Northern nobles, aided by Caucasian tribes, scourged the country, looting and carrying away the women. The King finally subdued them all, but tired of conflicts and the plotting of domestic enemies, some of them even members of the royal family, he retired to an island in the Lake of Sevan. His death came at a time when a state of comparative peace had been restored to Armenia (929).

King Abas (929-953)

Ashot II having no son, the throne was offered to his brother Abas. The new King had to resume punitive and defensive measures to suppress internal uprisings and quarrels, as well as foreign incursions. Despite these problems, Abas was able to achieve really constructive objectives, among which were the fortifications of Kars and the building of many churches and monasteries to replace those destroyed by invaders. He died after a reign of twenty-four years.

Ashot III (953-977)

The country was harassed by brigands when Ashot III, son and successor of Abas, took the reins of power. The new king, supported by some of his nobles, soon pacified his territory and brought it back to something like normality. He was then crowned at the cathedral of Ani, by the Katholikos Ananias, aided by the Katholikos of the Aghouans and forty bishops. Being a man of peace-loving temperament, he made no objection to his brother Moushegh's wearing a royal crown at Kars (962-988). This was the beginning of the division of Armenia — which to Ashot seemed the only way of insuring harmony with and among the turbulent nobles.

Tomb of Ashot III, at Horomos Mona near Ani

Creation of Seven Kingdoms

The extensive province of Vaspurakan was then ruled by Abousahl-Hamazasp (958-968). Upon his death, his realm was divided among his three sons. Ashot-Sanak obtained the largest part, whilst his brothers Gourgen-Khatchik and John Senekerim ruled over the districts of Antzevatziq and Reshtouniq respectively. As to the Sewniq, which lay beyond the Arax, and included the Lake of Sevan, it became independent in 970. The city of Lori, winning independence in 982, became the residence of the third royal branch of the Bagratids — the Korikians. Including some other kinglets, Armenia thus became a country of seven crowned heads, who were often engaged in brawls with one another or with their feudal lords. The northern part of the land recognized the nominal suzerainty of Constantinople; the south was under Moslem suzerainty. Nevertheless, the reign of Ashot III was a period of comparative security and prosperity.

157

Hamdoun a Moslem Invader Repelled

The King won a decisive victory over Hamdoun, a Moslem chieftain who had invaded Armenia after revolting against the Khalifa Al-Moti (946-974). He strongly fortified Ani and other strategic centers. But in that ever-changing Eastern political situation, we presently find him and his army of 30,000 men going to the assistance of the Byzantine Emperor Joannes I (John Zimiskes,[54] an Armenian by birth), who was then threatening the Arabs on the Tigris.

Ashot III became famous for his acts of benevolence, for which he is known as "Oghormadz," the Charitable. He constructed a number of churches, monasteries and hospitals, etc. His wife, Queen Khosrovanoush, rivalled her husband in piety and deeds of charity and generosity. She was the founder of the famous monasteries of Sanahin and Haghbat, in the Armenian province of Gougark, sixty miles south of Tiflis.

Sembat II (977-989)

After the death of Ashot, his son Sembat II was crowned in the cathedral of Ani. Sembat's energies were largely devoted to the embellishment and defense of Ani. Eight years of labor were required to complete the erection of a double city wall, flanked by round towers. Sembat's death occurred in 989, at the laying of the foundation of the magnificent Cathedral of Ani. His passing followed soon after that of his niece, whom he had married in defiance of the canons of the church, which forbade marriage of near relatives. Born at a time when many traces of Mazdeism were still left in the country and when custom permitted the Persians to conclude incestuous alliances, this king had transgressed the laws of his religion, thereby subjecting himself to the severe criticism of national historians.

Kars, a Center of Learning

In the kingdom of Kars, Moushegh died in 984. His son, Abas (984-1029), regarded in his youth as an indolent and frivolous person, proved a worthy ruler. A lover of arts and letters, he turned his attention to the education of his people and established many schools, where prominent men of learning were invited to teach.

---

[54] Hovhannes Tchimishkik by Armenian historians.

Chapter XXV
Magnificence to be Soon Followed by Calamity

Gagik I (989-1020)

Gagik I succeeded his brother Sembat II on the throne of Armenia proper. Under the rule of this king, the Bagratid dynasty of Ani attained the zenith of its power. The construction of the cathedral was completed, and the country was generously provided with new churches, chapels, monasteries and schools. Commerce attained a volume hitherto unknown. Nakhitchévan, Ardzen, Baghesh (Bitlis) and many other cities became important centers in which products of Persia, Arabia, India and even of China were exchanged for the merchandise of the West. Profiting by the era of tranquillity, Gagik centered his attention on commerce. Armenia became an intermediary mart between the Orient and Mediterranean countries, and was rewarded with an amazing increase of wealth.

Direct relations between the Moslem East and the Christian West were then impossible. There were two peoples who, by reason of their geographic position, could serve as intermediaries; the Georgians, masters of the route of the Caspian Sea, and the Armenians, inhabiting the plateau which dominates Iran and Mesopotamia.

Splendor of Bagratid Armenia

The chronicler Aristakes of Lastivert, a contemporary of both the splendor and the fall of the capital of the Bagratids, has left to us a picture of the kingdom of Ani before the invasion of the Seljuks. In his poetic, Oriental manner, he declares that Armenia at that time was like a great and smiling garden; fertile, verdant, clothed in velvety foliage, laden with flowers and fruit. "Its nobles in their gorgeous costumes and glittering array of armor and equipment, held sway in their baronial seats; the people danced and sang merry songs, the sounds of the flute, cymbals and other instruments gladdened the air. Old people in their crowns of white hair, the mothers pressing their children in their arms, the newly-wedded couple emerging from the church, all radiated happiness." "The Pontiff of the nation," he continues, "like a cloud charged with the graces of the Spirit, shed over the people a holy dew, creating new life in the garden of the church, whose walls were vigilantly kept by ministers whom he had ordained. As for the King, when he rode out of the city in the morning in his resplendent attire and pearl-laden crown, astride his white mare with her trappings of gold glittering under the rays of the sun, dazzling every eye, he was like a bridegroom or like the day-star, which rising above the world, attracts all eyes to itself, compels everybody to gaze upon it with wonder; while the numerous troops who marched before him in compact masses, rippling over the hills, resembled the waves of the sea, rolling over one another on the beach."

View of the ramparts and the principal gate of the City of Ani

Bagratids Minted No Coinage

Notwithstanding the opulence then prevailing in Armenia and the existence of copper and silver mines in the country, no coin seems to have been minted by the Bagratid princes. That right was in all probability reserved to the Khalifas, under whose suzerainty the Armenian kings ruled. Farther north, in regions where Byzantine authority was recognized, the rulers enjoyed the right of coinage. Copper and silver pieces issued by some of these are still in existence. The last Armenian King of Caucasian Albania, Koriké (1046-1082) minted copper coins.

Yet all these currencies were not sufficient for the needs of commerce. Most of the gold in circulation in the Near East, was that of Arabs and Byzantines. The silver coins used were the dirhems of the Khalifas and the old Sassanian and Roman dinars. As for copper money, all the mints of the Empire issued huge amounts of it.

Turmoil in Neighboring Countries

During the period while Armenia was enjoying peace, her neighbors were not so happy. The Khalifas were busy in suppressing rebellious emirs, while people to the north were engaged in wars against each other or against the Arab chieftains or Georgian marauders. In the West the Emperor Basil II (976-1025) was warding off threats from Bulgaria. Great numbers of Armenian families had been transported by the Greeks to Macedonia. Embittered by the Empire's harsh treatment, a considerable number of fighting men from among these Armenian exiles made common cause with the rebellious Bulgars, whose chief, Samuel, was born in the Armenian district of Dertchan, east of Erzerum. Samuel's forces, successful in the beginning, were badly beaten later by Basil, who became known as "Bulgarocton" (killer of Bulgars).

160

David of Taiq's Rebellion and Death

King Gagik deemed it wise to remain aloof from these affairs. Meanwhile David, to whom the province of Taiq had been entrusted by the Emperor, took advantage of the death of Bad, the Moslem emir of the Apahouni region, seized the fortress city of Manazkert and drove away the emir's troops and co-nationals. But the fleeing aliens, supported by the Emir of Azerbaijan, came back to recapture the territory, situated to the northeast of the Lake of Van. David, however, did not give up. Receiving aid from Koriké I, King of Georgia, and Gagik-Abas, King of Kars, he attacked once more and took possession of the contested districts. Despite his valiant deeds, David was the victim of a treacherous assassination plotted by his own Georgian nobles.

In 103 the King of Vaspurakan, Gourgen-Khatchik, died and was succeeded by his brother, John-Senekerim (990-1006), although the late king's sons were the rightful heirs to the throne.

Johannes-Sembat III Threatened by His Brother Ashot

Gagik I, King of Ani, whose death occurred seventeen years later, was succeeded by his son, Johannes-Sembat III (1020-1041). Corpulent in body and indolent in temperament, this prince lacked the qualities urgently required during this critical period in the Armenian homeland. Many feudal lords dependent on the suzerainty of Ani repudiated their allegiance, and the king's younger brother Ashot, energetic and valorous, claimed the throne for himself. In alliance with Senekerim, King of Vaspurakan, he marched on Ani at the head of a strong force. The Katholikos Petros Getadartz offered mediation, and Ashot was induced to withdraw, receiving the title of lieutenant-commander of the kingdom, and the promise of the throne on his brother's death.

View of the Castle of Ani

161

Ashot's Persistent Plotting

But Ashot was faithless. Being now closer to the court, he succeeded in creating a clique to work secretly in his behalf. He was further emboldened by the detainment of his royal brother as a prisoner by Koriké, King of Georgia. This was Ashot's opportunity to usurp the crown, had not King Sembat gained his liberty by ceding three forts to the Georgians. Having failed in these and other plots, Ashot fled to Constantinople, where he won the favor of Basil II and returned to Armenia, escorted by Byzantine legions. Sembat appeased him by giving him several territories on the Georgian and Persian frontiers.

Northeastern Barbarians

While Armenian seigneurs were thus engaged in factional struggles, a dreadful storm-cloud darkened the skies of the Orient. Barbarian peoples, intrepid and cruel, emerging from the plains of the Oxus River, had invaded Khorassan and the north of the Iranian plateau, driving before them the Persians, the Kurds and the Arabs. Nothing, it seemed, could resist these daring horsemen and skilled archers. Armenian historians called these nomads Scythians or Tartars, as being distant descendants of those hordes who, fifteen centuries earlier, had overrun Asia, likewise issuing from the boundless plains beyond the Caucasus, the Caspian Sea and the Bactrian mountains.

Emergence of the Turks

Simultaneously, the Seljuk Turks invaded Anterior Asia, spreading like a torrent overflowing its bed. The Turks had developed at the foot of the Altai Mountains, in those steppes where Turkomans still live today, where the Jaghatai, the primitive language of the Tartars is spoken. These people, sadistic and merciless, now converted to Mohammedanism, insatiable in their appetite for pillage, craved possession of the rich lands of both the Khalifas and the Greek Emperors. "The cruelties of the Arabs," says Jacques de Morgan, "were nothing compared to the horrors the Turks were to mankind." They advanced westward through mountainous areas where rich pastures for their flocks existed. The tribal masses followed the cavalrymen, carrying their household property, their wives and children, the aged and the loot from devastated countries. The onward wave was to halt only before the gates of Constantinople, where the forces of the Empire checked it for a considerable time.

First Clashes with Turks and Exchange with Sebastia

The first contacts between the Turks and Armenians occurred on the frontiers of Vaspurakan the province of Van. Shapouh, the oogeneral of Senekerim, put the invaders to flight in the first encounter. But the King, advised of the approach of the main army of the enemy and aware of his inability to cope with the perilous situation, ceded his kingdom to the Emperor Basil II, reserving to himself only the monasteries, with the villages upon which they depended for maintenance. In exchange the Emperor gave him the city of Sebastia (Sivas) in Cappadocia, and its territory, reaching as far as the Euphrates. The principality given up by Senekerim comprised 10 cities, 22 strongholds and 4,000 villages. Leaving these behind, he emigrated in 1021 to his new domains, taking with him his family and 400,000 of his subjects, almost one-third of the population at the time of Vaspurakan.

In his new kingdom, he enjoyed political security for some time, but the religious intolerance of the Greek clergy was still rife and its effects bore heavily upon the Armenian immigrants until the time when the Turks, always pressing westward, finally took possession of the country.

Turkish Defeat at Ani

As to the kingdom of Ani, its lands had been invaded by the Turks in the very year of Senekerim's departure from Van. At the gates of the fort of Betchni, north of Ararat, the enemy was checked by the Armenian army under the general Vassak-Bahlavouni, father of the famous statesman-school, Grigor Magistros. The Arab emir of Douin, Abu-Sewar, mindful of his own safety, allied himself with the Seljuks. The Armenian forces, united under David Anhoghin, chief of Gougarq and Aghouanq, gave battle against the Turks, inflicting upon them a crushing defeat.

The situation nevertheless remained ominous. The Armenians, though aided by small Greek contingents, were not equal to the task to stemming the ever-mounting flood rushing from the East. The Turks continued their westward drive, waging a pitiless war against valorous defense. A Kurdish governor, Khoudriq, after capturing the city of Berkry, to the northeast of the Lake of Van, dug a deep ditch, to be filled with the slaughtered bodies of Christians.

Emperor Harasses Armenia

The short-sighted Byzantine policy was another element in the plight of Armenia. Basil II, after landing at Trebizond and suppressing the rebellious Apkhazia, on the southeast coast of the Black Sea, took possession of Taiq, in northern Armenia in 1023, and then threatened the little state of Ani. King Johannes-Sembat, caught between Toghrul Beg, the Seljuk chief, and the Greek Emperor, sent the Katholikos Petros to the latter to implore his help, offering him the title to all his domain after his own death. The document bearing this promise, though kept secret during the reigns of Constantine XI (1025-1028) and Michael IV (1034-1041), gave the Greeks a legal claim to a territory extending as far as the Arax and even to the fortress of Kars.

Gagik II (1042-1045)

Johannes-Sembat III died in 1041. The death of his ambitious brother Ashot occurred in the same year. It was then that the new Emperor Michael V, "the

163

Calker," invoked the rights promised in the letter of Johannes to Basil II. The regents of the kingdom, however, refused to recognize the cession. The Emperor thereupon sent an army to Ani, with which Vest-Sarkis, the Armenian chief of the province of Sewniq, allied himself, in the hope of obtaining the throne of the little kingdom. This army and its Armenian collaborators laid siege to the capital, but were beaten and routed by Nationalists under the leadership of the old general, Vassak Bahlavuni. Gagik II, still a mere youth of sixteen, but brave, educated and intelligent, was thereupon crowned in the cathedral of Ani by the Katholikos Petros.

Turkish Reverses in Armenia

The Greek peril was now seemingly well-nigh averted, but a new terror, that of the Touranian-Seljuks, loomed on the horizon. The vanguard of this horde had already reached the northern plain of the Arax, camping on the banks of the stream called Hrazdan-Zanki which originates at Lake Sevan and empties in the Arax. Gagik, at the head of his army, lured them into a trap and almost destroyed them. The survivors recrossed the Arax and fled to the land southwest of Lake Urmiah, whence, reinforced by Kurdish tribesmen, they turned once more against Vaspourakan province. Here they were checked by an Armenian band under Khatchik, "the Lion." This heroic leader fell on the battlefield, but his sons, arriving with a greater force, routed the Turks and sent them fleeing towards Khoy and Salmas, on the Persian frontier.

Emperor Claims Ani, Gagik II Exiled

This Turkish onslaught had scarcely been repelled when Byzantine pretensions were intensified. Constantine X, Monomachus (1042-1054), who had mounted the throne through his marriage with the Empress Zoé, an Armenian by descent, put forth a claim to Ani and the entire district of Shirak. Upon the rejection of the demand by Gagik II, a Greek army invaded his territory, but was defeated before the walls of the capital.

The Emperor thereupon resorted to treachery to gain his ends. Corrupted by Byzantine gold, many Armenian nobles now advised their king to accept an invitation sent by the Emperor to come to Constantinople for a peaceful settlement of the disputed question. After being assured by the Katholikos and other leaders of their loyal adherence to his policy, Gagik II made the journey to the Byzantine capital. A magnificent reception was given him, but a short time thereafter he was summoned by the Emperor to relinquish his throne and cede to the Greeks the city of Ani and its territory. When he courageously refused to acquiesce, he was appalled at being shown a letter from the Armenian grandees, expressing their devotion to the emperors and their readiness to hand over to him the keys of Ani. Thus betrayed by his own people, Gagik gave up his kingdom, receiving as compensation the district of Lycandus in Asia Minor and the town of Bizou, in the vicinity of Caesarea (Kayseri). He was also granted the use of a palace on the Bosporus in Constantinople and a pension from the Imperial treasury.

Byzantine Persecution

Not satisfied with the extinction of the political life of the Armenians, the Greek clergy insisted upon their conversion to the Greek Orthodox faith. Meanwhile Armenia became economically the slave of the functionaries sent from the capital, who crushed the people under the burden of heavy taxes. The Armenian nobility, a favorite object of persecution, suffered the heaviest losses through systematic purges by the civil authorities.[55]

Gagik's Retort to Bishop of Caesarea

Gagik in exile suffered agonies upon hearing of his countrymen's woes. He himself was often subjected to insolent treatment by the ruling class. Even in Cappadocia the Greeks openly displayed their contempt for those Eastern Christians whose tenets differed in some slight degree from theirs. The orthodox Bishop of Caesarea, Marcus by name, lost no occasion to express his scorn for them. The bishop had a dog which he called "Armen," the epithet "dog" being a favorite slur hurled at the Armenians. Gagik, smarting under this insult resolved to punish the impudent prelate. In company with several friends, he went one day to call on the bishop. In the course of the conversation, Gagik expressed a desire to see the dog, and inquired the reason why he responded to the name Armen. "Because he is a pretty dog," replied the Metropolitan with thinly veiled insolence "and we call him the Armenian." At a signal from Gagik, his escort seized both the bishop and the dog, put them together into a large bag and gave the dog such a beating that the animal became wild and lacerated the bishop with its teeth, causing his death.

Murder of Gagik II
End of Bagratid Dynasty

From that time on, Gagik became an object of hatred by the Greeks. One day while he was strolling in the country west of Caesarea, some Greeks seized him suddenly, made him prisoner and a few days later hanged him on the battlements

---

[55] An inscription on stone, according to Brosset, engraved a few years after the occupation of Ani by the Greeks, indicates the degree of neglect to which the place had descended. "In the name of the almighty Lord and by the clemency of the holy Emperor-autocrat Constantine Ducas I, Bagrat, magistros, Katapan (governor-general) of the East, have desired to do good by this metropolis of Ani, when it had named as its tanouter (administrator) the Hypatos Mekhitar, son of Court; Grigor, Spathara-candidate, son of Lapatac, and Sarkis, Spathara-candidate, son of Artabaz." They suppressed the taxes named Vetzevor (one-sixth), sailli (on machines for threshing wheat), camen (on carts or chariots), and angarion (forced labor). "The catapan, whoever he may be, shall give six hundred measures of grain, and the administrators shall defray from their houses the cost of other presents. Because of great hardships suffered in importing goods, the wine merchants of Ani shall be exempt from tolls, whether they use carts or wagons. Any inhabitant who buys an animal for slaughter is exempt from tolls. Any porter of Ani is exempt from tax on half of his burden. The capuji (guardian of the gates of the city) shall be paid six dahekans of gold and three drams. . . ."

of the castle (1079). His sons, John and David, and John's son Ashot died soon afterwards, all by poison. Atom and Apusahl, King Senekerim's son, also perished by the Greeks at Sivas in 1080, according to Armenian chroniclers, along with another Gagik, the son of Abas, the last Bagratid King of Kars. The properties of all of them were attached to the imperial domain. This illustrious line of the Bagratids was thus destroyed by the Greeks, through shortsightedness and religious fanaticism, although the Bagratid name persisted until recent times.

Progress under the Bagratids

The way of life in Armenia made gratifying strides in the ninth and tenth centuries. Social welfare rose after a long period of misfortune. "Dozens of towns and hundreds of villages," says the historian Aristakes, "which had been ruined and abandoned, were revived and reconstructed." Industry and handicrafts flourished in cities. The increasing urban population needed more manufactured goods. An extensive market for woven stuffs was already in existence. The development of mines, known to the Armenians in remote antiquity, had been resumed by the Arabs in three zones — in modern Gumush-Khaneh for silver, in Spir for gold and in Allaverdi for copper. Special mention is made by Arab historians of the red dye, cochineal or al-kermes, used for dyeing various kinds of woolen and cotton fabrics in Armenia. Metallurgy, masonry, weaving, rug-making, pottery, carpentry and working in gold were thriving everywhere in the country. Among the artisans of Douin, the weavers of cotton, wool and silk — of shawls, scarves, spreads, pillow-cases and carpets, were especially renowned. Carpenters made wooden traveling paniers, farmers' tools and beautiful house furniture. Many objects of art were produced in Ani — silver and gold articles, rings, bracelets, belts, necklaces, earrings, church vessels and palace ornaments. Professor N. Marr, while excavating at Ani, discovered factories for copper-working and clay-baking. Ani and Douin were also celebrated for porcelain and copper vessels and containers and for embroidery and needlework as well as gold-tissued textiles. There were great numbers of wine-presses and oil mills in operation.

Growth of Cities

The removal of the rule of the Arab Khalifate from Armenia in the second half of the ninth century gave impetus to the effort aiming at complete independence of the country. With the exemption from payment of taxes to the Khalifas, economic advancement was hastened. Armed conflict, again raging between Byzantium and Persia at that time, made commercial transit across Mesopotamia and Syria impracticable, and Armenia was the gainer thereby, becoming the East-West trade route and giving her merchants the opportunity to serve as business factors in many countries — in the Greek Empire, in Arabia, Persia, Central Asia, India and China. Several cities of Armenia, such as Ani, Douin, Nakhjévan, Kars, Van, Amid (Diarbekir), Vostan, Manazkert, Bitlis, Khlat, Arjish, Karin and Ardzn, assumed special importance as centers of industry, commerce and culture. The historian Aristakes, describing the halcyon days of the period, dubs some of these cities with flattering adjectives; Kars, the Celebrated; Ardzn, the Magnificent;

166

Ani, the World-Famous. When, at the end of the eighth century, Ashot Bagratuni, "the Meat-Eater," grandfather of Ashot I, purchased from the Kamsarakans the district of Shirak and moved his residence there, Ani became the capital, and attained wealth and greatness during the reigns of Sembat II and Gagik I.

Agriculture and Husbandry

Agriculture played a vital role during the Bagratid period. Grain, cotton, rice, flax and grapes were the main products of the country. Many localities about the central part of the country were covered with farms, orchards and vineyards; granaries were filled with breadstuffs and jars with wine, while the pastures offered abundant grazing to herds of cattle and flocks of sheep. Wool production flourished, and silk and woolen textile manufacture attained a considerable volume. Irrigating canals were dug in many parts of the country to aid farming and horticulture. Metals and the manufactured articles of the cities, as well as horses, cattle, sheep, wool, medicinal herbs and roots were exported to other lands in large quantities.

Chapter XXVI
Destruction of Ani and Spread
of the Turkish Power

Fatuity of Imperial Policy

The alternate oppression and neglect of the Armenian kingdom by the Byzantine rulers was not only odious, but impolitic, even stupid, because Armenia, as an outpost of Christianity in the East, could, had she been kept strong, have arrested the Turkish wave for many years; but no one in the capital on the Bosporus seemed to comprehend this fact or see the impending danger to the Empire. The Greeks ruled in western Armenia and part of northern Armenia, the other part being under Georgian domination, while the Seljuks held the eastern part of Transcaucasia, and Arab emirs occupied the southern provinces. But this state of affairs did not last long. The Greeks, deprived of their best military resource — the Armenian element — were unable to maintain in the land of Ararat an army strong enough to check the new invaders. They were soon driven out by Alp-Arslan and by his son Melik-Shah (1072-1092), whose domains were shortly to extend from the Caspian Sea to the Indus River in the East, and to the Bosporus on the West. It was not long before two Ortokid dynasties were created in Armenia and Kurdistan, the former by Sokman, the Shah-Armen (or "King of Armenia") and the other by Il-Ghazi.

Toghrul Beg's Merciless Conquest

The conquest of Armenia by the Turks was not easily accomplished, however. From 1048 to 1054 Toghrul Beg hurled his hordes at the eastern provinces of the Byzantine Empire. His cousin Koutulmish and his nephew Hassan were defeated, but his brother Ibrahim ravaged Vaspourakan, then marching northward, took Ardzen, a city of 800 churches and of immense wealth. They gave the city over to flames, after plundering it and taking from the district 150,000 persons into virtual slavery.

In 1054 Toghrul Beg led his troops into the Van district and spread devastation everywhere. The King, Gagik-Abas, was defeated in battle and took refuge behind his city walls. The Turkish chief then turned northwestward and laid siege to the city of Manazkert, but that place was saved through a heroic resistance led by Vassil, the son of the city's Armenian governor. Toghrul took revenge by pillaging the city of Ardzké, north of the Lake of Van. Kars had been taken and half destroyed by Ibrahim, but its King Gagik-Koriké was safe in the Kars citadel, built upon an impregnable rock.

Imperial Palace Wars aid Turks

World conditions, on the other hand, were favorable to the Seljuks. With the death of Constantine Monomachus in 1054 the struggle between the new Emperor Michael VI and his rival, Isaac Comnenus, engrossed Byzantine attention, and Armenia, deprived of her princes, was unable to offer an effective resistance when Toghrul advanced as far as Melitine in western Armenia. At that point, he was compelled to retreat because of a shortage of provisions. The Armenians took advantage of this fact to deliver some telling blows upon the invaders in the mountain defiles, inflicting them serious losses. However, Toghrul captured Sivas in the following summer (1059), reduced it to ruins and slaughtered the major part of the population. The survivors were carried away into slavery, and the Seljuk army recrossed the Halys River (Kizil Irmak) with an immense train of booty, including wagons loaded with gold, silver and rich fabrics — for Sivas had been a commercial center of great importance.

Alp-Arslan Storms Ani

Alp-Arslan ("Bold Lion"), nephew and successor of Toghrul, was even more cruel than his uncle. He devastated the entire area of the Armenian plateau and the Lesser Caucasus. The city of Ani alone closed its gates against him with a courage born of despair. Bagrat, the duke, an Armenian, was then in command in behalf of the Emperor. Tired of fruitless assaults, Alp-Aslan was about to retire when the governor, fearing a new and more violent attack, ensconced himself in the citadel. Deserted by the Greek troops, the population began to flee along the valley of the Akhurian (Arpa-tchai). The Turks thereupon climbed over the undefended ramparts and entered the city on June 6, 1064. A frightful butchery followed, blood flowed in torrents in the streets, and in public places thousands fell by the sword. Those who had taken refuge in the churches perished and were buried in the ruins of the burnt edifices. Such survivors as were believed to be wealthy were tortured in an effort to force them to reveal the hiding places of their treasure.

"Men were slaughtered in the streets," says Aristakes of Lastivert, "women were carried away, infants crushed on the pavements; the comely faces of the young were disfigured, virgins were violated in public, young boys murdered before the eyes of the aged, whose venerable white hairs then became bloody and whose corpses rolled on the earth."

The dreadful holocaust continued for several days until the knight conqueror withdrew, leaving all in ruins behind him. Bagrat, the duke, and the Greek soldiers, had fled under cover of a storm. Alp-Arslan replaced them by a Moslem governor and garrison, and passed on towards Nakitchévan, followed by a caravan of booty and a multitude of slaves. Among the treasures seized from the Bagratid capital was the great silver cross which rose above the dome of the Cathedral. Alp-Arslan wanted to place it on the threshold of his mosque at Nakhitchévan, so that the "true believers" might enjoy the satisfaction of trampling upon the emblem of Christ every time they entered their sanctuary.

City of Ani Disappears from History

Never again did Ani rise from its ruin. It was in turn occupied by the Seljuks (1064-1072), by the Kurdish emirs (1072-1124), by the Georgians (1124-1126, 1161-1163), by the Tatars and the Persians, until its story was finally and completely ended by an earthquake in the year 1300, overthrowing what little remained of its former splendor. The inhabitants migrated to Georgia, to the Crimea, even to Moldavia and Poland.

Ani, "the city of a thousand churches," is now nothing but a wilderness, dotted with ruins, the abode of wild beasts; but the loneliness of the erstwhile metropolis gives an infinite charm to the vestiges of its past glory. On this rocky peninsula, bounded by deep ravines through which flow whirling streams, the dead city stretches out laden with mysteries, where only fragments remain of the great churches and frowning ramparts. Where princely mansions stood, there are now nothing but formless masses of rubble, hidden under thickets. Streets and public squares can scarcely be traced, but amid this tangled mass of ruins are still to be found bits of those superb sanctuaries, beautiful in their ordered lines, charming in their lacy sculpture and curious frescoes.

Tombstones at Ani

The majestic remains of the sacred edifices testify to the refined taste of the architects and kings of Ani. The double wall which, with its towers, its castle, its donjon, defended the city on the north, evokes a thousand reflections upon the links connecting Armenia with the West. And the traveler who visits this solitude is oppressed by a feeling of profound sadness as he recalls the horrors of which these places have been the theater — those massacres and plunders, a poignant account of which is left to us by the chronicler Aristakes.

The country surrounding Ani is arid and barren. The rocks are of rosy, brown and yellow hues; the earth a dull red. The hills seem still to bear the scars of the flames which destroyed the city, and of the volcanic tremors which completed its obliteration.

A few remains of the once-great wealth of Ani, saved from plunder, survive to the present day. In the treasure-vault of the Cathedral of Etchmiadzin are preserved some silver crosses, church ornaments and precious manuscripts. Other relics which were discovered in excavations in Ani, and piously kept there in a museum on the spot were wantonly destroyed in 1920 by the Turkish troops who invaded the new-born Armenian republic, a land which for a century had been Russian territory. That area still remains within the Turkish frontiers.

Turkish Mosque Built at Ani

The first Moslem ruler of Ani, Manoutchar, built in 1318 on the brow of the cliff above the Akhurian River, a mosque, the ruins of which may still be seen, and whose architecture was certainly inspired by the Christian monuments of Ani, more particularly by the church of Khoscha-Vank.

Armenia Major having lost her independence, several of her princes emigrated towards Greek territory; some accepted the yoke of the Seljuks while yet others embraced the faith of Islam. But the majority of the nation refused to quit the soil of their ancestors and tenaciously clung to its traditions.

Role of the Armenian Nobility

Greater Armenia had lived for a millennium and a half when she met with political death. Since her foundation, she had not ceased her struggle for independence; but her geographical position between two militaristic empires, doomed her to destruction. From the time of Alexander's conquest and the appearance of the Romans in Asia, always menaced by the Parthians, the Sassanids and the Arabs on one side, and the legions of Rome or Byzantium on the other, she was unable to beat off forever such mighty adversaries. Her nobles, her aristocratic leaders, although brave and warlike, did not possess that community of spirit requisite to carry the nation through such great perils.

When the children of Haik achieved the conquest of the country of Ararat, they were led by their tribal chiefs, a nobility of Armeno-Phrygian origin. But in the process of assimilating the conquered peoples of Nairi and Urartu, they found it advisable to respect the traditions of those vanquished populations, and the native chiefs of the land, who had once battled against the armies of Assyria, were therefore maintained in their lordly status in the new society. The result was such that a study of Armenian family names indicates a Urartean origin for a considerable number of the noble houses of Armenia. These two strains of nobility inevitably became antagonistic: one of them, the Armens, considering themselves the ruling class, the other, of the Nairi-Urartean stock lamenting the passing of the days of their domination.

171

Other divergent elements were added under succeeding foreign dominations —
Achaemenid, Greek, Parthian, Sassanid, Roman, Byzantine, Arab and Turk. The
nation's aristocracy was thus extremely diversified; interests and tendencies
became varied and opposed, all these resulting in competition, hatred, with the
consequence of great weakness for the whole nation. The nobles of Armenia were
valiant, but they subordinated the welfare of the State to their own personal
ambitions. The existence of seven small Armenian kingdoms at the time of the
Turkish invasion is a proof of this. Covered with mountains, difficult of access
and divided by nature into a multitude of districts, Armenia invited political
disunity.

Such divisions were exploited by neighboring alien powers. Byzantium
committed the gravest of errors by her hostility to the Armenians and by her
narrow sectarian policy, which finally brought about the ruin of Armenia and the
decline of the Greek power in the Near East. Byzantium seriously needed, not a
subject people on her eastern frontier, but an allied Christian kingdom; and there
she had a potential one in Armenia, stretching from the Tigris to the Black Sea
and from the Euphrates to the Caspian and the Caucasus, with ten million
inhabitants; a possible buffer state, capable of putting many legions of fighting
men in the field against the enemies of Christendom.

Tombstone of Hairapet, Bishop of Sewniq

A Foreign Appraisal

"The conception of such a state," says Jacques de Morgan, "would have meant the
salvation of the Empire; but in Constantinople, that capital wasted with palace

revolutions and wrangles over dogmas, the broad lines of Roman policy had been lost sight of. The result was that instead of consolidating the royal power of Ani, the Byzantines busied themselves in sowing discord among the Armenian princes, with eyes on their feudal territories they were unable to hold.

"Less exposed to Moslem attacks than their Araxian kinsmen, the Bagratids of Georgia managed to maintain their throne for six centuries after the fall of Ani; but these princes had the mighty Caucasian mountain fortress to repair to as a last resort whenever they were too hard pressed."

Chapter XXVII
The Barony of Cilician Armenia

Roupen I Organizes Revolt

Most of the Armenian nobles who had accompanied Gagik II on his journey to Constantinople, also followed their sovereign to his new domain, and so formed a small court around him. The majority of them belonged to the Bagratid family. One of them, Roupen, was, according to some chroniclers, of direct royal issue. He enjoyed considerable authority over his compatriots in the Tzamandos (Zamanti) district, and soon after the assassination of King Gagik, he organized a band of Armenian warriors and unfurled the banner of revolt against Byzantium (1080).

For centuries the persistent exactions and violence committed by the Greeks had incensed the Armenians against them. Differences of speech, traditions, customs and particularly of religious tenets intensified the aversion of these people to each other. However, the fall of the kingdom of Ani brought two parties into existence: one, the defeatist, resigned to submission to the Greek yoke; the other, still animated by national spirit and not forgetful of certain acts of treason, cherished dreams of vengeance and the recovery of national independence. The Byzantine Empire, on the other hand, worm-eaten by factional hatreds and religious bickering and threatened on all foreign fronts, was unable effectively to suppress popular uprisings in the provinces against the tyranny of the nobles and corrupt officials. As the Asiatic territories of the Empire had thus been deprived of security, the beginnings of the revolt of Roupen passed unnoticed.

The kingdom of Ani having already been subjugated by the Seljuk Turks, Roupen turned his eyes towards Cilicia, a country to which many Armenian chiefs and their people had emigrated from the national homeland.

Cilicia, New Refuge of Armenians

Cilicia, conquered by Arabs in the VIIth century, was partly recovered for the Empire in 964, when Nicephorus II (Phocas), reduced in turn Anazarba, Adana, Tarsus and Mopsuest (Missis). In 966, the Emperor's army extended its conquests further south, to Tripoli in Lebanon, Aleppo and Damascus. These expeditions, succeeded by that of Emperor John Zimiskes in 973, were real crusades, aimed at the delivery of the Holy Land from the Turks, as well as the recapture of the rich provinces of Syria. But the southern areas of Asia Minor, which had suffered most under the Khalifas, needed a reconstruction which would render them a solid bastion for the protection of the capital. Many Armenian chieftains had left their domains in their homeland to take refuge in Greek territory; and the Byzantine Emperors had availed themselves of this voluntary emigration by peopling the banks of the Euphrates on the east and the Taurus Mountain approaches on the southwest with this Christian element.

Coin of John Zimisces   Coin of Nicephorus Phocas

Oshin in Cilicia

One of these Armenian nobles, the nakharar Oshin, formerly lord of a fortress near Gandzak (Elizabethpol) in Caucasian Albania, had come in 1075 to Cilicia, where his kinsman, Abulgharib Ardzruni, governed Taurus and Mopsuest in the name of the Emperor Alexius I (Comnenus). Oshin was given a hereditary fief (domain), the district of Lampron (Nimroun Qala) on the Tarsus River at the Cilician Gates, the narrow pass leading from the Taurus mountain chain — a point of major importance for the security of Cappadocia. At that time the Arabs were in possession of Antioch.

Castle of Lampron (Cilicia)

175

Location

The frontiers of Cilicia are well marked by nature; no political demarcation other than that defined by its topography can be better imagined. On the west stand the mountain masses of Isauria and Cilicia Trachea, presenting the figure of a vast triangle, whose base to the north rests upon the plains of Lycaonia; on the east it is bordered by the Gulf of Satalia and on the third side by the western littoral of the Gulf of Pompeiopolis. The apex of this triangle is the promontory of Anemur, the farthest advanced point of Asia Minor towards the sea. Because of its natural position, Cilicia enjoyed an importance of strategic as well as commercial value.

The valleys of Seyhoun (Sarus) and Jahan (Pyramus) communicated with Coelesyria through the Syrian Gates, breaks in the Amanus range between Guzeldagh and Akmadagh, and through the Portella, the pass of Alexandretta and the shore of the sea. On the southeast was the city of Issus, where Alexander the Great vanquished Darius of Persia in 333 B.C.

Ayas, on the northern side of the Gulf of Alexandretta, became a much frequented port during the Middle Ages. Two commercial routes start from this place. One, through Lampron, served Cappadocia, while the other, through Gaban and Sebastia, reached Greater Armenia. Furthermore, a number of ports and anchorages on this coast, such as Megarsus, Alaya, and Side, offered safe shelters to vessels, and these landing places like Ayas, promoted the commercial relations of Cilicia with the littorals of Syria and the Mediterranean West.

Byzantine Policy

It was a part of Byzantine policy, therefore, to guard the defiles giving access to Cilicia, and this is why the Emperors favored the creation of small principalities in those regions. The immigrant lords from Armenia were known by the title of Ishkhan (ruler), corresponding with that of baron, which was later adopted by the Crusaders. Many Ishkhans had been settled in the Taurus and Amanus as well as in the plains when Roupen made his stand in the neighborhood of Caesarea, in the city of Cyzistra, where Gagik II was assassinated. Emerging from those parts, Roupen first moved westward and entering the difficult mountain heights in the north of Cilicia, he seized the fortress of Partzerpert (high castle), situated on a tributary of the upper Pyramus, about a day's march above Sis. That location became the cradle of the Cilician Armenian kingdom.

Death of Roupen

With no official title of authority, Roupen, nevertheless, issued a declaration of independence, and shortly afterwards, in the words of Hetoum the historian, "died in the peace of the Lord, after living a pious life, and was buried in the monastery of Castalon, leaving as successor his son, Constantin."

This fertile province of Cilicia, once so rich through its agriculture and commerce, had, as a result of the Arab invasions, been reduced almost to the condition of a desert. The survivors of Greek, Syrian and Jewish nationalities were concentrated in small groups in the ruins of the cities. Agriculture was carried on only in the shadow of the city walls and strongholds, where there was comparative safety.

Constantin I and Thoros I

The son of Rouben, Constantin I, who succeeded him and reigned from 1095 to 1099, and Constantin's successor, Thoros I (1099-1129) pursuing the designs of their predecessor, were concerned only with extending their domains, to the detriment of the Byzantines. They gradually spread their authority over the chiefs of the mountains around Partzerpert. Constantin had begun his reign by the capture of the fort of Vakha (Fékké), situated on the upper Seyhoun, which commanded one of the most frequented routes between Tarsus and Upper Cappadocia. The mastery of this mountain defile made possible the assessment of taxes on merchandise transported from the port of Ayaz towards the central part of Asia Minor, a source of wealth to which the Roupenians owed their power.

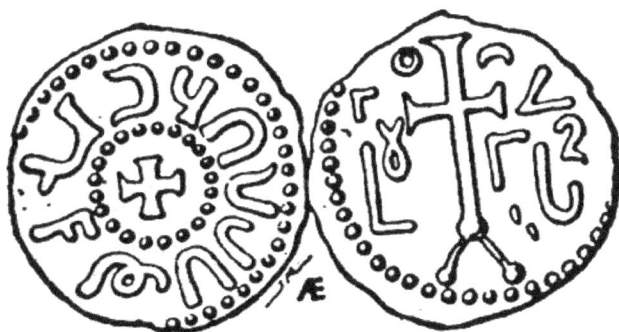

Coin of Baron Thoros

First Crusade

The Emperor was pondering the question of how to bring Armenokilikia, as it was called, under obedience, when the advent of the First Crusade upset his plans. Godfrey de Bouillon, leader of the Crusade, having crossed to Asia in 1097, entered Cilicia, and by following the route of Seyhoun, finally came to pitch his pavilions under the very walls of Vakha. The details of the Crusaders' march to Cilicia are given by the Armenian historian, Matthew of Edessa, as follows:—

"In 546 (1097), during the time of the two Katholikosi, Der Vahram and Der Barsegh (Basil), and in the reign of Alexis, Emperor of Romans, the army of

177

the Crusades set out in immense numbers; it comprised about 500,000 men. Thoros, the Governor of Edessa (a Greek appointee), was informed of the fact by a letter which they had sent to him; also the great Armenian chief, Constantin, son of Roupen, who occupied the Taurus, in the country of Godibar (east of Missis), and was the ruler of numerous districts. Constantin had come forth out of the ranks of the army of Gagik. The Franks advanced with difficulty across Bithynia. They passed through Cappadocia in wide spreading columns, and reached the steep slopes of Taurus. The great army passed through the narrow defile of that mountain chain to enter Cilicia, and after a stop at New Troy (Anazarba), it thence proceeded as far as Antioch."

Armenians Befriend Crusaders

The Armenians looked upon Godfrey de Bouillon as a savior. Had he not entered Asia against the will of the Greek Emperor, and was he not marching under the aegis of the Cross? Constantin, aware of the vast project devised by the Crusaders, saw in this a unique opportunity for deliverance from Byzantine suzerainty. He therefore did his utmost to assist the Crusaders, whose situation during the siege of Antioch would have been precarious had it not been for Armenian aid.

"The number of the Franks," continues Matthew of Edessa, "was so great that they felt the pinch of famine. The Armenian chiefs who lived in the Taurus, Constantin the son of Roupen, Pazouni, and Oshin sent to the Frankish generals all the provisions they needed. The monks of the Black Mountain (Amanus), also supplied them with foodstuffs." Pope Gregory XIII in his Bull of 1584, declared that "No nation came more readily to the aid of the Crusaders than the Armenians. They supplied them with men, horses, arms and food."

The Franks, for their part, duly appreciated the aid of their Armenian allies. Constantin was honored with the titles of Comes and Baron. Josselin, Count of Edessa, married the daughter of Constantine. Baudoin (Baldwin), brother of Godfrey, married the niece of the Armenian Baron, daughter of his brother Thoros. The mutual interests were thus consecrated by those marriages, and these Christians of the East entered into a vast feudal organization of the Crusades.

Thoros Drives Greeks Out

It did not take long for the Armenians to derive benefits from this accord. Encouraged by Tancred, Prince of Antioch, Thoros, son and successor of Constantin, followed the course of the Pyramus River, and seized the stronghold of Anazarba. This place, fortified first by the Emperor Justin I and then by the Khalifa Haroun al-Rashid, was considered impregnable. The city of Sis was the next to fall into the hands of Thoros. Churches and monasteries were constructed everywhere by this pious prince; Armenian colonists were induced to come and prosper under their national flag.

Coin of Tancred of Antioch

Repulses Turkish Invasion

Assisted by the Franks of Antioch, Thoros had conquered the major part of Cilicia, driving out the small Greek garrisons, when Turkish hordes penetrated into the heart of Cilicia and took Anazarba. Byzantines had been almost entirely dislodged from their former strongholds in the lower part of the country, and the Turks therefore believed that they could easily crush Armenian resistance. They coveted the possession of the Sultanate of Iconium and the southern shore of Asia Minor. Thoros repulsed and drove them back to the territory of Cogh Vassil (the Covassilio of Latin Chroniclers), another Armenian chieftain, who reigned at Marash. There too the invaders were defeated and once more forced to flee. Two years later, after ravaging the lands around Melitine (Malatia), they besieged the fortress of Harcan (Hajen), where they were again beaten by the Armenians. Their chief was captured and brought to Kessoun, the headquarters of the district, near Marash. Nevertheless, the Turkish marauders continued their depredations, especially in rural areas. The country suffered a major attack by the Seljuk Sultan of Iconium, Malik Shah (1107-1116). Thoros, however, after sustaining a severe reverse in the first engagement, won a decisive victory in the second, though it was a costly encounter. The Sultan retreated towards Kharput, looting and devastating everything in his way. The only stronghold that he failed to subjugate was the fortress of Dzovk, known to Strabo as Cybistra.

Baron Leon I Expands his Domain

Thoros died in 1129, and was succeeded by his brother, Leon I (1129-1137), who reigned eight years and expanded his rule over the plains, and even to the Mediterranean shores. Without the possession of seaports, contact with Europe could be effected only through the Frankish coastal cities in the southeast. But relations between the two former allies did not always remain as courteous as before. Thoros seems to have been slow in paying Baldwin the sum of 60,000

179

gold besants, his daughter's dowry; the Armenians complained of the exactions of the Crusaders, while the Franks accused their allies of calling upon infidels for help whenever they had the least pretense of discontent. A major cause of dissension between the Armenians and the Latins of Antioch was the ownership of the strongholds of the southern Amanus, and of the neighboring coasts of the Gulf of Alexandretta.

Treachery of Antioch

The fort of Sarouantikar, on the lower Jihoun River, dominated by Leon, was also a subject of dispute. Raymond de Poitiers, Prince of Antioch, demanded that place in 1136, claiming that it was a part of the Crusaders' territory. Raymond refrained from taking arms against the Armenian Baron, but chose a more despicable course; he lured Leon into a trap and held him prisoner. After two months of confinement, Leon obtained his liberty by consenting to harsh terms. Not only did he surrender the fortune of Sarouantikar, south of Marash, but also Mamestia and Adana; in addition he paid 60,000 gold pieces and gave his son as a hostage. He also pledged himself to assist Raymond against the Emperor John II Comnenus.

Baron Leon did not wait long to break the contract which had been extorted from him through treachery. He recaptured all the territories surrendered to Raymond and launched an attack against the Prince of Antioch and his ally, Foulques d'Anjou, King of Jerusalem. This hostility would have been fatal to both Armenians and Franks — both of whom were always menaced by the Turks — but Josselin II, Count of Edessa, who was related by marriage to Leon, obtained an honorable agreement for both sides in 1137. An alliance was then formed by them against the Emperor, who was then pressing his claims against Antioch as well as Cilicia.

Stepané at Marash

Meanwhile, the war against the Turks was in progress. "In 584 (1135)," says a historian, Michael the Syrian, "Baron Stepané, brother of Baron Thoros, having arrived under the walls of Marash, caused his troops to enter the city during the night. They were received in the houses of those inhabitants who were Christians. This surprise had been contrived by a priest of this city with whom Baron Stepané was in compact. At dawn his soldiers captured the place and slew the Turks who were within. Flushed with their victory, they insulted the guards of the citadel and molested their wives. God in His wrath therefore, would not deliver it into their hands. So they set the city afire, and taking away the Christians with them, advanced into the interior of the country."

Aboulfaraj describes the same events adding:— "The Turks, exercising humanity, showed a pacific disposition towards the Christians who had remained; and to the Armenian fugitives who had returned, they restored their houses, vineyards and fields. But an Armenian priest whom they (the Turks) suspected of being in connivance with his compatriots was flayed alive. After three days they cut off his tongue, hands and feet and threw him into the flames. The Armenians, incensed at this cruelty, put a number of Turks to the same torture."

Greeks Incite Turks

The hostility of the Turks towards the Armenians had in the meantime been nurtured by gold supplied by the court of Byzantium, which maintained, as ever, its designs of Cilicia and the principality of Antioch. Despite the alliance concluded between the Armenians and the Princes of Antioch, the Greeks invaded Cilicia, defying the Crusaders and Leon, and occupied all the plain of Adana and the Gulf of Alexandretta. The Baron took refuge in the Taurus Mountains, but at last found the situation hopeless, and surrendered himself to the conqueror. He was dragged away to Constantinople, where he died in imprisonment in 1141. His son Roupen, after being blinded, was assassinated by the Greeks.

Thoros II (1145-1169)

All Cilicia remained under Byzantine rule for eight years. The Latin principalities of Antioch and Edessa, often harassed by the Turks, were unable to assist their allies. One of Leon's sons, Thoros, a prisoner in Constantinople, had gained the favors of the Palace through his personal charm. He fled from the capital in disguise, on board a Venetian vessel, reached Cyprus and thence went to Antioch. There, Prince Raymond and the Patriarch Athanas VIII, supplied him with means by which to accomplish his adventurous design, namely, the shaking off of the Byzantine yoke. In company with a small escort he left Antioch and penetrated into the Amanus mountains, where some thousands of Armenian volunteers joined him. After several successful engagements with the Imperial troops, he recovered the ancient domain of his father.

Romantic Escape of Thoros

The chronicles of Vahram of Edessa thus describe the triumph of the young Baron:—

> "Those who were attached to the Emperor's palace claim that Thoros prolonged his sojourn until the day when a Greek princess who was in love with him gave him treasures which he took away with him. Reaching the mountainous part of Cilicia, he met an Armenian priest, to whom he secretly made himself known as the son of Leon. The priest welcomed him with joy. The Armenians who remained in the country and those who lived in the mountains, subjected to the oppression of the Greeks, had been most fervently wishing for the return of their old masters. Now being apprised by the priest of the return of their beloved prince, they readily united in greeting Thoros as their Baron."

181

While the Emperor John was subduing Cilicia and approaching Antioch, the Turks ravaged the adjacent Latin territories. The Byzantines had allied themselves with the Turks, so as to overthrow the power of the Frankish interlopers and destroy the Armenian baronies. But that unholy alliance was broken when the Moslems invaded the district of Kessoun, within the domain of the Empire.

Byzantine-Turkish Alliance violated

This rupture is described by Matthew of Edessa as follows:

"In 585 (1136), Sultan Mohammed, son of Amir Ghazi, son of Danishmend, came with a great army to the country of Marash, near Kessoun, and set fire to the villages and monasteries. . . . He deferred attacking the city, busying himself with diverting the water of the river, laying waste the gardens, making incursion here and there, and collecting his booty and putting it into security. However, the citizens of Marash, in constant fear of an assault, fell into such an excess of discouragement that one night they abandoned the outer ramparts; but their chiefs and the priests succeeded in reviving their spirits. . . . God did not command the infidels to invest and assault the place, and on Friday, which is the day of the passion of our Lord, Kessoun was delivered. The enemy burned the Garmirvank (the Red Monastery), the chapel and the cells of the monks, smashed the wooden and stone crosses and carried away those of iron and bronze, demolished the altars and scattered their fragments. He took away the doors with their admirable scrollwork design, as well as other objects, and transferred them all to his country, to show to his concubines and the populace. . . . Mohammed retreated upon learning that the Emperor of the Romans (John Comnenus) was speeding to the rescue of besieged Kessoun, and of our Count Baldwin, who had implored him on his knees for help. The Emperor, devastating the Moslem lands, was already approaching Antioch. After having deprived our Prince Leon of his sovereignty, he seized his cities, and fortresses and taking him prisoner, carried him off to the country of the Greeks, beyond the sea, on the frontiers of Asia."

Thoros II Reconquers his Barony

Whatever the conditions in which Thoros entered Cilicia, he found it occupied by many Greek garrisons. One after another, he conquered Amada (Tumlu-Kalessi), Anazarba, Adana, Sis, Aryudzapert and Partzerpert. The city of Edessa, however, was taken on December 23rd, 1144, by Imad-ed-din Zenghi. Thoros, unable to receive any aid from the princes of Antioch, was compelled to resist alone the Greek army of 12,000 men, commanded by Andronicus Comnenus, a cousin of the Emperor Manuel I, but inflicted a signal defeat upon that general in 1152. To avenge this humiliation, the Emperor resorted to stratagem, instigating an attack by Massoud I, the Seljuk Sultan, upon the Armenian Baron. The Seljuks, seated in the very center of Asia Minor, constituted a peril for the capital of the Greek

Empire; but Manuel's chief concern at the moment was the punishment of the Armenian Baron for the affront inflicted on him. Massoud invaded Cilicia, but Thoros parried this new danger by recognizing the Moslem Sultan as his lord paramount.

Turks Beaten

In 1156 upon some flimsy pretext Massoud again sent his troops against the Armenians. The invaders were repulsed by the Crusaders and the army of Thoros. Surprised in the defiles between the Amanus Mountain and the sea, the Turks suffered a bloody reverse. The remnants of their army retreated northeastward, devastating the districts of Marash and Kharput. But they were not slow in reorganizing and returning to the offensive, laying siege to the Castle of Till Hamdoun, in the vicinity of Sis. They were dispersed, however, when the Armenians took advantage of a pestilence raging in the foe's army and dealt him a telling blow. Masoud died and his son, Azzed-din Kilij Arslan II, concluded in 1158 a peace with Thoros, who continued to rule Cilicia and Isauria.

Knights Templars Defeated

Another storm now burst upon the Armenian horizon. Renaud de Chatillon, Regent of the Principality of Antioch, claimed from Thoros the castle of Gastim, a place of strategic importance commanding the defile of Portella. "Renaud," says the chronicler Michael, "had a dispute with Baron Thoros regarding a fortress which the Greeks had captured from the Frères (Knights Templars), and which Thoros retook from the Greeks. "The Frères," said Renaud, "fight for the common cause of Christians. Give them back that which belongs to them." A battle took place between the disputants, near Iskenderoun (Alexandretta), and many fell on both sides. Renaud was forced to return home, covered with humiliation. Later on, Thoros voluntarily surrendered to the brethren the fortresses in question, and the Knights in turn took oath "to assist the Armenians on all occasions where they needed help."

Renaud, who had attacked the Armenians at the instigation of the Greeks, felt justified in asking the Emperor Manuel to reimburse him for the expenses incurred in the campaign. The Emperor answered in such ambiguous terms that the Prince of Antioch resolved to indemnify himself at the expense of the Island of Cyprus. Both Crusaders and Armenians had been anxious to dislodge the Greeks from Cyprus, in order to secure a strong naval base there against Moslem incursions. Circumstances, however, did not permit its conquest just then. Renaud hoped to gain some satisfaction by a sudden descent upon the island, laying it waste, and looting its treasures.

Templars Invade Cyprus

In 1156 the Crusader ships disembarked upon the Cyprian coast an army composed of Latins and Armenians which, after crushing a feeble opposition, spread rapidly in all directions, plundering and kidnapping the rich, to be held for ransom. These acts of violence, though unjustifiable, were a natural retaliation for the intolerant and perfidious actions of the Greeks, often with Moslem aid, against the non-Orthodox Christians of the East.

Emperor Manuel of course could not tolerate the seizure of Cyprus. He sought revenge in 1158 by invading Cilicia at the head of an army of 50,000. He captured Anazarba, Till Hamdoun, Tarsus and Lamos, while Baron Thoros, unable to defend his country, retired to the castle of Dajikikar in the Taurus Mountains. Renaud and Baldwin of Jerusalem (husband of the Emperor's niece) interceded for Thoros, and regained for him the major part of his domain, on condition that he recognize the Greek Emperor's suzerain right. Thoros was then honored with the title "Palatin of Pansebastos."

View of the castle of Anazarbus

Stepané murdered
Thoros Massacres Greeks

Peace, however, was not yet well established. Disregarding all official pledges, Stepané, the Baron's brother, at the head of Armenian bands, laid waste the Imperial territories in the district of Marash. Andronicus, the Greek governor of Tarsus, resorting to stratagem, invited Stepané to a feast and killed him in the most cruel manner. Thoros, thereupon, ordered a massacre, to which a great number of Greeks within his borders fell victims. War between the Emperor and his vassal Prince would have broken out again had not Amaury I, King of Jerusalem, intervened.

Mleh Usurper

Disheartened by the country's misfortunes, Thoros abdicated before his death in 1169 in favor of his son Roupen, a minor, under the guardianship of Baille Thomas. But Thoros's brother Mleh, once member of the order of the Knights Templars, and now supported by Nour-ed-Din, the Turkish atabek (prince) of Aleppo, invaded the Armenian barony. Mleh at first agreed to a settlement offered by the guard of Roupen, by which he was to receive an equal share of the territory. But soon after this, the usurper repudiated his pledge and seized the entire territory. The Baille secretly carried Roupen to the castle of Romgla and put him under the care of the Katholikos Nerses (Shnorhali, "the Gracious"). But despite this precaution, the young prince was found dead not long afterward.

Mleh, who is accused by some chroniclers of apostasy and tyranny, had aligned himself with Moslem rulers, such as Salih-Ismail of Aleppo and Kilij-Arslan II of Iconium, defying both Greek and Latin states. Because of his military prowess, Mleh was finally recognized by Emperor Manuel in 1173 as the independent Baron of Cilician Armenia. But he had made a host of enemies by his cruelties in his country, resulting in his assassination by his own soldiers in the city of Sis in 1175.

Chapter XXVIII
Greeks, Crusaders and Moslems — Rise of Leon II

Treacherous Warfare

This period of Levantine history was characterized by a constant and bitter clash of conflicting interests. The Greeks cunningly embroiled the Crusader princes with each other and inflamed Moslem hostility against non-Greek Christians. They pretended friendships with formidable enemies, then suddenly changing their tactics, took up arms against their allies of yesterday. As for the Moslems, their treatment of Christians was not only contemptuous but merciless when they had the opportunity. The famous Saladin (Salah-ed-Din), Sultan of Egypt and Syria, issued a decree in Egypt forbidding "infidels" (Christians) to ride horses or mules and commanded them always to wear a belt in public, so that they may be distinguished from true believers. The Byzantines, despite the indignities to which they were subjected by the Mohammedans, sometimes heaped upon Turkish princes such honors that these only tended to increase Moslem contempt for all Christians.

Gaudy Display of Emperor

An account by Aboulfaraj of the welcome accorded to Kilij-Arslan, who spent three months in Constantinople seeking aid against his domestic adversaries, says that "twice a day food was served him on gold and silver plates which were left to him as gifts. On one occasion the Emperor, after dining with his guest, offered him all the battle service decoration as well as other gifts, not counting those presented to each of the thousand Turks who composed his escort." According to other chroniclers, feasts were given in honor of the Seljuk Sultan in an atmosphere of amazing splendor.

> "On a magnificently decorated platform stood a throne of massive gold, set with diamonds, jacinths and other precious stones, encircled by pearls of brilliant whiteness. Profusely distributed lights struck dazzling rays out of all these jewels. On the throne was seated the Emperor, dressed in a mantle of purple, upon which artistically combined diamonds and pearls formed admirable designs. Over his chest suspended to a golden chain hung a pink stone of the size of an apple. On either side were ranged the members of the Senate, in the order of their respective State functions. Kilij-Arslan, when escorted in, was astonished by such magnificence, but at length took a modest seat. During his stay at the court of Manuel, he lived in one of the palaces in the southern part of Constantinople. All the pleasures of the imperial city — equestrian combats, dramatic entertainment, spectacles of the circus, Greek fire — were offered him."

186

Thus the Byzantine Emperor treated the Seljuk chief who, entrenched in Iconium, was threatening all eastern Christendom, who, in 1148, had taken the city of Marash and violating his pledged words, slaughtered the knights, the Frankish bishop and priests and the major part of the populace. Instead of demonstrating to Kilij-Arslan the might of his legions, the Emperor chose to display only his wealth — which merely excited the visitor's greed and stirred him to action against the Crusaders and even the Greeks. Finally, the Emperor's worst error was that of supplying him with funds with which to turn against the Franks, but which were used against Byzantium itself.

Baron Roupen II (1175-1187)

Roupen II, son of Stépané and nephew of Thoros II and of Mleh, was elected by the seigneurs of Cilician Armenia to occupy the throne of the principality. The mighty Saladin, lord of Egypt and a part of Syria, was then preparing a campaign against the Crusaders. The Armenians meanwhile were threatened by Kilij-Arslan II; in fact, all the Christian principalities had to come then to grips with the Moslems. The new Baron of Cilicia feeling unequal to the struggle was constrained to buy peace in 1180; but scarcely had he withdrawn his forces from the frontiers, when the Prince of Antioch and Hetoum, the pro-Greek master of Lampron, instigated by Manuel, began hostilities against him. Roupen sent his brother Leon to surround Hetoum's mountain lair. Bohemund III, rushing to the aid of Hetoum, treacherously made Roupen prisoner, and the latter obtained his release only upon payment of 30,000 dinars as ransom and the cession to the Prince of Antioch of the cities of Adana and Mamestia.

Roupen, however, who had married Isabelle, daughter of Humphrey III, seigneur of Karak and Thoron, remained always friendly to the Crusaders in spirit. He was a just and good prince, and created many pious foundations within his domains. Shortly before his death, he abdicated in favor of his brother Leon, and retired to the monastery of Drazark.

Third Crusade Moves to East

Events of the gravest import were taking place in the East at this time. Saladin captured Jerusalem on October 2nd, 1187. Edessa and Acre had already fallen to the Moslems; Tripoli and Antioch soon followed. Unless the Western powers could come to their aid, the Crusaders and Cilician Armenia were doomed to early disappearance. The Pope exerted all his energy to bring about a new expedition. Accordingly, Frederick I, "Barbarossa," the German monarch — known as head of the "Holy Roman Empire," — and the Kings of France and England were moved to action. Frederick was given the leadership of the Third Crusade in 1189. Reaching Asia by way of Macedonia, the great army made a halt in Cilician Armenia, with Antioch and Jerusalem as its next objectives.

Leon saw in these formidable operations a unique opportunity to extend his authority and to obtain for himself a royal crown. He dreamed of playing the part of territorial and political intermediary between the Byzantine Empire and the

Latin principalities of the East. He, therefore, eagerly supplied the Third Crusaders with provisions, guides, pack animals and all manner of aid, besides pledging the cooperation of his army.

The Emperor Frederick was thus won over to Leon's cause, and promised him a crown, but a fatal accident delayed the consummation of this act. Barbarossa met his death in the icy waters of the Galycadnus River (Gheuk-sou), either in crossing it or while bathing. Leon then turned his eyes towards Frederick's successor, Henry VI, the new head of the Crusade. He also made an appeal in 1195 on the same subject, to Pope Celestine III who, as a spiritual sovereign, wielded more extensive and permanent authority.

Crusade Saves Armenia from Incursions

The arrival of this Crusade ushered in a new era for the Armenians. Greek legions as well as Turkish hordes ceased their incursions in Leon's domain. The necessities of a new situation were being considered by all the neighboring elements. The creation of a Kingdom of Cyprus was one of the striking signs of changing conditions. In the spring of 1191, Richard I (Lion-Hearted), King of England, who had left Sicily at the head of his crusading fleet, was forced by tempestuous weather to lay by in Cyprus, then ruled by Isaac Comnenus, a kinsman of the Greek Imperial dynasty, but who had declared himself independent of Byzantium. Being told that an English vessel had been shipwrecked upon his shores, Isaac hastened to the port of Limassol, hoping to lay his hands upon Berengaria of Navarre, the fiancée of King Richard, and Jeanne de Sicile, his sister-in-law, whose vessel had grounded, but getting clear again, had rejoined the English fleet.

Richard I in Cyprus

Incensed at this affront, the doughty Richard disembarked at Limassol, took possession of the entire island, and seized Isaac, with his family, and his treasure. The downfall of this despot was joyously hailed by the Latins because of his acts of espionage and treason in behalf of Saladin. Blithely installing Guy de Lusignan as the first King of Cyprus, Richard then proceeded towards the Holy Land.

Byzantines Antagonizing Christians

The meddling of Western nations in the affairs of the East during the first two Crusades had greatly ruffled the Greeks. They believed that any Moslem occupation of their territory would only be temporary; but they dreaded the outcome of the Crusades, especially the Third one, led by an emperor and two kings. Had they joined the Western forces, the Christian kingdoms of Syria and Cilicia would have survived, and Constantinople would probably never have fallen into the hands of a common enemy. But the fanaticism of the Greek Emperor greatly contributed to the fall of the Empire and the retrogression of world civilization.

188

Leon Plays Greeks Against Crusaders

Baron Leon displayed an astute diplomatic talent by balancing Greeks against Latins, though his ambition enough a crown induced him to lean towards the Latin side. On the other hand, Sultan Saladin had almost crushed the Western powers in the Levant, while the Greek Empire still enjoyed an imposing prestige, and, as a great ally or protector, could gratify Leon's ambition if it chose. This, however, never came about. The Armenian Church delegates who visited Constantinople in 1179 for the settlement of disputes between the sects, failed in their negotiations. The specified conditions on which Byzantine goodwill towards the Armenian nation might be obtained were these; (a) To recognize two natures in Jesus Christ; (b) To honor the fourth Council of Chalcedon; (c) To solemnize the birth of Christ on December 25th; (d) To celebrate mass with leavened bread and water mixed with wine; (e) To eliminate the formula, "Holy God . . . that hast been crucified;" (f) The election of a new Katholikos must always be submitted to the Emperor for his sanction.[56]

Papacy Favors Armenian Kingdom

The demands of the Byzantine clergy, seconded by the Emperor, compelled the Armenian Baron to turn towards Rome, to make common cause with the Western powers and to follow their fortunes in the Near East. In Rome, the creation of a native kingdom in Asia in harmony with the Latin spirit and culture was welcomed; it would provide the Crusades with a solid base, assuring the development of Christian states in Syria and Palestine, which might in due time dominate all Anterior Asia.

Western Europe generally believed that the Byzantine Empire would not last long. It was expected or hoped that it would be replaced by a Latin state, capable of preventing the Turks from entering Europe via the Bosporus. The conquest of Spain and Sicily by the Moors and their drive to the very heart of France in the eighth century had been a serious warning to Western Christians. Leon's ambition therefore found a favorable echo in the Papal palace as well as in secular courts. It was necessary, however, for that to be moderate in its demands for changes in the Armenian Church, for the people were strongly attached to its ancient rites and customs. The clergy clung to its prerogatives, and the nobles looked askance not only at the abandonment of religious isolation, but also at the creation of a royal authority to replace the seignorial allegiance which they were capable of selling to the highest bidder whenever opportunity offered.

Leon had received while with his maternal uncle, Pagouran, an education that was more Greek than Armenian, for the lords of Baberon and Lampron had remained loyal to the Byzantine Emperors. It is significant that Leon signed his name in Greek ΛΕΟ, followed (in Armenian) by his royal title, "Tacavor Hayotz," "King of the Armenians". It was indeed through his Byzantine contact that his

---

[56] These specifications are recounted in a letter of Katholikos Nerses to Bishop Michael the Syrian.

189

great political plans were developed. Aspiring to a higher and wider range of authority, he yearned to wear the purple and to treat on equal terms with emperors, sultans, khalifas and European sovereigns.

Leon Labors to Obtain the Crown

The negotiations dragged on for a long period. Leon appealed directly to the German Emperor, Henry VI. He also submitted his designs to other Crusader chiefs, winning the good will and support of all. Communications between Rome and himself became more frequent. The Pope received the Baron's ambassadors and sent his legates to Cilicia to discuss matters both political and religious. Already, half a century earlier, the subject of a closer relationship between the Armenian and Roman Catholic churches had been broached by Pope Eugenius III. Pope Lucius III sent a letter to the Armenian Katholikos, Grigor IV, Degha, in 1185, the translation of which by Nerses, Archbishop of Lambron, has been preserved.

Negotiations Between Pope and Katholikos

"In the year 634 of the Armenian calendar," says the Archbishop, "came Gregory, Bishop of Philippopolis, sent by the Roman Pope Lucius to our Katholikos Gregory. He brought the answer to the letter of our master (the Katholikos) and the book containing the customs and rites of the church, in Latin script." Four years later, in 1189, a letter which Pope Clement III sent to Baron Leon, urging him to participate in the deliverance of the Holy Land, began, "Clement, bishop, servant of the servants of God, to our well-beloved son, the illustrious mountain prince, apostolic greeting and benediction."

Greeks Still in Opposition

This correspondence with the Papacy did not prevent Leon from negotiating at the same time with the Greek Emperor Alexius II. In 1197 he despatched Nerses, Archbishop of Lambron and Tarsus, in company with one Baron Paul, to discuss ecclesiastical questions. It was on that occasion that the Archbishop reported to Leon, "After discussion with them (the Greeks), we found them ignorant, rude and dull, obstinate like the Jews, who do not wish to serve God through rebirth by the Holy Ghost, but through the ancient Scriptures. Grieved in our spiritual good-will, we returned confused and disappointed in our modest hope."

It was obvious that Leon was motivated by political interest and not by religious convictions. Had he found more tolerance in Constantinople, the Armenians would have been closer to the Greeks than to the Latins. The ritual terms which the Pope imposed upon the Armenian Church, in return for his support of Leon's ambition to kingship, were slight and acceptable. They tended still further to deepen the rift which separated the new Armenia from the Byzantine Empire.[57]

Leon Seizes Prince of Antioch

Nevertheless, the relations between Leon and the Latins had not always been friendly. Friction was frequent, especially with the neighboring principality of Antioch, the ill-defined frontiers of which afforded easy pretexts for disputes. A climax was reached in 1194 when Baron Leon, detecting a design to attack him plotted by Bohemund III, the Prince of Antioch, forestalled his adversary by luring him to an entertainment, where he was seized and thrown into confinement in the castle of Sis. The Frankish prince was released through the intervention of Henri de Champagne, Regent of the kingdom, but only on condition that all territory taken from Roupen II should be given back to the Armenians.

Leon Makes Ally of Antioch

As a further step in the development of Leon's far-reaching plans, an alliance was concluded with Antioch through the marriage of the Baron's niece, Alice, with Raymond, the eldest son of Bohemund. The marriage contract stipulated that should the bride give birth to a son, the child was to inherit the throne of Antioch. A boy was born and named Raymond-Roupen; but upon the untimely death of the infant's young father in 1198, while Bohemond was still alive, the latter's younger son, the Count of Tripoli, known as Bohemund IV, "the One-Eyed," took advantage of the heir's minority and seized the throne. Leon, furious at the usurpation of the rights of his grand-nephew, took up arms in the very year when he was receiving his long-coveted royal crown.

Artavasdus and Constantin V

---

[57] The loyalty expressed in Leon's letters to Pope Innocent III may be explained by the fact of the latter's supreme authority in the political world of the age. Among the Pope's vassals were many crowned heads, such as those of Portugal, Aragon, England, Scotland, Sardinia and the Two Sicilies.

Chapter XXIX
The Kingdom of Cilician Armenia —
Mongol Invasion

Leon I becomes King of Armenians (1199-1219)

On January 6th, 1199, Cardinal Konrad of Wittelsbach, Archbishop of Mainz, the delegate of Pope Celestine III, placed a royal crown upon the head of Baron Leon II, in the Church of Holy Wisdom (Sourp Sophia) at Tarsus. The Katholikos, Grigor Abirad (1195-1203) anointed the new sovereign, who assumed the name and title of *Leon I by the grace of the Roman Emperor (Henry VI), King of Armenia.* He thus declared himself a feudatory of Western Europe, represented by the German Monarch. A few years after his accession, however, Leon shook off this vassal status and began calling himself *"King by the Grace of God."*

Pope Names Terms

In sending the crown to the new king, the Pope had demanded that he subscribe to several conditions, all relative to divergencies existing between the rites of the Armenians and those of the Latins. "When you have adopted these rites," the Cardinal of Wittelsbach told him, "you will not have to trouble yourselves about the gifts and dues which you have to offer to the emperors and the Pope as tokens of Fealty for your crown. But if you refuse, I am instructed to demand of you very large sums of money in gold, in silver and precious stones."

The conditions were as follows:—

1. To celebrate Christmas and other feasts of saints on dates adopted by the Latins.
2. To recite in the church the prayers of the hours of the day and night — which practice had ceased in Armenia since the invasion of the Arabs.
3. To break fasting on the day before Christmas and Easter (Christmas Eve and Easter Eve) by permitting the use of fish and oil.

Leon called the Katholikos and the bishops together and asked them how to reply to the proposition of the Latins. Upon their refusal to accept the stipulations, he said, "You need not be disquieted. I will satisfy them for the moment by dissimulation." The bishops then gave their consent, and twelve of them signed the engagement.[58]

---

[58] Kirakos of Gandzak, the historian.

Golden Bulla of Leo I

Pope, Emperor and Khalifa Recognize Leon

The coronation took place with solemn pomp, in the presence of fifteen bishops, thirty-nine feudal barons and a great number of feudal knights.[59] The Khalifa of Baghdad sent presents. The assumption of a royal title was an act of great importance for the Byzantine government. Cilician Armenia was now shaking off its vassalage to the Empire; but a Byzantine denial of recognition of the new King would have been tantamount to defiance of the Crusaders. The Emperor, Alexius III Angelus, took the wiser course by sending Leon presents and a crown, accompanying them with this counsel; "Do not put on your head the crown of the Romans, but the one we sent you, because you are nearer to us than to Rome." It is believed by some that Leon had been given a crown three years before, in 1196, by the Byzantine Emperor.

The Frankish crown did not in any way modify the attitude of Leon towards the principality of Antioch. In 1203 he sent an expedition to enforce his claim against Bohemund IV, but his army was defeated by the Knights Templars, who were supporting the usurper.

After inflicting a decisive defeat upon the Sultan Melik-ed-Daher of Aleppo, Leon again took up arms against Bohemund IV and his allies, among whom were now enlisted the Templars. At the same time the Armenian King appealed to Pope Innocent III for adjudication of the dispute. The Pope delegated two Cardinals as arbiters. One of them, Cardinal Peter, made hasty and arbitrary decisions against the young prince, and finally, exceeded his authority by going so far as to excommunicate Leon. The Armenian King was not of a type to brook such

---

[59] According to N. Iorga, Leon was crowned "in the presence, and not by the hand, of Konrad, Archbishop of Mainz."

treatment. In retaliation, he expelled all Knights Templars and Latin clergymen from his domain and detained the Princes of Antioch and Tripoli in confinement.

Furthermore, without waiting for the reconsideration of the case by the King of Cyprus and the Patriarchs of Jerusalem and Antioch, as recommended by the Pope, Leon again laid siege to Antioch. A great number of its leading citizens were by this time turned against the usurper Bohemund. They opened one of the gates, through which the Armenian troops made a triumphal entry, to be welcomed with music and song. Thereupon, in 1211, the ceremony of the installation of Raymond-Roupen as the ruler of the principality took place, with the Latin patriarch presiding. Leon gave to Raymond-Roupen in marriage his wife's sister Helvis, the daughter of Amaury de Lusignan, King of Cyprus and Jerusalem. He also obtained from Otho IV, the German Emperor, the promise of a crown for his grand-nephew and protégé as King of Antioch.

Later on the ban of excommunication was lifted from Leon by Pope Honorius III, who also placed Raymond-Roupen and the state of Antioch under the protection of the Holy See. During his conflict with the Latins, Leon had entered into an alliance with Theodorus I (Lascaris), Emperor of Nicaea,[60] by giving in marriage Philippina, the younger daughter of his brother Roupen. Through this coup, the western and northern frontiers of the country were to be made secure against the Seljuks, who had already erected a kingdom in the center of Asia Minor.

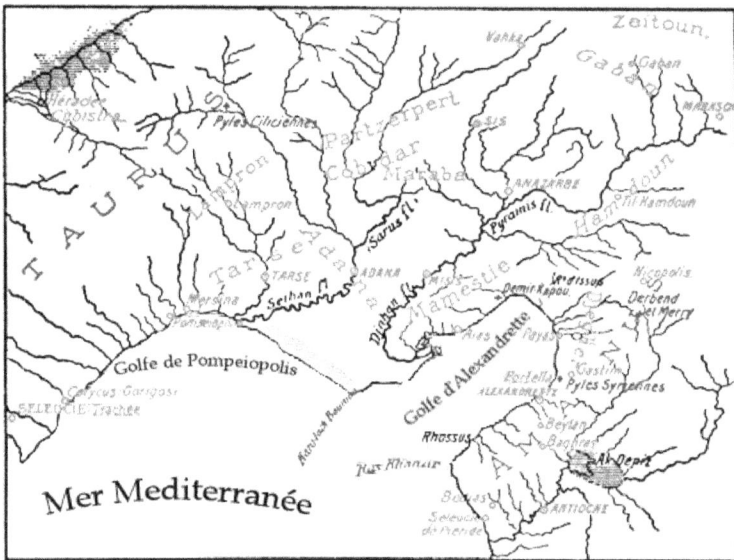

Cilicia

---

[60] In 1204 the Fourth Crusade had deposed the Greek Emperor Alexius V in Constantinople and set up a Latin Dynasty there, beginning with Baldwin, Count of Flanders, as Baldwin I. The Byzantines thereupon established their own government at Nicaea (modern Iznik). The Latin dynasty at Constantinople endured only fifty-seven years.

The Armenian King's policy, however, did not undergo a fundamental change. According to chroniclers, Leon had visited Cyprus on the occasion of King Richard's[61] marriage with Princess Berengaria, even acting as one of his groomsmen. He had also sent Armenian contingents to the aid of the French and English forces during their siege of Ptolemais (St. Jean d'Acre).

The Royal Court of Armenia

Leon organized his court and government after the pattern of those of Antioch and Jerusalem. He adopted courts of justice similar to the Assizes of Antioch — the Assizes of Jerusalem being in force among Christians of Syria and Palestine. The Latin and French languages began to be used by the clergy and court, together with the Armenian vernacular. The relationship between the Crown and the feudal lords became closer. Old titles and designations of rank were replaced by European ones, such as comte (count), baron, sir, countstable (connétable, constable); the last-named being an adopted form of the sbassalar, an agricultural or military commander. Leon created also two bailles (bajulus), in accordance with the practice of the Assizes of Jerusalem; one to protect and educate the future Queen, the other for the administration of the business affairs of the Crown. There were also a marshal, chamberlain, chancellor, a great cup-bearer (bouteiller), a grand courier (head of the King's messengers), all in accordance with the customs of the courts of Europe, though a few functionaries survived from Greek originals — such as the Proximos, a financial officer of the kingdom, and the Sébast and the Pansébast.

Leon reserved to himself the right of bestowing knighthood upon the feudal barons under his suzerainty. By the extension of the royal authority, a great number of semi-independent barons became subject to him, thus expanding the frontiers of the State and including seventy-two fortresses within an area measuring two days' march in width and sixteen days' march in length. Almost all the passes of the heights of Taurus and Amanus had been incorporated within the Armenian kingdom, and many of them entrusted to the care of European knights — the Templars, the Hospitallers and others.

Commerce of the Armenians

The economic development of his realm was another major object of Leon's concern. Situated between three competing elements — Latin, Greek and Moslem — Cilician Armenia enjoyed the advantage, from a commercial point of view, of serving as a link between East and West. The harbors of the Cilician coast, although not adequate for war galleys, afforded good shelter for such commercial vessels as came to cast anchor there. The Armenians, well acquainted with the trade routes of the Euphrates and Tigris, of Persia and India, had better knowledge than others of the value of Oriental goods in the western markets. They also came to an understanding with the Sultans of Iconium, the Khalifas of Baghdad and the Emirs of Aleppo with regard to duties on importations and

---

[61] Richard I of England (1189-1199).

exportations. After the fall of almost all Western Asia into the hands of the Moslem powers, the caravans began to move in comparative security between the Indus River and the Euphrates. The commerce formerly directed towards the Greek regions of Asia Minor were now gradually diverted towards Cilician Armenia, the new rendezvous of western navigators. Under Leon II, son and successor of the great first King, European merchants began to flock to Tarsus and Adana, and the harbor of Ayas was full of European masts. The republics of Venice and Genoa, whose business houses, once flourishing in Byzantine cities and on Syrian coasts, seemed now to be in decline, found a promising new field in Cilician Armenia. Both Venetian and Genoese merchants, always keen rivals with each other, were favored by a reduction of duties upon their transactions; they paid no more than one percent or nothing at all. But all others — those of Montpellier, Provence, Pisa, Sicily, etc. — had to pay from two to four percent *ad valorem*. However, when a later King of Cilician Armenia married a Sicilian princess, the Sicilian merchants were also placed upon the favored list.

The European merchants found in these emporiums all kinds of Oriental products — spices, perfumes, incense, soap, gems, raw silk, the fine textiles of India, the rugs of Iran and many other desirable articles. Out of this transit traffic, the Armenians derived immense benefit, the royal treasury being enriched by huge customs revenues.

King Leon is spoken of in Armenian history as "the Great" or "the Magnificent." He was endowed with superb qualities, indeed, and achieved notable successes in the political, military and economic advancement of his nation, although he was not always entirely scrupulous as to the means he used to obtain his ends. It should be understood that the ethical standards of the period were inevitably lowered by the incursions of barbarians and the bitterness of conflicting interests. However, Leon fully deserves the admiration of his people for his beneficent innovations, his pious and charitable foundations and his progressive legislation. He prohibited the sale of Christian slaves to non-Christians, he established asylums for lepers — then numerous in the East — and enacted many measures for the welfare and prosperity of his subjects.

Queen Zabel (1219-1252)

Before his death, Leon designated for the throne his daughter Zabel (Isabelle), born of his second wife, Sybille, the daughter of Amaury of Lusignan, King of Cyprus and his queen, Isabeau Plantagenet. The young princess was proclaimed Queen under the regency of Adam of Gastin. But Adam was assassinated by Ismaelites (Hashishins)[62] and the Baron Constantin, of the Hetoumian family was nominated as Baille or guardian. At this juncture, Raymond-Roupen, son of Raymond III of Antioch and Alice, daughter of Roupen III (who had been forced

---

[62] The "assassins" were a religious sect founded in Persia. A colony of them emigrated to Syria and settled in various places with their headquarters in Lebanon. They were noted for their secret murders committed in obedience to their chief, in whom they believed the Holy Spirit resided. The word *Assassin* comes from Hashishin. The men selected to do a murder were usually intoxicated with the drug hashish.

to abdicate as Prince of Antioch) set up a claim to the throne of Armenia and backed it by force of arms. But he was defeated and captured in the plain of Tarsus by Constantin, and executed. In order to clinch his military success over the Latins with a political stroke also, the Baille Constantin now (in 1222) arranged a marriage between the young princess and Philip, son of Raymond the One-Eyed, the Frankish Count of Tripoli. Philip's treacherous nature, however, soon made his position untenable. In violation of his sworn pledge to "adopt the Armenian way of life (Hayénag), to maintain the church and altar in Armenian fashion, and to respect everybody's right," he betrayed the interests of the Armenians and offended their sensibilities. He even despoiled the royal palace, sending to Antioch not only its ornaments and treasures, but the royal crown itself. He was deposed after a reign of three years and confined in a prison in Sis, where he died, presumably poisoned, two years later.[63]

The next step taken by the Baille Constantin leaves us in doubt as to his real motives. Zabel was then scarcely twelve years old but the Baille announced his intention of giving her in marriage to his own son, Hetoum. Some of the barons, resenting the idea of placing such power in the hands of Constantin, the master of the fort of Lambron, arranged the escape of the young Queen to Seleucia Trachea (Selefkeh), where her own parents were then living. The Knights Hospitalers, to whom the defense of the fort at that place had been entrusted by King Leon, were expected to protect the young princess, but when the Baille's troops came to invest the place, Bertrand, the Grand Master of the Order, then also on the defensive against the Sultan of Iconium, was compelled to yield. Zabel was removed to Tarsus and consented to marry Hetoum, her guardian's son, who, *ipso facto,* was to share the royal authority with her. The coins minted during that period bear the effigies of both Zabel and Hetoum.

Effigy of Hetoum I, King of Armenia

---

[63] Abulfaraj, the Syrian bishop, gives the following details; Philip endeavored to remove the Armenian barons and replace them with Franks. He despised the Armenians. He would not have his door opened for them until they had knocked ten times. Upon the plea of the nobles to be delivered from Philip, the Baille sent men disguised as hunters, who entered the King's bedroom by night and carried him away forcibly. His wife, Isabeau, wept, tore her hair and screamed, 'Sir! Sir!' she being very fond of her husband.

Hetoum I (1226-1270)

Hetoum I was a vigorous and handsome young man when he ascended the throne, and his reign was longer than that of any other king of Cilician Armenia. But the beginning of his rule was inauspicious. Sultan Kaikobad of Iconium (Konya) invaded the country, forcing Hetoum to make territorial and economic concessions. In fact, coins were even struck, bearing the name of the Sultan in Arabic on one side, and that of Hetoum in Armenian on the other.

Coins with the names of Hetoum I, and of Sultans of Iconium

Invasion of Jinghiz Khan

At this time appeared on the eastern horizon the terrible Jinghiz Khan (Genghis), the scourge of the 13th century, advancing with his hordes from the wilds of Mongolia towards the West. He had already devastated northern China, northern Persia, Greater Armenia and Georgia. All the princes of Asia Minor, Christian and Moslem, united their forces in the hope of repelling this dreadful conqueror. Jenghiz Khan eventually fell back to Kurdistan, where he was assassinated in 1227.

Oktai-Khan

But the Mongol peril was not yet dispelled. Oktai-Khan (1227-1241), son of Jinghiz, took up the work of destruction in the countries west of the Caspian Sea. This was a world disaster, unprecedented in its swiftness and ferocity. In 1235 almost the whole population of Gandzak (Elizavetpol), was exterminated by the Mongols. The pillage of Lori, Ani and Kars followed two years later, and in 1242

198

came the destruction of Karin (Erzerum), Caesarea and Sebast, all ruled by Kaikhosrou II, the Sultan of Iconium.

As the frightful wave of blood and fire approached his frontiers, Hetoum hastened to declare his submission to the Mongols. But their Khan, Batchou, demanded the surrender to him of the mother, wife and children of the Sultan of Iconium, who had taken refuge in Armenia. Hetoum regretfully submitted to the barbaric demand, upon which Kaikhosrov invaded Cilicia in revenge for this violation of the laws of hospitality. However, Hetoum, now supported by the Mongols, drove the Sultan away from his domain.

Coin of Hetoum I, King of Armenia

Alliance with Mongol King

The Armenian King, giving proof of his far-seeing diplomacy, then took another bold step towards the conclusion of an alliance with the all-powerful Mangou, the head of the Mongol princes. He repaired in person to the latter's court, was received by him with honors, and after concluding the alliance, returned home triumphant and confident.

Strange destiny for an Armenian King! — to travel the whole length of Asia to meet, in the depths of the mysterious wilds of Scythia, a barbarian overlord. Fortunate it was that the Armenian monarch had contrived to form an alliance with these pagan hordes which, after devastating the land of Ararat, were now turning their armed might against the Mohammedans.[64]

Mongols Destroy Baghdad

This step had been taken by Hetoum just in time; for, the gathering storm soon burst upon all Anterior Asia. In 1257 Houlagu Khan advanced as far as the center of Asia Minor, overthrew the Sultan of Iconium, then capturing Baghdad in 1258, slew the Khalifa, Mustasim, and his two sons. For forty days the Arab capital was given over to slaughter and pillage; nothing but ruin was left in the wake of the Mongol conquerors. Erzerum, Erzingan, Sebastia, Caesarea, Iconium, Martyropolis, Aleppo, Damascus, Edessa, Kharan, Amida (Diarbekir), all were devastated and their populations well-nigh exterminated. Christians, however, suffered less than Moslems, not only because of the pledge given to Hetoum by the Great Khan, but also through the intervention of the Princess Dokouz-Khatoun, Houlagou's wife, a member of the Christian sect of China called the Keraits, who had received Nestorian missionaries as early as 635 A.D.[65]

Houlagou disappeared from the scene upon the death of his brother Mangou, but his generals continued the work of destruction, though with less intensity because of a lack of unity among them.

---

[64] In his chronicle, written in French about a half century later, the nobly-born monk, Hetoum-Anton, gave the following account of King Hetoum's experience in the Far East;— The story about conversion is fictional.

"When Mangou Khan had listened to the plea of the King of Armenia in his presence and before everyone, he spoke as follows; 'Because the King of Armenia has come.... To you King of Armenia, we reply that we shall do all benignly, in order to comply with your entreaties. And in the first place, we being lord by the grace of God, will be baptized and declare faith in our Lord Jesus Christ, and will have all our house baptized, and will advise all others to be baptized and to accept the Christian faith, but without using any force, because faith and belief do not require force. To the second request, we reply that we and our people shall wish perpetual peace and friendship with the Christians.... To the Christian churches and their clergymen, be they in whatever condition, religious or lay, we grant the privilege of Franchise (exemption from certain taxes). They shall not suffer any sort of molestation. (p245)As to the matter of the Holy Land, we declare that we long to go in person and conquer it.... But because we have many other affairs, we give commission to our brother Alaoun (Houlagu Khan), who will accomplish this work and deliver Saint Jerusalem from the hands of the miscreants, and return it to the Christians ... and we give order to our brother to capture the city of Damascus and to destroy the Khalifa, our mortal enemy.'" Hayton (Hetoum) *"La flore des estoiles de la Terre d'Orient." Histoire des Croisades. Monuments Arméniens.*

[65] Orbelian, the Armenian chronicler, hails this lady with the epithet of "Most Blessed". Vardan Vardapet, another Armenian historian, writes: "In memory of our benevolent and kindly great Houlavou (Houlagou)."

200

Chapter XXX
The Memlouks Are Added to Armenia's Foes

New Scourge from Egypt

And now another scourge appeared on the scene to harass western Asia. The Memlouks were originally a cavalry corps established in Egypt from Turkish and other slaves sold to the Egyptian Sultan by Jinghiz Khan.[66] In 1251 they seized the government, made one of their own number Sultan, and held power for more than 250 years. Bibars, their Sultan (1260-1277), took the field in 1266 with the fixed intention of wiping out all the Latin states in Western Asia. He invaded Armenian Cilicia at the moment when Hetoum was again on his way to the Mongol Khan's court in quest of aid. The two royal princes, Thoros and Leon, strove to repel the foe, but their army was crushed, Thoros falling on the battlefield and Leon being taken prisoner. The Memlouks captured the most important centers of the country — Amuda, the fortress of the Knights Templars, Sis, Missis, Adana, Tarsus, Ayas — slaughtering the inhabitants as they went. Two years later, in 1268, Antioch itself fell to the Sultan. Almost every man in the city was butchered and the women were distributed among the soldiers. The booty taken was enormous.[67]

Hetoum finally obtained peace from the conqueror, though on very harsh terms. His son Leon was given his freedom in exchange for some forts on the frontier and the release of Sonkor al-Ashar (the Red Falcon), the Sultan's favorite friend, who had been captured by Houlagou. Soon after the return of his son, Hetoum, weary and disappointed, gave up the throne and retired to a monastery, where he died in 1270.

---

[66] Memlouk (Arabic) means "possessed", "slave", "serf".

[67] The strange savagery in the character of Bibars appears in his letter written after the event, to Bohemund, Prince of Antioch and Tripoli;—
"We took Antioch by the sword," he wrote, "on the fourth day of the month of Ramazan, in the fourth hour of Saturday. . . . If only you had seen your knights being trampled under the hoofs of horses, the plunder of your palaces, the weighing and distribution of your treasure, the purchase of your women and their sale, four for one dinar, if only you had witnessed the demolition of your (p247)churches, the smashing of your crosses, your richly bound Gospels put up for auction under the sun, the tombs of your nobility destroyed, your Holy of Holies trodden upon by Moslems, the bishops, priests and deacons immolated upon the altars, men of wealth reduced to misery and royal princes taken into captivity — if only you had seen your halls given up to the flames, your dead cast into the fire (and thus doomed hereafter to eternal fire), the churches of Paul and Gozma in ruins and rubble, then you would have cried, 'I wish that God had turned me to dust!' No one has survived to tell you all these things; I, therefore, give you the news."

Leon II (1270-1289)

His son Leon was endowed with many good qualities. He was pious, generous and sagacious. He encouraged scholars. The Bible and several works of former Armenian writers and translators were copied under his auspices. However, he suffered many griefs, domestic and otherwise. Pestilence took away a great number of his subjects. Among other harrowing circumstances were the intrigues of several of his feudal barons who wavered in their loyalty to the throne. And while he was laboring to improve the morale of his people, a formidable army, led by the emirs of the Sultan, invaded his country without the slightest pretext. Lacking adequate means of resistance, the Armenians were doomed to a dreadful fate. The city of Tarsus was taken, the royal palace and the church of St. Sophia burned, the state treasury looted, 15,000 civilians killed and 10,000 taken captive to Egypt. Almost the entire population of Ayas, Armenian and Frankish, perished.

Invasion by Bibars

A graphic account of that invasion is given by Makrizi, an Arab historian;—

"On the third day of the month of Shaban, 673 (Feb. 1st 1275), the Sultan left the castle of the Mountain, took the route of Syria and entered Damascus. From there he set out at the head of his soldiers and Arabs. . . . The Khazinadar (treasurer) and the emirs having made an incursion" (into Armenia) "by land, surprised the city of Missis and killed all its inhabitants. They had brought with them on mule dismantled boats, which were to be used in crossing the Jihoun and the Nahr-i-Aswad (Black River), but these were not needed. The Sultan at the head of his troops rejoined the two emirs after crossing the Nahri-Aswad.

"The army, despite numerous obstacles encountered en route, captured mountains and collected a prodigious spoil of oxen, buffaloes and sheep. The Sultan made his entry into Sis in battle array, and celebrated there a solemn feast. He sacked the city and demolished the palace, the belvederes and gardens of the takafor (king). A detachment sent by him to the defiles of Roum (Gates of the Taurus) brought in Tatar (Mongol) prisoners, among whom were a great number of women and children. The troops sent to the sea-coast seized many vessels, whose crews were slain. Other columns, in their drives through the mountains, captured and massacred the inhabitants and took quantities of booty. One division set out for Ayas, and finding that city undefended, despoiled and burned it. About two thousand Franks and Armenians from among its inhabitants who had taken refuge on the vessels in the harbor were drowned. An incalculable quantity of plunder was seized."

A contemporaneous Armenian writer, Vahram of Edessa, gives the following details in his rhymed chronicle:—

"They" (the Egyptians) "put to the sword all whom they caught on the plains. Only those who had taken refuge in fortified places escaped the carnage. All others, with no exceptions, were captured. Hemming in all our country, they laid the torch to everything. Tarsus the Great, the magnificent and illustrious city, was ruined. They burned the church of St. Sophia and gave the city over to pillage."

Leon Fights Valiantly

Armenia, however, was not yet completely beaten; her struggle against heavy odds continued relentlessly. Leon now efficiently supported by his nobles, succeeded in a few encounters. His uncle, the General Sempad, the grand old man of Armenia, marched to meet the Memlouks, whilst the King himself, with another force, undertook a detour to strike the enemy in the rear. Sempad lured his foes into a mountain pass and dealt them such a mortal blow that the bodies of the dead impeded the flight of the survivors (1276). Enraged at this reverse of his army, Bibars was about to launch a new expedition when he died from a wound received, according to some chroniclers, from an Armenian archer.

This victory, however, cost the Armenians dearly. They lost three hundred knights, and their General, Sempad, was accidentally killed when his horse hurled him against a tree. In appreciation of Leon's valorous deeds, the Mongol emperor sent him a superb sword, offering also to turn over to him all the lands in Mesopotamia which had been conquered by the Mongol armies. Leon declined this offer, however, pleading very justly that the responsibility of defending two kingdoms would be too difficult for him.

Battle of Homs

Cilician Armenia had enjoyed a peaceful breathing spell of nearly four years when hostilities between Mongols and Memlouks broke out again. Mangou-Timor, at the head of 50,000 Tatars, supported by a Christian contingent of 25,000 Armenians and Georgians, clashed with the Sultan Malek-Mansour of Egypt in the plains of Homs, Syria, in 1281.

The allies suffered a crushing defeat, and the conquerors, pursuing the Armenians, entered Cilicia.[68]

At length, through the mediation of the Commander of the Templars, a treaty of peace, to last ten years, ten months and ten days, was concluded between Leon II and the Sultan in 1285. But the terms imposed upon the Armenian monarch were

---

[68] Mangou-Timor, the general of the vanquished army, was put to death by the order of Abagha Khan, his own brother, and the Tartar legions who had brought about the disaster by fleeing from the field during the battle were condemned to wear feminine attire for the rest of their lives.

very harsh. He was to pay an annual tribute of one million silver dirhems;[69] to release all imprisoned Moslem merchants, indemnify them for their losses; to surrender the fugitives, to grant the Moslems full freedom to trade, even in purchasing slaves, whatever their nationality or religion might be. The Sultan, in turn, agreed to release prisoners and grant certain freedoms, except that he would not hand back fugitive Moslems or such Armenians as had embraced Mohammedanism. Leon was forced to subscribe to these onerous demands, but he enjoined the Genoese merchants of Cilicia from selling Christian slaves to Moslems or to nations dealing with them.

The remnants of the Latin principalities in the East were all in the same sad predicament as was Armenia. The chief concern of each was naturally the maintenance of its own existence; and there seemed no other way to achieve this than through compromise with the enemy. Certainly it could not be accomplished through armed resistance. Since the fall of Antioch the Armenian state was completely isolated from Christian or civilized contact; nevertheless, the peace treaty, harsh and humiliating though it was, gave it a respite of about eleven years, during which time Leon wisely carried on the work of relief and rehabilitation. Foreign vessels were again to be see visiting the port of Ayas, and commerce received a new impetus.

By his wife, Queen Ann (Kyr-Ann), Leon had eleven children, nine of whom survived him.

Hetoum II (1289-1297)

Christendom in the Levant was in a critical situation when Leon's son Hetoum II, ascended the throne. The Memlouks, now in possession of the principalities of Edessa, Jerusalem and Antioch, assumed an arrogant, even threatening attitude towards Armenia and the remaining Latin states. Melik Ashraf Kalaoun, the successor of Bibars, disregarding the treaty of 1285, demanded the surrender to him of the cities of Marash and Behesni. Urgent appeals by the Christians to Pope Nicholas IV and to King Philip IV of France were of no avail. The Crusading fervor was almost entirely extinct. Nearly twenty years had past since the last unsuccessful Crusade under Louis IX (St. Louis). Western European states were now competing with each other to win the favor of the Memlouks. King Alfonso of Aragon, King Don James of Naples and the Genoese Republic had already concluded treaties of commerce with them. And while Europe appeared to have forgotten its crusader colonies in the East, Kalaoun was pursuing his conquests, slaughtering male Christians and carrying their wives and children into captivity. Tripoli fell in 1289, and within two years Acre, Tyre, Sidon and Beirut suffered the same fate.

In 1292 Melik-Ashraf-Khalil, the son of Kalaoun, advanced to the Euphrates and invested Romgla, the residence of the Armenian Katholikos and a most important stronghold, which was being defended by Raymond, maternal uncle of Hetoum.

---

[69] The value of a dirhem was about 10 or 12 American cents.

After a siege of thirty-three days the place was taken, all the men were put to the sword, while the women and children, together with the patriarch Stepanos (Stephen), were taken captive. In the hope of staving off the complete destruction of his country, Hetoum abandoned to the enemy the cities of Behesni, Marash and Till Hamdoun.

Disasters in Egypt

Serious disasters — a deadly pestilence which swept the country, and bloody palace revolutions — now dealt severe blows to Egypt. Had any vestige of power or spirit remained in the Latin principalities, they could have taken advantage of this opportunity to revolt. But their morale was at its lowest ebb. Hetoum entered into negotiation with Melik Adil Zein-ed-Din Ketbougha (1294-1296), who had just seized the Egyptian throne from Nassir-Mohammed. As a result, the Moslem prince set free a part of the prisoners captured at Romgla, and restored the church vessels and relics taken from the same place.

King Thoros (1293-1295)

Discouraged by his many misfortunes, Hetoum abdicated in 1293 in favor of his brother Thoros and retired into a monastery; but in a short time he was forced again to take the reins of the state, at the instance of Thoros himself. This was for the purpose of making another appeal in person for aid at the distant capital of the Mongol Empire, now weakened by dissensions among the descendants of Jinghiz Khan. A truce having been patched up at the Tartar court, the old treaty of alliance with the King of Armenia was renewed. On his return to Sis, Hetoum was overjoyed at finding there two Byzantine envoys whose mission was to ask the hand of his sister Ritha-Marguerite for the associate Emperor, Michael Palaeologus.

Hetoum, more churchman than prince, and cherishing a real loyalty to the Papacy, longed to spend the rest of his life in spiritual seclusion; but he could not escape from his country's pressing political necessities. After the marriage of his sister — who now took the name of Xené-Marie — to the Byzantine sovereign, Hetoum went to Constantinople on a state visit to his brother-in-law, turning the Regency over to another brother, Sempad.

Sempad and Constantin (1296-1299)

But this prince forthwith proceeded to usurp the throne. Hastening homeward, Hetoum found himself arrested and put into confinement by Sempad. He was released, however, by another brother, Constantin, who imprisoned the usurper, but who, in turn, seized the throne for himself.

During the short period of Constantin's reign, a few months in 1299, the Egyptians made renewed incursions into Cilicia with two armies, one under the command of Bedreddin Bektash, and the other under that of Takieddin

Mahmoud. The forces of two other emirs, who were advancing towards Ayas, were almost entrapped in the mountains by the Armenians, and saved themselves only by headlong flight. Several forts and towns on the eastern frontier of the country also were captured by the emirs of Aleppo and Hama — who, however, had to evacuate almost all of them because of the approach of a Mongol army.

Coins of Sembat, King of Armenia

Hetoum II Returns to Power

Hetoum now ousted Constantin and took the reins of government again. Soon thereafter the Mongols reappeared in Syria, and supported by the Armenians, they won a great victory over the Memlouks near Homs (1299), drove them out of the valley of the Orontes and captured Damascus. This turn of affairs enabled the Armenians to regain all their possessions in Cilicia and vicinity. Four years later, however, the Egyptian Sultan took revenge near Damascus (1303) by crushing the allied Mongol and Armenian armies in the great battle of Merj-us-Safer. From the battlefield King Hetoum fled directly to Moussoul, where Ghazan Khan, the Mongol ruler, was then holding court.

For many years, Christian and Moslem priests had been competing with each other to win over the Mongol chiefs, each to his own faith. The precarious situation of the Frankish principalities of the Levant, due mostly to the growing indifference of Europe, and the increase on the other side of the military power of the common enemy, tipped the scales in favor of the Prophet. Hetoum and his successors were still being treated as allies by the Mongols, which fact served to intensify the irritation of the Egyptians against the Christians.

Hetoum Crushes the Foe

At this time Hetoum finally laid aside his royal power, and designated his nephew Leon III, sixteen years old, son of Thoros II and Marguerite de Lusignan, as his successor (1303-1307). But the young king had scarcely been crowned when an army of Memlouks under Kush-Timur menaced the country. The retired monarch, still Regent, emerged from his monastic cell once more, took the field in company with the youthful king in 1305, gave the marauders such a beating in the defiles of Bagras that few of them survived to reach their base at Aleppo.

Hetoum Attempts Church Union

One of the deplorable episodes in Armenia's long story of domestic friction occurred about this time. Some of her statesmen, backed by certain representatives of the higher clergy, had long favored a closer tie with the Roman Church, as proposed by the Papacy, in order to obtain more effective aid from Western powers. King Hetoum II, an ardent advocate of this idea, convoked a general assembly or synod at Sis in 1307, composed of forty bishops and many dignitaries, lay and clerical. They adopted a resolution, ratifying the desired union of the churches, despite vehement protestations from the people at large, including women, who now began to be vocal in national affairs. Some of the opposition leaders, unfortunately, were so intransigent as to betray their own leaders to the enemy.

Coins of Leo III of Armenia

Mongols Slay Leon and Hetoum

General Bilarghou, the representative of the Mongol Khan, who nursed a grudge against Hetoum for having prevented the erection of Moslem mosque in Sis, took advantage of this situation. He invited King Leon and the Regent, together with forty nobles, to Anazarba, as if for discussion of pressing political matters. As soon as the guests were inside the tent of the Tartar general, he unsheathed his sword and shouted, "Allah is great!" That was the signal for his soldiers to fall upon the Armenians and to slay them, including Hetoum and Leon, to the last man (Nov. 18, 1308).

Oshin (1308-1320)

Oshin, the fourth brother of Hetoum, who by a fortunate circumstance, was not present at this gathering, upon hearing of the dastardly murder of his brother and nephew, immediately placed himself at the head of a royal regiment and pursued the Mongol troops out of Armenian territory. He then returned to Tarsus, where he was crowned as King. His religious views were similar to those of Hetoum, and he thus aroused a violent opposition to himself among some of the nobles, beclouding and imperilling the early years of his reign.

The trend of thought of those days may be better understood from an incident recorded by the Armenian historian, Samuel of Ani;—

> This year (1309-1310), there convened at Sis, the capital of the Kingdom, a multitude of monks, priests and deacons, as well as Vartabeds (doctors of divinity), bishops and many people who refused to accept the use of water in the chalice of the mass, as well as other innovations. The King Oshin in accord with the Katholikos and the grandees, seized all of them and confined the Vartabeds in the fortress. He put to death a considerable number of men and women, and some priests and deacons; then putting the monks aboard a vessel, he exiled them to Cyprus, where most of them died."

Armenia in Cypriot Troubles

Amaury, Prince of Tyre, had married Isabelle, sister of Oshin; and because of this fact, the King of Armenia now found himself involved in the affairs of Cyprus. Henry II (de Lusignan), deprived by his brother Amaury of his right to the throne of Cyprus, had been exiled to Cilicia and detained there by Oshin. After the death by assassination of Amaury, Henry II was set free and reconciled with Isabelle.

The Kingdom of Cyprus was now the last remnant of the Latin power in the Levant, the Armenian King's dependable means of sending appeals to Europe. However, the West was no longer interested in the fate of Armenia; and the only help that Oshin could obtain consisted of 30,000 sequins contributed by Pope John XXII (1316-1334). During all this time the Egyptians and Turcomans continued their devastation in Cilicia, with the Armenians stoutly resisting in defense of their homes. But what could they hope for, isolated as they were in the midst of an ocean of enemies?

Leon IV (1320-1342)

Upon the death of Oshin his son Leon IV inherited the throne at the age of ten. His father had named Oshin, Count of Gorigos, as regent of the kingdom. This nobleman, a brother of Isabeau, first wife of King Oshin, was the uncle of the young sovereign. The Regent proceeded to make his own position secure by marrying Joanna, widowed Queen of King Oshin, also giving his daughter Alice in marriage to the little King, which ceremony required a special dispensation from the Pope.

Cilicia Harassed Again

Incursions by Egyptians, even by Tartar bands, now mostly converted to Mohammedanism, were still going on, undermining the vitality of the kingdom. Once again in 1322 the Pope intervened, appealing to Philip V of France and to the Mongol chief in Persia. The latter sent 20,000 troops to the aid of the Armenian King, a move which caused Sultan Melik Nasser hastily to conclude a fifteen-year peace agreement. But not without profit to himself, however; the treaty specified that half of the customs revenue of the port Ayas and half of the proceeds of the sale of salt to foreigners must be turned over to the Egyptian treasury.

Nevertheless, this new relationship with the Latin World and his appeals to Europe for help brought Leon no relief. Instead, Melik Nasser, that dreaded Damoclean Sword dangling over Cilicia, angered by rumors of preparations for a new Crusade under Philip VI of France, presently sent a large force to invade the country. Leon, who had taken refuge in the strong fortress of Gaban, in order to appease the foe was compelled to cede to him the entire territory lying east of the Jihoun River, together with seven other castles, also handing over 16,000 gold dinars (about 50,000 dollars), to indemnify the Egyptian merchants who had sold cotton to Venetian exporters, now fled from Ayas without paying their debts. And finally, to give full satisfaction to the Sultan, the Armenian King took a solemn oath, with his hand on the Gospel and the Cross, never again to have any dealings with the Franks, or to "send envoy or letter to the Pope of Rome." [70]

Latin Church Party

Having purchased security from the perpetual enemy at least temporarily, and at such tremendous cost, Leon IV cared little for the wave of resentment within the country, caused by his own arbitrary policy in religious matters. An Armenian Vartabed, named Johannes of Kerni, with the cooperation of a Dominican monk,

---

[70] Rainaldi, — quoted by Father Tchamitchian.

established in Eastern Armenia a branch of the latter's order called the "Unitor", — the object of which was to engraft Latin practices upon the Armenian church. These men introduced the Latin language into the Liturgy and declared the Armenian sacraments void; they rebaptized laymen and reordained the clergy. The movement was favored by the King, who thus became the leader of the Latin party, as opposed to the Nationalist party headed by the Katholikos Jacob II. The friction between the two cults assumed such proportions that the Katholikos threatened to excommunicate the King, but found himself check-mated when the King deposed him from office.

The young King's lack of proper education and his bad temper added much to the gravity of the national situation as he became of age. But though his conduct was reprehensible, history should not pass judgment upon him before considering the conditions in which he lived and acted. The caprice, arrogance, avarice and murderous lust for power of Oshin, his guardian, undoubtedly had a deplorable effect upon the young prince's character. Oshin had eliminated by death or exile all those who refused to cringe to him. Isabelle, his own sister and Amaury's widow, was one of the Regent's victims. Four of their five children lived in Cilicia; of these, two died, allegedly poisoned, and the other two were driven out of the country.

King Leon is Slain

Upon reaching maturity, the King found it impossible to endure his uncle's iniquities any longer. At last, in a fit of temper, he ordered the execution not only of Oshin, but of his brother Constantin, and finally of his own wife, accusing her of infidelity. In 1333 he married Constance Eleanor, daughter of Frederick II of Sicily and widow of Henry II of Cyprus.

The religious struggle within the kingdom was brought to a tragic end in 1341, by the assassination at the hands of Nationalist extremists, of Leon IV at the early age of thirty-two.

Chapter XXXI
French-Armenian Dynasty: End of Kingdom

Guy de Lusignan (1342-1344)

Having no male issue, Leon had chosen as his successor Guy de Lusignan, the fifth son of his father's (Oshin) sister Isabelle, who was living in the Greek islands at the time when his mother and brothers lost their lives in Armenia. The throne thus passed to a French petty royal family, and the preponderance of this foreign influence portended a great change in the national life. Guy, also known as Constantin II, nephew of Henry II of Cyprus and a close relative of the Imperial family of Byzantium, accepted the offer of the crown after some hesitation, and entered Armenian territory, escorted by an armed force.

The powerful neighboring Moslem states, uneasy over this change in the royal line of Armenia and at the tightening of the connections between that country and Europe, now sought a pretext for intervention by demanding payment of the annual dues which they had been collecting from Leon IV. Guy rejected their demands and for a time succeeded in thwarting their attempts to collect the money by force. Meanwhile, following the policy of his immediate predecessors, Guy was endeavoring to bring about a union with the Roman church, in the hope of receiving the military and financial aid so indispensable for the safety of his country. He sent two embassies to Avignon, France, the new seat of the Papacy, and convened an assembly to discuss the terms of the proposed union. The King's project was rejected by some of the nobles, who preferred to obtain peace through concessions to the Moslems rather than try to withstand them, relying on help from the West. During a riot fomented by his enemies, Guy, together with many of his Frankish bodyguards, was killed after a brief reign of two years. This, says the chronicle of Jehan Dardel, the friar confessor of Leon V, the last king, was "grand dommage pour la chrétienté que la mort d'un si bon prince, car il était hardy, preux et de moult grand entreprise."

Constantin III (1344-1363)

The nobles now elected Constantin, son of the Marshal Baghdin (Baldwin) of Neghr, who had died in the dungeon of the Emir of Aleppo in 1336. He was the first of the kings of Cilician Armenia in whose veins ran no drop of Hetoumian blood; but he was related to the royal house through his marriage with Marie, daughter of Oshin, the Baille, and Jeanne of Anjou.

The first domestic act of the new king was a shameful portent of his future course. With the intention of uprooting the Lusignan connection from the local scene, he confiscated all the property of the Lady Soultan, a daughter of King

211

Coins of Constantin III, King of Armenia

Gorgi VII of Georgia and wife of Jean de Lusignan, the brother of King Guy-Constantin II. The King then confined the princess, together with her two sons, Bohemund and Leon, aged five and two years respectively, in the island-castle of Gorigos. Warned of further treacherous designs of the King, the Lady Soultan succeeded in escaping, with her children, to the island of Cyprus on a fishing boat. The King of Cyprus, Hugues IV (de Lusignan), took the refugees under his protection, the little boys being the grandsons of his paternal uncle.

Invaders Ousted

The Armenians, compelled to battle during all this time against their enemies, once again lost the port of Ayas. The situation was growing worse day by day, and there were no signs of any intervention or aid from European powers. Thanks to the help of Dieudonné de Gozon, the Grand Master of Rhodes, the port of Ayas was given back to Armenia in 1347, but about the end of the same year the place was blockaded by the Egyptian fleet, and the Turcomans of Iconium (Konia) marched on Tarsus. Sultan Nassir, however, died about this time and disturbances arising in Egypt over the question of the succession weakened the Memlouks' war effort, with the result that the Armenians, in the next few years, recaptured Ayas, Alexandretta and other territory, and drove away all the marauding bands.

Later on, in 1359, the troops of Sultan Melik-en-Nasser Hassan invaded Cilicia, laid waste all the land and carried away an immense quantity of booty. The Moslems of Karaman in the meantime, besieged the seaport of Gorigos, which, however, was rescued in 1361 by King Pierre I (de Lusignan) of Cyprus.

Pierre I of Cyprus

The Cypriots thereupon equipped a fleet of one hundred and forty-six galleys, which was joined by the naval forces of the Knights of Rhodes and those of the Pope. Pierre, at the head of this great force, won some signal victories; the notion of inciting Europe to embark on a new Crusade began to seethe in his mind.

Accordingly, he set sail for Venice and thence to other capitals of the West, where he succeeded, with the support of Pope Urban V, in arousing some interest and obtaining a considerable sum of money.

Constantin IV (1365-1373)

In 1363 Constantin III died without leaving any heir. One party in the capital appealed to the Pope, claiming the succession for the heirs of Guy. Urban V, however, preferred Leon, a kinsman of Pierre of Cyprus. But the Nationalist party, scorning the Papal wishes, elected the son of Hetoum the Chamberlain, nephew of the Marshal Bohemund, the father of Constantin II, and enthroned him as Constantin IV. Pierre consented to the *"fait accompli"*, and lent the new sovereign his full support against his foreign enemies. Other Western nations — the Venetians, the Genoese and the Aragonians — remained neutral. They had signed commercial treaties with the Sultan of Egypt, despite Papal threats of excommunication against Christians who dared to trade with Moslems.

Raid on Egypt by Pierre I

Pierre I, undismayed by their indifference, organized an expedition and sailed from Venice in 1365 with a fleet of thirty galleys, carrying knights and soldiers of several nationalities — French, Italian, German, English and Greek. With this little army composed of 10,000 infantry and 1,000 horsemen, he made a landing at Alexandria, Egypt, and sacked the city, but abandoned it when a counter-attack was being launched by the Memlouks. From Egypt he turned northward and devastated all the Syrian coast, finally arriving in front of the Ayas, which he could not reduce because of the Armenian King's failure to give him assistance.

The King of Cyprus then returned to the West for additional subsidies and troops. While in Venice, he received a deputation which offered him the crown of Armenia. He took the matter seriously, for, sailing from Venice in 1368, he reached Cyprus with the intention of proceeding to Cilicia to be crowned king of that country; but he was assassinated in Nicosia, by some of his own nobles.

The death of Pierre emboldened the Egyptian, Syrian, and Anatolian foes to commit further ravages in the country. It was during this period of desperate and heroic resistance shown by the Armenians that there arose the intrepid figure of Libarid the Valiant, the last great Armenian general, whose very name spread terror and unwilling admiration among all the Moslem nations of the Near East.

As to King Constantin IV, he was, according to Jehan Dardel — not a wholly unbiased reporter — a tyrannical and selfish ruler, indifferent to the welfare of his country and to any possibility of its deliverance from its Moslem oppressors. He was finally assassinated in 1373, during a palace revolution. His wife, Queen Marie (Mariam), the widow of King Constantin II, who seems to have been always active in political affairs, sent ambassadors to his uncle, Philip of Tarentum (Southern Italy), titular emperor of Constantinople, and then to Pope Gregory XI, who endeavored to rally all Europe to the support of Armenia.

Unfortunately, a quarrel arising between Christian nations was to result in the loss, for all time, of the cause of Christendom in the Levant. Some petty wrangle over precedence between the Venetians and the Genoese flared up in Cyprus. The island was devastated by the Genoese, who then levied a tribute upon it of 40,000 sequins.[71] Upon the restoration of peace, Pierre II was crowned at Nicosia as King of Cyprus, and in Famagusta, as King of Jerusalem (January, 1372).

Pope Urges Aid to Queen

Leon, the only surviving grandson of Zabel (Isabelle) of Armenia, had been brought up in Cyprus. Pope Urban V had, as early as 1365, favored him for the throne of Armenia, but the prince had been detained in Cyprus by various intrigues and exigencies. Even before the assassination of King Constantin, the rebellious nobles had confided the regency to Queen Marie. In a letter written on February 1st, 1372, Pope Gregory XI informed Philip IV of Tarentum, that, "Marie, the Queen of Armenia, niece of Philip of Tarentum, requests that the Pope may come to her aid against the Moslems, who have put her realm in great danger. She has sent as ambassador to the Holy See, Johannes, Bishop of Sis, who expresses a wish that the Queen may find a husband from among the Latin princes, capable of defending and governing Armenia. The Pope urges Jehan, Prince of Antioch, Regent of Cyprus, the Venetians, the Genoese and the Knights of Rhodes to help the Armenians. He names Othon of Brunswick, a man combining the necessary qualities, to become the consort of Marie."

Leon De Lusignan Chosen as King

But the pontifical letter had no effect. Queen Marie thereupon sent to Pierre II of Cyprus a deputation consisting of the knight Leon of Hamous and two prominent citizens of Sis. The letter credential which the deputation presented was a request for the dispatch to Cilicia of Leon de Lusignan, as the rightful heir to the throne. It was concurred in by the Armenian nobility and clergy, and the two queens, Marie and Jeanne. But Leon, a feudatory of Pierre II, because of the fiefs of his wife, Marguerite de Soissons, was not able, however, to set out at once for Cilicia. The chief reason for the delay, as alleged by King Pierre, was the troubled state of the island due to the recent incursions of the Genoese; but another and major reason was the lack of funds with which to finance the journey.

The Armenian envoys returned home by way of Gorigos, the only port that had not fallen into Moslem hands. They were accompanied by the Knight Constant, equerry of the King-elect, and by Manuel the interpreter, to act as guardians of the royal treasury. Upon arriving outside of Sis, these man had to cross the lines of Bektimour, the Governor of Damascus, who had invested the capital — though he was later forced to raise the siege.

---

[71] A gold coin.

Leon Blackmailed for Permission to Leave Cyprus

Matters were meanwhile becoming worse for Leon in Cyprus. The piratical Genoese, now become the lords of the island, demanded as indemnity and interest, exorbitant sums from everybody — from King Pierre down to the humblest citizen. Leon, too, was forced to pay a "tax" of 280 gold livres (36,000 silver besants). His silver plate, his crown and wardrobe were seized, and restored only on payment of 300 ducats. The admiral of the Genoese fleet kept for himself the finest stone of the crown, a ruby. For permission to leave the island, Leon was compelled, moreover, to transfer to Catherine of Aragon, the mother of King Pierre, the fief of his wife, which yielded an annual income of 1,000 gold besants. Leon had also to undertake under oath not to enter the castle of Gorigos, on that west coast of Cilicia which was inhabited mostly by Armenians, but to land on the island. The Cypriots, to whom the main castle of Gorigos had been ceded by the Armenians, denied the local population the happiness of greeting their national sovereign. Leon resented this double humiliation by the Genoese and Cypriots, but refrained from expressing his feelings, for the reason that he might be forced to depend upon both for help against the Egyptians and Turcomans, who were blocking his way to Sis. By selling almost all his valuables, he obtained some cash, for which the King of Cyprus lent him a hundred gendarmes, under the command of the French equerry, Sohier Doulçart. This small force, with the addition of some cross-bowmen and archers recruited at Gorigos, was all that Leon could muster as an army with which to face his enemies. The Genoese admiral, even though he had accepted the sums of money which were sent to him, had refused to supply him with vessels with which to attack Tarsus by way of the river, "because of the trade agreement which the Genoese had made with the Saracens."

Castle of Gorigos

Leon Escapes from Cyprus

Pondering the dire consequences which might result from the groundless reports of projects attributed to himself in favor of King Pierre's rivals, Leon saw that he had not a moment to lose. He sent his wife and mother to the city of Gorigos, and, leaving the island where he had remained as he had promised, he set out with a few followers, under cover of the night, and arrived at a spot near the mouth of the Adana River, thirty miles from Gorigos. Doulçart, the knight, joined him the following day with twenty-five horsemen and as many arbalesters. Moving forward cautiously, the party had to avoid Tarsus; the rest of the journey was a hazardous one, the whole country being infested with hostile hordes. Leon procured guides from the bowmen, who were on foot, so that they might traverse shorter and safer mountain trails. Leon and his horsemen, twenty-five in all, rode two days and nights, almost without a halt. They dismounted before dawn at a distance of three miles from Sis, and sent a messenger to inform the city of their coming.

Leon V (1374-1375) Greeted with Joy

The citizens, led by the Katholikos, the bishops, priests and nobles came out in great number with music and dancing to welcome their king. They were transported with joy, for many of them had been so discouraged that they were planning to revolt, put the members of the Regency to death and surrender the city to the Moslems. Four days later, a force of a hundred and fifty armed men was dispatched to bring in the mother of Leon and the Queen. They arrived safely at Anazarba, and from there travelled to within a lieue (league) of Sis. Here, they were met by the King at the head of a procession of troops and conceptions, each one with a torch in his hand, making the occasion one of joy and festivity. Little did the jubilant throng dream that the church bells which rang for the coronation of Leon may be said to have tolled also the funeral knell of the last of the Armenian kingdoms.

Finds Empty Treasury

The first care of Leon, after the days of rejoicing, was an examination into the state of the treasury. To his bitter disappointment, he found it empty and the accounting unsatisfactory. Upon further investigation and after hearing testimony from government functionaries, he found that the members of the Regency — Mariam, the dowager of Constantin III and Baron Basile — were responsible for the defalcation. They deserved severe punishment, but Leon granted them pardon as a grace in honor of his coronation day.

Leon's Coronation

Leon's wish was that he be consecrated by a Roman bishop, but he found that this desire had to be modified. On September 14th, 1374, the coronation ceremony was performed twice in the cathedral of St. Sophia at Sis; first by the Archbishop of Narbonne in accordance with the Latin ritual, and then under Armenian rites by the Katholikos Boghos (Paul), Queen Marguerite of Soissons, the daughter of Jehan the Baille of Famagusta in Cyprus, was crowned in the same manner.

It is difficult now to say whether this double consecration was a political mistake on the part of Leon, but it certainly offended the Nationalist party and brought about unpleasant consequences.

Siege of Sis

Almost all important cities and castles in Cilicia, except Sis and Anazarba, were occupied by the troops of Melik Ashraf Shaban of Egypt; and two Turcoman chiefs, Davoud Beg and Aboubekr, each with eleven thousand warriors, threatened the very outskirts of Sis. Curiously enough, they did not conduct themselves like ordinary foes, but supplied the Armenians with the necessary provisions. Having received presents from Davoud Beg on his coronation day, Leon returned the courtesy and renewed the truce under the old terms. But a dissatisfied group precipitated a quarrel and Sis was subjected to siege for three months. The Frankish bowmen saved the situation by their skill, and the Turcomans were compelled to abide by the old agreement and to supply the capital with victuals, in consideration of the payment of the stipulated tribute.

The Renegade

There lived in Cairo at this time an Armenian renegade, named Ashot, son of Baron Oshin and brother of Constantin III's wife. The anti-Latin party among the Armenians, claiming that Ashot had a right to the crown, encouraged him to come at the head of an Egyptian Army, to take possession of his domain. Jehan Dardel has given the following picture of this invasion, although some scholars do not give full credence to the story.

Treachery in Sis

The Turcoman chief, Aboubekr, a satellite of Egypt, received orders from Cairo to starve the Armenian capital. Within the city, Leon's domestic enemies were secretly negotiating to deliver the city to the besiegers. The King, warned of the intended assault, gathered the population within the upper part of the city and in the castle, both well fortified.

The lower city did not seem likely to be able to hold out long, but the royal palace, surrounded by a massive wall and vast enough to shelter a considerable portion of the citizens, could adequately be defended. Within this enclosure, referred to by Dardel, as "the bourg", were other edifices, among them the metropolitan church of St. Sophia. Because of the ruggedness of the rock upon which they were built, the walls of the castle were irregular and unequal in height. These irregularities divided the castle roughly into three parts, each with flanking towers and bastions, resting upon the three principal pinnacles of the rock. Open spaces separated these distinct constructions, which, however, were connected by sunken ways cut in the rock and along the precipices. The southern side, where the donjon rose, was fortified more carefully than the other points of the stronghold.

Lower City Captured

On January 15th, 1375, Aboubekr, at the head of 10,000 men, captured the lower part of the city, which was given over to pillage, but the upper city and the castle remained impregnable. The anti-Latin faction had decided to obtain peace for themselves by submission to the Sultan. The Katholikos Paul (1374-1378), was one of the principal authors of this movement, thus "demonstrating," says Dardel, "that he preferred the temporal domination of a Moslem sovereign to the spiritual supremacy of the Pope."

Upper City Evacuated

In response to the appeal of the traitors, the governor of Aleppo, Seifeddin Ishk-Timour, sent 15,000 men to assist the Turcomans, and on February 24th the Egyptians were moving under the walls of Sis. More than 30,000 of the enemy thronged around the fortress, amid the ruins of the city and of "the bourg." Leon, anticipating the final assault, assembled the grandees and the clergy, made them all swear on the Gospel to remain loyal to the Christian faith and their sovereign, and promise to die for Christ. He then evacuated the upper city and set it afire by night.

Ruins of the Fortress of Sis

King Wounded

The enemy began the attack on the following day; but the only accessible point on the steep rocks was the platform which extended in front of the gate. The besieged put up a vigorous resistance, and the King himself was manning an arbalest when he was struck by an iron projectile which broke his jaw and knocked out three teeth. He retired to the castle to have his wound dressed, while the Saracens, considerably mauled, were retreating.

That same evening Ishk-Timour dispatched a letter, informing Leon, "that his lord, the Sultan, wants him (the King) to know that if he is willing to surrender the castle and become a Mohammedan, the Sultan will make him a Grand Admiral and restore his country." Leon's reply was that he would perish rather than renounce his God; but he offered to pay tribute to the Sultan as in the past, if the siege were raised and his possessions restored to him.

Traitor kills King's Guards

This rebuff infuriated the Moslem commander, who thereupon intensified the assault. In the meantime he was informed by traitors of the King's injury, and that the besieged were in a serious plight because the food supply of the fortress was exhausted. The Nationalists, moreover, won to their way of thinking the Cypriot knight, Matthew Chiappe, who had recently married the widow of King Constantin III. Chiappe was the sort who would stop at no treachery to effect his ends, even making an attempt on the life of the King. Together with a number of Frankish accomplices, he broke into the donjon where the King had his quarters, and killed Leon's Armenian guards to the last man. The King in great fear for the life of his wife and twin infant daughters, imprisoned in the donjon at that moment, took refuge in Queen Mariam's rooms. He offered to pardon the insurgents, but in vain, and a terrific struggle ensued. Four times the loyal Armenians attempted to enter the donjon, and each time failed.

Leon Yields

Meanwhile the rebels were letting the enemy in by means of ropes. A Jacobite friar, a companion of the Bishop of Hebron, who happened to be among the prisoners in the donjon, secretly let Armenians enter who took possession of the fort. Other conspirators instigated the mob to turn against the King, and determined to give the place over to the enemy, they admitted them into the outer works. Leon, wounded and in bed, had beside him only his wife and children and the faithful knight, Sohier Doulçart; a few soldiers still defended the donjon keep. Resistance being no longer possible, Leon sent an emissary to enemy headquarters.

219

Fall of Sis
End of the Kingdom

Receiving a letter of safe conduct from the Egyptian commander, Ishk-Timour, Leon, though scarcely able to walk, rose from his bed, his wounded head in bandages, and descended from the tower, accompanied by his family and escort. And so, on April 13th, 1375, only ten months after his landing on Armenian soil, Leon V gave up his sovereignty, and with it the last Armenian kingdom passed out of existence.[72]

The Memlouk general made a triumphant entry into the city of Aleppo with the captives in his train — the Armenian King, his Queen and children, the Dowager Queen Mariam, the knight Souhier Doulçart, his wife the Countess of Gorigos, the Katholikos Boghos I, many Armenian barons and dignitaries of Sis. These captives were forced, on many occasions, to prostrate themselves before the conqueror in public. From Aleppo, Leon was taken to Cairo, where he arrived in July. The coming of the Armenian captives brought on a three-day public celebration, noisy with the beating of cymbals and other instruments. Thereafter, yielding to the entreaties of prominent Armenian residents, the infant Sultan, or rather, his all-powerful minister Barquq, released Leon for detention, and allowed him a daily pension of sixty dirhems and privileges accorded to royal prisoners. Nevertheless, he was always under strict police surveillance.

It is through the chronicle of Jehan Dardel, the Franciscan monk, a native of Etampes in France, that the events of the short and tragic reign of Leon V are known to us. This monk's judgment upon the "Armins" (Armenians) is quite severe, but mature reflection upon the desperate state of the last defenders of the Christian kingdom against the Moslems and the famine that raged within the castle of Sis, may win for them some indulgence in their final recusancy.

Cilician Armenia Continuously Harassed by Foes

From the day of the unfurling of the banner of revolt by Roupen, to the hour of Leon's emerging from the castle for his capitulation, Cilician Armenia was a scene of almost perpetual warfare. Hundreds of times its towns and countryside were

---

[72] The Arab historian, Abul-Mehasen, writes of this event as follows;—

"This year the capital city of Sis was captured after three months of siege, by the Emir Ashiq Timour of Mardin, the Governor of Aleppo, and the Armenian State (devlet-al-Ermen) destroyed. May God be glorified! This good (p269) news was spread, and Meliq Ashraf (the Sultan) was enormously rejoiced by this great victory."

An Armenian eye-witness says; "How can one describe the outrages endured by our crosses and the Holy Books torn to pieces; and the demolition of the sacred altars?" Another witness, Bishop Zacharias, says, "Who can narrate by pen the mournful and lamentable happenings witnessed by my own eyes; the brilliant jewels and bright suns and stars and moons fallen down?" *(From Alishan's Sisouan).*

devastated by the invading Moslems, and its people slain or carried away into slavery. And the fall, one by one, of the Latin states of the Levant, inevitably undermined Armenian morale and fortitude.

For other wrongs suffered by the unfortunate kingdom, most of the blame rests upon the Armenians themselves. On many critical occasions, when the nation was threatened by a foreign enemy, religious intolerance and political and personal ambitions within the State, divided and betrayed it. The call to patriotic duty would have been more eagerly heeded by the Armenians, of course, had they not been disheartened by the action of their fellow-Christian nations, both near and to the west, who sacrificed spiritual and moral interests for the sake of temporal and material gain. It was not unusual for an Armenian landlord to be attacked by a Frankish baron — sometimes backed by a Moslem chieftain also. This explains why, several years after having been greeted as God-sent messengers, the "nation of the Franks" was referred to by Michael the Syrian in his chronicles as "oblivious of all benefactions lavished upon them."

De Morgan's Praise of Cilician State

"Whatever it may be, says de Morgan, "the Cilician state, founded by men from far off in the East and Europeanized through its contact with the Crusaders, has left a beautiful page in the grand epic of the Middle Ages. Despite troubles and wars, in the midst of the greatest dangers, the Armenians of Cilicia devoted themselves to literature and arts, built churches, monasteries, castles and fortresses and flourished in commerce. This principality, even in the midst of all the horrors of war, displayed a surprising vitality, by comparison with the timidity with which most other peoples of the Near East succumbed to the brute force of foreign conquerors. The heroic resistance which a handful of brave Armenians offered for three centuries, should command our recognition and admiration."

An Appraisal by Langlois and Others

That this last episode in the story of Armenia is full of romance, is admitted by all those who have studied the subject. In a passing remark about the monuments of Cilicia, Gustave Schlumberger refers to it as "the glorious kingdom of Lesser Armenia." Here is the testimony of Victor Langlois: "Numerous are those events, those brilliant traditions, — and however lamely we may follow the course of Armenia's victories and progress; however hastily we may examine the organization of her aristocracy and clergy; however slightly we may study her relations with the Western nations and the wars which she waged against the enemies, still shall we see that ... the historical documents of this country contain the memories of a glorious past."

Leon is Ransomed

Leon's life in Cairo was not a happy one. He lost by death not only his wife,

Marguerite de Soissons, but also his two children. In March, 1377, the King of Cyprus appealed to the Sultan for the liberation of Leon, but without success. In July of the same year, many pilgrims — nobles, knights, esquires and others — passed through Cairo on their way from Europe to Jerusalem. Among them was

View of the Castle of Sahi-Maran (Cilicia)

friar Jehan Dardel. He was invited to say mass for King Leon, engaged in long conversations with him and became acquainted with the story of his misfortunes and his hopes. He was finally persuaded to remain with Leon, as his chaplain and counselor and eventually became his ambassador. Bearing the royal ring and letters addressed to several of the sovereigns of Europe, Dardel left Cairo two years later, on September 11th, 1379. Arriving in Spain, he received from the Kings of Castile and Aragon considerable sums of money to be used toward the purchase of the liberation of Leon. These, plus 3,000 squirrel coats, a golden cup with silver and a gilt jar, at length obtained permission for Leon to leave Egypt. On October 7th, 1382, he sailed from the port of Alexandria, together with Dardel, upon whom, when they reached the Island of Rhodes, he conferred the title of Chancellor. From Rhodes he sailed for Europe, prompted not only by a desire to express his gratitude for assistance, but by new hopes for a betterment of his fortunes.

His life, thereafter, was like that of all exiled kings. The sovereigns of Castile and Aragon were generous towards him, the Pope of Avignon, Clement VII, whom Leon had preferred to the Pope of Rome, awarded to him the decoration of the "Golden Rose," and the King of Navarre, Charles II, whom he visited, lavished gifts upon him. But these favors cost the donors little and availed the wandering monarch nothing. Nowhere did he encounter any disposition to aid him in recovering his domain.

Leon as an Apostle of Peace

Paris, the capital of France, offered the ex-king a more extensive field for diplomatic activity. He was received by King Charles VI, in a manner due to kindred royalty. The appreciation in palace circles of Leon's "sagacity, moderation and penetration," was of more import and value to him than the annual pension, opulent lodgings and warm affection bestowed upon him. It was because of this confidence in his guest that Charles accepted a serious proposal submitted by him. In Leon's opinion, an Anglo-French accord was indispensable for the political rebirth of Armenia. But he observed with deep anxiety that the existing truce between these two powers was soon to come to its specified end. He hoped that he might utilize the respect felt for him by the French court to bring about an extended peace, and then appeal for their cooperation.

Having been given free access to the floor of the French Parliament, he attended the meeting in which the resumption of hostilities was discussed. The majority favored war. Those who were for peace requested the King of Armenia to become their advocate. Although "a prince of ardent spirit and great perspicacity," he had maintained silence until then, because his knowledge of the Latin language was defective and he spoke French with difficulty. However, he now took the floor and spoke as follows;—

> "Honorable Dukes, I must admit that the desire of revenge for injuries inflicted on one's homeland is a noble sentiment. And yet, with the permission of the King, I must say also that it would be advisable, even to forgo this legitimate revenge, to comply with established rules, and to avoid anger, which always leads to tragic ends. I think, therefore, that although your enemies have often violated truce pacts, you would in the present case be wise to beware of precipitate steps, and delicately invite them to conciliation. If they obstinately remain haughty and implacable, the justice of your cause will be more manifest. Your ancestors have ever adopted this policy. For my part, I shall be ready, if it pleases you, to undertake any mission in this affair, so that the sincerity of my word may be unquestioned. No friendly connection whatsoever binds me to the English, and yet an appeal by me may, perhaps, be more fruitful than one by a delegate from your own nation, against which they cherish inexorable hatred."

These utterances of Leon carried weight. He had been unfortunate during his brief reign, but he was not a stranger to the diplomatic field. Although short of stature, "he was great in valor, ardent in spirit and exceptionally clever in practical dealings. His exquisite civility won distinction for him. His external grace and decorum were the characteristic marks of princely lineage."[73]

---

[73] The quotations are from *"Chroniques de Religieux de St. Denys."* See also *Froissard* and *Juvenal des Ursins.*

Leon in England

The dethroned King of Armenia was at last dispatched to England as an envoy of the French Government. King Richard II considered it a rare honor, enjoyed by none of his predecessors, to welcome such an eminent prince to his realm. Attracted both by the luster of Leon's fame and the repute of his bravery, the English monarch was moved to offer him a reverential hospitality. He sent a number of high functionaries of the palace and dignitaries of the court to meet the guest, while he himself went forth with a mounted escort to the approaches of the city, where he greeted and embraced Leon affectionately, manifesting by words and countenance his joy over the arrival of the royal delegate.

A true delineation of the efforts of Leon for peace, is beyond our power; but we possess a precious document — the text of the speech delivered by him before King Richard and the Lords in Westminster Palace at the beginning of the year 1386. It is as follows;—

"I wish to tell you, not by way of flattery, but prompted by brotherly love, that the people of the Orient have until now admired your accomplishments, and they would not forbear to praise you, had you and France consented to achieve friendliness between you. But fate compels me, helas! to make a sorrowful and bitter confession. It was only because of your discord that the unbelievers were able to oppose me victoriously with their arms. I declare to you that I, once a king and now an exile, ruled in tears and mourning. The fickleness of force cast me into an abyss. Henceforth, the Crown is to me only a mournful adornment, and the royal turban once the decoration of my brow, will be as a veil of sacrifice, destined to immolation. O mighty princes! had you been willing to dedicate the support of your arms to Christ, the Christians of the East, who were saved by the blood of Christ, would not have been condemned to languish in grief, misery and slavery. The places long identified with the Christian faith, especially the Holy Cradle of Jesus in Bethlehem, and Zion, glorified through His miracles, would not have been subjected to the intolerable yoke of the Turks, Saracens and Persians. You, however, straying from the true course, have been supplying deadly weapons against the Christian world.

"Through a stretch of full sixty years, neither side can boast of anything but invasion and destruction of cities, the plundering or burning of villages and the imprisonment of the inhabitants of the countryside. The war was marked by alternate successes, the net result being only bloodshed. Tell me, I adjure you, which side is the winner? Let men of experience and erudition answer. If you boast of your victories, you must at least confess that their cost is too high. Should you count the French fortresses subjugated by you — all but one, by the way, lost already — your opponents might retort that it is better to preserve a country than to expand its frontiers. Illustrious princes, if I am to speak the truth rather than utter honeyed words, I shall not hesitate to declare that the motive

224

which has so far kept the flame of war alive, is your ambition to invade France. The kings of that country had, by long possession, assured themselves of the crown which they had so valiantly earned; and if the strength of a throne is based upon the obedience of its subjects, I must consider the throne of France unshakable. The hostility between the two nations has dragged on too long. In my opinion, both rivals should be implored to be satisfied with their vast territories, to cease the struggle between their peoples, so that they might be able to smite the enemies of Christ and to throw off the yoke of the Christians scattered through the Orient — those Christians who are day by day waiting for your help and humbly solicit it, O exalted princes!"

Here ended the exhortation of Leon. His audience was moved and felt deeply the urge of chivalrous sentiment and Christian duty. The English King, too, expressed his disposition towards new negotiations and willingness to postpone warlike preparations in accordance with the request of "our cousin, the King of Armenia," (nostre cousyn, le roy d'Armenye).

Leon returned to Paris, uplifted by ardent hopes. Once more parleys were held, but the desire objective, alas! was not realized. War was again declared and carried on with the usual fury and obstinacy.

Seal and signature of King Leo V of Armenia

Last Years of Leon V

Leon's later visits to the courts of European rulers were a series of glittering pageants. He was greeted at the wedding of the King of Castile as the best man, and was honored with the title of Chief Magistrate of the cities of Madrid, Villareal and Andujar. He received magnificent gifts and pensions from the Spanish monarchs, as well as those of France and England, and was everywhere promised aid in his political ambitions. None of it ever materialized, but he never ceased hoping until his death which occurred November 29, 1393, in the royal palace of Tournelle, in the Castle of St. Ouen, where he had spent his last years. His funeral was largely attended by royalty and nobility, who witnessed with curiosity the strange Armenian burial services, and the use of white mourning garb instead of black. He was buried in the monastery of the Celestins, but during the French Revolution, his ashes, together with those of other sovereigns, were scattered to the winds. His tomb was later placed in the basilica of St Denis. The epitaph thereon reads (in translation), "Here lies the most noble and excellent prince, Leon de Lysigne Fifth, the Latin King of the Kingdom of Armenia, who rendered his soul to God on the 29th day of November, in the Year of Grace, 1393. Pray for him."

Leon left two sons, Guyot, who became a military captain, and Philippe, who was ordained an archdeacon.

After the death of Leon, Jacob I, King of Cyprus, a kinsman and heir, assumed the title of "King of Cyprus, Jerusalem and Armenia." The last of the Lusignan family, Catherine Cornaro, the Queen of Cyprus, was the daughter of the Knight Marcus, grand-daughter of the Doge of Venice. On her death in 1510, the line of the Lusignans of Cyprus was extinguished, and the title of "King of Armenia" abolished.[74]

---

[74] The duration of the ten Near Eastern States of the same era;—

Frank Principality of Edessa	46 years
Latin Kingdom of Jerusalem	88 years
Principality of Tripoli, Lebanon	180 years
Principality of Antioch	169 years
Principality of Acre	187 years
Seljuq Sultanate of Roum (Konia)	213 years
Latin Empire of Constantinople	57 years
Greek Empire of Trebizond	258 years
Kingdom of Cyprus	295 years
Kingdom of Cilicia	295 years

The other captives from Sis, Katholikos Boghos and several dignitaries, had also been released. Ex-Queen Mariam, the Count of Gorigos, Cilicia and his princely wife Fimi, departed to Jerusalem and spent their latter years in the Armenian convent of Sourp Hagop (St. James). Mariam, also known as Maroun, had a daughter, Josephine Pinna, who passed away in Jerusalem in 1405. Their tomb is in the Armenian Convent.

Chapter XXXII
Armenia after the Loss of her Independence

Christians Humbled in Social Life

In 1064 — that is, nineteen years after the capture of Ani by the Byzantines, Greater Armenia was conquered by Alp-Arslan, the Seljuk. With the captivity of King Leon de Lusignan in 1375, Cilician Armenia ceased to exist. From that date down to the Russian revolution in 1917, the Armenians lost all vestiges of a political life.[75] For centuries past, especially in the Middle Ages, great numbers of Armenians have been compelled to take refuge in foreign countries.

The Arab type of conquest, though often accompanied by deeds of cruelty, was occasionally softened and tempered with some degree of tolerance, thanks to the restraining influence of the Byzantine power. The Emperors had never been so badly beaten by the successors of the Prophet as were the great kings of Persia. The tenets of the Koran too did not necessarily prescribe the extermination of "infidel" communities, so long as they continued to pay their capital taxes and made themselves useful in certain fields of occupation. As to slaves, whether captured or purchased, their status could not be questioned. Non-Moslem races were not, of course, eligible to military and political positions; they had to wear a special dress, to indicate their inferiority; their places of worship had to be of unpretentious appearance, with no bells, and to become now and then the scenes of sacrilegious deeds committed by non-Christian bands.

Turkish Domination in Armenia

After the capture of Ani Turkish domination extended to the slopes of the Caucasus Mountains, in the lands of the Kour and Arax Rivers. On the west the Seljuks advanced as far as Cappadocia in 1082, and that year the Ortokid Turks captured Jerusalem. Overcoming a sturdy resistance offered by the Armenians, Georgians, Imerethians and Mingrelians, the invaders occupied all the pasture lands, while their chieftains held sway in the towns. The forces dispatched by the Greek Emperors against them were inadequate, and served only to provoke reprisals.

Mongols and Jinghiz

Then came the Mongol incursions, spreading terror in Armenia and

---

[75] After the death of Leon, the following kings of Cyprus assumed the title of "King of Armenia"; Jacques I (1393-1398); Janus (1398-1452); Jean II (1452-1458); Charlotte and Louis de Savoie (1458-1464); Jacques II (1464-1473); Jacques III (1473-1475); Catherine Cornaro (1475-1489).

Transcaucasia. The Mongols left Central Asia in the middle of the 11th century. Advancing through the Siberian steppes and the Persian plateau, they subjected all the countries in their way. The vanquished tribes, mostly of Turkish blood and speaking the Jaghatay language, supplied the Mongol army with troops in such numbers that the original element gradually dwindled, and the chiefs alone of the Mongolian blood remained when their armies appeared in Transcaucasia. There even came a time when the Mongol language had disappeared, except in the courts of the Khans, and still later, the blood of the Mongol masters became mingled with that of their Tatar subjects, with whom they had no racial connection at all.

The exploits of Jinghiz Khan began in 1206. After subjugating the Turkoman tribes of the steppes, he destroyed the Kharizmian Moslem power in 1217, then expanded his rule over Khorassan, Persia, Iraq and northern India, almost all of which had once been parts of the Arab Empire. His generals, Soubada-Bahadour and Tchepah-Nouvian, pressed northward through Armenia and Georgia, to erect in 1223 the empire of the Kiptchaks, south of Russia, the home of former Turkish tribes of Comans and Petcheneks. Within less than twenty years from that date, Jinghiz Khan conquered also Moscow, Vladimir and Kiev, and advanced as far as Poland and Hungary, unchecked until he was beaten off in Illyria, on the eastern shore of the Adriatic, by Frederick II, the German Emperor, in 1242.

A considerable part of Armenia was already under the Mongol yoke, when Jelal-ed-Din, the Sultan of Kharizm, who had been driven from his own home by the Mongols, invaded northern Armenia and Georgia. He was slain by the Tatars in 1231, and his troops, after being merged in the Tatar army, settled themselves in the valleys. The Georgians retired into the Caucasus Mountains, and the Armenians into the massifs of Gougark and Gok-Tchay. The succeeding Mongol chiefs — Mangou Khan, Arghoun Khan, Ghazan Khan and others — ruled over all the region until the arrival in 1387 of that other great conqueror, Timour-Leng or Tamerlane, founder of the second empire of the Tatars.

Timour-Leng

The name of Timour-Leng (Timour the "Lame"), or Tamerlane, synonymous with death and devastation, spread terror among the Armenians. The inhabitants of Van, having refused to surrender, were atrociously punished after the city had been taken by storm. Thousands of them were thrown from the ramparts of the citadel. The men of Sivas, having fought for their city, were all put to the sword, save for four thousand soldiers among them, who were buried alive in a plain which has since been called Sev hogher, "the Black Ground." Children were trampled under the hoofs of the conqueror's horses, while women, tied to the tails of vicious steeds, were dragged until they perished.

The death in 1406 of the author of these frightful horrors was joyfully hailed throughout the world. By that time he had conquered the whole of Central Asia, from the Great Wall of China to Moscow. He had subjugated India, from the Indus to the Ganges, had wrested Syria from the Memlouks of Egypt, and had captured Sultan Bayazid of Turkey at Angora in 1402. The statesmanship and administrative skill attributed to him and his alleged patronage of science and art by no means counterbalanced his brutalities, such as the massacre of 100,000 prisoners, mostly Moslems, in the plain of Baghdad, or could make his death anything but a blessing to mankind.

Turkomans in Armenia

Armenia now became the prey of Turkoman dynasts: first, those of the Kaya-Koyounlou (Black Sheep) tribe, and then the Ak-Koyounlou (White Sheep). Iskender, of the Black Sheep dynasty, assumed the title of Shah-Armen. His brother and successor, Jihan-Shah dominated Azerbaijan, Van, Erivan and Georgia. It was during his rule that the seat of the supreme Katholikosate of the Armenian Church was transferred from Sis to Etchmiadzin (1441). The incumbent of the Cilician residence remained there, functioning as the Primate of that particular region. Jihangir, chief of the White Sheep line, who ruled over Mesopotamia and southwestern Armenia, had Diarbekir as his capital.

Ottoman Turks in Constantinople

Muhammed II, the Fatih (Conqueror), Sultan of the Ottoman or Osmanli Turks, captured Constantinople by storm in 1453. He treated the Armenians with tolerance and kindness. He ordered the transfer into his new capital of a large colony of Armenians and their settlement in six specified quarters within the walls. These were Kara-Gumruk, Matla, Tcharshamba, Tekké, Keumur Odalar and Akhir Kapou. Under official designation, they were originally known by the collective name of Alti-Jemaat (the Six Communities). The Conqueror regarded the Armenians as a progressive and industrious element, upon whose loyalty he could fully count. He summoned to the capital Bishop Hovakim, the Prelate of the Armenians of Brussa, a former Turkish capital, and bestowed upon him the rank of Patrik (Patriarch), with all the honors and privileges accorded to the Greek Orthodox Patriarch.

The rivalry existing between the two Turkoman tribes came to an end when Ouzoun-Hassan of the White Sheep took over the throne, proclaiming himself King of Persia, and obliterated the rule of the Black Sheep. His empire, stretching from the Oxus River to the Euphrates, included old Armenia and Georgia. This Ouzoun-Hassan, officially known as Mouzaffered-Din (1468-1478), was a follower of the Shiite sect of Islam, and wished to test his strength with Muhammed II, the conqueror of Byzantium, who belonged to the sect of the Sunni. He achieved his desire and more than he desired at the battle of Térjan in 1473, when Muhammed gave him a sound beating and put his Persian and Turkoman troops to flight.

Turko-Persian Wars

Through this victory the Ottomans became for the first time masters of a part of

Armenia, extending as far as Erzinjan. But this ill-fated country had yet to suffer many more devastations by rival foreign powers. Shah-Ismail I, founder of the Sefevi dynasty in Persia, marched against the Turks forty years later, in 1514. Forced to retreat from Erzeroum, the Persian troops devastated the entire country by fire as they left it. The Turkish army, led by Sultan Selim I, gave battle to the Persians on the plains of Tchaldiran, northwest of Tabriz and defeated them. Shah-Ismail was wounded and fled, leaving his treasure and his harem to fall into the hands of the Sultan. Tabriz was taken and the Persian Kings' gorgeous throne carted off to Constantinople. Shortly after this, Sultan Selim I (1512-1520) conquered Cilicia, Syria and Egypt, and sent Touman-Bey, the last Memlouk Sultan, to the scaffold.

The struggle between the Turks and Persians was resumed by Sultan Suleyman the Magnificent, who sent an expedition against Tahmasp, successor of Shah-Ismail. The Turks captured Van and Tabriz, but Tahmasp did not admit defeat, and by a strong counter drive, recovered Tabriz and invaded the Turkish frontiers. Suleyman thereupon led a great army in person, to capture Baghdad and retake Tabriz.

After a brief respite, hostilities between these neighboring countries again broke out under new sovereigns, Shah-Abbas I of Persia (1585-1628) and Sultan Mourad III of Turkey (1575-1595). The former was compelled to withdraw, yielding to the Turk the much-battered city of Tabriz, as well as Georgia and Persian Armenia (1585). Lala Mustapha, the Turkish general, carried away the boys and girls of Erevan, while his successor, Ferhad Pasha, erected in that city a fortress with the material brought from the ruins of churches, some of which he himself had destroyed. On various occasions during these troubles, the Armenians attempted to devise a plan for shaking off the foreign yoke; but nothing feasible developed in the secret conferences held by three successive patriarchs, Zacharia, Stphanos and Michael.

Persian Domination

The Persians, though they were an ancient race, the foremost in Oriental civilization, had adopted the Muhammedan religion. While they lived under the precepts of Zoroaster, they had developed some gentleness in manners and a sense of justice and tolerance which other warlike races and powers of Asia lacked. With the establishment of Ottoman government in Armenia, there grew up such a regime of intolerable exactions and severity that the leaders of the country in desperation sent envoys to Shah-Abbas I, imploring him to reoccupy their land and put an end to their sufferings.

Shah-Abbas seized upon this excuse to attempt a revenge for the reverses inflicted upon Persia by the Turks. He promptly invaded Azerbaijan, took the province of Ararat and advanced towards the West. He was brought to a halt, however, when confronted by a powerful force under the general, Sinan Pasha, sent against him by the new Sultan of Turkey, Ahmed I (1603-1617). Shah-Abbas, realizing his inferiority, had to give up Armenia, but not before he had burned

231

and destroyed everything within reach, reducing the country to a waste and making it useless for the victorious Turks. At the same time, he ordered the Armenians to Emigrate to Persia and settle there as colonists. The entire population of Eastern Armenia was thus deported, and those who were unwilling to quit their ancestral homes were forced to do so under the threat of whip and bludgeon, even of steel. Weary caravans did finally, after a long march, reach the banks of the Arax River, the crossing of which cost the lives of thousands. Those of the evacuees who could manage to evade their conquerors slipped away to the north, to seek refuge in Astrakhan, on the Volga River, to join eventually the preceding Armenian emigrants in Moldavia, Bukovina and Poland.

The main body of the deportees was, after a toilsome journey, herded through Azerbaijan and Kurdistan towards Ispahan, where Shah-Abbas established in 1605 an Armenian town, New Julfa, not far from his capital city. The King evinced a real sympathy towards the exiles, and as soon as they had settled in their new home, he proclaimed religious liberty within his realm. He himself occasionally attended the ceremonies of the Armenian Church, and did not tolerate any molestation of Christians by his Moslem subjects. Unfortunately, many of his successors failed to adhere to his wise policy, and under the influence of fanatical mollahs, mistreated the Armenians.

Meanwhile, war between the Persians and Osmanlis was being waged, with varying degrees of fortune. Finally, in 1620, the Turks were forced to cede eastern Armenia, including Etchmiadzin, to the Shah. The Sultan was deeply engrossed in his campaigns designed to conquer all Europe. Shah-Abbas confided the government of his new acquisitions to Armenian chiefs entitled Meliks, who enjoyed a considerable degree of independence. However, the rulers who succeeded this monarch perpetrated such acts of extortion and oppression as to prompt the Armenians to seek emancipation from the Moslem yoke.

Armenians Appeal to Europe
Israel Ori

In 1678 the Katholikos Jacob IV convened a dozen Armenian chiefs at Etchmiadzin and laid before them the suggestion of making an appeal to the Western powers for help in the liberation of Armenian provinces. In accordance with the decision of this conference, the Katholikos and several advisers set forth for Rome, where they hoped to secure the approval and sponsorship of their cause by the Pope. But the untimely death of the Katholikos at Constantinople, disheartened the other members of the delegation and prevented the execution of the project. Only one of the party, a young man of nineteen named Israel Ori, did not relinquish his mission. He went on to Vienna and thence to France, where he enlisted in the army of Louis XIV and was taken prisoner by the English. Upon his release, he went to Germany, where he gained the good will of Johannes Wilhelm, the prince of the Palatine, by promising him the crown of a liberated Armenia.

Ori returned home in 1699, intending to foment a revolution as the first step towards independence. Opposing the suggested union of the Armenian Church with that of Rome, the new Katholikos, Nahabet I (1696-1705), as well as the Patriarch of the Aghouans, Simeon IV, remained aloof from the movement. The leading secular chiefs thereupon selected the Vartabed Minas Tigranian, superior of St. James (in Gandzasar) to repair to Rome in company with Ori, with a letter addressed to Pope Innocent XII (1691-1700).

After paying homage to the Papal See, Minas and Ori proceeded to the Palatinate. Prince Johannes Wilhelm referred them to the German Emperor Leopold IV; but the latter, in turn, evaded responsibility by advising the delegates to appeal to Peter the Great of Russia. That dynamic sovereign became interested in the situation, and sent a mission to Armenia in 1700, though nothing came out of it. Disturbed by his failure to get quick action, Ori came back to Vienna, then went to Dusseldorf in Rhenish Prussia, and returned again to Russia in 1706. The Czar Peter now entrusted him with a mission to the court of the Shah; but the Persians, finally made aware of what had been going on in Armenia, merely quibbled and falsified to him in a polite way. Ori's death at Astrakhan in 1711 put an end to the activities of this clear-sighted soldier-diplomat.

Peter the Great

In 1722 Peter the Great sent an expedition to Persia and captured Derbend, but he recalled his troops just as they were besieging the fort of Shamakhi and signed a treaty of peace with the Persians. In the following years, the Czar ceded to the Turks the territories of Georgia and Qara-bagh, meanwhile advising the Armenians of those regions to emigrate into Russian territory.

Finding themselves neglected by the Russians, the Meliks now assumed the initiative. Qara-bagh arose under the leadership of the Armenian, David-beg, who had already mastered a part of the mountains. David, made cautious by Turkish interference from the West, acknowledged loyalty to Shah-Tahmasp (1722-1732), and was made Governor of Qara-bagh, now once more a Persian possession. On the death of David, friction arose over the patriotic leadership, of which the Turks took advantage to reclaim Qara-bagh. Mekhitar, the lieutenant of David, was assassinated by his rivals in 1730, and with his death the attempts of the Meliks to regain Armenian independence came to an end.

Renewal of Turko-Persian War

Taking notice that the Russian interest in the mountains of the Lower Caucasus had slackened somewhat, the Turks now resumed war against Persia. They took Erevan and Nakhjevan, and marched as far as Tabriz. After a decisive victory before Hamadan, they compelled Shah Tahmasp II to give up the provinces of Tiflis, Erevan and Shamakhi. Furious over this disastrous treaty, the Persian-Turkoman general Nadir dethroned Tahmaz II, replaced him with Abbas III, a boy, and took up arms against Turkey. A great battle fought on the banks of the

233

Akhurian River (Arpa Tchai) ended with the triumph of the Persians and the surrender to them of the Transcaucasian provinces.

The way was now open for Nadir, the general, to occupy the throne of Persia by usurpation, which he did in 1736. In recognition of the services rendered by the Armenians during the war, Nadir reestablished the privileges accorded to them by Abbas I. But hostilities with the Turks had now broken out again. Nadir-Shah advanced as far as Kars in 1743, and after a retreat to Erevan, he won a victory over the Sultan's army. Armenia, always an objective and the theatre of these quarrels, had to suffer terribly; ruins were heaped upon ruins, countrysides became deserted, and the inhabitants, exhausted by material and spiritual losses, began to depart in groups from their homeland, in a pitiful search for liberty under other skies. Nevertheless, the yearning for national independence still smoldered in the Armenian soul, despite all misfortunes. Appeals were made to Erekle II, King of Georgia (1737-1797), for the formation of a Transcaucasian state, which would include Armenia. Still brighter hopes were focussed upon Russia, where the great Empress Katherine II had seized the throne in 1762.

Katherine II

War between Russia and Persia was declared in 1768. The Empress, then heartily in favor of the independence of Armenia, had proposed that the crown of the new kingdom be given to Grigori Alexandrovitch Potemkin, the Armenophile general. The Armenians, led by their chiefs and by the Katholikos of Etchmiadzin, were preparing for a general uprising, when Ibrahim Khan, the Persian governor of the Transcaucasian districts, arrested the conspirators. The Katholikos of the Aghouans, Hovhannes X, died by poison in prison in 1768, and the others were kept in chains.

Dissension arose during those years between Ibrahim-Khan and the Persian Jevad-Khan, who was friendly towards the Armenians, and again eastern Armenia became a scene of bloodshed and devastation. In the meantime Persia, torn by civil war since the Ghajar-Turkomans' ascension to power, was on the brink of anarchy and ruin. Profiting by this state of affairs, the throne was seized in 1794 by the eunuch Agha Mohammed Khan, who invaded Qara-bagh two years later, captured Shousha and slaughtered many of its inhabitants, the majority of the victims being Armenians, because of their alliance with the local authorities.

The great power which had arisen in the North had been keenly observant of these developments. The Russian army swept southward in 1797 and pushed the Persian forces back across the Arax River, and annexed a large area of territory for the empire of the Czars. Qara-bagh did not obtain its independence, but was delivered for all time from tyranny. By the treaty of Gulistan, signed later on, in 1813, the Shah of Persia renounced in favor of Russia, all claims on the Khanates of Qara-bagh, Gandzak, Shaki, Shirvan, Derbend and Baku, also of Daghistan, Talish, Georgia, Iméréthia, Gouria, Mingrelia and Apkhazia. This treaty was violated by Fath Ali Shah, whose eldest son, the crown-prince Abbas-Mirza, after instigating the Muhammedans of Transcaucasia to revolt, undertook the invasion of the ceded area in 1826. The Russians retorted with a counter-attack, having the armed support of the Georgians and the Armenians, who were commanded by General Madatof, an Armenian, native of Qara-bagh. The Primate of the Armenians of Tiflis, Nerses of Ashtarak, later Katholikos, joined the movement at the head of a regiment. The army of Abbas was defeated and the city of Tabriz was occupied by the Russians. By the treaty of Turkmen-Tchai in 1828, Persia surrendered the Khanates of Erevan and Nakhjevan, their sole remaining possessions on the left bank of the Arax. Etchmiadzin, the spiritual capital of the Armenian people, was thus delivered from incursions, often humiliating and sacrilegious. However, the creation of an "Armenian autonomous province" under Russian suzerainty, which had been promised or hoped for, did not meet with the approval of the Viceroy of the Caucasus, General Paskevitch.

Peace with Persia was scarcely established when Russia felt it necessary to attack the Turks in the northwestern parts of Armenia. Under the Osmanlis, the yoke of subjugation had been heavy upon the Christians of western and southern Armenia. To the crushing exactions by Government officials were added the atrocities of the Kurdish tribesmen. Security of life and property did not exist. The news of a Russian campaign was therefore joyfully hailed by the harassed people, and their courage was revived to the point of aiding the army of liberation. General Paskevitch captured a dozen important towns and cities in Armenia — Kars, Akhalkalak, Akhaltzikh, Bayazid, Diadin, Alashkert, Hassan-Kala, Erzerum, Khnous, Baiburt, etc. The Czarist armies, victorious also in European Turkey, were threatening Constantinople when Western powers, intent on maintaining the integrity of the Ottoman Empire, interceded. By the Treaty of Adrianople in 1829, Russia was persuaded to restore to Turkey all her new acquisitions in Asia with the exception of the districts of Anapa, Poti, Akhalkalak and Akhaltzikh.

The Armenians were bitterly disappointed, and fearing Turkish vengeance for their adherence to the Russian cause, ninety thousand of them emigrated towards Alexandropol and adjacent Russian territories. This was a pitiful exodus; half of them died from starvation and exposure on the way. The survivors found themselves confronted with another oppression. The Russian administration, heir to the Byzantine policy of championship of the Orthodox Church, was not in sympathy with the faithful Armenian churchmen, who, being orthodox too, had clung to the autonomous existence of their own creed. Greek intolerance of bygone centuries seemed to have been transmitted in force to these Slavs of the East. Despite the periodical incitement of religious fanaticism by the Russian Orthodox clergy, the Armenians have always acknowledged their gratitude for the full security given to them within the Russian frontiers in those early days of the 19th century.

Treaty of San Stefano

War between Russia and Turkey broke out again in 1877, and the Russian Army of the East advanced as far as Erzerum. Once again the Christian inhabitants of western and southern Armenia were subjected to horrors at the hands of Kurdish hordes, raids which were instigated or connived at by the Turkish government. The Treaty of San Stefano, a suburb of Constantinople, where Grand Duke Nicholas, the Generalissimo, had halted, ended this war. It gave to Russia the following localities in Caucasia and Armenia: Batoum, Ajara, Artvin, Olti, Ardahan, Kars, Ani and Kaghziman. Erzerum and Bayazid had to be evacuated by the Russians. The Armenian generals, Madatoff, Ter-Ghoukassoff and Alkhazoff, were disappointed in their fond hope of placing their fellow-countrymen under the protection of Muscovite rule.

Following the massacres of Greeks in Constantinople in 1821 and in Chios in 1822, Sultan Mahmoud II (1808-1839) introduced some reforms in Turkey (Tanzimat — Reform Regulations). They proved to be ineffective. Soon after the Crimean War (1854-56), when Turkey had been defended against Russia by the allied forces of England, France and Sardinia, Sultan Abdul-Mejid, realizing his nation's need for European goodwill and friendship, took a further step by promulgating the Hatti-Humayoun in 1856. The massacre of Christians in Lebanon and Syria in that year and the repeated attacks on the Armenian town of Zeytoun in 1860 and 1878 demonstrated that the Ottoman Government was unable, or rather unwilling, really to reform itself and recognize the right of equality between its Moslem and non-Moslem subjects.

Zeytoun

The most provocative events occurred during the reign of Abdul-Aziz. As a French traveler, Victor Langlois, described the settling of these episodes in 1863, "The Armenians of Zeytoun form a confederation, placed *vis-à-vis* the Turks in a situation analogous to that of the Montenegrins (now merged in Yugoslavia). Ensconced on a mountain difficult of access, they have always lived outside the Sultan's authority. They have never been conquered; they wished their independence to be recognized or respected by the Turkish Government."

That Government attempted many times to abolish the autonomy, but on every occasion it met such a stiff resistance that it eventually withdrew its forces. Under a *modus vivendi* existing in 1862, the people of Zeytoun, then numbering 13,000, enjoyed certain privileges in return for the payment of tribute. Peace was disturbed, however, by Aziz Pasha, Governor of Marash, who, under the pretext of settling a dispute between the Armenians and the Turkomans of the village of Alabash, marched against the mountaineers at the head of an army of 25,000 Bashibozouks (Irregulars). After having a scout group of 70 mountain men slain and two Armenian villages burned, he met the main force of Zeytoun and suffered a crushing defeat, leaving about 6,000 dead in the cliffs and defiles, and saving himself only by headlong flight.

Appeal to Napoléon

In the hope of securing for themselves a lasting peace and the release from Marash prison of certain leaders who had been lured into custody by snares, the

236

Zeytounites in 1867 sent two delegations, one to the Turkish Government at Constantinople, the other to the French Emperor, Napoléon III. The former group were to explain the causes of the tragic occurrence and ask for redress; the envoys to Paris were to solicit the intercession of the French Monarch in their behalf, in his traditional capacity of protector of Levantine Christians. A prominent priest, a member of the Armenian delegation to France,[76] succeeded in stopping the Imperial carriage in a street in Paris by prostrating himself before it with a petition in his hand. Napoleon became interested in the matter and pleaded directly with Abdul Aziz, who was visiting France at the time and in fact, was a guest at the Tuileries. The result was that the punitive measures pplanned for the liquidation of Zeytoun and its 13,000 inhabitants by an army of 150,000 troops were countermanded.

But in 1878, during the reign of Abdul-Hamid II, and in the year of the Berlin Congress, the Zeytounites were again driven to take up arms because of exorbitant taxes imposed upon them. yielding to the intervention of the British and French ambassadors, the Sublime Porte adopted a milder policy toward the mountaineers and decreed a general amnesty for the "political offenders." However, there was a fly in the ointment; these liberty-loving cliffmen had to agree to the construction of a Turkish barrack upon the heights of their town. But the garrison proved of no avail to the Porte, for just after the Armenian massacres of 1894-1895, the Zeytounites rose up in arms again and fought off the Turkish army for four months, when the European powers once more intervened and made peaceful arrangements, through their consuls, who had visited the embattled spot.

The case of Zeytoun was but one symptom of the oppression and affliction prevalent throughout the Ottoman Empire. The emancipation of the Christian countries in European Turkey, such as Greece, Montenegro, Rumania, Bulgaria and Serbia, had been a warning to the Moslems against the creation of an Armenian state in Asiatic Turkey. The politicians of Stamboul had therefore been working towards the liquidation, by dispersal or otherwise, of the Armenian element from their soil. As one method, Kurdish tribes were instigated to swoop down from their mountain lairs whenever it suited their convenience and carry away from Armenian villages anything they could lay hands on, including young women. Deprived of bearing arms, these Christian populations of the plains could not defend themselves; but they were able at least to have their plight brought to the notice of their Church leaders in the capital of the Empire and of their fellow-nationals residing in Europe and America.

The Russo-Turkish war of 1877 offered an opportunity to the Armenians for official recognition of their cause. The Russian army of the Caucasus, commanded by General Louis Melikof, an Armenian, captured important cities in his ancestral land. When the Grand Duke Nicholas, at the head of the main army, reached San Stefano, in the outskirts of Constantinople, he took as his headquarters the mansion of the Dadians, a prominent Armenian family. The Ottoman Government then faced a grave danger. It was ready to make some

---

[76] Said to be Grigor Abardian Vardapet, assisted by Karapet Shahnazarian Vardapet.

concession in favor of the Armenians, if demanded by Russia, whom all the Christians of the East now looked upon as their saviour.[77] Since the beginning of the 19th century, the Christians of Armenia had pinned their hope solely on the "Keri" (uncle) — *i.e.*, Russia. The Russian Army was warned, however, not to advance further. The occupation of Constantinople could not be tolerated by Queen Victoria's government; the British fleet, still guarding the Eastern Mediterranean and the Suez Canal, was already at the gates of the Dardanelles.

The Porte was thus relieved and took courage; yet it had to subscribe to the Treaty of San Stefano on July 10th, 1878, Article 61 of which read;

> "Inasmuch as the evacuation by the Russian troops of the territories they occupy in Armenia and which are to be restored to Turkey might give rise to conflicts and complications detrimental to the good relations of the two countries, the Sublime Porte engages to realize without further delay the ameliorations and the reforms demanded by local requirements in those provinces inhabited by the Armenians, and to guarantee their security against the Kurds and the Circassians."

The Treaty of San Stefano would of course serve Russian interests — that was to be expected. Nevertheless, those interests did conform to justice, humanity and to the aspirations of the Christians under the Turkish rule. But the Conservative government of Great Britain, supported by Germany and Austria-Hungary, looked upon the treaty as a step towards Russian supremacy in the East. The Congress of Berlin in 1878, under the influence of the all-powerful Bismarck, the German "Iron Chancellor," deprived Russia of the fruits of her victory. Article 61 of the Berlin Treaty reads as follows;—

Treaty of Berlin

> "The Sublime Porte engages to realize without further delay, the ameliorations and the reforms demanded by local requirements in the provinces inhabited by the Armenians, and to guarantee their security against the Kurds and the Circassians. The Sublime Porte will periodically render account of the measures taken with this intent to the Powers who will supervise them."

The "joker" in the treaty is evident to the close observer. The Treaty of San Stefano would have permitted Russia to refuse to evacuate the Armenian territory occupied by it until the "reforms and ameliorations" were carried out; whereas the Berlin convention enforced Russian evacuation and entrusted Turkey with the duty of "reporting" periodically to the Great Powers as to the

---

[77] France, the traditional "protector" of the Levantine Christians, more particularly of the Roman Catholics, seemed to have relinquished this role after her defeat by Germany in 1871.

measures she had taken. Note also the replacement in the Berlin Treaty of the name of "Armenia" by the words, "provinces inhabited by the Armenians."

The Congress of Berlin was in session from June 13th to July 13th, 1878. But on June 4th, before the Congress opened its sessions, a secret agreement, known as the Cyprus accord, was entered into by Great Britain and Turkey. It provided that;—

> "In the event of Batoum, Ardahan, and Kars, or any one of those places being retained by Russia, and if any attempt should be made at any time by Russia to seize any other portion of the territories of His Imperial Majesty the Sultan, in Asia, as determined by the final peace treaty, England engages to join His Imperial Majesty in the defense of such territories by force of arms."

> "In return His Imperial Majesty the Sultan promises England to introduce such reforms (to be defined at a subsequent date between the Powers) as may be necessary for an orderly administration and the protection of the Christian and other subjects of the Sublime Porte; and in order that England may be in a position to assure the necessary means for the execution of her engagement, His Imperial Majesty the Sultan consents besides, to assign to her the Island of Cyprus, to be by her occupied and administered."

As soon as the Armenian Church authorities, Archbishop Nerses Varjabedian, the Patriarch of Constantinople at their head, learned that it was proposed to revise the Treaty of San Stefano, a delegation was sent to Berlin to ask that Armenia be placed under a Christian Governor-General, that a Christian militia be created and that there be a reorganization of the finances, courts and constabulary of the country. The delegation was composed of Archbishop Mgrditch Khrimian, ex-Patriarch of Constantinople, Archbishop Khoren Narbey of Beshiktash (Constantinople), accompanied by two lay secretaries, Minas Tcheraz and Stepan Papazian.

Chapter XXXIII
The Tragic Prelude

Armenian people Doomed

Article 61 of the Treaty of Berlin, far from promising any amelioration of the condition of the Armenians in Turkey, merely served as a pretext for inflaming the Turk's hatred of the Christian element and became, ultimately, the cause of its ruin. Sultan Hamid had cunningly instigated the idea of sending the Armenian delegation to Berlin (even with the privilege of using a secret telegraph code) in order that the Armenians, instead of being placed under the direct protection of Russia, became the nominal wards of the Six European Powers collectively. In fact, however, the Armenians by this move lost the friendship of the Colossus of the North. Furthermore, their delegates were not even given a chance to be heard in the Congress. On the other hand, Russia's huge sacrifices in the war were poorly rewarded, while Austria-Hungary gained the Turkish provinces of Bosnia and Herzegovina, which gave her supremacy in the Balkans, and an opportunity to the Germans to inaugurate their "push towards the East" (the *Drang nach Osten*).

With the signing of the Treaty of Berlin by the representatives of the Six Powers and the Ottoman Empire, there began the Turkish policy of the gradual elimination of the Armenians, the last Christian element aspiring to an autonomous existence. It is a fact that two separate Imperial Commissions, each headed by a ranking Pasha, with an Armenian assistant, made a tour in 1879 in the Eastern and Western provinces inhabited by Armenians, to investigate the local grievances. They even introduced certain reform measures, such as the induction of Christians into the gendarmerie. Seemingly, the dawn of a new era was being heralded, the Armenian activities along social, cultural, literary and educational lines seemed to gain grant impetus. But these very indications of a national or a community revival were suspiciously looked upon by the leaders of the ruling race. It was therefore not surprising that incidents and acts of misgovernment persisted. The mounted force of militia, composed of Kurds, called "Hamidiyé," after the name of the Sultan, for the defense of the eastern frontiers of Turkey, became in fact another instrument to terrorize the Christians of Armenia. Patriarch Nerses Varjabedian of Constantinople, an imposing figure upon whom the Sultan had bestowed the highest decoration and to whom the Ottoman Prime Minister and European ambassadors paid visits, made strong remonstrances and submitted reports on the misrule and hardships imposed upon his flock in their homeland. As a result on June 11th, 1880, two years after the signing of the Berlin Treaty, the ambassadors of all the Great Powers sent to the Sublime Porte an identical note, demanding the execution of the promised reforms. Then, finding the response of the Foreign Minister, Abedin Pasha, unsatisfactory, the ambassadors sent him a lengthy and documentary collective note, insisting upon immediate action towards the execution of the terms of the

61st article of the Treaty. The note, dated September 7th, 1880, was signed by Hatzfeldt (Germany), Novikov (Russia), Goschen (Great Britain), Corti (Italy), Tissot (France) and Calice (Austria- Hungary).

Diplomatic Pressure Ignored by Abdul Hamid

The Turkish reply to the note was nothing more than an acknowledgment of its receipt. Sultan Hamid was no longer concerned about such diplomatic pressure. Germany was insincere in it (as the Sultan knew) and Austria-Hungary followed the policy of Berlin. And Russia, in a spirit of revenge on Great Britain, was not particularly eager to see the carrying out of the specified reforms. Persecutions continued, systematically. The Armenians were dispossessed of their lands. They waited and waited, still hoping for the betterment of their lot through the good offices of the Powers. But their patience was of no avail; and in exasperation, they resorted, here and there, to armed resistance to the Kurds and to the iniquitous officials. A certain Kurdish chieftain, one Moussa Bey, burned Armenian villages, waylaid and robbed merchants and carried away young girls. Moved by the cries of the peasants, echoed through the Patriarch in Constantinople, the Turkish government summoned the chieftain to the capital for a pretended trial, but he was acquitted, despite overwhelming proofs against him.

Startled by the violent protestations in the European press against this travesty on legal procedure, the Sultan ordered the criminal back from his post for a second trial. This time he was "punished" by being sent on a pilgrimage to some town in Arabia, the Moslem Holy Land, for a period of time, theoretically to atone for his sins. But this faint triumph of the plaintiffs was not permitted to go unavenged. Its cost to the Armenians was the massacre, from August 21st to September 4th, 1894, of the Sassoun mountaineers, who had had the audacity to defend themselves against atrocious treatment by Kurds and Turks.

The Sultan's government was now dealing, not with rival foreign ambassadors whom he could play one against the other, but with secret societies which were exhorting their people to resistance, and occasionally supplying them with firearms. In one of his letters to his chief, the Premier, French ambassador Cambon wrote from Constantinople, "By dint of saying that the Armenians were plotting, the Armenians finally began to plot. By dint of saying that Armenia did exist, the Armenians finally came to believe in the reality of her existence, and thus, in a few years, secret societies were organized which exploited, for the benefit of their propaganda, the vices and faults of the Turkish administration; and which spread over all Armenia the idea of a national awakening and independence."[78]

Desperate Acts by Armenian Committees

Two "revolutionary" committees were formed outside Turkey; one in 1887 in Geneva, Switzerland, which was called "Hentchakist," after the title of the party's

---

[78] Documents Diplomatiques. Affaires Arméniennes, 1893-1897. No. 6.

monthly publication, the *Hentchak* (the Bell); the second, founded in Tiflis, Russia, in 1890, was called Dashnaktzoutoune (Federation), with a monthly organ, the *Droshak* (the Banner). Both parties numbered among their members fine, patriotic and sacrificing men, but rash and senseless demonstrations made by some of their leaders gave the Sultan a pretext for bloody reprisals. Moreover, the extreme socialistic doctrines injected by both parties into the movement of liberation alienated the sympathy of some friendly governments, especially Czarist Russia. However, public opinion in Western Europe and in Russia was stirred to such an extent by pro-Armenian groups and personalities that the Six Powers again united in forcing upon Abdul Hamid a project of reforms on May 11, 1895. The reforms were to be executed in the six Armenian provinces, Erzerum, Van, Bitlis, Diarbekir, Sivas and Kharput. Scarcely had the paper been signed when secret orders were issued from the palace of the "Red Sultan" for the general massacre which took place in 1895 and 1896. The number of the dead, almost all of them able-bodied men, reached 100,000 — according to the conservative estimate of the British Blue Book, 63,000.

Raid on the Ottoman Bank

None of the Powers signatory to the Treaties of reform projects dared to take any active measures in response to the cries of the victims of barbarism. A small group of Armenians in Constantinople, in desperation and in the hope of arousing Europe to action, made a daring attack on the Ottoman Bank in Galata in 1896, seized it and barricaded themselves inside, holding against the Turkish police and military forces. The young desperadoes, persuaded by the officials of foreign embassies, who guaranteed safe-conduct for each of them, gave up their conquest, and were shipped away to some European port. Even this factual demonstration failed to help the Armenian cause; but it gave the Sultan an excuse to intensify the persecution and to murder 8,000 Armenians in the Capital, under the very eyes of the Ambassadors.

It has been subsequently asserted, on good authority, that the Turkish secret police knew beforehand of the projected raid on the Bank, but the camarilla of Yildiz Palace permitted the attack, in order to inflame the Turkish populace of the Capital and to alienate the European sympathizers of the Armenians. By a coincidence, the British Fleet was at that time in the Aegean Sea, not far from the mouth of the Dardanelles.

Turkish Revolution and Constitution

Already an internal turmoil was simmering amongst the Turks themselves. During the next ten years, the secret society known as the Young Turks took the form of a party which called itself "Ittihad Vé Terakki" (Union and Progress). Its object was the overthrow of Sultan Hamid, whose despotism had exceeded all bounds, exasperating even the Moslems. Under the leadership of Niazi and Enver, the standard of revolt was raised in Macedonia in 1908. One after another, detachments of troops sent against the small band of rebels joined them, and to the amazement of all, "like leaves before the wind, the power of the Sultan was gone." The "Old Fox of the Yildiz Palace, making a quick about-face, side-stepped, proclaiming a constitutional government like that of 1876, which he himself had suspended four years after his accession."

Enthusiastic crowds of both Turks and Christians, believing that the millennium had come at last, joyfully embraced each other in public gatherings. An era of justice, equality and brotherhood had apparently dawned. The Ottoman Empire thenceforth would belong to all its citizens, without discrimination as to race or religion. However, the success of the Young Turks had to face a reaction. External and internal dangers threatened the new regime. Austria annexed Bosnia and Herzegovina, Greece seized Crete; Bulgaria, backed by Russia, declared herself independent. There were revolts in Albania and Arabia. And in the midst of all this confusion, the supporters of the Sultan set to work. The troops in Constantinople mutinied and killed some officers, declaring their loyalty to the Sultan-Khalifa and to the Sheriat (Moslem sacred laws). They renounced the new constitution and drove out the Ittihad. This counter-revolution was crushed by the arrival of the army of Macedonia, commanded by Mahmoud Shevket Pasha, who sent Sultan Abdul Hamid to Salonika, there to spend the rest of his life in the Villa Allatini. The Committee of Union and Progress was again in power, under a triumvirate, consisting of Enver, Talaat and Jemal. Javid, a Jew of Salonica turned Moslem, one of the founders of Ittihad, was entrusted with the portfolio of Finance. He was later believed to have played the traitor, selling to the Germans the control of the Baghdad Railway.

The Ottoman constitution was re-established, with Muhammed Reshad as the new Sultan-Khalifa. But the tragic destiny of the Armenians of Turkey seemed to have been inexorable. No ethnical group forming part of the Empire hailed with greater joy the proclamation of the constitution than did they. At the very moment when the Young Turks were menaced by the last abortive schemes of the Red Sultan, a new massacre took place in 1909 at Adana and in other parts of Cilicia, under the complacent eyes of the authorities, in concert with the Young Turks. Thirty thousand Armenians were butchered, cities were sacked and villages blotted out. The armed mountaineers of Zeytoun survived the holocaust, because they were prepared to exact a heavy toll before giving up their lives.

Turks Plan Extermination of Armenians in Turkey

Having entered the First World War in October 1914 on the side of Germany and her Allies, the Turkish Government decided to exterminate the entire Armenian population in Turkey, especially in the interior of the country, and thus settle the Armenian question once and for all. The war offered the best opportunity for the execution of this diabolical scheme, since the European nations were busy with the mortal conflict and therefore powerless to stop them from their intended barbarity.

The first signal was given by the arrest and deportation of the intellectuals of Constantinople and their subsequent murder in a remote area. Then followed the systematic massacres in towns and villages of all young and able-bodied

243

Armenians; the remainder, old people, women and children, were ordered to leave everything behind and march into exile. The columns started out accompanied by soldiers and by wild Kurdish horsemen who, on the way, indulged in brutality hard even to conceive, killing mercilessly and as fancy took them, and selling the women as slaves after bestially violating them.

After months of horrible torture the survivors reached the Mesopotamian desert where most of them died from hunger, thirst and the scorching sun. Over one million Armenians perished while the fiendish plan of destruction was carried out and another half a million succeeded in fleeing over to Caucasia or somehow surviving in Syria and in adjacent regions.

During those tragic days the Armenians defended themselves valiantly whenever local conditions permitted. Such examples of exceptional courage were to be seen in the self-defense of the Armenian population of Zeytoun, Sassoun, Van and Shabin-Karahissar. Remarkable was also the epic of the 4000 Armenians of Moussa-Dagh, who from the heights of this mountain drove back the Turkish assaults until they were rescued by French battleships.

Turkey profited with impunity by the crime of 1915 since Turkish Armenia was now completely evacuated of her population according to the original program of wholesale massacres and mass deportation.

"The attempts made to find excuses," says James Bryce, "for wholesale slaughter and for the removal of a whole people from the home leave no room for doubt as to the slaughter and the removal. . . . The disproval of the palliations which the Turks have put forward is as complete as the proof of the atrocities themselves." ("The Treatment of Armenians in the Ottoman Empire," by Viscount Bryce, London 1916.)

In the words of the historian Arnold J. Toynbee: ". . . the intermittant sufferings of the Armenian race have culminated in an organized, cold-blooded attempt on the part of the Turkish rulers to exterminate it once and for all by the methods of inconceivable barbarity and wickedness." ("Armenian Atrocities, The Murder of a Nation" by Arnold J. Toynbee, London, 1915.)

Chapter XXXIV
Armenian Mythology

Ara the Handsome

Recent researches and discoveries have proven that the legend of Ara, although subjected to many transformations, until the 4th and 5th centuries A.D., has its origin in Indo-European mother-sources. The Christian Armenians of the 5th century, took Ara as a man-hero, while the Armenians of the 3rd century, still pagan, had regarded him a god-like personality, or even a god.

Sammuramat is the Assyrian form of Shamiram. Erroneous statements are made by national and foreign historians, about Ara and Shamiram.

Aramis, not Barzanes, as Diodorus says, ruled Armenia at the time of the expedition of Ninus. Aramis, the king of Urartu, had formed a powerful federation of the kinglets of Armenia. He was defeated, but his successors carried on the resistance, and assured the recovery of independence for a considerably longer time.

The first mistress of Ara was an Armenian goddess: The three great ones were Nané (Sumerian-Babylonian, the Athena), Anahit, Astghik.

The ideology greatly developed in the Armenian paganism has no Avestic trait, because the ideal had no place in the Mazdeism, while in the Armenian temples of Armavir statues were erected in honor of the sun and the moon. Some scholars think to have discovered the worship of Triad (trinity) in the Armenian paganism. The edict of king Trdat, invoking Aramazd, Anahit and Vahagn, as the sources of power, and the existence in Ashtishat of the three famous temples, support this theory. The Urarteans also had three great gods — Haldis, Thiespas and Artemis. The same may be said of Zoroastrianism; Artashes cites three gods: Aramazd, Anahit and Mihr. Triad was recognized also by Semitics.

Anahit

Anahit's worship, probably borrowed from the Persians, was of paramount significance in Armenia. Iranians had no idol-worship in the beginning, but Artashes erected the statues of Anahit, and promulgated orders to worship them. The historian Berosus identifies Anahit with Aphrodite, while the Armenian mythology identifies her with the Greek Artemis. According to Strabo, Anahit's worship was dedicated to prostitution, while king Trdat extolls the "great Lady Anahit," the glory of our nation and vivifier . . .; mother of all chastity, and issue of the great and valiant Aramzd. Anahit-worship was established in Eriza, Armavir, Artashat and Ashtishat. A mountain in Sopheren district was known as

Anahit's throne (Athor Anahta). The entire district of Eriza, the Akilisene (Ekeghiats), was called "Anahtakan Gavar."

The temple of Eriza was the wealthiest and the noblest in Armenia, according to Plutarch. During the expedition of Antony, the statue was broken to pieces by the Roman soldiers. Pliny the Elderb gives us the following story about it: The Emperor Augustus, being invited to dinner by one of his generals, asked him if it was true that the wreckers of Anahit's statue had been punished by the wrathful goddess. "No!" answered the general, "on the contrary, I have to-day the good fortune of treating you with one part of the hip of that gold statue."

The Armenians erected a new golden statue of Anahit in Eriza, which was worshipped at the time of St. Illuminator. Religious prostitution, if it had existed at some previous period, seems to have been suppressed before that date.

The annual festivity of the month Navassard, held in honor of Anahit, was the occasion of great gatherings, attended with dance, music, recitals, competitions, etc. The sick went to the temples in pilgrimage, asking for recovery. The great king Artashes, taken ill, had sent an official to ask the goddess' help, but the king died before the return of the pilgrim messenger.

Mihr

Mihr or Mithra is the genius of the light of heaven and the god of truth. Derjan (Derzana) was the district where the Armenian Mithra worship was centered. Its famous temple was in the sacred village of Bagaritch. The Armenian Mithra does not seem to have become as prominent in Armenia as in Persia. Nevertheless, his name occurs frequently as a component part of many proper names, such as Mihran, Mihrdat, Mehruzhan, while the Armenian Mehian, a pagan temple, idol, altar, has also been traced to the same source. The Christian fire-festival of the Armenians is celebrated in February, a month dedicated to Mihr, and named — Mehekan. The Persian kings received a tribute of 20,000 steeds from Armenia on every festival of Mithra. Of all the Iranian deities, the cult of Mithra alone was diffused among western nations, and it waged stiff resistance against Christianity, but his vigor was exhausted in the fourth century.

Tir

The temple of Tir was a seat of oracles, as interpreter of dreams and defender of arts and letters. Tir was called the Scribe of Armazd, and disclosed the meaning of dreams as oracles. It was identified with both Apollo, the inspirer of divinations, and with Hermes, the messenger of the gods, inventor of the lyre, patron of eloquence and public treaties. One of the ancient Armenian months was called Tré, and several proper names are formed with Tir, such as Tirots, Tiran, Trdat, etc.

Tir, as an epithet of Scribe was believed to have the duty of registering the names of those about to die; hence the joke: "May the Scribe take you away" (Groghe dani kez).

Patriarch Eghishé Tourian finds connection between the pagan custom of obtaining new fire — the Ormizd fire — on New Year's eve, with Christian Candlemas, on which day, until recently, the Armenians used to build fire in the courtyard of the house, and enjoy dancing frolics around it. The Church festival, the Candlemas, is the transformation of the old Terentas, Persian Direndaz (bowman).

Astghik-Astlik

Astghik was second to Anahit in the rank of adoration among the Armenians. Her principal seat was in Ashtishat (Taron), where her chamber was dedicated to the name of Vahagn, that personification of a sun-god, her lover or husband according to popular tales.

Astghik, as the goddess of love, corresponds to the Greek Aphrodite. The rose among flowers and the dove among the birds were her favorites. Astghik's festival — the Vardavar — was celebrated at the commencement of summer. It now corresponds to the Christian Transfiguration, on which day the Armenians still hold some pagan, such as sprinkling water on each other, flying pigeons and playing games, etc. The word Astghik, meaning "little star," is the translation of the name of the Syrian goddess Beldi. A chapel was built by the Illuminator instead of the pagan sanctuary of the three gods — Anahit, Vahagn and Astghik — collectively called Vahévahian. It is now commemorated on the third Sunday of Easter, the "Sunday of the world-church" (ashkharhamadran Kiraki). According to a local tale, Astghik was in the habit of taking a bath in a stream every night; some romantic young men eager to see the goddess' exquisite beauty, lit a big fire on a nearby hill, but Astghik, in order to frustrate their design, caused the entire area, the plain of Mush, to be covered by a fog. Hence the name of Mush, which means mist, in Armenian — Mshoush.

Nané or Nanea

Nané, the daughter of Aramazd, was identified with the Greek Athenas-Pallas, the goddess of war and victory. She was recognized also in the old Iranian religion. The idol of Nané had been brought into Armenia and placed at the bourg of Til by Tigran the Great. Its worship seems to have been confined to that area alone. Its treasures, together with that of the altar of Anahit, were turned over by St. Gregory the Illuminator, to the holy service of the churches of God. The cult of Nané was of Elamite origin. "The story that Nané conceived miraculously, shows that the Mother Goddess of Phrygia herself was viewed, like other goddesses of the same primitive type, as a Virgin Mother," says Frazer.

Barshamin or Barshimnia

This was one of the idols transported by Tigran from Mesopotamia into Armenia, and housed in the village of Thordan, in Daranaghi. The brilliantly white idol was made of ivory and crystal, wrought with silver.

The name Barshamin is derived from the Phoenician Ba-al-shamin, in Aramaic form, meaning "lord of heavens," like the Bel of the Babylonians.

Vahagn

Vahagn, as national god, soon found himself at the side of Aramazd and Anahit with whom he founded a "triad." When Zoroastrian ideas were pervading Armenia, superseding the gods of the country, there was so much vitality in Vahagn's worship that Mithra himself could not obtain a firm foothold in that land, in the face of the popularity of his native rival.

Historian Khorenatsi's report of an ancient song gives a clue to his nature and origin:

> In travail were heaven and earth,
> In travail, too, the purple sea!
> The travail held in the sea the small red reed.
> Through the hollow of the stalk came forth smoke,
> Through the hollow of the stalk came forth flame,
> And out of the flame a youth ran!
> Fiery hair had he,
> Ay, too, he had flaming beard,
> And his eyes, they were as suns!

Other parts of the song, now lost, said that Vahagn fought and conquered dragons, hence his title Vishabakagh, "dragon reaper." He was invoked as a god of courage, later identified with Herakles. He was also a sun-god, rival of Baal-shamin and Mihr.

The Vahagnian song was sung to the accompaniment of the lyre by the bards of Goghten (modern Akulis), long after the conversion of Armenia.

The stalk or reed, key to the situation, is an important word in Indo-European mythology, in connection with fire in its three forms.

The name, originally Verethragna, the god of victory in Avesta, turned into Varhagn (the Zendic th becoming h in Arsacid Pehlevi), later on to take the form of Vahagn.

248

Vahagn was identified with the Greek Heracles after the latter's image was brought into Armenia by Tigran the Great. The priests of Vahévahian temple, who claimed Vahagn as their own ancestor, placed the statue of the Greek hero in their sanctuary. All the gods, according to the Euhemerian belief, had been living men; Vahagn likewise, was introduced within the ranks of the Armenian kings, as the son of Erouand (6th century B.C.), together with his brothers — Bab and Tiran. In the Armenian translation of the Bible, Heracles worshipped at Tyr, is named Vahagn.

Gissaneh (Kissaneh) and Demeter-Demetr

Agathangelos ignores the existence of these two idols in Taron. On the other hand, there must have been some ground for the tale about the fierce struggle of paganism, as reported by Hovhan (John) Mamikonian who lived in the seventh century.

Sandaramet

Sandaramet (Spenta Armaiti), one of the seven Amshaspents (the archangels), of the Mazdeian religion, was the daughter of Ahuramazda, representing the divine type of the virtuous woman. She was the spirit of piety and modesty.

The Armenian translator of the two apocryphal books of the Maccabees has identified Spandaramet with Dionis (Bacchus), a fact leading to the presumption that Spandaramet was regarded in Armenian paganism not as a goddess, but a masculine deity, lacking the moral traits of the Mazdeian Amshaspent. Being, in Avestic concept, the Spirit or the embodiment of the earth, Spandaramet, in the form of Sandaramet, became synonymous with earth, especially the underworld or hell. The word, in the form of Sandarapet, later on, came into use, meaning the chief or god of the hell.

The relation of this deity with Bacchus, the god of wine, is explained by the fact that wine, the most excellent product of earth, was an indispensable element in the mysteries of pagan festivals. Hence, the god presiding over the nightly drinking bouts would certainly have his lewd votaries male and female, — the bacchants and the bacchantes.

National and Foreign Gods

Nature-worship, such as the adoration of the sun and stars, was older in Armenia than the idol-worship. The statues of the sun and moon, erected in Armenia, as reported by Khorenatsi, should be classified among national idols, in the opinion of H. Gelzer. The seven temple-altars, the pantheon of the Armenian deities, seem to have been located in Bagavan (the town of gods), where the great national festival was celebrated in pomp, at the beginning of New Year, on the advent of the month of Navassard (New Year). Some writers erroneously believed that this celebration took place in Ashtishat or Vagharshapat.

Iranian Influence

The ancient Armenian religion was a form nearer to that of the Arsacid-Parthian kings. From that source have been borrowed the following:

Armazd, without its distinctly Iranian features.

Mihr-Mithra.

Spandarmet-Spenda-Aramaiti.

Vahagn-Verethragna.

Tir or Ture-Tir.

Anahit-Nahit.

These gods were not worshipped in Armenia, in the sense of their Iranian prototypes, there being neither Magi nor fire-worship in Armenia. There was no real identity between the old Armenian Pagan cult and the Sassanian Mazdeism, considering that the doctrine of Zoroaster was not in favor of idols.

Hellenic Influence

Idols were introduced into Armenia through Hellenic influence. Greek statues and even temple-priests were transported there by Artashes and Tigran the Great. The following are the gods of Armenia, identified as of Greek origin by the Greek translation of Agathangelos:

Aramazd — Zeus-Pater or Jupiter.

Mihr-Hephaestus.

Anahit-Artemis.

Nané-Athena.

Astghik-Aphrodite.

Tir-Apollo-Vahagn.

Vahagn-Heracles.

Syrian Influence

The deities of Syrian origin were:

Barshamin.

Astlik (Astghik).

Nané.

It was a custom among the Armenians to go on pilgrimage to the Syrian mother-goddess, Tharada, at Herapolis, offering her precious stones. The Armenian word kourn (pagan priest) is of Syrian origin.

Heroes and Legends

Artavazd.— The life of Artavazd, the son of Artashes, is wholly legendary; those legends were partly collected by Khorenatsi from the songs of bards and probably also from the records of the chief-Priest Oughub (Olympius). Artavazd's role has been one of fierce struggle against the Median tribe (the Mar) and their chief Arcam or Arcavan. Tigran the son of Erouand, is said to have killed Azhdhak, the king of the Medes, the grandfather of Cyrus, carried away his wife, Anoush and children into Armenia, and settled them at the foot of Mount Ararat.

This family was known in popular songs of the ancient era as Vishabazounk — the issue of dragons, because "Azhdahak means dragon in our language" says Khorenatsi. The progeny of the dragon, as related in the songs of the Goghten Canton, stole the child Artavazd, an implacable enemy of the Vishabazounk, now represented as demons, persecuted them relentlessly, to the point of extermination of the race.

Yeznik, the Armenian erudite and theologian of the fifth century, relates that, according to old tales, Artavazd was "detained by demons and is still alive, and that he will some day come out and dominate the world." Yeznik adds, "the infidels (the idolators of Armenia) cling to the superstitious hopes, like the Jews, who are bound to the expectation that David is to come, to construct Jerusalem, to gather together the Jews, and to reign over them."

Artavazd, a killer of dragons and their race, could not have been a person of vicious or demented type. His wars against the Mar people, or the dragons, remind us of the struggle which Feridun wages against the demons of Mazandaran, whose people, like the Mari colony of Ararat, were the issue of a foreign and savage tribe.

The Avesta (The sacred book of the ancient Zoroastrian religion) mentions Ahavazdah (Artavazd), an "immortal" personality, fighting a wild tribe of Touranian origin. J. Darmesteter referring to this says that in the Armenian

251

legend-songs, there is a king, Artavazd, who cannot die. Could not the immortal Ashavada have been adopted in Armenia? Patriarch Tourian answers the question of the French orientalist, by stating that Artavazd can positively be identified with the Ashavazd of the Avesta, who, as one of the undying souls, will wake from his sleep, to re-organize the world, and to carry out the work of Salvation, the miraculous work of Frashokereti (hrashakert in the Armenian).

The Avesta has also the tale of Azhidahaka, the evil spirit, killed by Thraetaona (Feridoun). From this story their springs the one of Zohak, the tyrant, the same Azhdahak finally became identified with Azhdahak (of Khorenatsi), the grandfather of Cyrus who was killed by our Tigran Erouandian in the fifth century B.C. According to Khorenatsi, "Persian worthless and foolish fables relate that a certain Feridoun (Hrouten) bound Purask-Azhdahak in bronze fetters and carried him to the Demavend mountain (in Tabaristan); that Feridoun fell asleep on the road and was dragged by Pursab to the hill; that Feridoun, awakening, carried Purasb into a cave of the mountain, chained him and placed himself before him as a barrier, where he still remains, with no power to devastate the world. A similar tale existed about Artavazd, with the addition that watchmen incessantly strike at the anvil, in order to remind us of the assurance that ironmongers harden the links of the chain.

According to a tale until recently prevalent among the Armenians, Mehr (Mihr), an intercessor deity, devoted to the work of redemption, had to be detained and chained in fetters.

Shamiram (Semiramis) and Ara the Handsome

The date, even the existence of Shamiran have been matters of conjecture among the scholars. Some of them put her as far back as 2000 B.C. as the wife of Ninus, the founder of Nineveh; others bring her down to the fourteenth or eighth or sixth centuries B.C.

Prof. Lehmann-Haupt, by putting together the results of archaeological discoveries, has arrived at the following conclusion: Semiramis was, probably, a Babylonian, for it was she who imposed the Babylonian cult of Neb or Nebu upon Assyrian religion. On a column discovered in 1909, she is described as "a woman of the palace of Samsi-Adad, king of the world, king of Assyria . . ., king of the Four Quarters of the World." Ninus was her son. The dedication shows that Semiramis occupies a position of unique influence. She waged war against the Medes and the Chaldeans. The legends probably have a Median origin.

Avoiding marriage, in order not to lose the power, she selected the attractive young men of the army, made love with, and destroyed them. This story is parallel with the Babylonian (Sumerian?) fiction, where Gilgamesh, the hero, rejects the goddess Ishtar, who had murdered all her lovers.

Popular etymology which connected the name of Semiramis with the Assyrian Summat, "dove," seems to have first started the identification of the historical

Semiramis with the goddess Ishtar and her doves. Her irresistible charm and sexual excesses (belonging only to the legends), and other features of the story, all bear out the view that she is primarily a form of Astarté.

The stories concerning Semiramis were later transported to Armenia. To her is ascribed the founding of Van, which tell of the enterprises of Menuas, Argistis and others, but do not mention any Shamiram, while every stupendous work of antiquity by Euphrates or Iran, seems to have been attributed to her.

The legend about the marriage proposed to the Armenian king Ara the Handsome, the rejection, and his death in the ensuing battle, are, partly, variants of the fiction of the Babylonian hero, Gilgamesh. Similar to them are the tales of Aphrodite and Adonis, and Cybele and Addis. In both cases the victims of the goddesses had been brought back to life by their killers. The temple at Zela, Anatolia, dedicated to Anahit, was built on a knoll, called Semiramic. Such hillocks as that one were, traditionally, the graves of the lovers of Shamiram.

Ara regained life, tradition says, at the village of Lezk, by the genii who licked his wounds. The village, situated near Van, on an eminence, had had a pagan temple, later replaced by the chapel of the All-Saviour (Amenaprkitch). Some connection is said to exist between the same Lezk, and the Armenian word lizel meaning *to lick, caress with the tongue.*

In the Armenian literature, Ara often has been depicted as a model husband, who, despite threats and allurements, remained loyal to his consort Nouard, setting a royal example to marital happiness, and confirming the traditional virtues in the Armenian family life.

Haik and Bel

Haik is regarded as the eponymous ancestor of the Armenian people. Bel or Belus, supreme god of the Babylonians and Assyrians, is identified with Nimrod or Neprot, who "was a mighty hunter before the Lord." (Gen. X.9). . . . Neprot demanded that he should be worshipped, but Haik, "brave and famous among the mighty," (in the words of Khorenatsi), disobeyed Bel, and departed with his family from Babylon toward the north, to Ararat. Bel followed him with an army, was engaged in war, and killed by Haik. This name became synonymous with "mighty one, the powerful, the athletic," haikapar, an adverb in the sense of *mightily, heroically.*

In the Armenian translation of the Bible, the constellation Orion is called Haik. "For, the stars of heaven and of Orion shall not give their light," (Isaiah, 13.10). "Canst thou bind the sweet influence of Pleiads, or loose the bands of Orion?" (Job, 38.31).

The canton of Hark in Armenia, where the family of Kaik or his predecessors, the "House of Thorgom" had settled, according to Khorenatsi, was also the place where the tyrant Bel was buried. The name Hark, meaning 'Fathers' in Armenian, had led ancient writers to certain conclusions, which are now contested. Some authorities believe that Hark is another form of Erech, one of the four cities founded by Nimrod. "And the beginning of his kingdom was Babel, and Erech, and Accad, and Calneh, in the land of Shinar," (Gen. 10.10). Erech in cuneiform inscriptions, Uruk or Arku, is the modern Varka, situated south-east of Babylon. Due to the multitude of ancient graves, the place was once regarded by Persians as a holy necropolis — city of the dead.

The story about Haik and Bel, Vahagn and Barsham of Syria, and Aram and the Barsham of Babylon, are the different phases of victorious struggles against Assyria and Babylon, by the forces of Aramé and other Urartean kings. They were also the echoes of the successful wars conducted against the Medes or the Mari, by Artashes (Artaxias) and Tigran the Great.

Chapter XXXV
The Feudal System in Armenia

I

A Vital Force

Feudalism was a powerful social and political organization in Armenia. Originating in remote antiquity, it survived the kingdom and the loss of independence. Its influence was both beneficial and baneful. It was one of the directing forces of its destiny, the other being the geographical determinism.

The conception of royalty in Armenia was opposed to the absolutism in the Persian, Byzantine and Arab empires, in which the autocracy was displayed in pomp and etiquette, the king remaining at a distance, as a divinized being — inaccessible, invisible, God's vicar. In Armenia the king was only the highest lord, "he who gives orders." King Trdat was described as "daring, magnanimous, vigorous, valiant and brave warrior." (Agathangelos). King Varazdat was "strong, robust," while his son Khosrov was physically insignificant, and known by the surname "kotak" — short of stature. Arshak II had a swarthy skin, excessively hairy.

The nakharars or princely lords of the country, constituted the most solid structure of Armenia. They were the real owners and masters. From the fourth and fifth centuries to the eighteenth the vestige of certain Armenian nakharars still lingered in some counries. On top of the class were the four bdeshkhs or satraps of the frontier princedoms, Nor Shirakan; Assorestan; Aruastan and Masqets. These princes were the descendants of formerly independent rulers. The nakharars maintained armies of their own, of various numbers, — thousands or ten thousands. They were called "lords of legions and flags." The entire country was known as the "Seigniorage of the kingdom of the Armenian land." The strongest of the nakharars were those of the Mamikonian, Sewnie, Bagratuni, and Ardzruni houses. The chief of the tribe or house was called ter, tanuter or nahapet. His authority, extended over all the inhabitants of the domain, was called also Ishkhanoutune, dynasty or dominion. The successor of a nahapet was called sepouh, patrician or knight. He helped the chief in councils, and possessed a seal. Under the oldest dynasty, the Arshakuni, only the son of the king succeeded to the throne. Later on, under the Bagratids, the brother was entitled to the right. The second rank of the society consisted of the inferior nobles, known as the ostaniks or azats (the free). The nakharars and the azats formed the principal armed forces of the country. They were identical with the knights of the West. They were called the "army of the noble legions" (azatagound banak) or "noblemen's troops" (azatazorq). In connection with a battle waged against the Persians in 371, at the foot of Mount Npat, Phaustus of Byzantium says: "When the heroic Armenians of the nobility armed with spear, overthrew the Persian lances, they shouted — 'Let it go to King Arshak, the brave!' and for every decapitated enemy they said: 'be a victim for Arshak!' " This was in revenge of the tragic death of the Armenian king in the Persian fort of Oblivion.

Land Ownership

Contingent hereditary possession of land, the fief, was called khostak. There were three kinds of land ownership: (1) Hereditary (haireniq); (2) Grants (pargevanq); (3) Acquired by purchase (gsakaginq). Freehold possessions, although hereditary, were subject to prestation — payment, and oath, for specific services of vassalage (dzarayoutune). A king might be dependent on, or a vassal of, another monarch for certain domains.

Classes of Service

Serfdom of a peasant to a nobleman existed in Armenia. The Armenian feudal organization had two kinds of service, — one, the service of nobles, of azats to the nakharar, and the service of nakharars to the king or to the satrap. Second, the peasant's service to his lord, by payment in cash or in kind. The land did not belong to the feudatory, who held by feudal tenure.

The vassal's bond in Armenia was similar to that in the West.

Acts and symbolic phrases and the taking possession of a princely domain, or of a high hereditary rank, were accompanied by royal investiture. The acknowledgement of fealty of a vassal to his lord or suzerain reminds us of the usage in Western Europe. The Mamikonian prince, Mushegh (Mushel) put his hand in the hand of the king, Pap, and took the oath.

The young Artavazd Mamikonian, the son of Vatché, the army commander, succeeded his father. He was called to the presence of the king, to be honored by the insignia borne by his dead father, and by promotion as the chief of the cavalry, because he was the representative of a famous lineage. All valiant men in his family had perished in the last battle. The command of the army was entrusted to Arshavir Kamsarakan, prince of Shirak and Arsharuniq, as well as to Andovk, prince of Sewniq, because both were married to Mamikonian princesses. The Katholikos Vrthanes, in concert with the king, charged Arshavir and Andovk with the duty of educating the young Artavazd, "so that he may be able to fill the place of his ancestors, and to accomplish great deeds for Christ, the Lord of all, as well as for his own Arshakuni lords." He had to protect the members of the House, and to follow their traditional sponsorship of widows and orphans.

The number of nakharars originally had been 900 or 400,[79] but many of them were assimilated in stronger ones. A parchment discovered by the Katholikos Sahak in the archives of Ctesiphon, has seventy nakharars listed, according to their official place of honor. Each one had to supply fighting men in case of need,

---

[79] According to N. Adontz the number should be put at around 50.

the figures varying from 50 to 20,000. The feudal chiefs were also invested with public functions, similar to the fief-offices of the West. The Bagratids enjoyed the honor (pativ) of crowning the king. Hence the exalted title, tagadir aspet, — "the knight who places the crown." The history Vardan tells us that the Byzantine emperor Basil I, the "Macedonian," sent an officer, Nicetas, to King Ashot Bagratuni, to remind him of his own Armenian origin, and to ask for a royal crown (876 A.D.).

Positions of Power

The head of the Mardpet family was the holder of another eminent position — Mardpetoutune, the administration of the royal household, the custody of the royal fortresses and the superintendence of the treasury. A mardpet, being in charge of King's household, was necessarily an eunuch. Under the Arsacids the Mardpet was called also "father of the king," hair-tagavori. He sat at the royal banquet above all the other nakharars.

The protection of the king's person and the command of his guard were the prerogatives of the Khorkhoruni princes, called the malkhaz, always equipped with lance and sword. The Gnuni family furnished the Hazarapet of Armenia, the minister of Financial and Rural Economy. Both the Khorkhoruni and the Gnuni houses were among the first to disappear from the scene.

The function of a hazarapet was higher in Persia than in Armenia. It was a sort of minister of the Interior, (not military); in fact, he was the Prime Minister or the Grand Vizier. The sparapet, in the Pehlevi spahpat, was a general, whose function, however, was hereditary, while the zoravar-general, was the factual commander in a given period.

The position of the Great Judge of Armenia was the appanage of the Katholikos, supreme head of the Church. He was also the authority of codifying the laws, while the nobles followed custom and tradition, and exercised their own rights over their vassals and the peasants.

Minor nakharars, the speouhs and other azats were charged with duties of lesser importance, such as those of senekapet (chamberlain), vorsapet (master of the hounds), takarapet (cupbearer), zinakir (squire, swordsman), shahakhorapet (master of the horse), karapet (the herald or precursor).

Clergy

The king was a nakharar himself, but more powerful than the rest. Only a lord, endowed with the hereditary rights of leadership. Airarat, the domain of the Arshakunis, was the largest and richest principality of Armenia. The members of the royal family, the sepouhs, assisted by those of the nakharars, the azats, formed a social class, and filled military, civil and judicial positions. The azats were exempt from corporal punishments for a crime or offence, but subject to payment of amends and to imposition of penitence. The clergymen were classified as azats. Justice in Christian Armenia was administered under Canon laws enacted by Church councils, such as those of Shahapivan and of Douin. The priests received fiefs in heredity. The canon law deprived ignorant and incapable priests of the right of possession of land and water for irrigation. The Church was enriched by donations in addition to the incomes of the pagan period. Peasants were required to pay tithes in cash or in kind. Judicial functions added to their income. The advantages of the clergy attracted low classes to the holy orders, so, priests and monks increased their numbers, stirring the resentment of the king and the princes. King Pap, an enlightened leader, took measures to restrain the excessive power of the Church. This is the main reason for the imputation of numberless vices to Pap by religious historians. Many a nobleman put on clerical garb, in the beginning of the Middle Ages. The function of the Katholikos and bishops was enormous. Under the Arsacids only the descendants of Gregory the Illuminator and of Bishop Albianos were eligible to the patriarchal throne. Katholikos Zaven, of the latter stock (377-381), "A wicked and envious" man, according to Phaustus, but "shining with virtues" according to other biographers (*Sopherq* by Alishan) wore the costume of higher nobility with short embroidered robes, and furs of ermine; and instructed the clergy to put on military vestments, instead of the monastic garb, long robes and skirt descending to the heels.

The artisans, as well as the shinakans (peasants) belonged to the class of anazats (non-free) or ramiks (plebeians).

Serfdom

Serfdom existed in Armenia. It was hereditary. According to an inscription at Sanahin, a certain nobleman donated to the monastery thirty peasants of Alashen Village, and one holy banner in white color. The serfs were attached to the soil. Their life was hard and toilsome, but they could be released on certain conditions. They were transferred by sale or gift or some contributions, in work or in koravar (field labor) for the chief.

The ramiks were subject to corporal punishment for crime or any misdemeanor. "The shinakan shall receive more strokes." He was sent, as a penalty, to serve in leper hospitals. On the other hand, the shinakan enjoyed certain rights and economic advantages. He paid as tax much less than the inferior nobleman, in contrast to the peasant of Russia and Georgia in the 14th century whose condition was much more painful. There the superior class paid four to ten times more than the serf. The peasants became well-to-do, even relatively rich. Under the Church laws, adopted by the council of Douin the priests could purchase land with no bond of heritage. Uninherited land and personal property were transferred, as donation or for payment, to the "Brotherhood of the Church," but not to shinakans.

The shinakan enjoyed certain personal liberties; he could not be forced to contract marriage against his wish. He took part in the deliberations of national interest. When King Tiran was blinded by the Persians (350), a General Assembly

258

was convoked for the adoption of certain resolutions. The meeting was attended by great satraps, ancients, governors, dynasts, nobles, generals, judges, chiefs, princes, except commanders (zoravars) and even by shinakan ramik (plebeian) peoples (351 A.D.). "Come," they said, "let us console each other, and defend ourselves and our country, and revenge our king." Thereafter, almost everybody in the land consulted with each other to find aid and assistance. Lazar says: "Vassak, the perfidious prince, never ceased writing to princes, to shinakans and to priests of Armenia." The chiefs of the class of the peasantry together with nakharars, came to Katholikos Nerses, complaining of the interminable wars waged by their king Arshak against the Persians.

In France and Western Germany of the Middle Ages, the feudal lord was satisfied merely by collecting the contribution of the peasants, in cash or in kind. In Eastern Germany and Poland the peasant was required to furnish his feudal lord with gratuitous man-power, too.

II

Peasantry Defended by Church

The system in Armenia was in accord with the first of these types, and yet, Church leaders in Armenia sought more alleviation of the economic life of the peasants. The Council of the village of Ashtishat (Taron), in 351 A.D., presided over by Nerses Katholikos directed all those in power not to over-burden (their men) with unlawful demands, and not to oppress them. The feudal chiefs were reminded that the laborers too had a lord in heaven. The Katholikos, likewise advised the servants to remain in proper obedience to their masters.

Armenia possessed a transit commerce, and some domestic barter business. However, under the Arsacids and the Arabs trade was mainly in the hands of foreigners. The captives carried away from Armenia by King Shapuh II of Persia in 368 A.D. were mostly Jews and partly Greeks and Syrians.[80] Many trade words

---

[80] The history of Phaustos, invaluable in many respects, gives inordinately high figures, due probably to some later copyist's caprice. Here is a list of Armenian and Jewish families deported by Shapuh from the various Armenian cities into Persia.

Artashat	9,000 Jewish	40,000 Armenian
Vagharshapat	-	19,000 Armenian
Erouandashat	30,000 Jewish	20,000 Armenian
Zarehavan	8,000 Jewish	5,000 Armenian
Zarishat	14,000 Jewish	10,000 Armenian
Van	18,000 Jewish	5,000 Armenian
Nakhjuan	16,000 Jewish	2,000 Armenian

used in the Armenian are of Syrian origin, such as: shouka (market), khanout (shop), caghout (colony). More than four centuries earlier (77 B.C.), 300,000 persons had been transplanted from Caesarea and vicinity into Armenia by Tigran the Great.

III

Currency

The need for metallic currency or coin was felt during the Arab conquest when the population suffered economic depression, due to the fiscal disturbances. "The infernal and insatiable avarice of the enemy was not satisfied by devouring the flesh of the Christians, the flower of the land, nor by drinking their blood. . . . All Armenia is suffering horribly because of the absolute lack of cash." (Ghevond). For that reason a class of citizens engaged in business, and consisting of both Armenians and strangers, came into being. The moral concepts and the interests of this new class were not in accordance with the spirit of feudal Armenia. "A money lover," says Thomas Ardzruni, "would rather have his neck wrung than give away one dang (mite, obol). If he sees the sun radiating its rays, by God's order, for the good of the world, he would say in his face, 'why don't you shed gold for me instead of light?' If he came upon a clear spring water he would say: 'I am not thirsty, and will not drink of your water, make silver flow for me.' " The same author believes that the city of Douin was destroyed by the earthquake because of "the stone heart of its population." Other contemporaries declared that business centers were all swelled and saturated by all sorts of impurities. The Katholikos Nerses, writing to the Bishops, rebuked "the hateful barbarous Nestorians who came to live in our country for commercial profits, and now, through their wicked, dirty and cursed profession, they are affecting our souls." The Katholikos pointed particularly to the ecclesiastics who had become dishonest merchants and usurers, instead of serving the church they seek gain." Hovhannes Mandakuni, the Katholikos of Ani, pronounced a malediction upon priests who were engaged in selling and purchasing.

Artisans in Metal

From the historian Ghazar of Parb we gather that a certain amount of business was carried on in mining products — such as gold, copper, iron, and precious stones. Artists and artisans of Armenia were famous for superb works of ornaments made of metals, inlaid articles, vestments embroidered in gold, tiaras. Smelting of gold and silver and mining of copper and iron were well-known in certain districts. The companions of St. Hripsimeh and St. Gayaneh coming from the West into Armenia, being all destitute, had no means of livelihood. One among them was efficient in the art of making glass trinkets, and small glassware, and collar-chains of glass. Through the sale of such articles the whole group's daily subsistence became assured. Professor N. Marr believes that the artisans of the country, constituting the majority of the urban population, had professional Brotherhoods or Unions.

Slavery

There was also a class of slaves in Armenia, that of strouks, the lowest social element, according to Anania Shirakatsi. This class consisted of war prisoners. The nakharars, as well as the monasteries, owned slaves, some of them purchased as chattels, others condemned as bankrupts. The status of the class was recognized by Church councils. The strouks were employed in agricultural labor or domestic service.

Money-Lending

Usury, the practice of lending money at exorbitant interest, was introduced into Armenia by strangers. The Katholikos Mandakuni says; "While the farmer prays God for rain to fertilize the seed and assure prosperity, those who thrive on usury wish for the people to suffer misery, famine and taxation. At the time of lending money the face of the rogue is joyful, but when the day comes to collect interest he has no sympathy for the debtor, the poor, dismayed debtor, he is not moved by his oaths and supplications, but remains implacable, unyielding, fiendish. The debtor is a slave in the eye of the creditor."

It should be noted that the urban population of Armenia was numerically much less than the rural. There were few large cities. The term qaghaq (qalag) originally meant a fort or rampart, around which rural communities grew up, The system of feudalism under the rule of lords or nakharars was anterior to that of monarchy. It was due to the decomposition of the older system of clans or tribes.

The terminology of the ancient language was adapted to the new social forms. The word azg now meaning nation or people, primarily designated a consanguineous group, houses or families of nakharars or the population of their domains. The word toun (doun), meaning house, designated a territorial unit — from the habitation of a clan, and later a state, — the Arshakuni toun or state — the state of the Armenian Arsacids. The original tanouter, chief of clan, became nahapet, the chief of a line, a ruler, a king.

The influence of the semi-feudal monarchy of Parthia was so great in Armenia as to create some confusion between the two peoples. Many terms of Armenian feudality are of Parthian origin, such nakharar, nahapet, sepouh, azat.

Three principal ethnic sources which participated in the formation of the Armenian seignorial class were attached to the Urarteans, Armeno-Phrygians and Parthians. The Armeno-Phrygians had a powerful aristocratic organization, according to A. Meillet.

Aristocracy

But the first fruits of the Parthian feudality could not prevail in Iranian surroundings, which were more favorable to the autocratic absolutism of the

Sassanids than to the aristocratic regime of the Arsacids. On the contrary, they found unparalleled conditions for prospering, in Armenia, a country naturally adapted to partition. The Armenian society became a powerful hierarchic organization, which is revealed to have been the oldest and the firmest feudality of history. This is how the nakharars asserted their exalted blood or nobility even before the kings. Manuel Mamikonian wrote to the King Varazdat, of a collateral branch of Arsacids: "We are your equals, of an extraction even nobler than yours." (Phaustos) Mushegh Mamikonian did not put away his sword before entering the tent of the Persian King. "Since my boyhood," he said, "I was brought up among kings, just like my ancestors and forefathers." (Sebeos). Another young nakharar, Shavasp Ardzruni said to Shapuh, the son of the Persian king: "I am of royal blood." Kings of Persia married the daughters of nakharars and gave them their daughters in marriage. Parantzem, the daughter of Andovk, nakharar of Sewniq, became the wife of King Arshak. King Tiran gave his daughter, Eranyak, in marriage to the Bagratid prince Trdat, the son of Sembatuhi, daughter of the Great Sembat. Trdat was brave and bold but short of stature and of pitiable appearance. This proved an unhappy marriage. Eranyak hated her husband, "she treated him with contempt and always bewailed that she, a beauty and of higher birth, was forced to co-habit with a man of disagreeable countenance and inglorious descent. One day, Trdat, growing angry, gave her a violent beating, cut off her blond hair, tore out the ringlets, and ordered her dragged away from the apartment. He then rebelled and passed to the strong parts of the land of the Medes. Arriving in Sewniq he heard of the death of (King) Tiran and remained there upon receiving that news." (Khorenatsi II.63).

The nakharars were jealous of their personal dignity and official rank in state functions. Besides blood relationship and old ancestry, they took pride in their personal valor and courage. The historian Matthew of Edessa, after recounting Gagik's fearlessness, adds: "that his men longed for nothing else but combats." Vardan Mamikonian said to his troops: "Nobody will believe that we have fled for fear of iron, that any member of our race has ever dreaded, that this family of ours, always devoted to the good of its neighbors more than for itself will forsake you; all this you know well, either through histories or by tradition of princes." (Ghazar). Shapuh, the Ardzruni general, after assuring his soldiers that he would put the Byzantines to flight, "fixed several cuirasses one on top of the other and striking all with his sword, shivered them into pieces." (Matthew of Edessa). Hovhannes Katholikos quotes the following lines from a letter sent to the Byzantines by Mushegh Mamikonian, "You wished to assassinate me treacherously. I tell you, do not awaken the sleeping lion, or the fox, forgetting his instincts. Otherwise, he who defeated 80,000 men, can also exterminate 70,000 of them. . . . Victory does not depend on the number of the soldiers; it is in the hands of God." There are many cases in which a few Armenians defeated the nation's enemy. Some of the military epics are obviously exaggerated, but whatever the real facts may have been, nakharars on many occasions have repulsed invading armies of much greater force than theirs. This superiority was due to several factors. Above all, the equipments of the noblemen's troops were better and could be used more effectively. They fought covered with shields — men and horses. A certain nobleman and his chestnut colored horse were so clothed in iron that the people took him and his mount for a metallic statue, whose eyes only remained open. The fighting apparel of Babik, prince of Sewniq, is described as follows: "Having taken his armament and decked his superb stature with a shining royal breastplate adorned with pearls, he put on a helmet topped by a tiger's head, and girded his waist with the sword. Then throwing a golden shield upon his left shoulder, and a strong lance in his right hand, he sprang upon his black steed and dashed on the enemy." (Stepanos Orbelian).

Warrior-Nobles

The Armenian warrior of the early fourth century is pictured by Phaustos as the man of the elite class "accustomed to the fatigue of combats, armed in all places, — lances, swords and hatchets. . . , expert archers whose strokes were sure. Men full of courage, never turning their back to the foe, iron-plated cavaliers, heads protected by a helmet, with flags and standards, and the sound of trumpets ringing." The attack of such heavy cavalrymen is said to have been irresistible. "Ashot the Great spread terror," declares Ardzruni, "his blow was so impetuous that he overthrew in death more horsemen together with their mounts, than those whom he slaughtered by sword. No enemy, not one, was capable of resisting him." Here is a description by Thomas, of a furious combat: "The sparkling of lances, and armours, the blazing of swords and the whiz of arrows resembled a conflagration, a thundering flame bolting out of the clouds; the mountain seemed to be all on fire . . . , the strangers (Arabs) suffered a terrific disaster."

Heavy armament required exceptional physical fitness, which, in fact, was possessed by the nakharars and azats. Of Prince Gourgen, Thomas says: "I ask myself in profound amazement, how could he sustain the burden of toil without sinking, while fervently rushing forward, to keep up the superabundant physical force required in endless combats."

There are many other testimonials to the same effect. This natural gift was further developed by training from an early age. "The Mamikonian princes particularly educated in the art, could use with the same dexterity, both the right hand and the left. They cleave the adversary in two by one stroke of the sword, hammering with such a force that in one instance the mace buried itself in an iron gate, and it has been impossible to pull it out until now." (Ghazar).

The spiritual atmosphere of the Middle Ages also has played a part in the moulding of the character of the Armenian military noblemen. They had formulated some kind of martial ethics in which generous and chivalrous principles, Christian faith, asperity (roughness of temper) and pride in their force were blended. Honorable death was achieved only in combat, in their estimation. Manuel Mamikonian, in his sick bed, displayed to a group of visitors, headed by the king (Arshak III) and the queen (Vardandoukht), the innumerable scars or wounds on his body. "No spot, even as large as a silver coin was left without the mark of injury. Then he said: 'Ever since my youth I spent my life in battles, all these wounds have I received in fighting, why would I not have been given to fall on the battlefield, instead of thus dying like an animal! I would prefer rather to die in combat in defense of my country, of the churches and of the servants of God. How happy I would have been facing death in defending my country for the safety of the churches and of the ministers of God. Also for the Arshakunis — the proper masters of our land, and for our women and children, for the devout people, for brothers, companions and intimate friends. My lot is now an ignoble death in bed.' " (Phaustos V.44).

Almost in similar words are depicted the fine accomplishments of the sparapet Mushegh Mamikonian, who had spent, a few years earlier, all his life in defense of his country, of the Christian Church, and his own lords and masters. He had not suffered even one furrow (kori) of Armenian territory to be seized by an enemy (Ibid. V.20).

The historian Aristakes of Lastivert, narrating the battle of Manazkert waged between the Byzantines and Seljuk Turks, in 1070, remarks: "The Armenian soldiers of the Emperor Diogenes Romanos, although inwardly detached from the party of the emperor, nevertheless, preferred death, so that they may leave the precious remembrance of loyalty and courage."

Chivalry

Certain gallant behavior on the part of the Armenian warriors must have impressed their enemies. Mushegh Mamikonian, at the head of 40,000 men, inflicted a crushing defeat (370 A.D.) on the Persian King of Kings, Shapuh, who was saved by flight on horseback. Among the captives were the Persian Queen of Queens, together with many other women of high standing. Mushegh was relentless toward the warrior chiefs, because his father, Vassak, had been mercilessly flayed alive by them. As to the captured women, "he warned his men against any kind of annoyance to them." Provided with palanquins they traveled comfortably, escorted by Persian guards, who were charged by Mushegh with the duty of delivering them to their king, safely and respectfully. Shapuh never forgot his opponent's chivalrous conduct. Mushegh, at that time had a white steed, The King of Kings made a habit, in the course of official banquets, to lift up the wine cup and say: "May the man of the white horse also drink wine!" He caused the portrait of Mushegh, mounted on a white charger, to be designed on a cup to have before him during entertainments, and always uttered the same words: "May the man of the white horse also drink wine." "Jermaktzin gini arptsé" — in the Armenian version (Phaustos V.2). A century later, the Armenian troops sent against the Persians, found them still unprepared on the battlefield. The Armenians did not attack; they granted one day's truce.

Despite the chivalrous deeds as cited above, retaliation of excessive acts was a traditional duty and honorable requirement. Unfortunately, the notion about revenge, as a social duty, was the cause of irreparable harm. Thus for instance, the houses of Manavazianq and Orduniq were annihilated. The peace-making efforts of King Arshak II and of the Katholikos Vrtanes were of no avail; both parties massacred each other. The survivors were exterminated by royal order.

264

Soon after that tragedy Mushegh had to suppress fourteen nakharars in revolt against the king Arshak, who in his turn was trapped in Persia later, owing to the defection of the nakharars. The sparapet Vassak Mamikonian, and Prince Andovk of Sewniq were the only ones supporting Arshak. While fervently loyal to the throne, the Mamikonians, as the commanders of the army, became the resolute defenders of the feudal privileges, according to Marquart. On several occasions they stood up against their king. Positions were changed by other families too, by the Bagratunis, Ardzrunis, and the Sewnis, as well as by the bdeshkhs (satraps) of Aghtsniq and Gougarq, etc., the nakharars, when embroiled with their king, appealed to a foreign power for protection — the Byzantines on the one side, and the Persians or Arabs on the other. King Khosrov III of Armenia (337-342), irritated by the treasonable acts of certain nakharars, promulgated an edict under which the great ones were to remain with the king, and their regiments to fight under the command of the generalissimo, not under their own nakharars. The spirit of insubordination, so often prevalent in the country, has been lamented by national historians — Ghazar of Parb, Hovhannes Katholikos, Sebeos, Ghevond. Even the clergy contended with the royal power, as a rival in authority and possessions. The city of Arshakavan was constructed partly as a refuge for those who escaped from feudal exactions, not for fugitives from justice, as the clerical historians have maintained. Arshak was not always an innocent ruler, but he was determined to build a strong monarchy, independent of foreign influence, and that is why he waged the thirty years' war against the Persian Empire. It is true that there existed in Armenia the idea of national unity, allusions to "All provinces," "all the regions," "all the places," "all lands of the Armenian speech," "all those under royal power," but that kind of unity did not imply a national sentiment or the notion of a fatherland vaster than the ancestral domain. The lack of that spiritual bond, of the modern concept of patriotism, was not confined to the Armenian society. Mad rivalries among the barons, and treason against the throne, or against the interests of the national homeland were in conformity with the ethics of certain periods of the past. Many a time have historians indicated the analogy of attitudes between the Armenian nakharars and the French feudal seigneuries. They show the injurious effects in France of the gradual parceling out of the royal domain in favor of new cadets, leading eventually to the disintegration of the State. The satrapal regime of Armenia contained in its very essence the germ of both its weakness and its strength. Fully adapted to the mountains of Armenia, having known how to attain the highest degrees of warlike skills and methods, this feudal organization, through three centuries resisted incomparably superior inimical forces. By its divisions and rivalries it sterilized its victories and finally disappeared, more through exhaustion than by enemy blows.

IV

Domestic Life

The lower classes in Armenia, peasants and certain artisans too, though untrained and badly equipped, took part in defensive wars. Sometimes they had to fight only by flinging stones. On few occasions we see them forming cavalry regiments. Domestic life in the country was very often disturbed by foreign incursions, or by wars between rival great powers. And yet, return to normalcy and progress toward prosperity were amazingly rapid. Through the increase of population and wealth "the farms were transformed into boroughs, and the boroughs into cities, to such an extent that even shepherds and ox-keepers wore silken tunics," says Stepanos Assoghik.

Luxurious Living

On the other hand, this same historian bemoans the moral effects of prosperity. "When we became fat and bulky, rich and refractory, forgetting God the creator of peace and donor of all blessings — the priests and the congregation, the great and the small, became guilty of excessive pleasures and of indulgence in wine, as the prophet has pointed out." In fact, the nakharars and azats, in marked contrast to the shinakans, displayed all the signs of luxury. The splendor of the great nakharars has been an object of general admiration. Here is the description of Vassak Sewny, the marzpan, by Yeghisheh Vardapet, in a reception by the Persian king at Ctesiphon. "On a day of great festival he (Hazkert) gave orders to invite to a banquet all the distinguished persons in the capital. The apostate (Vassak) was also invited. In observance of the customary court ceremonial he put on the vestments of honor which he had received from the king. He wore his turban, put on his golden tiara, girded on the solid gold belt incrusted with pearls and precious stones; with earrings on his ears, a necklace around his neck, the ermine fur over his shoulders. Thus arrayed with all his insignia, he repaired to the royal court, appearing as the most gorgeous and conspicuous among the guests." (Chap. VII). The princes of Sewniq were entitled "to sit upon a silver throne, to wear a pearl necklace and red shoes, to carry a gold staff with the name of their lineage inscribed on it. They had also the privilege of using a wild-boar seal to stamp documents. (Stepanos Orpelian) The Persian king Shapuh III (383 A.D.) sent to the Queen of Armenia (Zarmandukht, the wife of Pap) a crown, a mantle and a royal standard; and to Manuel Sparapet, a royal mantle; an ornament in gold and silver to attach to the eagle of the helmet; a headband to encircle his forehead; a breast brooch usually worn by royalty; a scarlet tent with an eagle insignia atop; a large tapestry with azure canopies and a golden table-service for his banquet hall." The mighty nakharar of the Mouratzan house, the minister of Artashes I, had the privilege of wearing the crown in pearl, two earrings, the purple buskin for one foot only, also the right of using a golden spoon and fork, and to drink from a golden goblet, accompanied by music.

The following footnote by Langlois is of considerable interest: "Procopius likewise speaks of the costume worn by the satraps[81] at the time of Justinian who reconstituted the administration of the country. . . . This costume was composed of a mantle of wool, not of sheep but of some sea-shells called pinna in Greek, and of a vestment in purple, with gold embroidery. The mantle was clasped by a golden ornament carrying a precious stone, to which were attached small golden chains with three sapphires; a silken tunic adorned with gold laces; finally purple

---

[81] Satrap, from the Zend khshatrapa, meaning ruler of a province. A governor of a province under the Persian monarchy.

boots reaching the knees, a special privilege of the Roman emperors and Persian kings."

Heroism under Privations

The living standard of the nobility in normal times may be deduced from the narrative about the condition of the wives of the exiled nakharars after the battle of 451, as recited by Yeghisheh.

> "They were all dressed in the same manner. Everybody slept on the floor ... the straw mats had the same brownish color and the pillows were of the same black. There were no cooks to prepare particularly choice dishes for them, nor especial bakers to provide them in the manner to which the nobility had become accustomed, but everything was common to all. ... No one poured water on the hands of another, nor did the young offer towels to their elders. No soap ever came into the hands of the refined ladies and no (fragrant) oil was offered. ... No spotless platters were set before them, no cup-holders were offered for their enjoyments; no herald stood at their doors. ... The curtains of the nuptial chambers of the newly-weds became covered with dust and smoke, spider-webs were woven in their sleeping quarters. ... The lofty seats of their residences were destroyed. ... Their mansions toppled and fell, and their fortified shelters were demolished. Their exquisite flower-gardens were dried up and withered, and the fertile vines uprooted. ... Their treasures were confiscated and nothing was left of the jewelry which once adorned their faces.

> "The delicately brought up ladies of the land of Hayastan, used to soft cushions and litters, went always on foot, and bare-footed to houses of prayer. Those who had been fed on calves' brains and the tender meat of game since childhood, now lived on herbs like animals. The skin of their bodies darkened, because in daytime they were burnt by the sun, and all through the night they lay on the ground."

Many other texts confirm the richness of the nakharars' mansions. When Dame Sophia Ardzruni, daughter of King Ashot I, heard of the assassination of her husband, Derenik, she ordered her household to go into deep mourning. "The golden tissues of door-curtains forming the brightly colored arched entrance to the chambers were taken away, and replaced by black and inferior material. ... All windows exposed to light were closed in her wonderful apartments" (Thomas Ardzruni).

Armenian architecture is another test of the human taste of Armenian nobility. Noteworthy is its interest in public edifices, in churches, monasteries, shrines, and palaces. Aghtamar, the chief island in the lake of Van, was the site of several monuments, of a "supremely surprising architecture." The Prince Gagik Ardzruni embellished the burgh of Ostan on the coast of the same lake, by building palaces, churches and beautiful passages, adorned with statues. The mural decorations of the church of Aghtamar were remarkable indeed.

In the realm of literature we know Artavazd, the son of Tigran the Great, was the author of tragedies in the Greek language. Grigor Magistros was the most eminent among the nakharars, a grand seignior, diplomat, soldier-poet, a man of universal knowledge in the 11th century. But, in general, the Armenian kings and princes spent their time, when not engaged in war, in hunting and feasting. Hunting was done in many ways — "traps and nets to snare the galloping animal, by dexterous shooting with the bow, or by attacking with daggers in the manner of the gladiators, after chasing herds of enormous boars." (Ghazar of Parb).

Zeno, the son of Polemon, king of Pontus, aspiring to the throne of Armenia, in order to win the favor of the nobles of the country, had adopted their customs and usages — their huntings and entertainments. (Tacitus).

Chapter XXXVI
The Armenian Church — Early History

Origin

The Armenian Church acknowledges the Apostles Thaddeus and Bartholomew as the First Illuminators of the Nation. According to tradition, the ancient churches of Artaz (Maku) and of Aghpak (Bashkalé), in southeastern Armenia, contain their graves. The mission of Thaddeus is said to have extended through the years 35 to 43, and that of Bartholomew from 44 to 60. Critics however, hold that these accounts are borrowed from Greek (or Syriac) sources of a later date. To the see of Artaz tradition also had ascribed an early line of seven bishops, covering a period of 127 years. Their names are given as Zementos, Zacharia, Atrnerseh, Moushé, Shahen, Shavarsh and Leontius. Tradition also gives to the see of Sewniq a series of eight bishops — Kumsi, Babylas, Moushé (later on transferred to Artaz), Movses, Sahak, Zrvandat, Stepanos, and Hovhannes. It is generally maintained that Christianity reached Armenia first through Antioch, then from Edessa and Nisibin.

The historian Eusebius mentions a letter dated 254 A.D. from the Patriarch Dionysius of Alexandria to Bishop Mehrouzhan (Mitrozanes) of the brethren in Armenia. The Armenian records of martyrology contain many names of converts of both sexes, some of them of princely blood, who gave their lives for their faith in the time of St. Bartholomew and at the beginning of the second century. The Latin Church venerates the memory of St. Acacius, martyred with ten thousand converts near Mount Ararat during the reign of Hadrian.

According to Tertullian (155-222), the earliest of the ancient ecclesiastical writers and the creator of Christian Latin literature, Armenia was one of the countries whose languages were heard on the day of Pentecost. The text of the Acts the Apostles in the ordinary Bible mentions Judea as situated between Mesopotamia and Cappadocia; "And how hear we every man in our own tongue, wherein we were born? Parthians and Medes, and Elamites, and the dwellers in Mesopotamia, and in Judea, and Cappadocia, in Pontus and Asia. . . ." (Acts II.8.9). The name *Judea*, erroneously inserted by some copyist, undoubtedly should be *Armenia*. Judea was not a foreign country; it was the country in which they were situated at the time, and to hear its language spoken would be naturally expected. Tertullian's own words were:

"Upon whom else have the nations of the universe believed but upon the Christ who is already come? For whom have the nations believed — Parthians, Medes, Elamites, and they who inhabit Mesopotamia, *Armenia*, Phrygia, Cappadocia, and they who dwell in the Pontus and Asia and Pamphylia, sojourners in Egypt and inhabitants of the reign of

269

Africa which is beyond Cyrene, Romans and wayfarers, yes, and in Jerusalem, Jews and all other nations . . . ?"

("Answer to the Jews," Chap. VIII)

Augustine, the greatest of the ancient Church fathers, confirms the correct reading of Tertullian. This evidence and the persecutions carried on by three consecutive kings of Armenia — Artashes, Khosrov and Trdat himself — indicate that a considerable number of persons had been converted, even before the preaching of Grigor Loussavoritch.

Official Conversion of Armenia

Armenia was the first country in the world to adopt Christianity as a state religion. The conversion and baptism of King Trdat, the royal family, the nakharars and the army, together with thousands of the people, took place in the year 301. [82] The conversion of the Emperor Constantine was much later; modern authors place his baptism in the year 337. Eusebius says that in 311 Maximin Daia, one of the four participants in Roman Imperial authority — the others being Constantine, Licinius and Maxentius — and a bitter enemy of Christianity, declared war against the Armenians because they had renounced paganism.

Grigor Partev (Gregory the Parthian), through whose preaching this tremendous change was accomplished, is said to have been related to the Arshakouni (Arsacid) kings of Armenia. His father, Prince Anak, an Arsacid prince, had in conspiracy with Artashir, the Sassanid, assassinated Trdat's father, King Khosrov of Armenia, as related in a previous chapter. Anak was slain while trying to escape, and the child Grigor was carried to Roman territory for safety from reprisal. Trdat, the legitimate heir, was also taken to Caesarea for similar reasons, and twenty-three years later recovered his father's throne, aided by the Emperor Diocletian. Grigor was brought up in the Christian faith and educated in Caesarea; he, too, returned to Armenia after the reestablishment of the national kingdom.

The causes which prompted Trdat to declare Christianity as the national religion are matters of conjecture, but we may not be wrong in assuming that he had followed the general trend in the Roman world. However this might be, the fact is that to Grigor Loussavoritch's untiring efforts is mainly due the triumph of the Gospel over the pagan religions in Armenia. He was duly chosen to be the head of the Church of Armenia and sent to Caesarea, the Cappadocia metropolis in 302, for special consecration at the hands of the Archbishop Leontius. Grigor established his residence at Hashtishat (Taron), where he built a church and a palace.

---

[82] Trdat was baptized on Jan. 6, 303, Christmas Day, according to the Patriarch Maghakia Ormanian.

Grigor's Long Ascendancy

Grigor organized and controlled the church for a quarter of a century. To him are ascribed canons, homilies and liturgical services. Twelve episcopal sees, with priests converted from paganism as titulars, and four hundred urban and rural dioceses were created by him, and preachers sent to neighboring countries — Georgia, Caspio-Albania and Atropatene. He died in 325, the year of the Council of Nicaea. His younger son, Aristakes, unmarried, succeeded him, took part in the Council of Nicaea (modern Isnik) and was one of the signatories of the Acts. At Aristakes' death in 333, his elder brother, Verthanes, of that Council, took over the post and held it until 341. His successor was his son Houssik (341-347). Because of the refusal of the sons of Houssik to enter holy orders, the patriarchal see devolved upon Parén, a kinsman of Grigor's family. Later on, by the election of Nerses, Houssik's grandson (353-373), the line of succession reverted to the family of the Illuminator. [83]

Royal Opposition to the Church

A party supported by princely houses had been opposing the newly organized Church, which King Trdat had enriched by territorial grants. Acts of violence are recorded, during this period, and probably as a consequence of this, the Church control passed to the house of Albianus, which had formerly supplied priests for the pagan religion. The patriarchal authority reverted once more to the family of Grigor when Sahak, son of Nerses and of the Partev or Parthian lineage, was elected Katholikos in 387 and ruled until 439.

Spiritual Awakening

Despite political hindrances, the spiritual awakening was strong enough to assert itself. The Church in the fourth century was well organized, but lacked an element of vital importance — a written language. The Armenian language was not provided yet with an alphabet. The Greek language prevailed in the schools of Caesarea, and the Syriac in Edessa, then a Persian territory. Grigor was obliged to appoint foreign teachers to head the schools which he founded. The Bible and the Church Services were read in the Greek and Syriac languages. It was difficult, under such circumstances, to uproot pagan worship and customs from the mountainous districts on the one hand and from satrapal mansions on the others.

But inasmuch as the people were ignorant of both Greek and Syriac, an oral translation of the Scripture service was made for them in the Church. A class of translators (Targmanich) had to be created to serve during the Church services,

---

[83] The number of bishops attending the Council at the summons of Constantine seems to have been considerably less than the traditional 318 — really only 221. The great majority of them came from the eastern provinces of the Empire. The outsiders were four or five — one Goth, one Crimean, one Persian, and "Restaces" (Aristakes), the Armenian, the son of Gregory the Illuminator, with perhaps another Armenian bishop." (*Cambridge Medieval History,* Vol. I)

to interpret the passages of Scripture which were read aloud by the class of readers (Verdzanogh). These men explained the prayers and the readings used in the Service, and instructed the people in their mother tongue. "If we were to note the differences in translation between the psalms used in the offices and psalms found in the text of the Scriptures, we would find two translations; one dating from the fourth century, for popular use, and the other the fifth century based on the Greek text."[84]

Monastery of St. Varag at Van

Beginning of Armenian Literature

Mesrop-Mashtots, a disciple of the Patriarch Nerses and formerly a secretary at the Royal court, conceived the idea of an effective missionary movement for the diffusion of Christianity in Armenia. But lacking an alphabet, the task could not be carried out. With the backing of the Patriarch Sahak, Mesrop submitted his suggestion for a written language to the King, Vramshapouh. The monarch cordially endorsed the plan and contributed liberally towards its accomplishment. Mesrop made several trips to neighboring centers of learning for consultation with scholars, and finally, in 404, he succeeded in creating an alphabet which with thirty-six characters reproduced the sounds of the spoken Armenian.

The next work, to be taken in hand immediately, was the translation of the Bible into the new written language. A group of scholars from among the Translators was selected by Sahak and Mesrop. The translation of the Old Testament was

---

[84] *The Church of Armenia,* by Ormanian.

made using both the Greek text of the Septuagint and the Syriac version, the latter being followed to a lesser extent. Almost thirty years were required to complete the work, before the end of which, in 433, Sahak had made a final revision of the translation, comparing it with a Greek copy sent to him by the Patriarch of Constantinople. Next, they devoted their time and energy to the translation of the books of the liturgy, such as the Divine Liturgy, the rituals of baptism, confirmation, marriage, funerals, the daily offices and the calendar.

While following closely the liturgy of Caesarea, Grigor had borrowed liberally from the national customs and pagan rites, giving them a Christian character.

The Armenian Church in the Fifth Century

Sahak was deposed in 428, and an anti-patriarch named Sourmak was nominated by Bahram V, the Persian King. Two others, Birkisho and Shimuel respectively, succeeded him. Then once more, in 437, Sourmak returned to the post. Sahak had been permitted in 432 to return home from Ctesiphon, and was welcomed by the nation as its spiritual head, although divested of his civil and juridical functions. The Council of Ephesus, held in 431, had condemned Nestorius, and the Christian world was agitated by dogmatic controversies. Armenia could not hold aloof from the wrangling. The books of Theodore of Mopsuest (Missis), the precursor of Nestorius, were secretly circulating in the country. Sahak received from the Patriarch of Constantinople the decisions of the Council of Ephesus. He summoned a council at Artashat in 435, and sent a letter to Proclus of Constantinople, refuting Theodore's errors. Sahak died in 439, and Mesrop, who had charge of the spiritual leadership of the nation, followed him to the grave six months later.

In previous chapters we have depicted the vital part played by these two pre-eminent leaders, through whose inspiration and achievements Armenia was able to struggle against the mighty Persian Empire. We now turn to the other strife which the Armenian Church was called upon to wage for centuries against the great Christian power of the West, Byzantium; a strife that was dogmatic or doctrinal in theory, although to a large extent it was fundamentally political.

Claims of Supremacy

According to the Greeks, the see of Armenia was under the jurisdiction of Caesarea because of the episcopal consecration of St. Grigor at the hands of Leontius, Archbishop of Cappadocia. The Armenians dispute this claim, pointing to the Apostolic origin of the Armenian Church. Only two provinces in the Roman Empire, known as First Armenia (Sebast) and Second Armenia (Melitene), had recognized the authority of the Archbishop of Caesarea, or of the Exarch of Pontus. Greater Armenia, under Persian suzerainty, had always maintained independence in ecclesiastical matters. The sons and immediate successors of St. Grigor — Aristakes and Verthanes — had gone to Caesarea for consecration. Subsequent incumbents probably did the same. However, the practice ceased in 374, when Sahak became Patriarch, he having been consecrated by local bishops.

The ill-feeling caused by this secession (or insubordination, as the Greeks would regard it) assumed inordinate proportions by reason of the negative attitude taken by the Armenians towards the Fourth General Council of the Church, which was held in 451 in Chalcedon, the modern Kadikeuy, a suburb of Constantinople.

Council of Chalcedon (451)

The zeal displayed by the Archimandrite Eutyches of Byzantium in opposing Nestorius gave rise to heated disputes regarding the nature of Christ, and stirred up strife between the sees of Constantinople, Alexandria and Antioch. Emperor Marcianus held the Fourth Council for the purpose of arresting the ascendency of the monophysite (one-nature) doctrine promulgated in 449 through the influence of Dioscorus, Patriarch of Alexandria at the Synod of Ephesus. That council had adopted the formula of St. Cyril, *one nature of the Incarnate Word God.* Nestorius of Antioch, Patriarch of Constantinople (428-440), who believed in a purely moral unity between the two natures, had been condemned by the council. A special synod, held upon the initiative of the Patriarch Flavianus at Constantinople in 448, also condemned Eutyches, who had "carried the union so far as to make it a blend and a confusion of the two natures, . . . and the giving of a heavenly origin to the body of Christ." At another special synod held at Ephesus in 449, the followers of Flavianus and Nestorius were condemned. In the following year, Pope Leo I called a synod in Rome to condemn both Eutyches and Dioscorus, and succeeded, moreover, in inducing the Emperor Marcianus to summon the Council of Chalcedon (451), where about 600 bishops gathered. Most of the western bishops could not attend, as Europe was then in turmoil because of Attila's invasion. The council reaffirmed the Nicene and Constantinopolitan creeds and the Ephesian formula of 431, and accepted the Christological statement contained in the *Epistola Dogmatica* of Leo I. The council also rejected both Nestorianism and Eutychianism, and stood upon the doctrine that Christ had two natures, each perfect in itself, and each distinct from the other, yet perfectly united in one person, who was at once God and man. The first session of the Council was tumultuous, and abusive epithets were exchanged. It was presided over by the Legate of the Pope; Imperial commissioners directed the order of business, opened the meetings, laid before the council the matters to be discussed, demanded the votes and closed the sessions. It continued for three weeks, and the final record was formally subscribed to in the presence of the Emperor.

Discipline, Parish Organization

In addition to the creed, the council promulgated thirty canons against clerical abuses and in favor of social improvements of practical import. One of the canons conceded to the see of Constantinople second rank among the Patriarchates. Others had the safe guarding of the interests of the Patriarchs as their aim. The Patriarch of the New Rome — Constantinople — was seeking predominance over the older see of the Church. The Patriarch of Alexandria, jealously proud of the eminent part played by his predecessors in oecumenical councils, could not tolerate the ambitious designs of his new rival. He claimed that the works accomplished in Nicaea by Athanasius and at Ephesus by Cyril could not be undone by the Bishops of Constantinople and Rome, who were in alliance against Alexandria, supported by the armed forces of Marcianus, the Emperor-general. Leo himself was naturally apprehensive of the pretensions of Flavianus, and did not subscribe to those canons of the council which defined the various jurisdictions or threatened the precedence of Rome.

The Council of Chalcedon was technically a success, and did in fact accomplish some tangible results, but its work was not sufficiently complete to obviate further controversy. Rebellions in Palestine and Egypt were the immediate consequences of the decrees of the council against Dioscorus and the Monophysites. The episcopate of the Graeco-Roman world was divided into two camps, and their flocks indulged in violent recriminations. The subtle distinctions laid down as between the unity and duality of natures did not suffice to calm men's minds.

At a new council held at Antioch in 476, the doctrine of Chalcedon was declared doubtful, and the Emperor Zeno forbade the giving of support to the decrees of the Fourth Council. In 482 he issued the Henoticon (edict of unification or reconciliation), wherein he denied all authority to the council. Finally, the Emperor Anastasius, by a decree dated 491, reversed the decisions of the Council. Through these executive measures the Emperors sought to combat Nestorianism, which enjoyed full liberty within the confines of the Persian dominions, where a prosperous Syrian element resided.

Armenia Shaken by Disaster

Armenia remained unconcerned with these quarrels until the beginning of the sixth century. The country was in mourning for the death, exile and dispersion of hundreds of her prominent leaders, lay and clerical, as a result of the desirous Battle of Avarair in 451, which was fought just eighteen weeks before the opening of the Council of Chalcedon. When the sorrow and agitation had subsided, the Armenian Patriarchs had neither the time nor the disposition to give serious thought to matters outside their own jurisdictions. The first occurrence which brought the Council of Chalcedon to the attention of the Armenians took place during the incumbency of the Katholikos Babken (490-515). Those Syrians living in Persian Mesopotamia who had remained loyal to the orthodox doctrine of the Council of Ephesus, were being harassed by Nestorian zealots. They asked for guidance from the Armenians, who had remained in strict adherence to the anti-Nestorian preaching of St. Sahak. The Nestorians were hostile to the Church of Alexandria, whereas the Armenians had maintained their attachment to the Church. The Emperor Marcianus, whose handiwork was seen in the Council of Chalcedon, had refused the aid against the Persians solicited by an Armenian deputation. Furthermore, the council had later been disavowed by the two successors of Marcianus, Zeno and Anastasius.

A synod of Armenian, Georgian and Albanian bishops, held in Douin in 506 under the presidency of Babken, reaffirmed the profession of faith of the Council of Ephesus and rejected everything that savored of Nestorianism, including the acts of the Council of Chalcedon. The Synod at the same time condemned Arius, Eutyches and Macedonius. Later, the Greek and Latin churches recognized the Council of Chalcedon as the Fourth Oecumenical Council, but the Armenian Church stedfastly upheld its original conservative declaration of 506 in Douin.

Political Element

When speaking of theological or dogmatic subjects, which periodically disturbed Armenia, one should not overlook the political element usually underlying or influencing them. The country passed successively under Persian, Greek and Arab rulers, for whom religious professions of dominated peoples were of great importance. The Armenians insisted upon loyalty to their established principles, yet avoided, as much as possible, any position or action calculated to offend the ruling power and thereby compromise their own safety.

From 428 to 633, the larger part of Armenia was governed by Persian marzbans. Thereafter, for a short period — from 633 to 693 — the marzbans were replaced by Greek curopalates. Then came the period of Arab domination for more than a century and a half (693-862). The Greek Emperors, even after abandoning Greater Armenia, strove to exert pressure on her people to accept the Chalcedonian profession. The Persians and the Arabs, desirous of winning the Armenians away from the Greeks, held out alluring promises to them. The Armenians would not and could not accede to the Greek demands; and the idea of collaboration with non-Christians was repugnant to them.

The excitement occasioned by the Council of Chalcedon had not yet subsided when Justinian mounted the throne in 527. He endeavored to please the orthodox followers of the Ephesian doctrine, and at the same time restrain the tendencies of the Chalcedonian party. The new Council of Constantinople, summoned by Justinian in 553, finally settled the Chalcedonian question, reaffirming the idea of the two natures in Christ, yet defining it as it was defined at the Council of Ephesus. The Armenians did not feel the need of new definitions, and the Synod of Douin, which assembled in the following year (554) under Katholikos Nerses II, proclaimed once more the Ephesian doctrine, as in opposition to Nestorian errors and Chalcedonian claims.

The negative attitude of the Armenians towards the Chalcedonian profession was resented by the Greeks, at whose instigation the Georgians, led by Bishop Kurion, seceded from the jurisdiction of the Armenian Katholikosate, to join the Patriarchate of Constantinople. This event had unfavorable repercussions upon the Georgian church centuries later, when the Russians came to dominate the Caucasus. Her separate existence had no longer any *raison d'être*, because of the identity of doctrines which justified the absorption of the Georgian church by the Russian. On the other hand, Greek attempts at installing anti-patriarchs for the

276

Byzantine portion of Armenia invariably failed, because of the inflexible opposition of the Armenians to the Chalcedonian formula.

Revival of Chalcedonian Activities

Official pressure to effect a union of the Greek and Armenian churches was revived by the Emperor Heraclius, who had succeeded in defeating and sweeping away the once-victorious Persians and recovering the relic of the Holy Cross, which they had carried away from Jerusalem. On his second visit to Karin, Armenia, in 632, Heraclius held a conference with the Katholikos Ezr (Esdras) and his bishops. As a result of these negotiations the Armenians accepted a formula which was in keeping with their own faith, save that it passed over in silence the Council of Chalcedon. The event was solemnized by the celebration of a mass, at which Greeks (including the Emperor), and Armenians took the communion together. Despite this demonstration of harmony, the Katholikos had excited popular indignation by his submission to the Emperor, to such an extent that until a very recent date his name appeared in the list of patriarchs with the initial letter inverted. This stigma, however, was unjust. Neither the Katholikos nor the Emperor favored the Chalcedonian doctrine in its extreme form. The Emperor was a defender of the monothelite doctrine which held that Christ had but one will.

Arab Invasion Begins

Political surprises were soon to bring about new changes in the situation. The Katholikos Nerses III, surnamed Shinogh (Builder) ascended the throne just as the Arabs began to invade Armenia in 641. The national leaders were perplexed, unable to decide upon a course to be followed. Nerses himself was for Greek rule, but the military commander, Sembat Bagratuni, and Theodore Reshtuni, considering the Greeks to be weak and unreliable, were inclined to favor submission to the Arabs. The Emperor Constantine IV, in retaliation, marched into Armenia at the head of an army, having as his first objective the imposition of his religious authority. The Katholikos succeeded in appeasing the wrathful monarch, but a new Synod, assembled at Douin in 645, after the withdrawal of the Greek forces, resolved again to reject all but the first three councils. Nerses had to modify his vacillation and maintain a passive attitude with regard to the more realistic anti-Greek policy of Theodore Reshtuni.

This confused condition of affairs continued after the death of both leaders, Nerses and Theodore. During the patriarchate of Sahak III (677-703), the Arabs had become firmly established in Armenia, and there was no arena left for Graeco-Armenian disputes. However, the Khalifas would naturally appreciate the adoption by the Armenians of a religious policy in opposition to Greek idea. Sahak III undertook a journey to Damascus to visit the Khalifa, but died on the way, in 703. His endeavor was rewarded, however; the Khalifa granted most of the privileges which he had expected to ask for.

The Katholikos Hovhannes (John) III, of Otzoun, surnamed Imastasser (the Philosopher), wrote against the heresies of the time and introduced disciplinary and liturgical reforms. He is the author of a code of canon-law. He cultivated friendly relations with the Khalifas, and obtained from them concessions for the benefit of the church and nation. The Synod of Manazkert, convened in 726, under the presidency of Hovhannes, and composed of Armenian and Syrian bishops, decided "the great question of the corruptibility of the body of Christ, which had been raised by the orthodox monophysites. It had caused a split between the Syrian and Armenian churches." (Ormanian)

With the creation by the Khalifas of Armenian vassal principalities in 862, Armenia had begun to enjoy administrative autonomy, and the church functioned under peaceful conditions. Utilizing this opportunity, Patriarch Photius of Constantinople attempted once again to resume negotiations with the Armenian Church. His move has by some writers been ascribed to "an intention of winning support against the Roman Church with which he had quarreled." However, his letters to the Katholikos Zakaria (855-878) and to Prince Ashot Bagratuni, inviting them to accept the decrees of Chalcedon, led to no result.[85]

Armeno-Syrian Synod

The Armeno-Syrian Synod held at Ctesiphon under the eye of Khosrov Parviz of Persia rejected the decisions of Chalcedon (614-616). But the selfsame decisions were accepted in the Armeno-Greek Synod of Karin in 632, presided over by the Katholikos Ezr, in the presence of the Emperor Heraclius, conqueror of the Persians. The third council of Douin (649), held under the Katholikos Nerses II, on the invitation of the Emperor Constans II and the Greek Patriarch Paul II, declared itself in favor of monophysitism, despite the solid argumentation of David, the Armenian philosopher. This attitude, however, was dictated by the famous nakharar Theodorus Reshtuni, who favored Arab friendship. Consequently, Nerses allied himself with diophysitism as soon as Constans II's return to the offensive sheltered the Katholikos against the wrath of Theodorus (653). But this reconciliation was as little durable as the successes of Greek arms. The same was true of the agreement accepted by Katholikos Sahak III, whom Justinian II had taken to the Constantinople as a hostage

---

[85] The following comment by the British scholar, F. C. Conybeare, sheds a light on the subject from another angle; "The ties with Greek official Christendom were snapped forever, and in subsequent ages the doctrinal preferences of the Armenians were usually determined more by antagonism to the Greeks than by reflection. If they accepted the Council of Ephesus in 430 and joined in condemnation of the Nestorians, it was rather because the Sassanid Kings of Persia, who thirsted for the reconquest of Armenia, favored Nestorianism, a doctrine current in Persia but rejected in Byzantium. But later on, about 480, and throughout the succeeding centuries, the Armenians rejected the decrees of Chalcedon and held that the assertion of two natures in Christ was a relapse into the heresy of Nestor. From the close of the fifth century, the Armenians have remained monophysite, like the Copts and Abyssinians, and have only occasionally broken their record with occasional short interludes of orthodoxy." (Encyclopaedia Britannica, 1910, "Armenian Church.").

in 690. Two years later, in the council of Trullo[86] the Greeks passed censure upon the Armenians for their use of unmixed wine in holy communion and for the matagh, or sacrifice of animals.

Under Umayyad Arab Rule

The first conquering Arabs adopted a moderate policy towards the Christians. In consideration of the payment of one dinar, they guaranteed the life, property and freedom of worship of the Christians. By separating from the Greeks, Theodorus Reshtouni even obtained an exemption from tribute for three years. The situation of Christians and Moslems, however, was not the same; the testimony of the former against the latter was not admissible in court. A Moslem was fined only 5,000 souzehs for killing a Christian. Any attempt to revolt was cruelly suppressed; an example is the burning of 1,775 Armenian hostages in the churches of Nakhjavan and Khram. The Ostikan (Arab governor) residing in Douin could keep watch upon the Katholikos and the Armenian sub-governor, who likewise resided in the city. The Katholikos Hovhannes Otznetsi, a subtle politician, in order to win the good will of Khalifa Hesham (724-743), called upon the potentate with his beard sprinkled with gold powder, but letting the hair cloth he was wearing appear under his rich dress. He asked a larger religious liberty for the Armenians, and the exemption of taxes on the clergy; and this being granted, he, in return, drove away from Armenia all the Greek warriors and inspectors.

Patriarchal See Transferred

Etchmiadzin, the original residence of the Katholikos of "all the Armenians" (Amenain Hayots), did not remain identified for long with the capital, Vagharshapat. After the fall of the Arshakuni kingdom, both the Marzban and the Katholikos were installed in 425 at Douin, at the foot of Ararat, not far from Etchmiadzin.

Douin, which was the residence of the Bagratuni kings before they moved to Ani, remained the patriarchal see until it was invaded by the cruel and savage Youssouf, the Arab governor of Atrpatakan, who had rebelled against the Khalifa. Katholikos Hovhannes V, the historian, who had gone to negotiate with him, was detained as a hostage. For a long time after his liberation on payment of a huge ransom, he wandered about the country, because Douin had been destroyed in 893, partly by the enemy and partly by an earthquake. Finally in 927, Hovhannes fixed his domicile at Tsorovanq, a monastery near Van, the seat of one of the four Armenian kings whom the Khalifa had crowned, following the adage, "Divide and rule." From there the patriarch followed the king to the island of Aghtamar, in the lake of Van.

---

[86] Trullo, a misnomer, pertains to two councils held in the trullus or domed chamber of the imperial palace at Constantinople, in 680 and 691 A.D. The latter, called by Justinian II, established 102 canons for the discipline of the church, allowing the marriage of priests. The first Trullan council, 680, condemned monophysitism. Trullus, in Low Latin, means a dome.

After the death of Hovhannes V and the three succeeding patriarchs, the Katholikos Anania (943-967), a wise and able administrator, left the island and settled in the town of Arkina, near Ani. His successor, Vahan Sewnie (967-969), was suspected of being a Chalcedonian. A synod assembled at Ani deposed him and elected Stepanos III. Disputes which had arisen between these two, the kings of Ani and Van taking opposite sides, were quieted only after their deaths. Khatchik I, the new incumbent (971-992), courageously defended those of his flocks living in the Byzantine domains against Greek clerical encroachments, and consecrated bishops for them, in defiance of the impositions of the Greek clergy. Khatchik, after the cathedral and patriarchal palace at Arkina had been built, undertook the construction of a new residence at Ani, but he did not live to enjoy it. It was first occupied by his successor, Sarkis I (992-1019), whose inaugural ceremonies gave the people of Ani their last opportunity to enjoy a spiritual festivity; for the successor of Sarkis, Petros I (1019-1054), was finally forced out of the residence when Ani was captured by the Greeks in 1046.

Historians reproach Petros for an alleged unpatriotic act. Hovhannes-Sembat, the weakling son and successor of King Gagik of Ani, concerned only with his own personal security on the throne, agreed to the cession of his kingdom at his death to the Emperor Basil II. Petros is said to have brought about this secret transaction during a visit to Trebizond, in Greek territory. Twice relinquishing the office with changes of residence, he reoccupied his seat at Ani in 1036, despite the opposition of the king. When Hovhannes-Sembat died, leaving no issue, the legal heir was his brother's son, Gagik, who was fifteen years old. But Vest Sarkis, minister of the deceased king, sought the throne for his own son, while Vahram Pahlavuni, the General of the army, defended the right of the young heir. Of course the Emperor Michael IV ("the Paphlagonian") claimed Ani on the strength of Sembat's deed, though his claim was disputed by the Tatars and the King of Gougark. Vahram was able for a time to stave off the greedy claimants, foiling all the intrigues of the Katholikos and Vest Sarkis, but was at length forced to yield the capital to the Emperor's army in 1046. The Katholikos was at first treated courteously by the Greeks, but he was presently invited to Constantinople, where he remained for three years in urbane detention. He was then sent to Sebast (Sivas), where he died in 1054.

His nephew and successor, Khatchik II, was also summoned to Constantinople, where he was urged to reveal the hiding place of the treasures of Petros and to bring about the union of the two churches, but he did not yield to pressure on either point. After three years of forced sojourn in the Byzantine capital, he was sent to the town of Thavblour, near Derendeh, in Armenia Minor, where he died in 1065.

280

Chapter XXXVII
The Paulikians and the Tondrakians

Points of Difference

In addition to the political troubles which beset Armenia during the eleventh century, the Paulikian sectarians known to Armenians as the Tondrakians (those of Tondrak Village) created a new form of internal disorder. The cardinal point of Paulikianism was a distinction between the God who made the material world and the God of Heaven, creator of souls, who alone should be adored. Paulikians rejected the Old Testament, and in the New, gave their approval chiefly to the Gospel of St. Luke and the epistles of St. Paul. They did not believe in incarnation. Christ, to them, was an angel, and baptism and eucharist consisted in hearing his words. They also rejected any hierarchy, the cross, pictures and all ritual. They were fanatically hostile to all forms of worship. Professor Conybeare of Oxford thinks Paulikianism was a continuation of Adoptionism.[87]

The sect was founded in 657 by one Paul of Samosata — or in the name of St. Paul — at Kibossa, in western Armenia. The Katholikos John III ("the Philosopher") summoned two synods to take measures against them, one at Douin in 719, another at Manazkert in 726, but with little effect. They were persecuted by the Emperors Constantine IV and Justinian II, but were protected by Leo III and Nicephorus I, in return for their services as soldiers. When persecutions were renewed under Michael I and Leo V, they rebelled and fled to the domain of the Khalifa, who encouraged them. During the reign of Basil I they invaded Asia Minor with the Khalifa's troops, even to the outskirts of Constantinople. Their stronghold was Tephrike (Divrik), which was ultimately destroyed by an imperial army in 871. Constantine V and John I (Zimiskes) transplanted large numbers of them into Balkan countries, to kill or be killed by the enemies of the Empire. Philippopolis became a Paulikian center on European soil. The movement spread into Asia Minor, Syria, Mesopotamia and especially Greater Armenia, where the sectarians were called Tondrakians.

Despite official suppressions and punishment, the votaries of this cult offered stiff resistance to civil and religious authorities. Recent Armenian critics represent them as an expression of protest against the social system, an uprising against the exactions of princes and feudal lords, of peasants against aristocrats.

---

[87] An 8th-century heresy, teaching that Christ, in respect to His divine nature, was doubtless the Son of God, but that as to His human nature, He was only *declared* and *adopted* as the Son of God.

Popular demonstrations and armed conflicts were not unusual in the plain of Ararat, in Aghouank (Albania) on the northeast and in the Aghtsnik on the southwest. Even after their exhaustion in Armenia and Asia Minor, the Paulikian deportees in the Balkans did not relent. The rise of the Albigenses and other Manichaean heresies is ascribed to their propaganda. "They shook the East and enlightened the West," says the historian Gibbon. Conybeare believed that he had found descendants of Paulikian communities in Russian Armenia. The discovery of a book containing their profession of faith, "The Key of Truth," led him to picture them as a simple, godly folk, who had clung to an earlier form of Christianity.[88]

Orthodox historians of the eighth to twelfth centuries accuse the Paulikians and their followers of armed collaboration with Moslem enemies and of detestable practices, such as devil-worship, evil nocturnal rites and pagan customs. Grigor Magistros, the Imperial governor, within whose jurisdiction Tondrak lay, called the place Shnavank, "Monastery of Dogs," "where men dressed in clerical garb lived in company with a multitude of prostitute women." Not content with such verbal and written castigation, Magistros sent a strong police force to purge this source of scandal and corruption.

"The Paulikians," says Professor C. A. Scott, "have been celebrated uncritically as early Protestants against Catholic abuses, of they have been condemned unheard as deadly heretics. A just estimate will be arrived at only when all such pre-suppositions have been laid aside, and when to the Greek sources . . . have been added the Armenian, and further, when the literary relations between the Greek sources have been thoroughly sifted."

Bishop Hacob of Hark, accused of being a sponsor of or sympathiser with the sect, was, after two trials and acquittals before the ecclesiastical court, nevertheless, degraded by the Katholikos Sarkis. At Kashi, a mob identified with the Tondrakians destroyed the great cross of the village. The perpetrators of the sacrilege were severely punished and even tortured. In circumstances such as these, the Armenians followed the example of the Greeks in their harsh chastisement of fanatical sectarians, whose acts were said to have degenerated into crimes against public welfare and morality.

Patriarchal Seat in Cilicia

Convinced of the futility of further attempts at absorption of the Armenian church into the orthodox Greek orbit, the Emperor Constantius Ducas in 1065 finally sanctioned the nomination of Grigor Vahram, son of Grigor Magistros, as the Governor-general of the Empire, a post also filled by the son. A condition attached to the nomination was that the new Katholikos, Grigor II, Vkayasser (the Martyrophile), should not remain in Armenia. He was therefore obliged to

---

[88] This work, copied from an Armenian manuscript in 1782, was translated into English by Conybeare.

take up residence at Dsamentav (Zamintia), in the new state of King Gagik of Kars, and later, of Amassia.

The patriarchate of Grigor II extended over forty years (1065-1105), but was not marked by any conspicuous accomplishment. He was gifted with an excellent intellect and broad learning, but had assumed his office, not because of any particular qualification or desire for it, but only to fill the vacancy, and also because he was the best candidate upon whom the Greek Emperor and the Armenian nation could agree. He made tours in the Holy Land and Egypt, leaving the performance of his official duties to subordinates, among whom his nephew, Barsegh (Basil) of Ani, displayed peculiar ability and succeeded his uncle upon the latter's death. Although supposed to reside in Zamintia, Barsegh actually lived within the confines of Cilicia, then being filled with Armenian refugees, fleeing from Tatar invasions of the homeland. The monastery of Shugr, in the Sev Ler (Amanus, Black Mountains), became a favorite home for Barsegh. He died of an accident in 1113, and was succeeded by Grigor III, Pahlavouni, then only twenty years old. The youth of the new Katholikos encouraged Bishop David Tornikian to assert his claim to the see of Aghtamar, where several patriarchs had sat temporarily. David was sufficiently strong-willed to enforce his claim, despite an adverse decision rendered at a general meeting held in Cilicia by many bishops, princes and a multitude of lay and clerical delegates, estimated to number 2,500.

Egyptian Sultan Seizes the Katholikos

In 1125 Grigor moved his residence eastward to Dzovk-Sof, also known as Dluke, north of Aintab. Still later, in 1147, he found a safer refuge in the fort of Hromkla (Roumkala), on the west bank of the Euphrates, which he had bought from the wife of a Latin count, Josselin, lord of Germanicus (Marash). For a century and a half Hromkla remained the patriarchal seat, until Sultan Kalaoun of Egypt captured the place in 1293 and carried away as prisoner the Katholikos Stepanos IV. The see was then transferred to Sis, the Armenian capital. In 1375 the kingdom of Cilicia was overthrown by the Memlouks of Egypt, and 66 years later the patriarchate of "all the Armenians" returned to Etchmiadzin, 540 years after its departure from Douin in 901.

Chapter XXXVIII
New Effort Towards Church Unity

Contact with Latins

The Armenians, subject to incessant aggression and strain from all sides, looked for some support from other Christian nations. But though desirous of brotherly understanding and cooperation, they have always resisted all external attempts at religious domination or proselytizing. They often remained alone and isolated, yet cultivated friendships in the hope of making their own standing recognized and respected by others.

A series of unionist negotiations with the Greeks and Latins continued, sometimes simultaneously, during the existence of the Armenian kingdom of Cilicia (1080-1375). The Katholikos Grigor II (1065-1105), in the course of his travels — undertaken for research in the history of martyrs — endeavored to procure an *entente* with the churches of Jerusalem, Constantinople and Alexandria. An unfounded account of his having made a trip to Rome arose from confusion of the names Rome and Roum, the latter referring to Hromkla, "the castle of Romans or Romians." A closer relationship with the Greeks happily put an end, at least temporarily, to imperial oppressions.

The first official contact between the Latin and Armenian churches took place in the Council of Antioch in 1141, held under the presidency of Cardinal Albericum, the papal legate. The Katholikos Grigor III (Pahlavouni) accompanied the Cardinal to Jerusalem in 1143, where another council was convoked. In reply to proposals for union with the Church of Rome, the Katholikos declared that nothing of vital importance separated the two churches. Pope Lucius II sent ecclesiastical gifts to the Katholikos, who in turn dispatched presents to him through a delegation. Doctrinal and ceremonial differences were made subjects of discussion at Viterbo, Italy, under the new pope, Eugenius III, who occupied the Papal throne in 1145. Eugenius wrote to the Katholikos, requesting him to adopt the usages of the Roman Church.

In 1165, Bishop Nerses Shnorhali, brother of the Katholikos, met Prince Alexis, the imperial governor-general, at Mopsuest (Missis) in Cilicia, to discuss reunion of the Greek and Armenian Churches. Both men were well versed in doctrinal matters.

After verbal conferences between the two, Bishop Nerses set down in writing the fundamentals of the Armenian faith and the liturgical practices of the Church, for presentation to the Emperor. The document was dignified in tone. Avoiding any criticism of the Chalcedonian doctrine, it explained that the term, "one nature," used by the Armenians, in the sense accepted by St. Athanasius and St. Cyril, was because of the "ineffable union" of the two natures with one another.

Nerses Writes to the Emperor

Some time after the receipt of the letter of Nerses, the Emperor invited him to Constantinople for an interview. Nerses, having meanwhile succeeded to the Patriarchal throne after Grigor's death, was unable to undertake the journey, but promised a visit later. In his answer, he again emphasized the desirability of mutual concessions;— "If God wills that we converse with one another, let it not be as the master with his servants and the servants with their master . . ."

Referring to the practices peculiar to the Armenian Church, such as the use of unleavened bread, wine without the admixture of water for the Communion, also the celebration of the feasts on different dates, Nerses said that the Armenians had retained the early customs.

The Emperor Sends a Delegate to Katholikos

In 1170 Emperor Manuel I sent two delegates for a discussion with the Katholikos. They were Theorianus Magistros and John Utman, an Armenian, Abbot of the Monastery of Philippopolis. After the close of the discussion, Nerses wrote to the Emperor, saying that the Armenians admitted their error in thinking that the Greeks leaned towards Nestorianism, just as it was an erroneous belief of the Greeks that the Armenians followed Eutyches. At the request of the Imperial delegate, he again wrote out the profession of faith of the Armenians. On his return to Constantinople, Theorianus submitted a report to the Greek Emperor, ascribing to Nerses complete agreement with the Greek position.

Second Mission

In recognition of this (alleged) achievement, Theorianus, again accompanied by Utman, was sent to Cilicia on a second mission in 1172. On this occasion, they brought a memorandum comprising nine demands for the Armenians to accept.

Nerses sent letters of acknowledgment to the Emperor and the Patriarch, and promised to convene a synod, but died before it could meet. His successor, Grigor IV, Tgha (the Youth), was as desirous as Nerses of establishing peace between the Churches. In his acknowledgment of the letter of condolence sent by the Emperor, he begged him to lighten his demands. The emperors complied with this request when negotiations were resumed in 1177. He admitted that the Armenians did not confuse the two natures, and that their faith was orthodox. A letter signed by the Patriarch Michael and seventeen bishops and metropolitans also acknowledged the orthodoxy of the Armenian Church.

Dissensions Among Clergy

The Katholikos Grigor summoned the bishops and abbots to Hromkla for a meeting. But the clergy of Greater Armenia were not in sympathy with the idea of any union. Headed by Barsegh, Bishop of Ani, the Abbots of the monasteries of

Haghbat and Sanahin and others criticised the Katholikos for sending a profession of faith to the Emperor without consulting them. They insisted that confession of one nature of the Word God incarnate, as received from the Church Fathers, should be defended. They could not understand why these Greeks, while admitting that the Armenian dogma was orthodox, had sent a different formula for acceptance.

In reply to their opposition, the Katholikos reminded them of the precepts of love and charity, not to hate one another or insult and curse. He rebuked their criticism of the Greeks, saying, "The Greeks have invited us once and twice; should we not meet them courageously, and either agree with them or make them agree with us? If they insist on the two natures, we should refute and chide them. If they change, we shall gain brothers. Even if nothing is achieved, the Armenians will at least have shown their good will."

This appeal had only partial success. The Bishop of Ani and several other prelates of Greater Armenia came to the synod at Hromkla in 1179. The Synodal letter sent to Constantinople explained the Armenian faith without mentioning the two wills and operations, but accepting the formula of "two natures" and stating what had already been explained by Nerses regarding the human and divine wills and operations. The letter ends with an expression of willingness to bring about a union, "for truly we have one Lord, one faith, one baptism, one God and Father."

This letter reached the Capital after the death of Emperor Manuel. His successor rejected the policy of moderation, and reverted to the oppression of the Armenians. When negotiations were resumed in 1196, the Greeks insisted upon the imposition of all the nine points originally presented. The council which met at Tarsus displayed a spirit of goodwill and a desire for reasonable collaboration. But despite the concessions made by the Armenians, the Greeks remained obdurate. Even a visit to Constantinople by Bishop Nerses of Lambron did not relieve the situation.

Armenians Unyielding

A fundamental fact is that the Armenians were determined to preserve the independence of their church. In accordance with the ninth clause of the memorandum presented by Theorianus, the Katholikos was to be appointed by the Emperor; but the Armenians were not ready for such submission. How could they forget the bullying attitude of the Greeks? "Your clergy and your people," wrote Nerses to the Emperor, "consider it an act of justice ... to hate and insult us. Order them to renounce such offensive actions and come to us in love and peace. ... Let there be an end to the reasons for which, until now, our people have fled from you. Our churches and altars of God are ruined, our sacred objects are destroyed, our ministers are subjected to ill treatment and calumnies, the like of which we do not even suffer at the hands of the enemies of Christ who are our neighbors. Such deeds not only fail to unite those who are separated, but bring dissensions even among those who are united."

Chapter XXXIX
Leaning Towards Unity

Leon II favors Latins

Encouraged by the appearance of the Crusaders in the East, the Armenians began looking to the Latins rather than to the Greeks for friendship. The promoter of this policy was Prince Leon II, whose objective was the restoration of the Armenian kingdom in the new homeland of Cilicia. The Prince was supported by the patriarch Grigor IV and the brilliant Bishop Nerses of Lambron. However, the clergy of the Eastern provinces, then under Moslem rulers, were opposed to any concession to either Latins or Greeks. Nevertheless, the desire for rapprochement was predominant. Prince Leon, in his endeavor to gain the royal crown which was being promised him by the Emperor Frederick Barbarossa, sought an intermediate ground hoping for harmony without estranging the Easterns whom he needed for the realization of his bold political designs on Armenia Major. But the Eastern divines remained suspicious and unyielding. Refusing to recognize the new Patriarch, Grigor VI, Apirat, they elected Barsegh (Basil) II of Ani.

Relations More Strained

Another difficulty was that the closer intercourse between the Armenians and the Latins irritated the Greeks, and the Emperor Alexis Angelus, by way of corrective, resorted to persecution. Bishop Nerses of Lambron was sent to Constantinople in 1197 in an effort to bring about a friendly understanding, but his labour was in vain. The negotiations with the Latins were more successful. Henry VI, successor of Barbarossa, agreed to bestow the royal crown on Leon. The legate of the Pope demanded the acceptance of some form of union before any royal investiture took place. Despite the opposition of the Armenian clergy, Leon succeeded in procuring the approval of the twelve bishops, and his coronation took place on January 6th, 1199. The legate placed the crown on his head and the Katholikos anointed him.

Latin influence was dominant during the long Patriarchate of Constantine I (1221-1257). The Armenian people, realizing the political, social and economic advantages to be derived from a connection with the West, became more and more reconciled to the policy of their lay and spiritual leaders. King Leon died without male issue in 1219, and his daughter Zabel, sixteen years of age, was crowned queen. Her first husband, Philip, Prince of Antioch, provoked the Armenians by his pro-Latin and other extravagances, and was seized and confined in a fortress, where he died. Her second husband, Hetoum (Ayton), son of the Regent, Prince Constantin, was crowned as King.

Wise Policy of Hetoum and Katholikos

Hetoum and the Katholikos Constantin rendered great service to the Nation in furthering a close relationship with the Latins without creating any public provocation. Meanwhile, they were also careful to keep on good terms with the Greeks, by negotiating with them through the Bishop Hacob I, Gitnagan (the Erudite). The successors, both of the King and the Katholikos, continued the policy of harmony with the Latins, without sacrificing the independence of the Church. But King Hetoum II (1289-1305) proved to be such a pro-Latin zealot as to cause internal conflicts. The Katholikos Constantin II, who had opposed the King's policy, was deposed. His successor, having been carried away by the Egyptians, did not have time to act, but Grigor VII of Anavarza, who occupied the patriarchal throne in Sis, was ready to introduce into the Armenian Church some Latin innovations. He summoned a Synod in 1307 to obtain approval of his plans, but died before it met. The next Katholikos, Constantin III of Caesarea, adopted and proclaimed the syllabus of Grigor VII.

From this time on, the attempts of the Kings and high clergy to bring about a church union continued. The political situation of the country, however, prevented any relaxation of the resistance to amalgamation. The Egyptian Sultans, who aimed at predominance in the coast-lands of the Eastern Mediterranean, deeply resented any European influence on the little Christian kingdom of Cilicia, and seized upon the slightest pretexts to invade that country, whose hope for adequate military aid from Europe remained a mere fantasy.

Return to Etchmiadzin (1441)

The Kingdom of Cilicia fell in 1375. During the half-century incumbency of the seven succeeding Patriarchs, the moral standard of the see suffered a lamentable decline. The succession to the Pontificate was obtained through bribery or violence, and extortion was in consequence a means of recoupment of outlays. The Patriarchate of Aghtamar, in eastern Armenia, faced with the decay of the see of Sis, assumed leadership to remedy the situation, and perhaps to strengthen the prestige of their own position. The theological school of Sewniq had become a center of learning under such able divines as Hovhannes of Orotn, Maghakia of Khrim and Grigor of Tadev. This sort of intellectual activity, reinforced by other considerations, gave rise to the idea of the reestablishment of the Patriarchal throne at its original home, Etchmiadzin — which at that time happened to be enjoying relatively some measure of security under Persian domination.

A general council, composed of 700 ecclesiastical and lay members met at Etchmiadzin in 1441 and voted a resolution to effect the change. Grigor IX, Moussapekian, who was Supreme Patriarch at the time, preferred, however, to remain at Sis with a limited zone of jurisdiction, and approved of the election at Etchmiadzin of Kirakos of Virap.

Unfortunately, the rosy hopes for a new era of peace and progress within the Church did not materialize. Patriarch Kirakos abdicated in 1443, to be succeeded by Grigor X, Jelalbekian, then by Zakaria of Aghtamar, and then once more by Grigor X. From that time on during the next two centuries, the Patriarchs were constrained to have one or more coadjutors. This system, which was adopted in order to satisfy the ambition of certain Bishops, had also a beneficial result; it simplified the order of succession, the senior coadjutor being immediately enthroned upon the death or retirement of the incumbent. The disturbed political situation of the country had made almost impossible the convocation of complete and untrammeled electoral assemblies.

Symbolic Relic of Dignity

The possession of the relic believed to be the right Arm (Atch) of St. Grigor Loussavoritch (the "Enlightener") had, since the early centuries, been considered an appanage to the Patriarchal dignity. Consecrations were performed with the "Holy Atch." The predominance of Etchmiadzin over Sis could be confirmed only by the presence there of this relic. Zakaria of Aghtamar carried it away with him when he was driven out of Etchmiadzin in 1447. The foundation of the Patriarchal See of Cilicia dates from 1477, when Bishop Karapet of Tokat, the anti-Patriarch, began to boast of the possession of a pretended Holy Atch (Arm).

Inner Conflict and Oppression

From Grigor Jelalbekian (1443) to Movses III's election in 1629, Etchmiadzin was a scene of conflict and confusion. There were no less than thirty pretenders to the Patriarchal seat, some of them already coadjutors. With the sale of the holy office by the Persian khans and the torture of priests, the Church's degradation had reached its lowest point.

A faint ray of light appeared with the advent of Katholikos Michael of Sebast in 1540. He held the contestants in check and adopted progressive measures. Being particularly interested in the new art of printing, he sent Abgar of Tokat to Venice for study in 1552, with a letter of recommendation to Pope Pius IV. By 1564, several books had been printed in Armenian, although we find other Armenian books printed up to 1512, but they were produced by European printers, sponsored by Armenian merchants. The movement spread far and wide — to Rome, Constantinople, Etchmiadzin, Ispahan, Amsterdam. In the last-named city the first completed Armenian Bible, illustrated, was printed in 1666 by Oskan Vartabed.

Awakening in 17th Century

Despite many drawbacks, the Armenians of the East were the first to strive towards intellectual light. Of notable import were the reforms achieved in Etchmiadzin by the Katholikos Movses III, though his tenure of office was short, only from 1629 to 1632. He succeeded in obtaining permission from the Persian King for certain needed reforms, such as the cessation of extortions and reduction of taxes. His successor Philibbos continued his progressive policies, and traveled to Turkey where through his influence he settled the controversial matters of Constantine and Jerusalem patriarchates. Movses tried also to improve the financial situation of Etchmiadzin and to that end irrigation and hydraulic projects were carried out.

Hacob III (1655-1681) repaired to Constantinople in 1664 to grapple with certain problems, especially the proselytizing campaign of a Roman priest, Clement Galanus. An Armenian vardapet, Thomas of Aleppo, pro-Latin, had usurped the post of the Patriarchate of Constantinople, but he was soon expelled therefrom in an outburst of popular indignation. Hacob also had to face Eghiazar of Aintab, who proclaimed himself anti-Katholikos and Patriarch of Jerusalem and Constantinople. Hacob again journeyed to Constantinople where he died in 1680 under the strain of his overwhelming task. The anti-Katholikos was legitimately elected and did some praiseworthy work before his death in 1691.

Simeon of Erevan
A New Era

From the Katholikos Nahapet of Edessa down to 1763, all his successors, ten in number, gave of their best for the high position of the see. The most distinguished of them was the last of the ten, Simeon of Erevan, whose innovations may be said to have opened up a new era. He established legal registration of the real and personal properties of the Monastery, insured the protection of other interests of Etchmiadzin, effected the enrichment of the Seminary's curriculum and the founding of a print shop and a paper mill. He was also the author of the Armenian Church calendar, and instituted a chancery for the official records. The Katholikos Ghoukas (Luke) of Erzerum (1780-1799) endeavored to implement the projects of Simeon. He also formed a permanent council of Bishops as advisers to the Supreme Patriarch. The embellishment of the interior of the Cathedral at Etchmiadzin was another of his projects.

Relations with Russia

The tranquillity necessary to such spiritual and intellectual enterprises was, however, of short duration. Etchmiadzin was almost continually at the mercy of avaricious and tyrannical Persian Khans, making life unbearable for the Armenians. The result was that they began to seek Russian protection. A number of families took refuge in Russian territory, and thus came about a closer relation with the Tsarist empire of the North. Archbishop Hovsep Arghoutian won the sympathy of the Empress Catherine II (1762-96) and her son, the Tsar Paul I (1796-1801). It was not long before the Russians began taking more drastic measures. They declared war on Persia, occupied Erevan and Etchmiadzin, and an Armenian contingent of volunteers, with Archbishop Nerses Ashtaraketsi in command, joined the Russian army. Generous promises, implying the creation of an autonomous Armenia, were made by the Emperor Nicholas I (1825-55), but proved to be mere empty words. Russian generals on the scene discouraged the idea of Armenian independence, and in 1836 Etchmiadzin was placed under Governmental control by a regulation known as "Polozhenia." At this, Armenians throughout the world expressed some resentment, but eventually discovered that State supervision had its advantages. The Armenians in the Caucasus and in the other parts of Russia were all enjoying peace and security in business and the arts, and had made notable progress in cultural fields.

Between Russia and Turkey

In 1903 the Russian Government assumed a threatening attitude because of certain political demonstrations staged by Armenians. All the properties of the Armenian Church in Russia were confiscated and their schools were closed. The oppressive measures had attained fearful proportions when they were revoked in 1905. Steps taken by the Russian orthodox clergy caused great concern to the Armenians in Russia and abroad. Armenians in Turkey did not conceal their irritation, even advocating a pro-Turkish policy, until the black days of the Armenian tragedy of 1915, planned and executed by the Young Turk leaders, restored the Giant of the North to the former place of "Keri" — uncle.

Etchmiadzin Still Center

Church. Since Ephrem (1809-1831), nine Katholikosi have succeeded each other — Hovhannes VIII (1832-1842), Nerses V (1842-1847), Madteos (1848 The patriarchal See of Etchmiadzin, which was occupied by Ephrem at the time the Russian annexation, still remains as the residence of the Supreme Head of the Armenian-1865), Kevork IV (1866-1882), Magar I (1885-1891), Mkrtich I (1892-1907), Madteos II (1908-1911), Kevork V (1911-1931), Khoren I (1933-1938), Kevork VI (1945-1954), and Vazken I (1955-).

Armenian Religious Denominations

The Armenians are divided into three faiths:—

1. Those who belong to the National Armenian Orthodox Church, mistakenly called by others, "Gregorians." The majority of the Nation are members of this Church.
2. Members of the Roman Catholic Church. The main difference between these two faiths lies in the fact that the Roman Catholics recognize the Pope of Rome instead of the Katholikos of Etchmiadzin as their spiritual head.
3. Those who are affiliated with some branch of Protestantism — mostly Congregationalist.

Hai-Horoms

There were, before World War I, a few thousand Armenian-Greeks, calling themselves Hai-Horom, who spoke the Armenian language, but professed Greek Orthodox doctrines. They lived mostly in the district of Eghin, on the Euphrates, and around Gheyveh, on the Ankara railway line. They were originally members of the Armenian National Church. Those Armenian Emperors who sat on the throne of Byzantium were Hai-Horoms; they had to take the oath of allegiance to the Greek Orthodox Church upon assuming the crown.

Moslem Armenians

There also exists in Turkey a large community of Moslem Armenians, forcibly converted during centuries of persecution and massacres. Most of them still retain Armenian customs and traditions. Thousands were added to these converts to Moslemism in various parts of Turkey during the massacres of 1894 and 1915.

Old Words and Customs

A great number of agricultural, architectural and home-life words used by Turks are of Armenian origin. A few of the Christian customs still practiced by Moslem women before the Armenian deportations were these:— Making the sign of the Cross on the dough; bringing sick children to the Armenian Church, for the priest to read to Gospel over them; sending gifts to the Church and asking for prayers by the Sabbath congregation.

J. A. Tavernier, the French traveler, wrote in 1665:— "From Tokat (Asia Minor) to Tabriz (Persia), the country is inhabited by almost none but Christians; one should not be surprised if, in the cities and in the countryside, fifty Armenians are found for one Mohammedan."

In Armenia were found the roving bands of Armenian Gypsies, known as Tchingans or Poshas. They spoke the Armenian language, also an idiom allied to the Sanscrit of India.

Patriarchate of Constantinople

Sultan Muhammed II, after conquering Constantinople in 1453, granted the Greek patriarch privileges connected with religion. A new Armenian colony brought to Constantinople in 1461 was placed on the same footing as the Greek element, with Bishop Hovakim of Brussa as their Patriarch. The Armenian Patriarchs of Constantinople gradually extended their influence over all the provinces of Turkey, even including the dioceses of the Patriarchate of Jerusalem and the Katholikosate of Sis and Aghtamar.

Creed and Differences

The chief doctrinal points of the Armenian Church are as follows:—

1. Rejecting the Filioque, it asserts that the Holy Spirit proceeds from the Father alone, not from the Father and the Son.

2. It rejects the decision of the Council of Chalcedon with regard to incarnation.
3. In reciting the Trisagion, it retains the addition, qui crucifixus pro nobis — "who hast been crucified for us."
4. It denies purgatory, but prays for the dead, consecrating to this devotion the day after Epiphany, Easter, the Transfiguration, the Assumption, the Exaltation of the Cross, the Feast of St. Vardanians and Green Sunday (the second after Easter), dedicated "to the memory of the myriads of martyrs dead during the World War of 1914."

The Nicene Creed

The Symbol adopted by the Armenian Church, that of the service, is the Athanasian formulary which was born during the council of Nicaea. The Church has another symbol, too, adopted later which appears in the ritual, to be pronounced by the ministers of the Church on the occasion of their ordination. Its difference from the first is by paraphrased formularies, the principal one of which concerns the nature of Jesus Christ. They profess the monophysitism of the Council of Ephesus, quite different from that of Eutyches. The latter's name, together with that of Arius, of Macedon and of Nestor, are solemnly anathematized by the Church.

The differences separating the Armenian Church from the Greek Orthodox lie in the rejection of the Armenians of the Council of Chalcedon, and in non-recognition of the following councils — although the points defined by them were not rejected *ipso facto*.

This formulary would at first view seem independent of that of Nicaea, so that many scholars, Armenian and foreign, do not recognize any subordination of the one to the other. On the contrary, the two documents have been regarded as not only alike, but even identical. The Armenians lay claim only to the priority of their symbol or credo. They charge that an allegedly ancient Greek translation, supposedly written by St. Athanasius, is a counterfeit. Others hold the contrary belief. Evagrius the monk, who died in 399, used it in a treatise, of which an Armenian translation is in existence. In a letter to the Syrians, dated 504, Katholikos Babken used the symbol of Nicaea, but in a second letter he employed the above formulary. In the preceding century, Katholikos Sahak had inserted this symbol in his reply to Proclus. There have been later unauthorized compilations of the formulary. The one now recited in all the Armenian churches has a slight difference from the above.

The following declaration of faith of St. Gregory the Illuminator concludes the profession of faith:—

"And now we glorify him who was before all eternity, worshipping the Holy Trinity and Godhead of the Father, of the Son and of the Holy Ghost, now and ever, and unto unending times. Amen."

Name of the Church

The Armenians make use of the ethnographic term, "the Armenian Church" (Hay Yekéghétzi), or "the Church of Armenia" (Hayastanyaitz), or of "the Armenians" (Hayotz Yekeghetzi). The words *holy, apostolic, orthodox* have no official authorization. After the Russian occupation of Etchmiadzin, the word Loussavortchakan (Illuminatorian) was placed in front to specify the denomination of the Church and the word rendered in Russian by the term *Gregorian*, taken from the name of the Illuminator. The designation, Armeno-*Gregorian* Church had thus been recorded in the Russian *pologenia* (regulation) of 1836.

"Seeing that so much stress is laid on the need of a doctrinal designation," says Maghakia Ormanian, formerly Patriarch of Constantinople, "could not that of Oughapar (Orthodox) Church be adopted? ... We should be complying with common practice if we were to adopt the expression *Oughapar Armenian Church.*"

Armenian Catholics

First Appearance

Roman Catholicism was introduced among the Armenians of Cilicia as far back as the thirteenth century. Long afterwards, in the early nineteenth century, the activity of Latin missionaries in Turkey, meeting opposition from the native Armenian clergy, created discord and bitter quarrels between the two parties. A pamphlet urging National unity, printed in Constantinople in 1820, had an appeasing effect for a short time; then passions rose again and assumed treasonable proportions. Families inclined to the Roman Church were accused of disloyalty to the Sultan, and were subjected to many hardships. They were saved from persecution by the intervention of European diplomats, especially those of France. Finally in 1831, Armenians of the Roman Catholic faith were authorized by the Sultan to organize their own community, with a Patriarch, independent of the Armenian hierarchy. The situation was improved in 1846, when a group of educated young men from among the Catholic Armenians, founded in Constantinople a Society, having as its object the cultivation of tolerance, the conciliation of parties and the promotion of education among the Armenians. By a happy coincidence, the Armenian Mekhitarist Fathers of Venice and Vienna, who acknowledged the Pope as their supreme head, were rendering invaluable service to their Nation through schools and publications, diffusing enlightenment and inspiring patriotism.

The first Katholikos of the Armenian Catholics was elected in 1740 and given residence in the monastery of St. Mary of Bzemmar in Lebanon. Later, during the Patriarchate of Antoine-Hassoun of Constantinople, that See of Bzemmar was transferred to the Turkish capital, and in 1866 the Church's two chief officers were united in the person of Archbishop Hassoun as Patriarch Katholikos.

Armenian Protestants

American missionaries first appeared in Palestine and Syria in 1824. Two Armenian bishops, Hacob and Dyonesius, unfrocked because of peculations during their administrative duties in the monastery of Jerusalem, had, after a short affiliation with the Roman Catholic Church, adhered to the American movement. In 1830 Dwight and Smith, Presbyterian missionaries, traveled together in the provinces of Armenia. In 1831 a Mr. Goodell established his headquarters in Constantinople and began a systematic labor among the Armenians. The first Protestant Church, under the auspices of American Congregational missionaries, was organized in Constantinople in 1838, with the cooperation of Armenian ex-priests from Nicomedia. Mr. Schneider was then in charge of the field of Brussa, and Mr. Johnston of that of Trebizond.

The spread of this new doctrine was rapid. The Armenian patriarch of Constantinople, Stepanos Aghavnie (Stephen the Dove), a man of pacific temperament, looked upon the movement with little anxiety. The notables of the nation, dissatisfied with his forbearance or indifference, created in 1839 the office of Coadjutor in the Patriarchate. The man chosen for this post was Bishop Hacob Seropian, who, in an excess of energy, exiled four leaders, three of whom had had no part whatsoever in the Protestant movement. The three were Phizica Boghos, a man of learning, Thomas, a vartabed, and Kevork, a priest. Upon Stepanos's retirement from office, Hacob succeeded to the throne of the Patriarch. He forbade attendance at American schools by children, and hurled excommunication at those who were in sympathy with the dissident and disloyal members of the National church.

These threats and penalties did not serve their desired purpose. The preachings, publications and educational enterprises of the missionaries gained prestige from them and attracted more adherents. Another school was founded at Bebek, which was destined in after years to become Robert College. Meanwhile, the Patriarch's aggressive policy had suffered a check as a result of pressure on the Sublime Porte by the diplomats of America, England and Prussia.

Hacob now changed his tactics and had recourse to weapons of a moral and persuasive nature. He began paying special attention to the schools of his own church, and particularly to the Jemaran (Academy) of Scutari. He also became engaged in another and most crucial struggle within his own flock. Resenting a dictatorial attitude of the Amiras — the wealthy and influential Armenian grandees — Hacob assumed the leadership of the popular or middle class front, which was mostly represented by the heads of various trades and crafts (Esnafs). The struggle was to end after twenty years with the establishment of the Constitution of the Patriarchate.

The denominational controversy did not survive as long as that. Patriarch Matthew inaugurated a series of debates, in which learned men from each side took part. In one of these meetings, the utterances of an Armenian Vartabed were so sarcastic and insulting with regard to the Virgin Mary, the Cross and baptism that the Patriarch unfrocked him and published a bull against the Protestants. Again diplomatic pressure was brought into play. The British Ambassador, Sir Stafford Canning, not only remonstrated with the Grand Vezir, but wrote a letter to Patriarch Matthew, reproaching him for his intolerance. Matthew answered him in writing and then called upon the Ambassador in person to explain his actions. The Ambassador had already been persuaded to modify his views to some extent through the mediation of Bishop Horatius of the Anglican Church of Constantinople. In a subsequent report, the Bishop characterized some elements of the movement as "a mixture of atheists and radical factions, destroyers of Church canons and of original truths." But whatever the factual details may have been, the cause of freedom of worship was to triumph at last. At the behest of Lord Cowley, the British Ambassador, seconded by the Ambassador of Prussia, an Imperial edict was promulgated in 1847, authorizing the creation of the Protestant Millet (nation) of all non-Moslem races, with a Vekil (representative or head) of the community.

Chapter XL
The Armenian Language

Where First Known

Armenian is the idiom first known as being spoken in the sixth century before Christ by the people living in the mountainous regions of Ararat, the Lake of Van, the southeastern shore of the Black Sea, and the sources of the Euphrates and Tigris Rivers.

Of Indo-European Origin

It is an Indo-European language; that is, an outgrowth with variations, of a long-vanished tongue, represented also by the Indo-European, the Hittite, the "Tokharian," the Slavic, the Baltic, the Albanian, the Greek, the Celtic and the Italic (Latin and Osco-Umbrian). But it is as independent of all the others as are, for example, the Greek and the Germanic. It is isolated, not paralleled by any language of similar aspect, as the Slavic is with the Baltic, or the Italic with the Celtic. In its earliest known form, it appears to have had no dialects. From the beginning, it has been manifested in one form only, and the modern speech does not present any trace that would indicate the existence of dialects greatly differing from one another even in the fifth century A.D. In any case, these tongues do not contain anything to imply Indo-European peculiarities unknown in the classic Armenian. For at least a thousand years it was not written, and therefore, there are no documents in existence to enlighten us about its origin and about the influence exercised upon it by the idiom spoken by the natives of the area which was later occupied by the Armenians.

Theory of Thracian Origin, via Phrygia

Some Greek historians say that the Armenians must have been Phrygian colonists — the Phrygians themselves being of Thracian origin. J. Marquart has even placed their habitat in the north of Thessaly. But the little that is known of the Thracian language does not confirm this theory linguistically. It appears evident that the Armenian tongue was brought to the country later known as Armenia between the tenth and the sixth centuries B.C. What influence did the language of the previous inhabitants have on it? Unfortunately, scholars have been unable to find any clues which would determine what Armenian words whose etymology is still unknown could have sprung from the speech of the natives. No doubt many words were adopted bodily. It is therefore probable that the linguistic tendencies of the ancient inhabitants of the country have in a large measure determined the destinies of the Armenian.

Resemblances to Georgian, Caucasian, etc.

In fact, the general aspect of the Armenian phonetic system resembles that of the Southern Caucasians, the Georgians and other near neighbors. As another remarkable similarity, the Southern Caucasian languages have numerous declensions, but no grammatical gender; while the Armenian, despite the dropping of the final letters, has preserved almost all the cases of the Indo-European declension, but has no trace of genders, which were lost before the fifth century A.D.

We have no account of the development of the language during the long period of time between the Indo-European era and the stabilization through writing of the classic Armenian. The Vannic cuneiform inscriptions were written in an idiom differing from the Armenian. The Hittite inscriptions have now been deciphered, and the language does not appear to have any close relation with the Armenian.

Borrowings from Other Languages

Contacts with subdued nations and later, with conquering ones and others, introduced a great many foreign elements into the Armenian language. In the early centuries of the Christian era, the Armenians were frequently under Iranian domination. For more than three centuries the country had an Arshakid dynasty, and during that time the nobility had a strong Parthian flavor. Hence the numerous Iranian words in the Armenian vocabulary, whose forms indicate that they were borrowed, not from the old Persian, but from an archaic Pehlevi. There are so many Iranian elements in the Armenian *vocabulary* that the language was for a long time regarded as an Iranian dialect. However, the Armenian *grammar* remained almost free from the influence of the Persian, which has neither declension nor gender. The Syriac and Greek words found in the Armenian proceed from ecclesiastical and scientific borrowings and are of little linguistic importance. Many Greek words have strayed into the Armenian indirectly through borrowings from the Pehlevi.

Grabar, or Written Language

The introduction of Christianity into Armenia and the desire for evangelization brought into existence the Grabar or written language, in classic form. Like the Gothic and the Slavic, the Armenian was first written by a scholar who put into words its system of grammar and a vocabulary facilitating the translation from Greek of the sacred books and writings, expressed in an alphabet well adapted to the phonetics of the tongue. The irregularities of writers accused of vulgarisms, like Lazarus of Parb (Ghazar Parbetsi), are chiefly lexical. Where grammatical, it is by no means certain that they were perpetrated by the authors; they may be innovations by writers or copyists. Almost all the existing manuscripts of these authors were written no earlier than the Middle Ages. Certain translations of philosophical text in an artificial style, almost always imitations of Greek originals, have also peculiarities, manifestly novel, which are departures from the originals.

Phonetic Variations East and West

Because of the absence of ancient dialectal differences, it cannot be determined in what region the classical Armenian was evolved and stabilized. As the language of scholars and the Church, the classic Grabar has remained in use to the present time. It passed gradually out of popular use in the Middle Ages, being replacedamong the people by the modern common vernacular (Ashkharhabar, from Ashkharh, "world," "country") which was in general use in the fifteenth century. It is to be noted that there are a number of phonetic variations between Eastern and Western vernaculars of the modern Armenian, as for example the sonorous labial, guttural and dental letters, b, g, and d, heard in the East, are in the West turned into p, k and t. For example, the word Grabar, so pronounced in the East, would in the West be pronounced Krapar. Sourb Grigor in the East become Sourp Krikor in the West. The Eastern is nearer to the classical Armenian.

Grabar passed out of use in the eleventh century, in which epoch texts of a dialect (Armenian of Cilicia) were used.

Byron a Student

Among the students of the Armenian language we must not forget the English poet, Lord Byron, who for some time lived in San Lazar, Venice, and had as his teacher Father Pasquale Avcherian, with whom he collaborated in compiling an Armenian-English grammar. In a letter written to a friend on December 5th, 1816, Byron expressed himself as follows, ". . . . I find the Armenian language — which is twin, the literal and the vulgar — difficult but not invincible; at least, I hope not. I shall go on. . . . It is a rich language, and would amply repay anyone for the trouble of learning it. . . ."

The Armenian language and literature undoubtedly offer to the philologist, to the students of Oriental-Christian literature and to the theologians, a vast field for research. Often, for example, the ancient Armenian versions, in the absence of the Greek originals, become definitely precious, particularly if one takes into consideration their accuracy. The adaptability of the Armenian language to the peculiarities and nature of the languages in the original texts, is indeed remarkable.

When the Armenian version is done by men of genius and good taste instead of some humble and anonymous monk, it becomes a notable work of art. It is sufficient to remember the stupendous version of the "Oraisons Funèbres," of Bossuet, and the "Georgics" of Virgil, and of the "Sepolcri" of Ugo Foscolo, made by Father Arsen Bagratuni.

Under this aspect, the Armenian language and literature are seen as really a language and literature of translations, though original and admirable works in Armenian are not lacking.

Chapter XLI
Armenian Literature

Ancient Armenian Literature

Two objectives prompted Mesrop in the accomplishment of his great work; the diffusion of the Christian faith in his own country, and the emancipation of the Armenians from the influence of foreign preachers. The first works translated from Greek and Syriac texts were those devoted to religion and piety — the Old and New Testaments, the writings of Ephrem the Syrian, the Hexameron (six days of creation) of Basil of Caesarea, the homilies of John Chrysostom, the Ecclesiastic History of Eusebius, History of the Conversion of Edessa, the (apocryphal) correspondence of Jesus with Abgar by the Syrian Laroubna, the Syriac liturgy and that of St. Basil. The original works composed in Armenian were those of Korioun, Yeznik, Agathangelos and Phaustus. There are hymns attributed to Mesrop and Sahak.

No Written Literature before Mesrop

No Armenian literature in writing existed before Mesrop's era. Movses of Khoren (Khorenatsi) cites certain names as of historians dealing with Armenia; Mar-Apas Katina (identified by some critics with Berosus), Olympus (Ughicub) of Ani, the archpriest of Hormuzd (Aramazd), Bardesan and Khorohput, Iranian annalists. Khorenatsi's statement as to the existence of such historians as these has been disputed by some authors, but their opinion is debatable, because Armenia, in the stage of civilization which she had then attained, could not have remained without possessing any inscribed annals at all. The upper class of her population was highly cultivated; life within the royal court and satrapal mansion was colorful and rich in the display of artistic taste. There were men of letters among the nobility; Tigran the Great's son Artavazd had written tragedies and treatises in the Greek language which Plutarch mentions with praise; Vrouyr, a man of royal blood, was a distinguished poet; Parouyr, a native of Göksun, Cilicia, the Proeresios of the Greeks and known as "the prince of orators," was a teacher of elocution in Rome; Gregory of Nazianzen, his pupil, speaks of him in admiration.

Oral Hymn Composers

Nevertheless, the real Armenian literature of those days is to be traced in the oral hymns composed by the songsters, of which a few fragments only have been quoted by Movses Khorenatsi and Grigor Magistros. These chants were numerous, various and very popular. For centuries they lingered on people's lips, despite the efforts exerted by the Church Fathers to eradicate them as heathen relics. That old poetry vibrated with epic inspiration; it sang the powerful and serene gods; *Aramazd,* "the source of mankind," "the father of the gods and all heroes," "the architect of the universe," "the creator of heaven and earth," "the wise," "the valiant"; *Mihr,* the invisible fire, son of Aramazd, the essence of universal life, the god of light and heat; *Nana,* the goddess of maternity, the patroness of the family; *Astrik,* the goddess of beauty and wisdom, the patroness of virgins; *Anahit,* goddess of fecundity and of wisdom, "the pure and immaculate lady," "the mother of chastity. She is the glory of our Nation and its protectress. Through her the Armenian land exists, from her it draws its life."

Anahit, the Golden Mother

Many images and shrines were dedicated to Anahit, under the name of Oskémair, the Golden Mother. The name Anahit was borrowed from the Zoroastrians. On her festival day a dove and a rose were offered to her golden image, hence the day was called Vardavar, "the Flaming of the Rose." Her golden statue in Erez (Erzinjan), was captured by the soldiers of Antony.

Upon the introduction of Christianity, the festival of Anahit became the Feast of the Transfiguration of Christ. This is also the Armenian "water-day," on which occasion the people amuse themselves by throwing water at each other. On that day, the people had to show the progress they had made in art and in other occupations during the year. Races and other competitions took place, the victors being crowned with wreaths of roses. When the doves were flying, the High Priest sprinkled the people with the water of Aradzani (the eastern tributary of the Euphrates), and the people in turn sprinkled each other. The origin of this custom dates back to the traditions of the Deluge.

Vahagn, God of Force

Vahagn was the god of force, the lover of Astrik, who battled with dragons. He was credited with a miraculous birth; the fires of Heaven and earth and the sea, crimson in the light of dawn, travailed to bring him into being. Vahagn cleared Armenia of monsters and saved it from evil forces. His exploits were known also in the abode of the gods. Having stolen grain from the barns of King Barsham of Assyria, he ran away and tried to hide himself in Heaven. The grain he dropped became the Milky Way, which is called in Armenian, Hartgogh — "Galaxy or Milky way," "Tack of the Chaff-Stealer." Venus, the Roman goddess of beauty and love, was also the wife of a fire-god, Vulcan.

Romance of King Artashes

The theme of another song referred to by Khorenatsi is the romance of King Artashes. Addressing himself to Sahak Bagratuni, his patron and Maecenas, he wrote as follows; "The deeds of Artashes are known to thee through the epic songs which are chanted in the province of Goghten"; that is to say, his founding of Artashat (Artaxata),[89] his alliance by marriage with the royal house of the Alans, his sons and their descendants, the loves of Satenik with the Vishapazounq (progeny of dragons), who were of the race of Astyages (Azhdahak), his wars with them, the overthrow of their dynasty, their slaughter, the burning of their palaces, the rivalries of the sons of Artashes, the intrigues of their wives, which further fomented the discord among them. "Although these things are well known to thee through the epic songs, I will, nevertheless, narrate them again and will explain their allegorical meaning."

Another epic stanza, consisting of only four lines, refers to Queen Satenik's love for Argavan, the chief of the Medean prisoners, whom Artashes heaped with honours. The passage implies that Satenik was desirous of getting certain herbs — khavart and khavardzi — from under Argavan's pillow. If she could put them under her own pillow, Aragavan's affection would be insured.

One of the Artashes epics was sung by minstrels as late as the eleventh century. Here are some of its lines, as set down by Grigor Magistros. They are supposed to be expressions of the king in his last moments, during a foreign campaign;—

"Who will give me the smoke of the chimney and the morn of Navasard,[90] The running of the stag and the coursing of the deer? We sounded the horns and beat the drum As is the manner of kings."

Funeral Songs for King Artashes

The obsequies of Artashes were celebrated with great splendor. He was much beloved by his subjects, some of whom committed suicide at his grave. Professional female mourners (Yegheramayr) and singing maidens, dressed in black with hair dishevelled, followed the hearse, clapping their hands and moving in a slow dance. The funeral songs depicted the life of the deceased, his stature, the manner of his death and his domestic relations. The song called upon the dead man to arise from his slumbers. It rebuked him for remaining deaf to the prayers of the survivors, and vouchsafing neither word nor smile to them. Then came laudatory epithets addressed to the dead, and finally, farewells and messages through him to deceased relatives.

Sasma Dzur

Of all the epics from which Khorenatsi gives fragments, the only one that has survived among the people in complete form, with numerous variants, is *Sasma Dzur*. the Bible contains the following reference to the story; "And it came to pass as he (Sennacherib, King of Assyria) was worshipping in the house of Nisroch, his

---

[89] According to Strabo, it was built upon a design given to Artashes by Hannibal, the Carthaginian general, who had taken refuge in Armenia.
[90] Navasard was the Armenian New Year.

god, that Adramelech and Sharezer, his sons, smote him with the sword, and they escaped into the land of Armenia" (2 Kings, XIX, 37 and Isaiah XXXVII, 38).[91]

The epic related the doings of the two brothers and their descendants in Armenia. It is still handed down orally among the Armenians. Khorenatsi says that he himself heard these poems sung to the accompaniment of various musical instruments. The love of the old pagan religion and manners continued in the province of Koghten — abounding in orchards and vineyards — where the old poems were chiefly sung, long after the introduction of Christianity. These poems prove that the Armenians, even under Paganism and when they had no alphabet, had a perfected poetical language, which, in its construction, imaginative force, brilliancy and grammatical development, bears the impress of literary culture.[92]

Liturgical Poetry

Armenian literature contains a volume of religious poetry, represented by the *Sharakan,* the compendium of church hymns and chants. Some of them were written in the fifth century, and they were enriched by later additions, down to the thirteenth century. The oldest author known by name is Komitas the Katholikos (619-628). Sahakdukht, a noblewoman of the eighth century, wrote Sharakans and composed music. Modestly concealed behind a curtain, she gave singing instruction to both sexes. "They were angelic songs on earth," says the historian Ghevond Yeretz (Leon the Priest). Singers and musicians who were also poets were called in Armenia "philosophers."

Petros Getadartz, the Katholikos, visiting Constantinople in 1050, took with him a company of singers, whom he presented as a gift, for the service of the Byzantine Court. The twelfth century Bishop Khatchatour of Taron invented musical notes, quite unlike and unrelated to European ones.

Hymns

Armenian hymns, somewhat plaintive and monotonous in the Eastern style, have nevertheless a peculiar charm and often rich color. Great tenderness, hope, devotion and supplication are their characteristics. A vein of mysticism runs through many of them, especially those written by Grigor Narekatsi (951-1009), who think his name from the monastery of Narek, south of the Lake of Van. Narekatsi wrote elegies, odes, panegyrics and homilies. He is famous also for verbosity. In one passage the word "God" is embellished with ninety adjectives. The influence of Arabic literature is noticeable in the Armenian of this period.

---

[91] According to cuneiform inscriptions, only one, Arad-Ninlil, of the five or six sons of Sennacherib, committed the crime. His name has been corrupted to Adramelech. Sharezer, his alleged accomplice, the Nebo-Sar-Esher of the cuneiform inscriptions, was the prefect of Markashi (Marash). They were pursued and defeated near Karkemish, and took refuge in the land of Ararat about 700 B.C.

[92] See *Armenian Legends and Poems,* by Zabelle C. Boyajian and Aram Raffi, London, 1916.

Narek, the Book of Prayer, was once regarded with veneration but little short of that accorded to the Bible itself.

Some pagan melodies must have found their way into the hymn tunes of Christian Armenia.

Folk Tales, Fables, etc.

The unwritten literature of Armenia consisted mainly of folk tales, fables, proverbs, and riddles. It appears to have been a custom in ancient times for a man to meet on the bank of a stream or in a public park the girl whom he wished to marry, and propound a riddle to her. A correct answer would assure marriage.

Fortune-Telling

Charm-verses, used for fortune-telling, gave rise to another and extensive sort of literature. Once a year, on the eve of Ascension Day (Hampartzoum), young maidens who want their fortunes told, decorate a bowl with certain especially selected flowers. Into this bowl each girl casts a token — a ring, a brooch, a thimble. After filling the bowl with flowers of seven different kinds and water drawn from seven springs, they cover it with an embroidered cloth and take it by night to the priest, who says a prayer over it. Then they put it out in the moonlight, open to the stars, where it remains until dawn. At daybreak, supplied with provisions for the whole day, they go out of the village, carrying the bowl, to the brink of a spring, gathering on the way various kinds of flowers, with which they deck themselves. Arriving at their destination, they first play games, dance and sing; then they take a little girl, too young to know where the sun rises, who has been previously chosen for the purpose and dressed gaily for the occasion, and who does not know to whom each token belongs. They cover her face with a richly-wrought veil, so that she may not see the objects in the bowl, and one by one she draws the articles out of it. While she holds each in her hand, someone in the party recites a charm-song, and the owner of the token just drawn takes the song which accompanies it as her fortune.

Word-of-mouth Folklore

Armenia must have had much word-of-mouth folklore, which the elders recited during the long winter evenings to family groups and friends sitting around the hearth, describing deeds of valor by tribes and individuals. These treasures unfortunately have been lost, and have been partly replaced by Hebrew legends, through the ill-conceived zeal of the founders of the early Christian Church in Armenia, as in the entire Christian world of those days.

Clergy and popular Poets

The literature of Christian Armenia was cultivated for the most part by the clergy; nevertheless, despite the intolerant spirit which had prevailed, the taste for ancient memories was deeply bred into the masses, and therefore the link between pagan poetry and the new culture was not entirely broken. Through the renaissance of that spirit in the fifteenth century, there sprang up in Armenia, even among the clergy, a class of popular, non-religious poets.

All foreign specialists in the study of the Armenian language agree in attributing to it an honorable place among the best interpreters of human thought. The translation of the Bible is regarded as a remarkable literary monument.

Ancient Poetry

The ancient Armenian poetry dealt with the exploits of heroes, historical or legendary — Haik the mighty, of noble figure, with curly hair, bright eyes, powerful arms, brave and renowned among the giants; Aram, who captured the Medean tyrant Nukar, and with his own hand nailed him through the brow to the top of the tower of Armavir; Ara, the handsome, so loyal to his wife Nevart that he refused the hand of Shamiram (Semiramis), Queen of Assyria, who was so enamored of him that she fought a combat with him, endeavoring to take him by armed force; the King Tigran, who killed the tyrant Azhdahak of Media; the King Artashes II, who raised his country to an exalted plane of power and prosperity. Artavazd, the sullen and impetuous prince, cursed by his own father, the kindly Artashes, was precipitated by the genii of Mount Massis into a profound abyss, where he lives through all eternity, chained to a rock; for, "should he ever come out, he would destroy the world." The Armenian poets sang lastly, Torq, the giant who symbolized Force by crushing rocks with his hands, and sketching eagles on stones with his nails, who one day sank many vessels in the Sea of Pontus by throwing into it from a hill-top huge stones, which raised a tempest. Such are the traditions which reflect old Armenian memories, mixed with Oriental and Occidental fables. These chants, according to Victor Langlois, had been composed at various times by rhapsodists or popular bards who had free access to royal courts and aristocrats' palaces. We gather from what Khorenatsi says, that these oral poems of antiquity formed a complete epic, similar to the Shahnameh of the Persians. And yet they might have been isolated productions, such as songs of love, of dance and marriage, and sacred hymns dedicated to the gods.

Another View

Armenian poetry, as a form, offers certain characteristics of the Orient, but it also displays an intimate affinity and profound relationship with the art of the Occident. This popular poetry embraces all varieties — love songs, lullabies, children's songs, badinage, satirical couplets, prayers, funeral chants, dance motifs, songs of festivity and of weddings, tales in verse, national and historical chants, emigrants' laments and various others which glorify nature, extol the work in the fields, praise the birds, the seasons, etc. There are also popular epics, the most beautiful of which is that of David of Sassoon, the champion who, by his herculean strength, subdued lions and tigers, and who killed the tyrant Msramelik (King of Missr — Egypt) and freed his native land of the oppressor's yoke.

305

St. Grigor Loussavoritch, the Illuminator

To the founder of the Armenian Church is attributed the compilation of Hajakhapatum (Stromatis) a series of discourses, in Greek, on doctrinal, dogmatic, moral and canonical subjects. To him also is ascribed the authorship of hymns in honor of the maiden martyrs, Hripsimeh, Gayaneh and their thirty-three companions.

The Armenian word Hajakhapatum might be interpreted as "frequently delivered narrations" or sermons, "Stromata" in Greek. Father K. Zarbhanelian and others are not certain as to Hajakhapatum having been edited in Greek, in which language St. Grigor was trained in Caesarea. We know that the schools established by King Trdat taught the Greek and Syriac languages.

Analyzing the style and trend of the work, some critics find it a mediocre production of doubtful origin and of a date later than the Council of Nicaea (325). Patriarch Tourian, a modern scholar, after refuting P. Vetter's opinion that *Hajakhapatum* was written by Mesrop Mashtotz, concludes his essay with these words;— "Should we assume it to have been compiled about the last part of the previous (fourth) century, it must have been the product of an alien writer, translated into Armenian afterwards."

All records of St. Grigor's marvelous enterprise are silent as to his book until the middle of the fifteenth century, when a certain Archdeacon Grigor of Jerusalem used the expression Hajakhapatum. This fact is another bit of proof against the contention that St. Grigor was the author of the book, and in favor of the view that he was a man of action in defense of the new religion rather than a devotee of abstract speculation.

Zenob of Clag

Zenob of Clag, a Syrian priest, had accompanied St. Grigor from Caesarea to Armenia to assist him in the evangelization of the country. He was appointed Superior of the Monastery of St. Karapet — the Baptist — in the vicinity of Nine-Springs (Innaknian) of a stream in Taron.

The book of Zenob contains a letter of St. Grigor to Patriarch Leontius of Caesarea, thanking him for the relics of St. John the Baptists, by whose miracles the idols of Gissaneh had been demolished after a bloody battle. He thanked him also for sending to Armenia the anchorites Anton and Gronides. in his reply, the Patriarch of Caesarea congratulates St. Grigor upon the conversion of Armenia, he having received the details from certain travelers.

Zenob had been requested by Grigor to write the narrative of the assassination of King Khosrov, the disclosure of the relationship of Trdat with Grigor, the latter's incarceration in a dungeon, and his release to cure the King and to establish the Christian religion in Armenia.

Zenob's book, written in Syriac, has been subject to alterations and interpolations by copyists and translators, especially by Bishop Hovhan Mamikonian. Considered a compendium of absurdities by many critics, it has been praised by others for its interesting accounts of events.

According to Zenob, the pagan priests serving Kissaneh were black and long-haired, Indians by race, and because Kissaneh was tressed when he was compelled to accept Christianity, they made a habit of leaving a long tress of hair on the heads of their boys, in memory of their old cult. Such a custom prevailed in the Mamikonian family, whose home was in Taron, but Phaustus thinks it was common to all Armenians. Speaking of Artavazd, the son of Vatché Mamikonian, he says, "He was yet very young, and as such, in accordance with the religious custom of the Armenians, his head was shaved all around, retaining only a long tress of hair."

The Christians believed that the temple of Kissaneh was the "Gate of Hell and Sandaramet, the seat of a multitude of demons. As to Demeter, it was only known that he and Kissaneh were brothers.

Patriarch Yeghisheh Tourian believes, on the authority of the French savant Sylvain Levi, that the story of Zenob cannot be entirely discarded. The efforts from 256 B.C. onward, towards the spreading of Buddhism in Hellenic lands may have had repercussions in Armenia, resulting in the establishment there of the worship of Kissaneh (Indian) and Demeter (Greek). The German orientalist, Lassen, saw on Armenian soil the traces of a Buddhist-Hellenic religious syncretion.[93]

Agathangelos

Agathangelos, who is sometimes called a Greek, sometimes a Roman, was allegedly born in Asia Minor, within the bounds of Byzantine dominion. At the command of King Trdat, whom he is said to have served as secretary, he wrote a *History of King Trdat and St. Grigor*. This work covers a period of a little more than a century — 226 to 330 A.D. — which includes the reign of the valiant King Khosrov of Armenia. He describes the events as if by an eye-witness, but close study indicates that he had some sources for a part of his chronicle.

A few authors have disputed the very existence of a person of this name, the meaning of which is "evangelical preaching." Agathos means literally "good," and angelus "angel." This objection never brought forth a rejoinder. The appellation "Agathangelos" was not uncommon at that time. On the other hand, we have the fact that he was an object of veneration. Zenob and Khorenatsi call him "sincere and truthful." For Parbetsi he was "a God-blessed man." As for the book, it holds a very high place in the Armenian literature. The author was probably not

---

[93] In the development of religion, the process of growth through the coalescence of different forms of faith and worship.

proficient in literary Armenian, so he must have written in Greek, which he had mastered, along with the Latin.

The existing Greek copy of Agathangelos is a translation from an Armenian text, though the two do not entirely agree. The Greek contains pages which do not appear in the Armenian. There exists also an Arabic version of this ancient book. Alfred von Gutschmid is of the opinion that the *History of Agathangelos* is not the work of a single person, but is rather a collection of the writings of various authors of different periods. this view has been propounded by various scholars, from Cardinal Baronius and Fathers Papebock and Stilting to Langlois and Armenian experts.

That the Greek text was translated from the Armenian has been demonstrated also by linguistic proofs. Patriarch Tourian has cited a few nouns and place-names in the Greek text in their original Armenian forms;—

Yeraksh, the river, instead of the Greek Araxis:

Npat, a mountain, instead of the Greek Nipates:

Ekelisene, a province, instead of the Greek Akilesene:

Manya ayrk, a mountain cave, instead of the Greek Apelaion manes.

Aspet, a knight; Maghkhazoutune, a civil position of rank; and Spaskapetoutune, high-stewardship, all have the same form in Armenian and Greek.

The present text of Agathangelos is the work of several writers or copyists, who lived one and a half centuries after him, and reduced the historical work to a hagiographical compendium. No copy of the original Armenian translation has yet been discovered.

The earliest known manuscript, dated 1293, is now in the Library of Etchmiadzin. The Library of the Mekhitarists of Venice has several manuscripts, the oldest of which is dated 1634. Much older than this is 8th or 9th century manuscript, in middle Ergatakir and palimpsestic[94] text, now in the Mekhitarist Library of Vienna.

Phaustus of Buzant

Phaustus, sometimes called "of Buzant" (Pavstos Puzantatsi), a Greek by origin, wrote a *History of the Armenians* covering a period of sixty years from 330 to 390 A.D. Having lived in Armenia from his very early years, Phaustus became a naturalized Armenian, and attaining a Bishop's rank in later years, was

---

[94] A palimpsest is a parchment or tablet which has been used twice or three times, the earlier writing having been wholly or nearly erased.

admitted among the officials of the Katholikos under Nerses the Great. The work of Phaustus, written in Greek, before the introduction of the Armenian alphabet, was translated into the latter language. This history, although it contains many fantastic narratives and figures, is nevertheless a picturesque work, valuable as a mirror of some aspects of the life in Armenia in the fourth century and abounding in colorful descriptions. Phaustus is said to have been born in the town of Buzanda (modern Bozanti) in Cilicia, not in Byzantium, as his surname would seem to indicate.

Sahak the Great

St. Sahak Parthev (the Parthian) was the son of the Katholikos Nerses the Great. As an issue of St. Grigor, he inherited the Patriarchal See in 375 A.D., while he was yet in adolescence. He probably began his education in Caesarea. He covered a span of fifty years on the throne, with short intermissions because of political troubles. He trained a considerable number of disciples to serve as evangelists. He himself attracted large audiences whenever and wherever he preached, in cities and countryside. His literary works included the wonderful translations from the Scriptures, as well as ritual and ceremonial writings, especially pertaining to the Holy Week. He died in 439, and was buried at Ashtishat, in the district of Taron.

Prohaeresios or Proyeresios

Fourth century Greek authors mention a number of Armenian students who had gone to Athens and Rome to acquire higher learning. Proeresios (Parouyr Haygazn, the Armenian) stands at the top of the list. In his student days, he was so poor that he and his friend Hephaestion, having only one decent garment between them, wore it on alternate days. The name of Parouyr, unknown to Armenian authors, was first mentioned by Eunapius the Greek, his contemporary. According to this witness, Parouyr was endowed with unusual physical excellence — beauty of countenance, robust constitution and a titanic stature.

Attracted by the fame of this genius of erudition, the Emperor Constantine II[95] invited him to his palace in Gaul and entertained him magnificently, though the guest was very simple and ascetic in habits. He was sent by the Emperor to Rome, where he became an object of popular veneration, culminating in the erection of his statue, which bore the inscription, "Regina rerum Roma, Regi Eloquentiae" (Rome the Queen to the King of Eloquence).

The Emperor Julian, "the Apostate," a scholarly man, raised to the purple against his desire in 361 A.D., greatly admired Parouyr, and in a letter spoke of his "exuberant and overflowing stream of speech . . . mighty in discourse, just like Pericles. . . ." In the hope of winning Parouyr to apostasy, Julian maintained him

---

[95] Son of Constantine the Great. When the Empire was partitioned at his father's death in 337, he received as his share Britain, Gaul and Spain.

in a professorial chair, dismissing all others; but Parouyr remained loyal to his faith, and voluntarily resigned his lucrative post. He died at the age of 95. His pupil Eunapius had said several years before, "I saw him at 87, old and white-haired, silver-shining, as he used to say, but very active, the like of which I had never seen among the aged. I took him for an immortal being."

Among his admiring pupils were St. Basil of Caesarea, a great prelate, St. Gregory the Theologian, another celebrity, and Libanius, a famous non-Christian philosopher and rhetorician.

Mesrop Mashtots

Mesrop, son of Vardan, was a native of the village of Hatzekats, in the District of Taron, succeeding Sahak as *Locum Tenens*. At first in military service, he was later appointed secretary of the Royal Chancellery, for correspondence in the Persian language. He had gained proficiency in the Syrian language in Edessa, after graduation from school in Armenia. He was destined, however, to win the undying gratitude of the Armenian nation by devoting the best part of his life to the spiritual and educational needs of his fellow-countrymen. Encouraged by the saintly Katholikos, he chose as his first field of activity the district of Goghten, the modern Akoulis (Ordupat) near the Persian side of the Arax River.

His efforts were amply rewarded. The task undertaken in Greater Armenia having been consolidated, there now remained Byzantine Armenia as an object of concern. The Greek clergy opposed the establishment of Armenian schools. Mesrop, accompanied by Vardan Mamikonian, was delegated by the Katholikos to visit the royal court in Constantinople. They were graciously received by the Emperor Theodosius II and their request was generously granted by the monarch and the Patriarch Atticus, a native of Sebast (Sivas), and of Armenian origin. An Imperial edict authorized the establishment of Armenian schools, with subsidies from the civil list. Finally, Mesrop was honored by the titles of "Ecclesiasticos" and "Akumit," and Vardan with the military rank of "Stradelat."

No literary works by Mesrop are known, with the exception of a few sharakans and prayers. The ritual of the Armenian church known as "Mashtots," is ascribed to a Katholikos Mashtots, whose tenure of office was only seven months in the year 897. According to Father Zarbhanelian and several ancient chroniclers, the main compiler of the book of the Armenian ritual was Mesrop Mashtots. Patriarch Ormanian holds a different view, conferring the honor on Katholikos Mashtots. This worthy cleric, the Bishop Superior of the monastery of Sevan, was a "real anchorite" with a "philosophical mind." For forty years he took only bread and water as nourishment. His death in 897, was brought on, says Ormanian, by the abrupt change in his way of life from that of a hermit to that of the highest dignitary of the Church. The compilation of the ritual had been achieved before his elevation to the Katholikosate. Ormanian reminds us of the heavy responsibilities of Mesrop Mashtots; requiring his full attention. Furthermore, even had the work been done by this Mesrop, the naming of the ritual would have been in honor of Sahak, his superior. Ormanian calls attention to the differences in the orthography of the names — "Mashtots" for the missionary-educator, "Mashdots" for the devout and saintly abbot.

After the Invention of the Alphabet

The invention of the Armenian alphabet was soon followed by the translation of certain parts of the Bible, starting with the first verse of the Proverbs of Solomon; "To know wisdom and instruction; to perceive the words of understanding . . ." Mesrop's collaborators at that time were Rhupanos and two former disciples — Hovsep (Joseph) Baghnatsi and Hovhan Yegeghetsatsi. The original text was in Syriac.

The first Armenian letter-types, known as Ergatakir, are in the shape of the present capital letters, as written by an iron pen or style. In the ninth century they were somewhat altered, the curves being replaced by rectangular forms. In the twelfth century appeared the "Bolorkir," the present printing letter's shape, to which was added in recent times another modified form known as the italic or running-hand.

The French Armenist, Auguste Carrière, discovered in Egypt a piece of papyrus with inscriptions in Armenian characters and Greek. Father H. Dashian believed that the papyrus was the sheet from the notebook of an Armenian resident of Egypt who was studying Greek. The date of the notebook could not have been later than the first half of the seventh century — before the Arab invasion.

The complete translation of the Bible into Armenian Grabar or classic, was made from the Greek Septuagint by the Katholikos Sahak with the collaboration of his able assistants. A second translation was made 25 years later from a revised copy brought from Constantinople by the Armenian student-translators known as "Targmanitch".

The Golden Age of Armenian literature, with a brilliant record of 45 years, was the achievement of the Translators' school.

Yeznik

Yeznik, a graduate of the Sahak-Mesrop school, completed his linguistic, theological and philosophical training in Edessa and Constantinople. He returned home in 432, bringing with him the canons adopted by the Council of Ephesus and a true, correct copy of the Bible in Greek. He was commissioned by Sahak and Mesrop to revise the "hastily made" first Armenian translation, bringing it into accord with the new text. *The Refutation of Religious Sects* by Yeznik, attacks non-Christian beliefs, such as that of the Magian preachers, of Greek philosophers and of the heretical Marcion. Yeznik's writings contain borrowings from various foreign authors, yet the *Refutation* is declared to be a gem, a splendid specimen of the Golden Age of Armenian literature, because of the unexcelled perfection of its language and style.

Korioun's Life of Mesrop

Most of the Armenian historians and chroniclers, from the fifth to the fourteenth century, represent documentary interest concerning not Armenia alone, but also the Byzantine Empire and the nations of Asia. Korioun, the earliest Armenian-language historian, writing in the fifth century, has left a *Life of Mesrop* which contains many details of the evangelization of Armenia and the invention of the alphabet. Having received his early education under Mesrop, Korioun went to Byzantium for higher studies, returning to Armenia with other students in 432. Later, he was appointed Bishop of Georgia. He has been listed among the junior translators. His style is original, but somewhat obscure due to grammatical irregularities. To him have been attributed the translations of the three apocryphal books of the Maccabees.

David the Invincible

David, "the Invincible" (Anhaght), was born in the canton of Harq, Taron. He was the son of Khorenatsi's sister. While tradition places David among the great figures of Sahak-Mesropian schools who had been sent to Athens for higher studies, Greek Fathers, admiring his rare eloquence and erudition, ignore his Armenian nationality. Even in early years in Athens he won triumphs over competitors in impromptu discussions on scientific and philosophical subjects. For this reason he was honored by the titles of "philosopher," "the omniscient," "thrice grand" and "invincible." His works include originals and translations. Among them are the *Panegyric on the Cross, Rules of Philosophy, Instructions to Rhetors* and the *Grammar of Denys the Thracian.*

Yeghisheh

Precise data regarding the life of Yeghisheh (Elisha) are lacking. Incidental and sparse accounts of later dates represent him as an armor-bearer or aide-de-camp to Vardan, the Generalissimo, as an attendant, secretary, vicar, etc., who devoted his latter years to an ascetic life, during which he wrote the *History of Vardan and of the Wars of the Armenians.* First the province of Moks-Moxuan and then a cave opening upon the sea of Reshtounik (Lake of Van) have been named as the places of his seclusion. His work, an epic in prose, in which fiction is sometimes mingled with history, is placed in the first rank of Armenian classic literature. Some commentators have called him the Armenian Xenophon. Yeghisheh's task was not the pleading for a faction or party when he brands Vassak, the nakharar of Sewniq. In his religious zeal, he vigorously attacks the renegades in faith and exalts all who had contributed to the triumph of Christianity, including those who fell in the battle in 451, among them the martyred general, Vardan Mamikonian. Yeghisheh's book was written probably about 470. His claim to having been an eye-witness of events described by him should not therefore be taken literally.

Movses Khorenatsi

Movses of Khoren, to whose *"History"* we are indebted for all the information we have regarding the fragments of the Armenian epics and legends, was born in 410 A.D. He was one of the fortunate young men who were sent abroad for higher education. Upon his return from Alexandria, in whose great library he had been studying, he was shipwrecked and taken to Italy. He visited Rome, and from there went to Athens and Byzantium.

After his return to his homeland, he retired into solitude, because of the persecution organized against him by the ignorant clergy, who were unsympathetic towards all students educated in the West. According to a recent theory, Khorenatsi aroused public resentment by his adherence to the formula adopted by the Council of Chalcedon in 451 concerning Christ's nature. He altered his stand on the subject in later years, however, and thus obtained the bishopric of a diocese, which placed him in a better position to write his *History of Armenia.*

Some critics, both European and Armenian, question the veracity of much of Khorenatsi's work, and place him in the eighth or even the ninth century. Most modern critics believe that the History bearing his name, although a work of great value, cannot be that of Movses, "the Philosopher," of the fifth century, but a compilation made by one or more writers in the seventh, eighth or even the ninth century. There are others, however, who firmly believe Khorenatsi to be a fifth century historian, whose book has been garbled by later hands. However this may be, all are unanimous in declaring the History a most valuable document, not only for its poetic language and picturesque style, but also for the epic and legendary fragments and traditional accounts concerning the Near and Middle East, which corroborate Latin and Greek authors.

To Khorenatsi, who has variously been called "The Armenian Herodotus," "Father of Historians" and "Father of Poets," have also been attributed several works on rhetoric, hymns, grammatical and doctrinal treatises.

Ghazar Parbetsi

Ghazar Parbetsi, well known for his *History of Armenia,* and his letter addressed to Vahan Mamikonian, the Marzban of Armenia, had completed his studies in Byzantium in the second half of the fifth century. His narrative of events covers a period of 95 years, from 390 to 485, the first year of Vahan's rule. In the introduction to the book, written about 490, he points to himself as the third historian after Agathangelos and Phaustus. The second of his three chapters deals with the battle of Vardanians, on which he obtained his information from Prince Arshavir Kamsarakan and other eye-witnesses, and perhaps from records. His letter to Vahan is a self-defense against the imputations of venality raised by the monks, which had caused his dismissal from the Cathedral of Vagharshapat. Traces of popular or vernacular expressions in this letter have been noted by philologists. Parbetsi defends Khorenatsi, "the philosopher of blessed memory," who, he says, "met with much opposition and annoyance from the unlettered clergy, who called this enlightened man a heretic, and in their ignorance found fault with his books, besides showing many acts of unfriendliness towards him."

Hovhan Mandakuni (403-490)

One of the last representatives of the school of Sahak-Mesrop, Hovhan Mandakuni was 75 years old when he was elevated to the Katholikosate in 478. He served until 490. He was a perfect leader and wise politician as well as an eloquent orator. Several sharakans and prayers now in use are ascribed to him. He had the good fortune to greet Vahan Mamikonian in the Cathedral of Douin in the happy occasion of his nomination as Marzban of Armenia by the King of Kings. In his sermon he urged as a Christian duty good will and tolerance towards those who had been disloyal to the Armenian national interests. During the protracted struggle against the Persians, Mandakuni had been a champion of the national cause.

The literary style of Mandkuni is remindful of the earliest translators of the Golden Age. He was noted for the regulations of liturgy, divine service, holy orders, baptism, marriage, etc. Following the example set by Greek church-fathers, he emphasized the rules of decency and modesty, especially in theatrical performances.

Anania of Shirak

Anania of Shirak (Shirakatsi) is the only one among the early seventh century authors who produced scientific works, most of which, however, have been lost. An astronomical treatise entitled, *Concerning the Skies*, a collection of mathematical problems, a translation entitled *Of Weights and Measures*, a *Chronology* and a few discourses on feast days and calendars constitute Anania's surviving works. In recent years some critics claimed Shirakatsi to be the author of a "Geography" which had been attributed to Khorenatsi. We learn from his autobiography that he studied with the Greek master, Tucykos, in the city of Trebizond, and himself taught a group of pupils after returning home.

Movses Kaghankatuasi

Movses, an historian, was born in the village of Kaghankatouq, province of Outi, Aghwania (Caucasian Albania), and died after 685 A.D. The chronicle of the following three centuries, contained in the third book of his work are additions by another Movses, the Dashkhurantsi, of the tenth century.

Like the *History* of Sebeos, the work of this Movses was not known until the middle of the nineteenth century, although his name was mentioned by others as one of the very eminent writers. Since the discovery of this manuscript, he is considered an authority on northern tribes, especially those of Aghwania or Albania. According to his own statement, he had accompanied Viro, the

314

Katholikos of Aghwanq, as an attendant while traveling to the tent of the terrible chief of the Khazars. Much later, a second journey to the same court under another monarch, proved a beneficial one.

The unyielding spirit of the Aghwans impelled the Roman triumvir Pompey to subdue them by force of arms in the first century B.C. Although half-civilized and warlike they gradually moved towards the southwest and settled peacefully in the Armenian provinces of Outi, Artsakh and Paytakaran. In certain regions they gained prominence, despite their religious and cultural dependence on the Armenians. St. Grigor, the Illuminator, converted the Aghwans to Christianity and appointed a Katholikos for them in the person of Grigoris, one of his grandsons. Grigoris suffered martyrdom at the hands of a heathen mob in 342. Mesrop Mashtotz avenged him by returning good for evil. After having endowed the Iberians (Georgians) with an alphabet and a number of schools Mesrop left for Aghwania, and receiving encouragement in his mission from the authorities there, he was rewarded with gratifying results. On the other hand oppressive measures taken by the Byzantines compelled the Aghwans to adopt the Chalcedonian decisions. In the course of the eighth century the Armenian and Aghwan Churches held two united convocations in Partav, then a flourishing seat of the Aghwan Katholikos. The city, now in ruins, is known as Barda, not far from the Caspian sea-coast.

The Aghwan language, now almost forgotten, survives in a narrow area in Outi, on the banks of the River Kour. The close contact with the Armenians modified the Aghwan speech, which has been described as originally harsh and guttural.

The work of Kaghakanduatsi, known as *The History of the Aghwans,* ends in 685 A.D. It is of particular value because of information it contains about the manners, customs, religious concepts and ethnic divisions of Caucasian tribes — Huns, Khazars, Alains or Alans, Mazcouts and others, more than a dozen all told.

The *History,* beginning with the Biblical stories of Adam and Noah, points to Japhet as the ancestor of the nation, and depicts its "glorious" events, past and contemporary. Faulty chronology, which creates confusion, and an occasional disregard of grammar are compensated by the author's warmth of expression and beauty of style.

Sebeos

Sebeos, the Bishop of the Bagratids, wrote the *History of the Emperor Heraclius* (610-641), a valuable work, narrating Byzantine and Armenian affairs, military, political and ecclesiastical.

Hovhan Mamikonian, 7th Century

Hovhan (John) Mamikonian wrote a history of Taron as a continuation of Zenob of Clag's work on the same subject.

Hovhan of Otzoun (650-729)

Katholikos Hovhan of Otzoun of Otznetzi (in Tashirq) known as "The Philosopher," whose pontificate lasted from 716 to 728, was venerated for his saintly life and deep learning, even by the Arab conquerors. He wrote hymns, sermons, canons and ecclesiastical rules, his discourse against the Paulikian sect deserving special notice.

Ghevon the Historian

Ghevon (Leon) (720-790?), a priest, the only Armenian historian of the eighth century, has left a brief account of events during a period of 125 years, ending with 790, and mostly concerning the Arab invasion of Armenia. It contains a translation of a long letter supposedly written by the Emperor Leo III (718-741) to the Khalifa Omar II.

Shapouh Bagratuni

Shapouh Bagratuni, son of Ashot I and a military commander, wrote the history of his time, especially that of his princely family. He was the first lay Armenian to write a book in his native tongue. He was the father of Queen Mlkeh, the wife of King Gagik of Vaspurakan (Van). His name is well known through a Gospel especially written for his daughter's use, it being the second in antiquity (906) of the six oldest surviving manuscripts in the Armenian language. The first one, dated 887, is now in the State Library at Erevan. The manuscript gospel of the Armenian monastery of Jerusalem bears the date of 602, though this is still a matter of doubt and controversy. Of the *History* of Shapouh, no copy has so far been discovered.

Katholikos Hovhannes VI (840-931)

Katholikos Hovhannes VI, the historian, has left a record of his times — for the most part a sombre story with only occasional brighter glints — prefaced by a brief sketch of Armenian history from the beginning. He seems to have used Khorenatsi's work as a guide.

Thovma Ardzruni

Thovma (Thomas) Ardzruni wrote the history of his princely and illustrious house, under the orders of Grigor, "the Lord of the Ardzrunis and the Prince of Vaspurakan." Later hands have made additions to Thovma's original text, which ends with 905, the time of King Gagik of Vaspurakan (Van). This author had a searching mind and extensive knowledge. He made journeys in person to ascertain the truth of unproved statements. The sources of his information concerning the earliest periods were fifth century scholars such as Mambreh, his brother Movses and Theodorus — none of whose works now survive. Of special interest is Thovma's description of the primitive society of the almost inaccessible mountains separating the district of Taron from that of Aghtzniq (modern Bitlis). "The people of this region have been called Khoyt (rough), because of the rudeness of their manners and speech," yet they were known as hospitable and friendly towards strangers. They had the habit of reciting the Psalms according to the early translations of Armenian Vardapets, which they knew by heart.

Grigor Narekatsi (950-1010)

Grigor, younger son of Bishop Khosrov Antzevatsi, born in the village of Narek, district of Rshtuni, south of the Sea of Van, was devoted to monastic life from an early age. He became a famous writer and a saintly figure. He was even persecuted by jealous clericals because of his popularity.[96]

While still young, Grigor wrote a commentary in simple style on the "Song of Songs" of Solomon. He later produced eulogies and panegyrics which were considered sublime. They were dedicated to St. Mary, to the Apostles, to the Cross of the Monastery of Abaran and to St. James of Mdzbin[97] (Nissibin). Meanwhile he also wrote to the Superior of the cloister of Gjav, cautioning him against the Paulikian heresy.

Narekatsi's masterpiece is the *Prayer-book* (Aghotagirq), known as the "Narek," a penitent's lamentations in 95 chapters. In the language of Patriarch Tourian, "The work is an expression of anguish, a cry of wicked and unclean souls, as well as a voice of longing and of soaring towards eternal holiness and sublimity. His meditations, for the most part buried under a mysterious obscurity, now and then burst out like a flash of lightning which illuminates the tenebrous depths of a sorrowful world. Had the sincere words and ardent faith of a repentant sinner been less mixed with literary art and rhythmical lines, the entire work might have been less obscure. Nevertheless, his poetic zeal for conversation with God has enriched the language with a new zest, influenced by the strange tendencies of his time."

"The Prayer-book of Narekatsi," says Father Zarbhanelian, "although mysterious and difficult to understand, is marvelously beautiful, and has such a sweetness of style, that both Armenian and foreign philologists are unanimous in vouching that no such work has yet been seen in other nations."

---

[96] The story was told that when messengers from the Katholikos of Ani (Barsegh or Basil), came to investigate certain heresies charged to Narekatsi, they were invited by him to dinner during a Lenten week. The main dish was roast pigeon, of which the guests declined to partake. Thereupon Narekatsi ordered the pigeons to take flight, which they did, with extraordinary effect in favor of the host.

[97] Mdzbin, a fortified town, was in the district of a borderland on the southwest of Armenia. The monasteries of Gjav and Abaran are located in the province of Moqs, in southern Armenia.

A French scholar, Eugene Boré, traveling in Armenia in 1838, altered his course in order to visit the ruins of the Monastery of Nark. In the mind of this savant, "Narekatsi's name ranks as that of the most profound doctor, most nearly perfect writer and most tenderly pious saint of the Armenian Church." The writings of Narekatsi reveal a vast knowledge of theological and Biblical subjects, of Armenian history, and of the ancient customs of the Church.

Of some twenty authors dealing with Narekatsi, the most elaborate text of Narek was published in Buenos Aires, Argentina, in 1948 by Archbishop Karekin, then the Primate of South America, and now Patriarch of Constantinople. This 386-page volume, of large folio size, also comprises a translation into modern Armenian, each page of the modern version facing the classic original.

In his analytical, 46-page introduction, the erudite editor portrays the recluse of Narek — the moralist, preacher, teacher, and idealist, as often engaged in conversation with God. Another rendition of the immortal Prayer-book into modern Armenian was made by Patriarch Torgom of Jerusalem, a venerable and profound scholar and fervent admirer of Narekatsi.

Other writers have expressed the following interesting views regarding the author of Narek.

That his manuscripts have been altered, and subjected to interpolations or mutilations by ignorant and audacious copyists.

That he was not a pessimist; he was rather an optimist, with reliance on God's infinite mercy for the sinner.

That in non-religious verse, he was more of a troubadour than a poet.

That he was never influenced by foreign art or concept, whether Persian, Arab or Greek. All his background was national — *i.e.*, Armenian, which might be further specified as Narekian.

That his world was not exclusively internal or speculative; he searched for facts about his surroundings. His description of a ship-wrecked sailing vessel, for example, displays broad knowledge of the subject. It should be remembered that the sea or lake of Van was not far from the Monastery of Narek.

Taking into account all these opinions and evidence, competent authorities, including Patriarch Yeghisheh himself, admit that Narekatsi's Prayer-book remained for more than 900 years the magic wand for good, which charmed, enchanted, healed and guided multitudes towards the heavenly heights.

Grigor Magistros (990-1058)

Grigor Magistros, linguist, scholar and public functionary, was another writer of Narekatsi's period. A layman of the princely Pahlavouni family, he was the son of Vassak Pahlavuni, the general who had defended the city of Ani against the Greeks. Grigor served some time as Governor-general of the province of Edessa. The Byzantine Emperor Constantine I (Monomachus) bestowed upon him the title of Duke. He studied both sacred and secular literature, Oriental as well as Greek. He collected all Armenian manuscripts of scientific or philosophical value that were to be found, including the works of Anania Shirakatsi, and translations from Callimachus, Andronicus and Olympiodorus. He translated several works of Plato — *The Laws,* the *Eulogy of Socrates, Euthyphro, Timaeus* and *Phaedon.* Many ecclesiastics of the period were his pupils.

Foremost among his writings, are the *"Letters"* numbering eighty which shed much light upon the political and religious problems of the time. His poetry bears the impress of both Homeric Greek and the Arabic of his own century. His chief poetical work is a long metrical narrative of the principal events recorded in the Bible. This work, we are told, was written in three days at the request of a Mohammedan noble, who, after reading it, became converted to Christianity. Grigor was almost the first poet to adopt the use of rhyme introduced into Armenia by the Arabians. Unfortunately, his language is often almost unintelligible, because of artificiality and unusual words, especially when he deals with philosophical, scientific or mythological subjects.

Here is a fable written by Magistros, as related to him by the peasants;—

"The lark, fearing that Heaven would fall, lay on her back, holding her feet up towards the sky, thinking she might thus prevent the catastrophe. Some laughed at her and said, 'With your spindle legs, you want to become a tree, O bird, with a mind capacious as the sea.' The lark replied simply, 'I am doing what I can.' "

Stepanos Assoghik
Oukhtanes, Aristakes of Lastivert

Stepanos (Stephen) Assoghik (992-1019) wrote a *Universal History* (up to 1004 A.D.) in which events relating to the Bagratid period occupy a considerable place. Oukhtanes is another historian of Armenia, of the same period. Aristakes of Lastivert, the "Armenian Jeremiah," mournfully relates the story of the disastrous events of which he had been an eye-witness: domestic frictions, massacres, pillage and intrigues leading to the downfall of the Bagratid dynasty. He devoted two chapters to the activities of a certain religious sect,Paulicianism, spread out from the Tondrak, in Armenia.

Hovhannes Sargavak

Hovhannes Sargavak (Deacon John) (1045-1129), honored for his erudition by the title of Sophestes (Philosopher) and appreciated by King David of Georgia, became the Superior of the Monastery of Haghpati in Armenia. He reformed the Armenian calendar, and has left mathematical studies besides doctrinal, ritual and devotional works. He collected over fifty manuscripts, theological and philosophical, and had them recopied by his pupils, after having corrected errors made by previous copyists. Hovhannes, also known as the Vardapet (Doctor), had his library in a cave, where he studied day and night. He died in 1129. His gravestone, under the belfry of St. Mary's Church at Haghpat, still bears his name — Sophestes Sargavak. The historian Alexander Yeritziantz, found a few Armenian manuscripts in petrified condition in 1873 in the cave of Karni, which is believed to have been Sargavak's study and library.

Eleventh-Century Vernacular

By the end of the eleventh century, there was developing a vernacular of the people (the Ashkharhabar) in which books for popular use began to be written. The Grabar, or ancient Armenian, continued to be the language of the Church. The "Golden Era" of ancient Armenian literature was of short duration — only twenty-five years — but the influence and inspiration of the period bespeak a quarter-century of marvelous activity.

Nerses Shnorhali

Katholikos Nerses Shnorhali (1100-1173), grandson of Grigor Magistros, born in Sof (Dzovq), on the mountain Duluk (Doliche), northwest of Aintab, was the most noted author of the "Silver Age" of Armenian literature. He earned the title, "The Gracious," because of the purity of his life, the eloquence of his sermons, and the elegance of his literary style. He was also known as "Klayetzi," after the name Hrom-Kala or Hrom-Kla, the Roman fortress on the west bank of the Euphrates which became the Patriarchal See, purchased from the widow of Josselin Courtenay, the last Prince of Edessa.

Nerses, an issue of the illustrious Pahlavuni (Pahlavid) house, received his early religious training in Karmir Vanq (the Red Cloister), on the Black Mountains or Amanus, known as Ghiavour Dagh. At the age of eighteen he was ordained priest by his elder brother Grigor III, the Katholikos. He was so popular that the nomination was approved by all. He became famous even among Greeks, Latins and Moslems.

He was strongly in favor of an entente with the Greek Church. While still a bishop, he had an interview in Cilicia with Prince Alex, the brother-in-law of the Greek Emperor Manuel, and also wrote three letters to the Emperor concerning the doctrines of the Armenian Church. The Emperor, on reading them, was delightfully surprised, and sent a messenger to the Katholikos, requesting him to permit his brother to make the journey to Constantinople.

But the death of Grigor in 1165 prevented this. Nerses Shnorhali, succeeding him, wrote to the Emperor of his inability to present himself at the Palace, reiterating his desire for harmony between the Churches. Manuel thereupon dispatched Theorianá, the famous scholar, to Hromkla, with a letter in reference to the desired union. Answering to the Imperial script, Shnorhali refuted certain errors ascribed to the orders and dogmas of the Armenian Church. In a later, shorter note, he explained in what sense the Armenian Church professes the one nature in Christ, in conformity with the doctrine of St. Cyril of Alexandria (376-444).

To keep his people informed of his negotiations with the Emperor, the Katholikos sent to the bishops and doctors of Armenia and her neighbors, copies or summaries of these papers. He had imparted the news of his brother's death by an encyclical letter addressed to the clergy, to monastic superiors, bishops, princes, civil and military officers, to farmers and women. The language of this document is impressive yet plain and clear, and full of allusions to the life, customs, morals, and defects of his flock. Particularly significant is the following remark of the Spiritual Head of the Nation;—

> "Our people possess no royal and populous city where, occupying the patriarchal and doctrinal seat, we might teach the divine commands to our brethren in the manner of the first patriarchs and doctors of divinity. Forced to dwell 'in this grotto', we rather resemble deer in flight from hunters and dogs."

Nerses Shnorhali was a prolific writer and preacher. He sent numerous administrative circulars and special letters — such as the comforting message to the inhabitants of Edessa, who suffered from an epidemic of leprosy. Several married priests, one in Constantinople, another in Armenia, and a third whose domicile is unknown, assured an attitude of hostility towards the saintly Katholikos, endeavoring to undermine his policy of harmony. Shnorhali refuted their charges in a vigorous but dignified answer.

The great Katholikos had planned the convocation of an assembly for the discussion of the project of Church union, but he died in 1172 before his desire could be realized. His death put the movement in abeyance. The Emperor Manuel expressed his deep sympathy with the Armenians for their great loss.

Among the many prayers written by Shnorhali is one composed of twenty-four verses in prose, corresponding to the twenty-four hours of the day, beginning "Havadov khosdovanim—" ("Faithfully I confess—"). This has been translated into thirty-six languages and printed by the Mekhitarist Fathers of Venice. He also wrote commentaries on some parts of the New Testament, and edited "A commentary on a Eulogy of the Holy Cross," written by David the Invincible. The style of David, always enigmatical and obscure, was here utterly incomprehensible. Vardan Vardapet, of the Cloister of Haghpat, requested and received from Shnorhali an explanatory interpretation of the discourse. He also wrote "An Elegy on the Capture of Edessa from the Crusaders," by Atabeg of Moussul (1144), with an appeal to the five capitals of the world and to the Patriarchs of Jerusalem, Rome, Constantinople, Alexandria and Antioch. This poem is a source of information upon the times of the Crusades.

Also should be mentioned "Jesus the Son," an historical compendium of the Old and New Testaments in verse. Father Alishan finds it remindful of Milton's *Paradise Lost*. Neumann calls it a masterpiece. Jacob Villote characterizes it as "certainly divine." Shnorhali left yet another poem of an entirely different kind, "About the Sky and its Ornaments," written at the request of the Armenian physician and astronomer, Mkhitar Heratsi.

A great figure in the Silver Age of Armenian literature, Shnorhali wrote in the Armenian vernacular, to be read or chanted by the common people, even by the armed guards of the fortress. *A History of Armenia* in abridged form, rhymed, written in his teens, has won high praise. Among his many accomplishments must be mentioned his proficiency in musical art. He composed songs and taught them to the garrison of the castle, so that they might be used in replacement for discarded tunes. They begin with quotations from the Psalms of David. These are now parts of the morning and evening canticles of the Armenian Church.

His songs and sharakans are still sung in the Armenian churches. He wrote in all about 1500 lines comprising long poems, mostly in rhyme, as well as couplets of short lines, musical and sweet. One of his poems narrates the history of Armenia from the days of Haik up to his own time. King Leon III, 150 years after this poet's death, asked Vahram Raboun Vartabed to consequent the poem from the death of Shnorhali to his own time, 1275. Vahram wrote the desired sequel in 1,500 lines. "It is a bold act to continue the work of Nerses the Gracious," he apologized, but added that, aware that black threads are sometimes introduced into gold-thread embroidery, he consented to undertake the labor.

Foreign Influence Hellenist School

The Seleucians, by founding cities east of the Euphrates River, took the first step towards founding of Hellenistic culture in Armenia. Artavazd, son of Tigran the Great, wrote tragedies and discourses in the Greek language. A half-century — 550 to 600 A.D. — has been designated as the period of the Hellenistic School of Armenia, though scholars are not in full agreement as to the dates. Translations from the Greek of several works earlier than the sixth century are cited as proofs against them. In some of them Greek words have been adopted in composition, grammar, and syntax. This usage prevailed to such an extent that the translations are slavish and unintelligible, making necessary the aid of the Greek text itself.

Philhellenism has been attributed even to Sahak and Mesrop. The Katholikos Gute, enthroned at the age of 75 in 467, was famous as "full of Armenian learning; even more in the Greek." Armenian students were entranced by Greek culture. They specialized in non-religious and profane works, too, such as the

Discourses of Aristotle and the *Introduction* of Porphyry. According to M. Abeghian, there were three cycles of Hellenism in Armenia — 1) from 450 to 475; 2) from 552 to 564; and 3) from 600 on. Another computation dates the beginning from the compilation of the *Grammar* of Dionysius of Thrace, in the second century B.C. H. Manandian classifies the translations into three groups. Khorenatsi's Hellenistic leaning is indicated also by the title, "Philosophos," bestowed upon him. The Syriac equivalent of the word is "Philosopha," the form adopted by the Armenians. M. Abeghian deals at great length with Khorenatsi's work on Rhetoric and Poetry — Pitoyits Kitq in Armenian, Xreia in Greek. This was the art of developing the life of a person or any profound subject in a treatise. Khorenatsi offers Demosthenes and Plato as figures and Justice and Honesty as principles on which to construct the writing.

Nerses Lambronatsi (1153-1198)

Nerses of Lambron, Bishop of Tarsus in Cilicia, a member of the illustrious Hetoumian family, composed a number of works in vigorous style upon doctrinal questions. Having been severely criticised by the Eastern Armenian clergy because of his borrowings from the Latin ritual or mode of worship, Nerses answered them in a letter addressed to the Prince (later King) Leon. He compares his alleged innovations in the Church to the adoption by the Armenian aristocracy of European or Frankish manners and customs, which he himself considered progressive steps towards European refinement. His name has been entered among the Saints of the Roman Catholic Church, in recognition of his advocacy of the union of all Christian denominations.

Mekhitar Kosh (1130-1213)

Mekhitar Kosh (Thin-bearded), the erudite vardapet, was an author of distinction besides being a preacher and a teacher. The most important of his works is the *Law-Book,* the first judicial treatise in the Armenian language. Mekhitar Kosh is well known also for his fables, 190 in all, which have won for him the title of "The Aesop of Armenia." The following is a specimen;—

> "The owl sent matchmakers to the eagle, asking his daughter in marriage in these terms; 'You are the ruler of the day, I am the ruler of the night. It will be well for us to form an alliance in marriage.' The proposal was accepted. But after the marriage, the bridegroom could not see anything by day, and the bride could see nothing by night. Therefore the falcons ridiculed them, and their marriage was unhappy."

This fable was intended as a warning against marriages between Christians and heathens.

Madteos Ourhayetsi

A native of Ourha, the ancient Edessa, a cultural center, Abbot Madteos spent the major part of his active life there. He was the superior of Karmir Vanq (the Red Convent), near the town of Kessoun, east of Marash, the seat of Baldwin, the Latin prince. Madteos Ourhayetsi is said to have been slain during the storming of the city by the cruel Atabeg Zanghi of Moussoul in 1144.

The literary and historical knowledge of Madteos was limited, but his veracity has not been disputed. He is almost the only source of certain information about the political and ecclesiastical events of his time and area. A man of strong convictions, he was bitter against Greeks and Latins, especially against Frankish settlers, whose avaricious and imperious rule and ingratitude he condemns. He was a fervent Armenian patriot, lamenting the martyrdom of his people and exalting their heroic deeds. To him we are indebted for the record of two documents of importance — 1) a letter from the Byzantine Emperor Zimisces, to King Ashot I, the Bagratid; and 2) a discourse delivered in the cathedral of Aya Sophia, Constantinople, in the presence of the Emperor Constantine Ducas by Gagik II, the exiled Bagratid king, concerning the doctrinal divergence between the Greek and Armenian churches.

Ourhayetsi's work is rather chronological, covering two centuries from the second half of the tenth through the second half of the twelfth. He relates much about the early Crusades, and the battles between Byzantines and Arabs for the possession of parts of northern Syria and eastern Asia Minor. Byzantine authors such as Getrenos, Zonaras and Anna Comnenos are well versed in their particular spheres, but uninformed regarding Edessa and neighboring lands which are treated by Madteos. His chronological mistakes have not been disregarded, however, by Patriarch Tourian.

Ourhayetsi, never tolerant towards Greeks and Latins, is also unsympathetic towards Syrians, judging by allusions made by Abulfaraj at a later date.

Mekhitar Heratsi

Mekhitar Heratsi of Her (Khoy, Persian Armenia), was a famous Armenian physician of the twelfth century, who left a medical book entitled, *The Malarials' Comfort*. The book had been written at the suggestion of the Katholikos, Grigor Degha (1173-1193). This prelate's predecessor, the Katholikos Nerses Shnorhali, had dedicated one of his poems to the physician.

Vanakan Vardapet (1200-1250)

Hovhannes Vanakan Vardapet, born in the province of Aghouank (Caucasian Armenia) was the founder of a school and library in the monastery of Khoranashad. Two historians, Vardan and Kirakos, were among his disciples. Together with a number of his pupils, Vanakan had been a prisoner of the Tatars in 1225. Later, when released, they all resumed their work. Vanakan died at the age of 80 and was buried, in accordance with his own request, in that section of the cemetery "where are the graves of the poor." He left several homilies, but the

History of the Tatar Invasion, a valuable source of first-hand information on the fateful events, as attested by his contemporaries, has been lost.

Vardan Vardapet Areveltsi

Vardan Vardapet Areveltsi (of the East) (1200?-1271) has been honored with such epithets as thrice-exalted, erudite and great Sophestus. Having left his home in Armenia for a pilgrimage to Jerusalem, he was entertained by King Hetoum and the Katholikos Constantine as a guest in Cilicia from 1241 to 1246. His literary remains include Commentaries on Daniel, the Pentateuch, Psalms and Songs. His principal and most important work is his *History* which begins with the Creation and ends in 1264, when he was sent by King Hetoum to the headquarters of Hulagu, the Tatar Khan, on a politico-religious mission.

Vardan Aykegtsi

Vardan Aykegtsi (Vardan of Aykeg) was the author of various works, among which are his *Fables* and a *Geography*, both of which have been mistakenly attributed by some to Vardan Areveltsi. Born in Marata, a Syrian village near Aleppo, Vardan lived for a time in Duluke (Doliche). Driven from there, he went to the monastery of Aykeg, in the Black (Amanus) Mountains. His *Fables*, commonly known as Aghvesagirq ("The Book of the Fox"), are said to have been only in part from his pen, many additions having been made by others. He died in 1250.

Sembat Constable

Sembat, born in 1208, brother of King Hetoum I, was trained as a soldier and appointed Marshal, corresponding to the Frankish Constable of the age (Comes Stabulis, French Connétable). His name appears on the records of many of the wars of Cilician Armenia. From 1248 to 1250 he was away from home, having been sent on a political mission to the court of the Tatar Khan. At the age of 69, in a victorious battle with the Egyptians, he was fatally injured when his horse crushed his leg against a tree while he was hotly pursuing the enemy commander.

Sembat also studied history and jurisprudence, and left valuable translations on these subjects. His *Annals*, an abridgement of the *Chronology* of Matthew of Edessa, with additional notes, was twice translated into French, as a source of information regarding the Crusades. Considerable value has also been attached to Sembat's translation of the Code of Laws of the Latin King of Antioch (*Assises d'Antioche*).[98] His edition of the Law-book of Mekhitar Kosh, rendered in the vernacular idioms of the western Armenians and adapted to the requirements of the new times, has been considered even more important.

---

[98] No copy of the original text of this book has yet been discovered. The students of Frankish medieval jurisprudence have had recourse to the French translation from the Armenian of the Constable, made by Father L. Alishan.

Kirakos Gantzaketsi (1200-1272)

Kirakos was a disciple of Vanakan, together with whom he was for a time a prisoner of the Tatars. Vanakan was freed on the payment of ransom by friends. Kirakos, however, remained longer, to serve the Tatars as an interpreter, and finally managed to escape.

He is the author of a *General History* relative to events from 303 to 1265. The last part of his book, dealing with the invasion of the Tatars and their cruelties is the more detailed. His work contains interesting and unusual sidelights about the Greeks, Persians, Arabs and Mohammed. He also speaks at length of the Aghouan neighbors of Armenia and their ecclesiastical connection with Etchmiadzin and Douin. Of especial value are his descriptions of the manners and customs of the Mongols. Kirakos is regarded as reliable in his frank and impartial statements of facts. His allusions to the gallantry of King Leon the Magnificent towards women are well known by the educated public.

Many additions to the Sharakan or Hymn-book by various composers from different centers resulted in confusion. As pointed out by the late scholar Manoug Abeghian, it was mainly through the efforts of Gantzaketsi — as well as of Vardan Vardapet — that the Church authorities succeeded in correcting this anomaly.

During the lifetime of this writer, the political tribulations of the Armenians had brought their intellectual and cultural level to a very low point.

Some of the stories reported by Kirakos seem fabricated, and the literary quality of his writing is considered below par by some critics, who, nevertheless, must admit the genuine merit of his work.

Hetoum, the Historian

Hetoum, the Aytonus or Hayton of some western chroniclers, Lord of Coricos, a seaport of Cilician Armenia, was a scholar, linguist and theologian. His name is internationally known through his *History of the Tatars,* usually under its French title *La Fleur des Histoires de la Terre d'Orient.* While a guest at the palace of Pope Clement V at Poitiers, he translated this work orally from his Armenian text, dictating it to a certain Nicolas Falcon, who compiled the book. It was later translated into Latin, Italian and Spanish. The work is full of interesting information concerning the farthest Orient, China, Persia, Armenia and western Asia. As a guide to these distant parts of the world, Hetoum of Coricos has been considered second only to the great Venetian traveler, Marco Polo. His later years were spent in Cyprus, where, in 1305, he had joined the religious brotherhood of Prémontré, under the name of Friar Anton.

King Hetoum II

Hetoum II, King, statesman, warrior and monk, was also a man of literary attainments. He left a *Memoir* in rhyme, an historical sketch of the Hetoumian dynasty, from its foundation to his own days. He later joined a religious order, the Franciscans, assuming the name of Iohannes. A colored portrait of him has been discovered in Venice, with this inscription, B. Iohannes, Rex Armeniae, Seraphicum habitum suscepit, Anno 1294. (The Blessed John, King of Armenia, took the Seraphic (Franciscan) habit in 1294). A silver seal, made during his monastic life, a rare specimen, is now preserved at the Mekhitarist Monastery of St. Lazar, Venice.

Stepanos Orpelian (1258-1305)

A native of Sewniq, Stepanos was issued from the ancient family of Sissakan and for twenty years was Bishop of that province. After many years of research and gathering all the information available, he wrote a *History of Sewniq*, which is his principal work.

In this book are described the important political and religious struggles in Armenia, the foreign invasions with some reference to the Tatars. A student of religion, history, rhetoric and music, he obtained his ecclesiastical degree of Vardapet from Bishop Nerses, the Superior of the Monastery of Glatzor, a famous center of learning.

He was one of the champions of conservatism within the Armenian Church against the alleged innovations through Latin influence in Cilicia; and yet he was diplomat enough to enjoy three months' hospitality in 1286 at the court of the liberal King Leon II and in the palace of the Katholikos Constantine, by whom he was raised to the rank of Bishop — in his own words, a Metropolitan. Armenia Major and the adjacent countries were at that time in the grip of famine, as the result of merciless persecutions and devastation by the Tatars and other barbarian tribes. Under these conditions, Orpelian declared "death blessed desirable and blessed, life odious and miserable." Then, together with Nestor, the Patriarch of the Chaldean or Assyrian Church, and his twelve bishops, Stepanos was received by Arghoun, the Tatar Governor-general of Persia and Armenia, and given a cordial welcome, gorgeous ecclesiastical robes and a decree exempting the monasteries and churches from the vexatious taxes imposed upon them by local functionaries.

Hovhannes Erzngatsi (ca. 1250-1326)

Hovhannes Erzngatsi (John of Erznga or Erzinjan) was nicknamed Blouz, probably because of his short stature. The little that has reached us of his voluminous works reveal an exceptionally gifted scholar, with treasured knowledge of vast scope. Living mostly in the latter part of the thirteenth century, he was also the last of the higher class of the Armenian authors of the ancient and medieval ages. Erzngatsi wrote hymns, commentaries, odes, eulogies, a *Martyrology*, an astronomical treatise on *Celestial Elements*, and a grammar. He was personally known and honored in almost every center of learning in Greater Armenia and Cilicia. As an outstanding orator, he was the main speaker on the occasion of the conferring of knighthood on Hetoum and Thoros, sons of King Leon II, which was celebrated at Sis in 1284. Having studied Latin, apparently at an advanced age, he translated certain parts of the *Theology* of Thomas Aquinas into Armenian.

Yessayie Netchetsi (1264?-1338)

Yessayie Netchetsi, famous for his erudition and for his virtuous life, was also known as an enthusiastic defender of the National Church. He was the Superior of Gaylatsor Monastery, where he had over 300 students. Nitch is a village where he was born in the district of Taron.

Thovma Medzopetsi (1379?-1446)

Thovma Medzopetsi (Thomas of Medzop), was the abbot of the Monastery of Medzop, near the town of Arjish, whose remains are on the northern coast of the Lake of Van. His annals give valuable details on the deeds of Lang-Timour (Timour the Lame), the most powerful and most dreaded conqueror after Jenghiz-Khan. He also describes the quarrels in which Timour's sons, Shah Rokh and Miran Shah, engaged with Kara Youssouf, the Turcoman, and his sons, Skandar, the Lord of Tabriz and Shah Mahmoud of Baghdad. A large part of Thomas's history has been translated into French by Félix Nève, of the University of Louvain. Thoma of Medzop died in 1446. Besides some devotional and chronological works, he left also a history of the reestablishment of the Cathedral of Etchmiadzin in 1441, a thousand years after the death of Katholikos Sahak, during which time the incumbents had to change their residence from district to district, because of political, military and other exigencies.

Arakel Tavrizhetzi (ca. 1594-1670)

Arakel Tavrizhetzi (Arakel of Tabriz), a vardapet, is regarded as the best historian among those who wrote between the early fourteenth and the early nineteenth centuries. The marked place he holds is due, not to his literary style, but to his good order and method in recording facts. His work embraces sixty years, covering rather more than the first half of the seventeenth century, during which time eight Ottoman Sultans warred against the Persian monarchs, Khudabendeh, Shah Abbas I and Shah Sefi, with the object of occupying the Armenian provinces. In mournful words, Arakel describes the five years' famine as a result of those wars and of the terror spread by the Jelali marauders. The deportation by Shah Abbas I of the inhabitants of Jugha (Julfa) and of the Arax Valley, to the interior of Persia, forms an epic in his *History*. As spots of bright relief, he mentions some reforms and reparations accomplished by the three successive Katholikosi of Etchmiadzin — Movses III, Pilibbos and Hagop V. Of other interesting matters contained in Arakel's book we may cite the list of the then existing famous monasteries and scholars, and reports on the Armenian settlements in Julfa, Poland, etc.

Armenian Troubadours

Most of the Armenian Troubadours (ashough)[99] were influenced by Moslem popular poetry, to which they in turn contributed, by composing and singing in the Turkish, Georgian, Persian and Kurdish languages. Something of their own national temperament and Christian mentality must certainly have been introduced into the Moslem poetry. The ancient Armenian translations, however, do not show any trace of imitation of foreign poetry; their only sources of inspiration were the Armenian popular songs. Among the best troubadours known so far, we may cite Frik, Hovassap and Ghazar of Sebastia, Naghash Hovnatan, Keropeh, Ohannes, Djivani and Nahapet Koutchak. This latter, the most original of all, was born probably in the fifteenth century. There are ecclesiastics, however, who have imitated the troubadours, such as Constantin of Erznga, Hovhannes of Telgouran, whose colorful and vibrant verses are likewise full of noble thoughts and sentiments.

Sayat Nova (1712-1795)

A gifted Armenian ashough, son of Aroutin of Aleppo, born in Tiflis. He sang in Georgian, Turkish, and Armenian. Had entree even to the Georgian court. Has written touching love songs and others based on high principles. A widower at 60, he became a monk. When Persians invaded Tiflis, he took refuge in the church, saying, "I will not deny Jesus; I will not quit the church." He was slain there.

Despite their struggle for existence, the Armenians from the fifth to the fourteenth century never ceased to contribute to the literary and scientific movements. Spiritual liberty was always preserved in the monasteries, even among unspeakable horrors. The Armenians were seldom blessed by those long periods of peace and quietude which the nations of the West, the Byzantines, Arabs and Persians enjoyed during the stormy centuries of barbarism. And yet they must have had enough moral force not to abandon intellectual pursuits throughout the Middle Ages.

---

[99] The word ashough is from the Arabic asheq, a lover, a troubadour, a person inflamed by love, who travels, wanders here and there, playing on a violin or other instrument and singing of beauty.

Chapter XLII
Modern Armenian Literature[100]

Constantinople, Tiflis, Venice, Chief Centers

After the extinction of their political life, in the old homeland as well as in Cilicia, the Armenians established colonies in many lands, carrying with them the love of their language and literature. In their various alien environments, their thoughts turned with deep veneration to their ancient authors, whom they considered the champions of their national independence. Great numbers of Armenian literary centers came, therefore, into being all over the world. The remoteness of these from each other and the environment in which they developed, must naturally have influenced the direction in which each of them advanced. The Russian spirit and the German language — which was then fashionable in the land of the Tsars — exerted their influence on the Armenian communities in Moscow and Tiflis. In Constantinople, Smyrna, Venice and other Western communities, the French, Italian, and Greek cultures became models, while the study of the French language and literature became predominant in the Armenian high schools of Turkey.

The new literature thus began to develop in all branches — drama, fiction, epic poetry, satire. Works on history, archaeology, philology, sociology, science, law, politics, etc., appeared on bookshelves. Among the centers in which modern Armenian literature blossomed and flourished were Constantinople, Smyrna, Jerusalem, Etchmiadzin, Tiflis, Moscow and Vienna, with Venice topping all of them. The Monastery on the island of St. Lazar, in close proximity to Venice, which the Senate of that Republic had granted to the Congregation of

---

[100] For the compilation of a list of outstanding Armenian literary men, the author acknowledges his indebtedness to several well-known writers, ancient and modern. Among others, particularly grateful thanks must go to H. Thorossian for his excellent *Histoire de la Littérature Arménienne*, which has been of invaluable assistance.

The latest period of Armenian literature has presented a delicate problem. The number of writers is so great, both in the Eastern and Western fields, that the author has had to confess his inability to draw up a suitable list from among them. He therefore called on a group of competent Armenian writers in New York to assist him in the task.

Their selection is presented on these pages. The generally extensive knowledge and the excellence of the style of the writers on the list made the choice a difficult one, and various other considerations have also entered into the selection.

Mekhitarists in 1717, became until the middle of the nineteenth century and beyond an intellectual beacon for the Armenians of the world.

17th Century Renaissance

With the seventeenth century, there burst forth a renaissance of Armenian literature, when writers in Russia, and later on, in Turkey, ventured to use the vernacular (ashkharabar), rather than the classical language. Abbot Mekhitar, himself the founder of the St. Lazar Congregation, had compiled a grammar of the modern Armenian speech. Books, pamphlets and periodical publications helped towards this transformation by popularizing the National and foreign works, which were until then within the reach of only a few men of erudition. The effect of this movement on the welding of the thought and sentiment of the masses and in creating a public opinion, was most remarkable.

Mekhitar, the Abbot (1676-1749)

Mekhitar was born in Sivas, his baptismal name being Manoug. His early training was entrusted to Armenian nuns, and he was ordained a deacon at the age of fourteen. Spurred by a keen desire for learning, he journeyed to Etchmiadzin, but was disappointed in his expectations there. Three months later, he went to the cloister of Lake Sevan, where he found solace in a vision of St. Mary. On his way back to Sivas, he stopped at Erzerum, and at the request of the Superior of the Monastery of Passen, remained there a year, instructing the students. At the end of that time, deciding that the environment was unfavorable, he returned home. But the exertions of travel were too much for his frail constitution, and he fell ill. For a year, his eyesight was threatened. When he recovered his health, he was consecrated Vardapet at the age of twenty. With wide knowledge and effective eloquence, he began to preach. He was now ready for the realization of his favorite objective — the creation of a brotherhood for service in the spiritual and intellectual fields.

With the hope of visiting Rome, Mekhitar left Sivas in 1695, his first stopping place being the port of Alexandretta. There he boarded a boat for Cyprus, but during his short stay at Alexandretta he had contracted malaria, which made him unwelcome on board the vessel. A good Samaritan rowed him ashore, whence he was taken by others to the Armenian monastery of St. Macar. There, through the summer months, he suffered from neglect and contempt on the part of the so-called pious ascetics.[101] The sickly, penniless priest returned to Sivas and retired to the monastery of St. Nishan, near that city. In 1696 Mekhitar made a trip to Constantinople, calling there upon Khatchadour Vardapet, a famous scholar, for advice and aid. The latter could not be granted for lack of funds.

---

[101] On Sunday, Sept. 8th, 1901, the two hundredth anniversary of the founding of the Mekhitarist congregation was celebrated there on the monastery grounds by the pupils of the Orphanage of Nicosia. An artistic monument to the memory of Abbot Mekhitar was constructed by the graduates of the institution as a souvenir of the event, and dedicated in 1931.

While in Constantinople, Mekhitar gathered a dozen disciples, and translated and published several books, among them *The Imitation of Christ,* by Thomas à Kempis.

Suspecting him of being a Latinist agent, the patriarch of Constantinople, Avediq, planned to have him imprisoned, but Mekhitar took refuge in the monastery of the Capuchins (mendicant friars). Here, in company with his disciples, he formally founded a religious order dedicated to St. Mary, on September 8th, 1701. Shortly afterward he sent a few of his disciples to Morea (Peloponnesus) in Greece, then under Venetian rule. He then escaped to Smyrna, and a little later, to Morea, at the very time when the Turkish police were searching for him. The Venetian government gave the Mekhitarist order a large tract of land on which to build a church and a monastery, and the order was placed under the protection of the Pope.

When Morea was threatened by the Turks, the congregation was transferred to Venice in 1717, and because the Senate could not legally donate land or buildings to religious institutions, the Island of St. Lazar, on which there was already an ancient church, was transferred to that body. There had been an Armenian colony in Venice since the thirteenth century, enjoying privileges or grants such as a bridge and a cemetery. Among them were commission agents, printers and ship-owners. They helped the new congregation financially. The monks prayed, worked, and studied. As expressed by Victor Langlois, they stood on European soil, "with eyes turned towards the Levant, the cradle of the Armenian race."

When Mekhitar died, the once-barren island had been transformed into a center of Armenian culture. "Mekhitar was a model of sanctity and studiousness," says Fr. Janashian, "his disciples saw in him a pattern of the real and learned master. He taught to work with collective effort and academic character. The beautifully printed Bible which he published and the magnificent Armenian Dictionary he compiled demonstrate this." (*History of Modern Armenian Literature,* Venice, 1953.)

The printing of the Bible was a colossal achievement. Mekhitar was not content with the Bible of Oskan Vardapet, printed in Amsterdam in 1666. Oskan's corrections were made according to a Latin text. Being desirous of comparing it with a Greek text, Mekhitar obtained a copy of the "Seven-Language Bible," printed in Paris in 1645, containing the Hebrew, Syriac, Greek, Latin, Arabic, Chaldean and Samaritan texts. The comparison and printing of the work occupied three years. Also among Mekhitar's works are a *Grammar of the Classical Armenian, Book of Virtues,* a *Grammar of Modern Armenian,* etc. He took great pains in purifying the language from its latinization by the Unitors, without injuring the sensibilities of the Romanic zealots. His name has received international recognition, and the Roman Catholic Church has elevated him to the rank of Beatitude.

Michael Tchamtchian (1733-1823)

Foremost among Mekhitar's pupils was Father Michael Tchamtchian, author of a *History of Armenia.* Although based upon national and foreign sources, the authenticity of which has been attacked by recent critics, Tchamtchian's work has great value as the first systematized and chronologically set compendium of twenty centuries of the history of Armenia and neighboring countries. Moreover, he merits recognition for his untiring perseverance which, even under unfavorable conditions, accomplished the printing of the three large volumes in a little more than five years (1781-1786).

Injijian and others

The Geography of Ancient Armenia, by another of Mekhitar's pupils, Father Lucas Injijian, is one of several monumental works of that author. Fr. Agontz Cuver, also a geographer; Frs. M. Aucher (Avkerian), Kh. Surmelian and G. Avetikian produced in collaboration the great "Dictionary of the Armenian Language" in two large volumes. Arsen Bagratouni, an eminent poet, author of "Haik the Hero," and of the "Grammar for Advanced Students" and the translator of Homer, Vergil, Racine, Voltaire and Alfieri; Archbishop Edward Hurmuz, poet and translator of Vergil's *Aeneid* and Fenelon's *Telemachus*, and Father Eghia Tomajan, translator of Homer's *Iliad* and *Odyssey* must not be omitted.

Others to be mentioned for their varied literary accomplishments are the Fathers Basile Sarkissian, G. Zarbhanelian, H. Thorossian, S. Eremian, S. Eprikian, A. Ghazikian, G. Der Sahakian, V. Hatsouni, S. Der Movsessian.

Ghevond Alishan (1820-1901)

Another Mekhitarist scholar of stature is Father Ghevon (Leontius) Alishan. He was born in Constantinople and given the baptismal name of Keropeh (Cherub). At the age of twelve he was sent to St. Lazar Seminary. Returning to Constantinople after graduation, he was ordained priest in 1840.

He appears next in Paris as a professor in the Mooradian College, of which he eventually became the Dean. In this capacity, he was a source of inspiration to great numbers of Armenian students from Turkey, Egypt, Persia and Russia, some of whom later filled high governmental positions, or served the Armenian nation as professors, journalists and spiritual leaders.

In 1872 Alishan retired from educational and administrative work, and devoted his time thereafter to scholarly research and activity — archaeology, geography, mythology, philology, poetry, etc. and published many books, from his own pen or translations, and several valuable manuscripts. His ardent patriotism and vast erudition made him the most popular writer of his time. His fiftieth anniversary in religious and literary work was celebrated in 1890. He died in 1901 at the age of 81.

Of the fully one hundred works of Father Alishan, perhaps the most elaborate ones are, *Souvenirs of the Homeland — Shirak; Sissouan, Ayrarat, Sissakan, Hayapatoum* in two volumes.

These works — philological, geographical and historical — have a decidedly poetical cast. In fact, Alishan's rightful place in literature would be among the poets, even though he wrote mostly in prose. His language — the classical, the modern and the vernacular — has an original and individual tone. Several of his works have been translated into European languages, among them *Sissouan* into French. A. Tchobanian says of him, "His chant is the sublimest, the richest, the most vigorous and the most diverse that the Armenian lyre has sounded in modern times." As some critics see him, fervent patriotism dominated Alishan's writing, at the expense of scientific objectives. Nevertheless, despite his charming originality, he seems to have been influenced at times by Chateaubriand, Lamartine, Hugo, Goethe and Schiller.

Vienna Group

The Mekhitarist Congregation of Vienna, which had its beginning in 1774, has been interested more particularly in philological and historical studies, and has published translations from works in the German language. Their polyglot printing press capable of turning out artistic work is considered one of the best in the Austrian capital. The Mekhitarists of Vienna have produced many eminent scholars, such as S. Tornian, H. Katerjian, M. Karakashian, A. Aydenian, G. Menevishian, G. Sibilian, S. Dervishian, H. Dashian, G. Hovanian, G. Kalemkiarian, and N. Akinian.

Archbishop Arsen Aydenian (1825-1902), was of encyclopedic mind and mastered ten languages, ancient and modern. He was conversant with the pure sciences — mathematics and cosmography — also the fine arts, including music, design and engraving. Western scholars admired the universality of his culture. His great work, a *Critical Grammar of the Modern Armenian Language* is a masterpiece on Armenian philology.

Another star in the Vienna constellation was Rev. Hagopos Dashian (1806-1933) He was a first-rank scholar. His head, it was said, was a library, comparable with that of Alishan. We have from him studies on Agathangelos, Pseudo-Callisthenes, Armenian Paleography, the Legend of Abgar, etc. Special attention is due to his stupendous *Catalogue of the Armenian Manuscripts of the Mekhitarists of Vienna* and his *Study of the Armenian Classical Language,* originally outlined by Fr. K. Spenian.

Awakening in Turkey

The first step towards the diffusion of modern Armenian literature in Turkey was taken by Apcar of Tokat. He had founded an Armenian press in Venice in 1565, forty-three years after the one established there by an Italian. In 1567 Apcar, assisted by Arakel, the monk, set up a printing house in Constantinople, too. Others followed their example, publishing books mostly for use in churches.

Yeremia Keumurjian

The outstanding of the new period in Turkey was Yeremia Keumurjian, called Tchélébie, a title of honor given by the Turks to Christian laymen of high standing. Yeremia, a member of an aristocratic Armenian family, was a man of culture, well versed in the Turkish, Greek and Latin languages, as well as in his own mother tongue. He wrote a *History of the Ottoman Sovereigns* and a *Description of Istambul*; he translated parts of the Armenian history of Khorenatsi into Turkish, at the request of Turkish scholars. He died in 1695.

Hovhannes Golod and Others

Hovhannes Golod, Patriarch of Constantinople from 1715 to 1741, himself an erudite man, encouraged the enterprises of printing and book-publishing. Patriarch Hagop Nalian (1741-49, 1752-64) was a theologian and writer of distinction. Grigor Peshtimaljian, who died in 1837, was a lay educator of renown, as well as a poet and grammarian.

Nahabed Roussinian (1819-1886) and Others

Armenian literature in Turkey was strongly influenced by nineteenth century writers of France, where a considerable number of young Armenians had received their higher education. Foremost among these was Dr. Nahabed Roussinian, who championed the cause of the modern Armenian language (Ashkharhabar) as a medium in public schools, instead of the classic Grabar. He succeeded in achieving his objective, but he failed in his grammatical innovations. In reform movements in general, as well as in administrative and educational branches, Roussinian had distinguished associates, such as Hagop Balian, Mgrditch Agathon and Krikor Odian. These men also played important roles in the affairs of the State. Garabed Panosian, an outspoken journalist, was another advocate of progressive ideas. His proposals in 1864 for certain canonical reforms, the institution of divorce, for example, raised a storm of protest on the part of Church authorities. Mgrditch Beshiktashlian (1828-1868) left his mark upon his national literature as a professor of the Armenian language, and particularly as a poet and playwright, reviving heroic Armenian deeds and figures of the past. Another poet and playwright, versed in European classics, was Thomas Terzian. Archbishop Khoren Narbey, eloquent preacher and brilliant personality, was also a linguist and poet — lyric and elegiac.

Writers of Smyrna

The city of Smyrna, half Greek and half European in culture, the adopted home of a small Armenian community, was another hive of intellectual activity. In 1840 it gave birth to the weekly *Arshalouys Araratian* (The Dawn of Ararat), founded by

335

Lucas Baltazarian. Other periodicals that followed were the *Arpee Araratian* (The sun of Ararat), *Dzaghik* (the Flower), *Meteora* and *Arevelian Mamoul* (The Eastern Press). Madteos Mamourian, editor of the last-named monthly, as well as Grigor Tchilinkirian were translators of several European works — the *Werther* of Goethe, Walter Scott's *Ivanhoe,* Victor Hugo's *Les Misérables,* the novels of Dumas, Eugene Sue, etc. Among the prominent literary figures of Smyrna in the nineteenth century were Stepan Oscan, Caloust Constantian, Grigor Mserian and Mesrop Nubarian.

Mgrditch Khrimian

An Armenian provincial literature in Turkey, representing the genuine national spirit of the people, came into being through a clergyman of Van, destined to become during his lifetime (1820-1907) the most popular of Armenian personalities. This was Mgrditch (Baptist) Khrimian, known as the "Hairik" — Dear Father or Papa — who in 1871 was elected Patriarch of Constantinople and in 1892 Katholikos of Etchmiadzin, the Supreme head of the Church. A self-educated man, not versed in any European language, Khrimian studied in his own language sufficiently to become familiar with the progress of human thought in general, and in particular, with the treasures of Armenian literature, ancient and modern, and the multifarious aspects — religious, political, social and philosophical — of the contemporary situation of the world. In 1854, while still in his native district, he entered into the priesthood in the monastery of Aghtamar, on an island in the Lake of Van. His progressive tendencies were resented by the brethren, so he left them and gave himself to independent service. For several years he traveled extensively, to Constantinople and other Armenian centers in Turkey and the Caucasus. His sermons, as well as his written messages won for him public admiration and affection.

He established a printing press in Van, and put forth a periodical called "Ardzwee Vaspourakan" — "The Eagle of Vaspourakan." Next in Mush, he started another journal under the title of "Ardzwig Tarono" — "The Eaglet of Taron," Taron being the province in which Mush is situated. He was the first apostle to awaken the Armenian aristocracy and the intelligentsia of Constantinople and Tiflis to the right appreciation of the peasants and townsmen of the National homeland. The latter element, the urban lower class, was represented largely by the porters and servants who came to the city to toil for years, enduring a hard, even wretched bachelor life, to enable them to return home at last with a few pounds earned at the cost of great privation. Through the forceful pleadings of Khrimian, these unfortunates became objects of consideration, as the guardians of the best traditions of the past and the cherished hopes for the future. Among Khrimian's literary products were: *An Invitation to Ararat*; *An Invitation to the Holy Land*; *A Family of Paradise*; *The Pearl of the Heavenly Kingdom*; *Sirach and Samuel*; *Grandfather and Grandson*. He also published pamphlets depicting the abject misery of the Armenians in the interior of their country, and he even hinted at persecutions instigated or perpetrated by the Turkish Government itself.

Garegin Serwantzdian (1840-1892)

Ranking next to Khrimian among the provincial writers comes Bishop Garegin Serwantzdian, born in Van and educated under Khrimian. While on a mission from the Patriarch Nerses of Constantinople in 1879, he traversed various parts of Armenia, risking his life among Turkish and Kurdish fanatics, while collecting precious material on ethnological and topographical subjects. His "Thoros Aghbar," "Horod Morod," "Grotz Brotz," and five other books were avidly read in every Armenian center in Turkey and Russia. The "Thoros Aghbar" (Brother Thoros) is the name of a waterfowl which he saw plunging into a lake in Armenia, disappearing and reappearing again and again, apparently in search of something in the water, but always failing. The bird's untiring persistence inspired the author to delve deeper and deeper into research until he had gathered many valuable items of folk-lore — sometimes from colophons and manuscripts, or from stories, songs, benedictions or maledictions, all crumbs left from remote antiquity. Bishop Serwantzdian's labors saved cultural traditions which otherwise would have been lost forever, since their living guardians had been eradicated by the Turks in 1915.

Other provincial writers who cultivated local and native literature were Boghos Vardapet Natanian, Hovhannes Haroutunian (Telgadintsi), H. Mirakhorian, and Kegham Der Garabedian.

Khatchatour Abovian (1805-1848)

The first novelist in Armenian literature was Abovian, who, in 1840, wrote his novel, *The Wounds of Armenia,* an expression of the people's soul, in popular language. The work was not published until many years after the death of the author.

Abovian's birthplace was Kanaker, a village in Erevan province, rich in beautiful scenery. He received a primary education at Etchmiadzin Monastery, then attended Nersessian Academy at Tiflis. Before graduation, he was called upon to serve as a secretary of the Katholikos. He also had the good fortune to accompany Professor Parrot, the German explorer, in an ascent of Mount Ararat.

Soon afterward, in 1830, upon the recommendation of Professor Parrot, he entered the University of Dorpat, Estonia, where he studied for six years. Returning to Etchmiadzin, he opened a school. But he soon became a target for persecution, because of his modernistic and supposedly Protestant ideas. Transferred to Tiflis, he suffered the same harassment there. He then obtained a position in the provincial school, married a German girl and became the father of a boy.

Moving to Erevan, he enjoyed friendly treatment after the death of the Katholikos, Hovhannes of Garpi, leader of the reactionaries. But he did not realize his hopes under the new Katholikos, Nerses of Ashtarak, and another source of grief developed in his home. His plea for divorce was denied by the

Church, and Abovian, discouraged and melancholic, vanished in April, 1848. The cause of his death — if it was death — remains a mystery. It has been variously called suicide, assassination by a Persian foe, or by order of the Russian Czar Nicholas I, to whom are ascribed the murders of Lermontov, Pushkin and other liberals.

His Works

Abovian's first works were poems in ancient, classical language, patriotism being the dominant subject. The best among his numerous productions is the novel in popular language, *The Wounds of Armenia*. Following this came *Filial Love, Forerunner of Education, Zankie, Agnes and the Daughter of the Turk*. Several of his works remain unpublished. *The Wounds of Armenia* is based on an actual incident, the abduction of an Armenian girl in Kanaker village during a war between Russia and Persia. While narrating the heroic deed of the central figure, Aghasi, it incidentally depicts popular beliefs and customs. The villagers' enjoyment of the hilarity of a carnival is rudely interrupted by a raid of the farashes (armed attendants) of the Sardar (Governor) of Erevan, whose object is to kidnap the beautiful Takhuni from the arms of her weeping mother. Aghasi arrives just in time, kills four of the soldiers and saves the girl and her mother.

The rescue did not, however, go unpunished. Hassan, the Sardar's younger brother, destroys several Armenian towns and villages, only a few of them resisting. The rest of the novel pictures combats with the Persians, Aghasi and Hassan being the respective leaders. Abovian calls his book an historical novel, giving it the sub-title, *Lamentation of the Patriot*.

Critics find faults in the work, such as repetitions, incongruity, insufficiency of moral issues and expatiation. But he is nevertheless considered the forefather of Armenian fiction.

Mesrop Taghiatiants (1803-1858)

Born in Erevan. Trained at Seminary of Etchmiadzin. Went to Constantinople, then to Calcutta. Taught in Girls' High School in that city, published a monthly, *Azgasser* (The Patriot); wrote history, fiction and poems imbued with high patriotism.

Bedros Tourian (1851-1872)

Born in Constantinople. Showed his talent for poetry at an early age; wrote exquisite lyric poems, but suffered poverty. He died at 22, an object of affection and admiration.

Krikor Odian (1834-1887)

Born in Constantinople. Statesman, intimate of Midhat Pasha, who restored the Ottoman Constitution. Odian fled to Paris for fear of Sultan Hamid's enmity. From Paris he contributed to the Armenian press of the capital. His style was elevated, and he had a rich vocabulary. Known as "the Eminent Exile," he died in Paris.

Hagop Melik-Agopian ("Raffi") (1835-1888)

Born near Salmasd, Persian Armenia. The most outstanding Armenian novelist. Attended Armenian and Russian schools in Tiflis; then studied on his own. He attempted a business venture but soon failed in it. From 1872 to 1884 was a staff-writer for *Mshak*. The Russo-Turkish war of 1876-7 supplied him with material as an eye-witness of the refugees' sufferings. As an advocate of freedom for Armenians of Turkey, his name became popular. He chose to be a schoolteacher from necessity, but wrote many patriotic novels, among them *Jelaleddin*, *David Beg*, *Samuel*, *The Demented* and *Sparks*. He died in Tiflis.

Hagop Baronian (1842-1891)

Native of Edirneh, European Turkey. A humorist from an early age. While working as a bookkeeper, he published many periodicals, such as *Euphrates*, *The Bee*, *Theatre*, *The Children's Friend*, etc. Through his knowledge of the Greek and French languages, he was familiar with the satirists, old and new, as well as with mythology. His writings always stirred laughter, but his object was to rebuke at the same time the loose life of the people, especially of Constantinople. Some of his humorous works are *The Honorable Mendicants*, *Uncle Balthazar*, *The Oriental Dentist*, *Khikar* (Ahikar), etc.

Grigor Ardzrouni (1845-1892)

Born in Moscow, son of a wealthy general, his home languages were both Russian and French. Graduated from State Gymnasium in Tiflis, he then studied physics in St. Petersburg, where he began to be interested in Armenian affairs. Returning to Moscow, he wrote for Armenian periodicals. Having contracted tuberculosis he went to the south of France. After recovery, he took political and philosophical courses in Germany, then studied literature at St. Lazar, Venice. On his return to Tiflis, he launched the *Mshak,* a weekly, then daily publication. Despite reverses and suspensions, this paper survived, even for some time after Ardzrouni's death. It was a progressive newspaper, its aim being the salvation of the new generation and the awakening of national consciousness. It ceased to appear in 1920.

Gabriel Soundoukiantz (1825-1912)

Born in Tiflis. The greatest representative of Armenian theatrical literature. Author of several plays, his masterpiece being "*Bebo,*" a drama that leaves a deep impression.

Kamar Katiba (Raphael Patkanian) (1830-1892)

Born in Nor Nakhitchevan on Don; trained by his father, he received higher education at Lazarian Institute, Moscow. After one term at Tiflis as a teacher, he went to the University of Dorpat, Estonia, to study languages, thence to Moscow University. Leaving college, Katiba founded his own periodical, *Husis* (The North), which was short-lived. Later, he was principal of the Diocesan school at Nakhitchevan. He wrote poems, songs, and text-books, also made translations from Russian and German. His poem, "Mayr Araxi Aperov" (On the Banks of Mother Arax), is still sung by Armenians. The heroic deeds of the ancestors and the cruelties and sufferings endured by his countrymen were his favorite themes. He heralded an era of popular awakening.

Srpouhi Dussap (1842-1901)

Born in Constantinople of an Armenian mother and a French musician father. Inspired by Beshiktashlian's songs, she became a writer, as well as the founder of the Society of Dbrotzasser (School-Lovers). She wrote three novels — *Maida*, *Araxia* and *Siranoush*. As a pioneer feminist, she aroused some resentment, but in the end she became popular with poets and intellectuals.

Rhetheos Berberian (1850-1907)

Born in Scutari, Constantinople. Educator, poet, linguist and eminent author. Having mastered the classic Armenian, he adorned with it his romantic poems. At nineteen he translated Lamartine's "Death of Socrates" and other poems. Berberian College, founded by him, attained high prestige.

Eghia Demirjibashian (1851-1908)

Born in Constantinople, son of an artisan. Graduated from Nubar-Shahnazarian College. An early devotee of fiction, when still a youth his name began appearing in periodicals. For a living, he worked as a clerk in the offices of Public Works, but his yearnings were intellectual, and he was unhappy. His melancholy condition induced his kinsmen to send him to Marseilles, France, to study business law. He preferred philosophy, however, and founded a paper in French. Returning to Constantinople, he wrote articles on various subjects. His thinking was a strange mixture of the pessimistic, positivist, skeptical, poetic and theosophic. Despite such vagaries, he commanded public affection. Readers eagerly sought his articles, and schools were anxious to have him as teacher or principal. His career was brief, however. He had lost father, mother and brothers, and loneliness so affected his mental faculties that he was confined for a time in a hospital at Yedi-Kouleh. He committed suicide shortly after his discharge.

Arpiar Arpiarian (1852-1908)

Graduate of Moorat-Raphael, Venice. Talented novelist, journalist, correspondent of *Mshak* of Tiflis. Prolific writer, author of *Red Alms, Blessed Family*, etc. Worked in London, Paris, the Caucasus and Egypt. Once jailed as revolutionist in Constantinople. Finally assassinated in Cairo by a political partisan.

Missak Medzarentz (1886-1908)

A young poet of particular charm and originality. Occupies a high rank among the best Armenian poets of the West. Has left a collection of poems, *"The Rainbow"* and *"New Verses"*.

Rouben Zartarian (1874-1915)

Born in the province of Kharput. Had an active political life. He later devoted his time to writing. He left legends, idyls, stories, in a beautiful language and charming style.

Krkior Zohrab (1861-1915)

Born in Constantinople; received his education in public and Roman Catholic high schools. He studied law and practiced it brilliantly. He was also a man of letters, one of the most eminent of his time. His charming personality attracted friends, both men and women. In disputation, he usually carried his point, but found it hard to control his temper. In the dark days when the Turkish menace was growing, when a deputation was on its way to Berlin, he attacked the Patriarch Nerses and his advisers; and in the Ottoman Parliament, of which he was a member, during a debate on military service for non-Moslems, he spoke in favor of it, but sent his wife and children to Paris on the following day.

Just before the First World War, the Turkish Cabinet, under the so-called Ittihad (Union and Progress), had decided to destroy the Armenian population. Zohrab, a member of the Ittihad and of the Parliament, and an intimate of Talaat Pasha, boldly fought against the execution of this horrible design, but all in vain. He himself was one of the 250 intellectuals of Constantinople doomed to perish on the road to exile.

As an able and eloquent attorney, he had won the confidence of clients of all nationalities. And yet ambition and innate urge moved him to seek expression in literature, where his accomplishments were preeminent. His works were numerous — essays, novels, editorials, plays, criticism, satires, polemics, even poems. To mention a few of his novels; *A Vanished Generation, Voices of the*

341

Conscience, The Life as it is, Mute Sorrows, etc. Aggressive, at time contradictory and unreasonable, yet he had multitudes of ardent admirers.

Daniel Varoujan (1884-1915)

Known by his poetical works, *Shuddering, The Massacre, The Nation's Heart, Pagan Chants, Chants of Bread,* etc. Emotional as well as realistic, his varied talents are magnificently displayed through the rich resources of the Armenian vocabulary, of which Varoujan was a master.

Adom Yarjanian (1877-1915)

Known by his pen name *Siamanto.* Lyric poet, sentimental dreamer, has left some beautiful pages. Author of "*Heroically,*" "*Red News from my Friend,*" "*Invitation of the Country.*"

Maghakia Ormanian (1841-1919)

For twenty-eight years tutored in the theological institutions of Rome. Ormanian forsook the Roman church, and became a vardapet of the Armenian Church in 1879. After serving in and near Constantinople, he was appointed Arachnord (prelate) of the Diocese of Erzeroum, where he served for seven years. In 1887 he was appointed Dean of the Seminary at Etchmiadzin, but the unfriendly attitude of the Russian Governor-General shortened his stay. Returning to Turkey, he was named Vice-Abbot of Armash, near Izmit, and Dean of the Seminary there. After the first massacres, he was the only one among the higher clerics to be acceptable as Patriarch of Constantinople. Ormanian was the author of *Azgapatoum* (3 volumes), a history of Armenia with respect to the Armenian Church, *Hamapatoum,* a concordance of the Gospel, and *The Armenian Church, its Doctrine and Administration.* Besides treatises in Armenian, he has also published books in French and Italian.

Hovhannes Toumanian (1869-1923)

A beloved popular poet, he wrote songs, poems and tales, among which are the well known *David of Sassoun, Anoush,* and *Sack of Lori.*

Erouand Odian (1896-1925)

Native of Constantinople. Mostly self-educated by travel. He might have been called a successor to Baronian, the satirist. Fear of terrorists caused his flight to Athens. Then he worked in Paris, in London and Egypt, where he joined *Azad Bem* (Free Pulpit), a weekly. Among his many humorous writings are *The Usurer, The Go-Between Priest, A Mission to Dzabelvar* and *The Parasites of Revolution.*

Minas Tchéraz (1852-1929)

Born in Constantinople. Graduated from Nubar-Shahnazarian College. In early youth he published the *Ergracound* (Globe), a periodical. After holding positions in national councils and educational committees, he was made secretary of the Armenian delegation sent to Berlin under ex-Patriarch Khrimian. In 1889, Tchéraz, then principal of the Central College, fearing arrest by the Turkish police, left Constantinople for London. There, as an unofficial agent of the Patriarchate of Turkey, he worked for the Armenian claims. He published a monthly paper, *L'Arménie,* in French and English; also wrote for French papers on Armenian culture and the role of Armenia in world history.

Shirvanzadé (Alexander Movsesian) (1858-1925)

Native of Shirvan district, Aghwanq. A gifted fiction writer and a dramatist, one of Armenia's finest. He received an appointment to a State office in Baku, but later relinquished the post and induced the Mardasirakan (Philanthropic) Society to establish a library, with himself as librarian. His early writings had appeared in *Mshak*. Through his novels he became a public hero; but on the charge of being a revolutionary, he was imprisoned and exiled to Odessa. Armeno-Turkish troubles caused him to move to Paris, where he attended lectures at the Sorbonne. Upon the birth of the Armenian Republic he visited the United States; then after a lengthy stay in France, he returned to Armenia and lived in Tiflis until his death. Among his works are *From the Memoirs of an Agent*, *The Guardian's Fire*, *For the Honor*, *A Married Woman*, *Vain Hopes*, *The Chaos*, *The Possessed*, etc.

Eghisheh Tourian (1860-1930)

Patriarch of Constantinople and later of Jerusalem. An intellectual giant, he was well versed in French, English, Hebrew, Greek, Latin and German and so deeply engaged in scholarly research that he had little time for the publication of his writings. Some of them were printed by his former disciples at the Jerusalem Seminary. They included Armenian history, Armenian paganism, mythology, and ancient Armenian literature. He compared in part the Armenian translation of the Bible with the Greek text. His *Collection of Studies and Criticisms* (posthumous, 1935) is a precious chrestomathy.

Papken Gulesserian (1868-1936)

Born in Aintab. After a course in Vardanian High School, he received religious training and order in the Convent of Armash, where he wrote *A Critical Study of Eghisheh*. Ordained bishop at Etchmiadzin. Among his works are *Islam in Armenian History*, *Hovhannes Golod*, *History of the Katholikosate of Cilicia* (in part), etc. Bishop Papken visited the United States in 1916 and published the *Taurus* monthly. Thence went to Jerusalem and for five years lectured to upper classmen in the Seminary. Finally he became Coadjutor Katholikos of Cilicia at Antelias.

343

Torkom Coushakian (1874-1939)

Called to occupy the seat of the Patriarch of Jerusalem, he edited the *Sion* monthly. The financial condition of the monastery of St. James was greatly improved under him. Patriarch Torkom published a masterly translation into modern Armenian of the classical *Narek*. He wrote also the biographies of Katholikos Khrimian and Patriarch Tourian. He had been appointed by the Katholikos Kevork as the General Executive Director of the world-wide celebration of the fifteenth century of the invention of the Armenian alphabet. He subsequently published an exhaustive compendium of the speeches and studies made on that occasion in various countries.

Vahan Tekeyan (1877-1945)

A journalist and a prominent national figure of high principles. Accomplished poet, author of *"Cares," "Wonderful Resurrection," "From Midnight to Dawn," "Love,"* etc.

Zabel Essayan (1876-1947)

Born in Constantinople. Followed courses in literature in Paris. A talented writer; author of several novels of high literary quality; *Well-bred People, My Exiled Soul, Prometheus Released.*

Avetis Aharonian (1866-1947)

Born in Iktir, at the foot of Ararat. A distinguished writer. Author of some 30 novels, dealing mostly with the misery of the Armenian people. Was President of the Armenian Delegation at the Paris Peace Conference, after the First World War, and signed the Treaty of Sèvres, in 1920.

Arshag Tchobanian (1872-1954)

Graduated from Armenian Central College of Galata. Poet, critic, and realistic novelist; he was unexcelled among Armenians who wrote in French about his native land. Jacques de Morgan's History of Armenia was compiled at his suggestion. His monthly review, *Anahid*, contained many literary gems. Among his works are *Chants Populaires Arméniens, Trouvères Arméniens, La Roseraie d'Arménie*, in 3 volumes. He met death in Paris in a traffic accident.

Eroukhan (Ervant Srmakeshkhanlian) (1870-1915)

A talented writer, his style has a characteristic beauty. The subjects of his novels are taken from the life of the humble class. Among his works are, *The Daughter of the Amira, Legitimate Son*, etc.

Avetik Isahakian (1875-1957)

Born in Alexandropol (Leninakan), died in Erevan. A great and most popular, beloved poet. Author of charming poems; *Songs and Wounds*, *Abu Lala Mahari*, translated into many foreign languages.

The list of prominent Armenian writers of our times is long, indeed; the following names should at least have a mention here: Berj Broshiantz, Mikael Nalbandian, Stepan Nazariantz, Sembat Shahaziz, H. Hovannisian, Vahan Terian, E. Tcharentz, T. Demirjian, Nar-Dos, Mouratzan, V. Papazian, S. Bartevian, Dikran Gamsaragan, M. Gurjian, Anais (Yevpime Avedissian), etc.

Chapter XLIII
Architecture in Armenia

By Arshag Fetvadjian[102]

Mixture of Religious Art

After having been ruled for centuries by feudal princes independent of each other, Armenia was reconstructed in 150 B.C. as a kingdom, under a Parthian dynasty known as the Armenian Arsacide (Arshakuni).

At this time there were several religions existing side by side in Armenia, with the gods of Greece in the ascendency. There were statues of Artemis, Herakles and Apollo set up at Armavir. Other images, including those of the Olympian Zeus, Athene, Hephaistos and Aphrodite, were brought later and placed in the stronghold of Ani (Kemakh). Representations of the native divinities which most resembled them were placed alongside them. The temple in the Ani stronghold, where Zeus was housed, had been consecrated to Ahura-mazda, the father of gods. Athene found a home in a temple of Nina (Naneh) at Til. Artemis was placed in the temple of Anahit in Eriza; while to Aphrodite was assigned another temple at Ashtishat, in the house of the goddess Astghik.

---

[102] The renowned artist, Arshag Fetvadjian, was born in Trebizond, on the Black Sea, in 1866. From an early age he evinced a keen interest in painting and archaeology. He entered the Imperial Fine Arts School in Constantinople, won the Prix de Rome, went to that city to study in 1887, and later, to the Imperial Arts Academy in St. Petersburg. Returning to the Caucasus, he specialized in Armenology, and exhibited his paintings in Tiflis. For twenty years he traveled in Armenia, reproducing on his canvases churches, chapels, monasteries, palaces, gravestones — in all, more than 2,000 architectural and artistic subjects.

Mr. Fetvadjian came to America in 1922 and died in Boston in 1947. Under his will, all his paintings and drawings were bequeathed to the State Museum of Soviet Armenia. "Fetvadjian Month" was recently (1958) celebrated at Erevan, with an exhibition of his works. Many invaluable relics of Armenian art and architecture of the sixth to the thirteenth century, which had escaped the ravages of time were destroyed during the last incursions of 1917-1921, and would have been eventually forgotten had it not been for Fetvadjian's meticulously exact paintings of them, made while they were still in existence.

The above article, sent by Mr. Fetvadjian at our request, was originally published in the *Journal of the Royal Institute of British Architecture* in 1922.

After the importation of the Greek images, the temples presumably remained native in character. Up to the present time, the only evidence regarding art under the Hellenophile kings is the beautiful head of a Greek goddess in the British museum, found at Sadakh (the village Sadagha in Turkish Armenia, near Erzinjan).

Near Erevan there is the ruin of an edifice of Roman style for the pantheistic idol cult fashionable in the days of the Arshakists. It is said to have been built by King Trdat as a summer residence for his sister Khosrovidoukht.[103]

Development of Armenian Architecture

Church of St. George at Ani

In my collection I have two water-colors which are faithful pictures of the ruins of the churches of Ererouk and Tekor, both built in the sixth century. The Tekor Church was damaged by lightning in 1912, after 1,500 years of existence. These two monuments are nearly identical in plan, details and technique, and also in the sculptures and decoration of their façades. The interiors are bare. They are examples of a charming archaism, and are generally supposed to be the work of

---

[103] Strzygowski gives some details of this building. In the British Museum is a fragment, in a debased Hellenic style, which is said to be from the Palace of Trdat.

masters who had been apprenticed to Syrian architects. I think, however, that the art of these two structures represents a step in an evolution, of which the genesis remains unknown.

One particularly notices in these drawings the engaged columns which directly support the springers of the arches; the plinth of expanding courses and the elliptical cupola. The cupola, externally enveloped in masonry, shows a lack of experience; and the low tambour which supports it is also remarkable, for later this feature was developed to an extraordinary degree. The Church of St. John at Puragan and the Sourb-Nshan at Kassakh are other examples of contemporary churches. The more ancient houses of worship are larger and more sumptuous than later ones, which fact may be traced to the relatively greater prosperity of the country at an early time than later.

The Church of Avan, near Erevan, dated 577, has a central cupola, supported on eight round arches. Possibly it once had also four small cupolas at the angles. There is likewise a little basilica at Kassakh which seems very ancient. It is of the same age as a church at Eghivard, which dates from 574.

Originality of Religious Architecture

From the hour when Armenia became riper for the task of creating a Christian architecture, its churches were of a specific type; they are in no sense imitative works. Constructed when and where the word of a prince was law, they reveal an artistic taste and a powerful technique to those of the Syrian masters from whom, as certain scholars assume, the Armenians learned their architectural art. In Syria there was an immense heritage of artistic tradition — Egyptian, Phoenician, Greek and Roman — and at the flowering time of Christian art, the land was still flecked with examples of ancient architecture. Syrian masters were in contact with artists of many countries. The architects of Tekor and Ererouk had not this advantage, and therefore deserve to be held in greater esteem.

The monuments of the second architectural period of the Christian era in Armenia were basilicas, sometimes having a cupola; or constructions on a central plan, always surmounted by a cupola; or churches of tri-apsidal plan, the invention of which Strzygowski attributes to Armenians; and finally, churches in the form of a cross. The following are the churches of this period; — St. Gregory of Douin (601-611); church at Avan (beginning of seventh century); two churches at Vagharshapat, Sainte Hripsimé and Sainte Gaiané (618 and 630); the old church in the citadel of Ani (622); the Cathedral of Bagaran (631); St. John at Bagaran (631-639); St. Anania at Alaman (637) and the Cathedral of Mren (638-640).

Notwithstanding the disturbance caused by the Arab invasion around 648 A.D. and after, Armenia, still rich and prosperous, maintained by her own resources her culture, art and industry. A number of *chefs d'oeuvre* of architecture were created during the time of her quasi-political vassalage to the Arab Khalifate. Armenian masters strove to create works captivating in originality, though modest in dimensions. While fighting off Arabs with one hand and with the other repelling the incursions of the Byzantines, who sought to bring Armenia under the confession of Chalcedon, monuments of architecture without precedent were erected — such as the following:— The Church of Our Lady of Masters, a construction of quatrefoil plan (650); the churches of the great and little Artiks (650); the Church of Adiaman (650-660); St. Stephen in Akrak; the large Church of Arouj (Talish); the great Church of Eghivard, Our Lady of Ashtarak; the Holy Apostles at Agori; St. Stephen of Maghart; the fine structure of Our Lady of Talin, on a tri-apsidal plan (690); the lesser Church of Talin, of cruciform plan surmounted by a cupola; Our Lady of Petchni; St. John at Brnakot, in Sewniq, the Church at Nakhjavan — these remarkable structures were all created between 650 and 700 A.D.

Church of St. Stepanos and the Monastery of Maghard

As artists, the Armenians were content to remain within the limits of humble proportions. Some of these buildings in toto might be placed with the great galleries of modern museums. The work of each district had its own distinct characteristics. Each master was a creator, *not a copyist,* varying ever by the force of true originality. The architects were particularly ingenious in adapting cupolas to all kinds of plans. They harmonized art with convenience and reality.

Armenian Influence on Byzantine Architecture

The fierce struggle for overlordship in Armenia between the Arabs and Byzantines had caused many princes, nobles and soldiers to remove permanently

349

to the territory of the Byzantine Empire known as the Armenian "temon."[104] This emigration may very probably have influenced later Byzantine architecture. On the other hand, there is less likelihood of influence in the opposite direction. Armenia, as intolerant as Byzantium on these questions of faith, drove all dissenting Armenians from the country in 719. Under such circumstances, it is difficult to believe that Armenians had much admiration for the architecture of Byzantium.

In the eighth and ninth centuries Armenia had little leisure for advancing the traditions of art and culture. Nevertheless, the mountain fastnesses to which many princes had been forced to withdraw gave to their architects a new field for their skill in constructing churches and convents dedicated to the memory of their ancestors, where masses were celebrated for the souls of the departed.

A monument discovered at Ani during the excavations of 1910 was probably built during the century of desolation. A part of a beautiful church of Otzoun is dated 718, and a portion of that at Banak belongs to the same century. Later, the Arabs again returned to their earlier policy of practical alliance with the Armenians, and about the beginning of the tenth century, the famous Church of Aghtamar was built by the architect Manouel, the crowning achievement of the labors of this time. The same architect constructed the artificial port on Lake Van. During the ninth and tenth century centuries, the following were built:— The Church and Convent of Narek, the Church of the Saviour at Taron; Churches at Ashtarak, Mazra, Horomos, Noratouz, Dariounk, Oughouzli, Soth, Makenatzotz, Vanevan, Salnapat, Sevan, Keotran (near Erevan), Taron (St. John the Baptist), Ishkhan, the Convent at Shoghak. These are marvels of form and richness of decoration.

Dynasty of the Bagratides in the Tenth and Eleventh Centuries

The Arab Khalifate, at that time in difficulties, was ready to be conciliatory, and the dynasty was left free to devote its energy to internal culture. The Architects of the tenth and eleventh centuries have left us a large number of remarkable monuments. Among these are the metropolitan church of Ani, a veritable museum of fine and original buildings; the group of churches at Sanahin, with the convent buildings, the convents of Horomos, with a noble group of civil constructions around them; the splendid Church of Marmashen; the convent of Haghbad; the elegant group of five miniature churches at Khtzong; the remarkable church of the Holy Apostles at Kars; the ornate church of Arkina, the severe Karmir-Vank and distinguished church of Goushavan, the Church of Irind, with its central plan, and that of St. Elias, of the citadel of Ani (which is identical in form and contemporary). The aristocratic church of Bdjni and the sober Our Lady of Tzpni; St. Stephen at Vorodn; Our Lady of Khotakeratz; the humble church of Pravadzor; the cathedral of Karin; the architecture at Gntevank; and the church of Havoutz Thar.

---

[104] In Greek, meaning multitude of people.

Notwithstanding the prosperity, relatively speaking, of this era, an attempt was made to observe in building the modern proportions which would accord with the old traditions. In the interiors as well as on the exteriors of the churches, the walls are formed of wrought slabs in regular courses. As in more ancient construction, I have never remarked in the buildings of the Bagratid era any trace of painting. Sculpture in low relief frequently decorates the façades. The monuments of this epoch do not show motives borrowed from Arab art.

Eleventh and Twelfth Centuries

When the Bagratides were succeeded by the Zakarean princes in 1012, the artistic life of Armenia seems to have been little interrupted, although there were with the Byzantine Empire, and the Turks made their first appearance in the country in 1060. Architecture continued in a series of buildings which, in graceful originality and ingenuity of conception, yielded nothing to the works of the preceding era. The Prince Ivané, brother of Zakaré and generalissimo of the Georgian army, evidently won the good will of tradition-bound Byzantium by his confession of the Creed of Chalcedon. This prince made some attempts to bring the Armenians back to Byzantine orthodoxy, but those faithful to their creed would not be drawn away from the traditions of their national art.

Among architectural works of this period are, the Church of the Shepherds, before the wall of Ani, of which I have a water-color drawing; the churches of Horomaiz; the Church of Our Lady in Haridj, etc. Noteworthy are also Khota-Vank at Ani; Haghardzin; Koussa-Vank; Khatra-Vank; the Holy Cross at Zarinji; the church of the Convent of Shkhmourat and St. Gregory of Tesekh; the churches of Cosha-Vank; Hartz-Hankist at Banantz; Keghart (Airi-Vank); Kepair; Bzavatzor; and Saghotzor (Sevortiaz); the church of the Mother of God at Sanahin; of Spitakavor at Zenjirli; of the Convent of Srvegh and of Vaghahas.

All these monuments are living documents for those who are willing to complete their study of Christian church art. Many other lesser works of the twelfth century also remain in Armenia.

In the thirteenth century, the fourth renaissance of architecture, hundreds of structures were sown over this land, and the style of these works shows great vitality and intelligence.

Those which I have been able to study in detail are usually well preserved. A characteristic of the works of this period is found in the narthexes of the churches. This novelty, begun at Horomos in the eleventh century, in the day of the Bagratid King Hovhannes Sembat, now became general. In the room were numerous monolithic columns with bold capitals; the ceilings were covered with fine carvings, the doors were magnificent and the windows fantastic. Sculptured memorial tablets to persons of distinction are there, especially if they were benefactors of the church. These halls, called Cavit or Jamadoon, are mausoleums provided to satisfy the pious desire of those who wished to be buried in the shadow of the sanctuary. The Armenian Church did not permit burial in the sanctuary itself, and the jamadoons are supposed by some students to have been devised for this purpose.

The thirteenth century ended in turmoil. Architecture, after a century of enthusiastic support by patrons and work by the artists, inclined towards decadence, in consequence of the failure of security. The fourteenth century was a time made dark by the apparitions of the Turko-Tatar hordes, when all culture and art became impossible.

Characteristics of Armenian Architecture

Carving: The Architecture of Armenia was essentially a stone art, and the decorations are in accordance with the nature of the building material. Sculpture held a prime importance, both on the inner and outer faces of the walls. Ornamental surfaces are usually carved in what may be called a *champlevé method,* which is both ancient and characteristic of all the schools of the classical Near East. Such carved decoration was engraved, as it were, on the surface, which it covered like embroidery; and the method seems peculiarly appropriate to the quality of the stone used. Many fragments found in excavations show the use of some animal and vegetable forms, such as eagles, bulls, serpents, heads of angels, lions and rams, pomegranates and grapes. At times, large surfaces, say ten yards long by six yards high, are covered over with carpet-like patterns made up of polygonal and star-shaped slabs covered with intricate carving.

Walls: The faces of walls are as perfectly fitted as modern parquetry of oak; the filling is rubble, with excellent mortar. The courses of the facings vary in height. Roofs are covered with wrought stone slabs.

Ceilings and vaults: The ceilings in the great narthexes built during the period from the eleventh to the thirteenth century are constructed of slabs laid horizontally with consummate skill. The naves of the churches are usually covered with tunnel vaults; these are built in sections, inclined at an angle. Vaults with spherical surfaces were commonly used in the seventh century; and other forms appear in the period from the ninth to the eleventh century.

The simple semicircular arch is not found in Armenia, though common in Byzantine architecture.

The stilted arch is the most usual form, and is common in all the epochs of Armenian art.

The horseshoe form of arch is current in the oldest buildings of Christian Armenia, as remarked by Texier and others.

The pointed arch exists only as an illusion obtained by a slight modification of the round arch at the crown.

A segment arch is found in the west front of the Church of Our Lady at Bagnair, a *chef-d'oeuvre* of the tenth and eleventh centuries.

The tunnel vault is both ancient and common.

Ribbed vaults are also common.

Flat ceilings were often highly decorated with carvings. No examples of painted decoration have been found except some fragments of plaster at Ani.

Stalactite work, suspended from ceilings and walls, sometimes covers the whole surface of a cupola. These elements are worked out in variations which become veritable symphonies in stone. Contrary to a prevailing idea that this medieval type of decoration is an Arabic invention, I believe that it is of Armenian origin. In Armenian only do I find the most daringly contrived specimens of this kind of sculptured architecture, covering sometimes entire surfaces of canopy-shaped ceilings of the church narthexes and inner surfaces of corona-like cupolas.

Other Kinds of Architecture

So far I have spoken only of the *architecture of worship* in Armenia. There remains still the *architecture of defense*; i.e., buildings for military and strategic purposes. There are hundreds of strongholds, among the most ancient works of the constructive art, perched upon well-nigh inaccessible, awe-inspiring heights of this mountainous country.

Besides these, there is the *Funerary architecture* — cemeteries full of memorials for the departed, richly, elaborately ornamented tombstones, elegiac mausoleums erected *in eternal memoriam*, of kings, princes and men of high rank.

There is also the *architecture of buildings of public utility*, which includes hostelries for the accommodations of caravans and travellers, and bridges, often of monumental grandeur, spanning streams 300, 400 or 600 feet in breadth.

Finally, the *architecture of man's residence* — royal palaces, dwellings of princes, citizens, etc., of which we can say little, lacking archaeological evidence. The architecture of the peasant's abode in Armenia, continues to be unchanged and of the same type as described by Xenophon in his *Cyropaedia*, fourth century B.C.[105]

---

[105] During the winter months of 1892-93, in Vienna, the late Archbishop *Mesrop Magistros*, then a newly-graduated philologist from the University of Yourievo, upon request of the Imperial Institute of Scientists, wrote a monograph upon the architecture of the peasant cottage in which he was born. This book was translated into Armenian.

Chapter XLIV
Armenian Sculpture and Painting

Reliquary at Etchmiadzin

Foreign element

Ruins of pagan temples in Armenia remind us of Roman monuments, with traces of foreign influence, Syrian or Byzantine. An example is Zwartnots, with its capital, and the eagles with spread-wings. The capitals of the Ani Cathedral display variants. Figures testify to Western and Eastern elements.

Attention has been attracted by cross-stones, called "khatchkar", some of them as old as the fifth century. Most common are geometric motifs, with figures of Christ, Mary, and biblical events, such as Daniel in the lion's den and legends of Gilgamesh the hero. One khatchkar bears the figure of Anahit. Church façades or windows are decorated with the figures of angels. In one of them is seen the mounted knight Manuel Amatuni, fighting a lion. A sculpture in Mren portrays the founder of the church, David Saharuni and his wife, introduced to Jesus and disciples.

Tombstones

Aghtamar Church

Another precious example is the church of Aghtamar, built in 920. Here is a frieze of animals and scenes of hunting and of grape-gathering, with King Gagik plucking grapes. On another façade, is portrayed Christ holding the Gospel, with an inscription of the sentence — "I am the light of the world." On a window, we see an inscription that reads — "And Adam gave them names of all the animals and wild beasts." The artist meant the Garden of Eden, but did not forget the later saints — the Illuminator, Thaddeus, Bartholomew, etc., and the main biblical events.

King's Statue

A notable fact is the Egyptian influence as evidenced on the Gospel of Queen Mlkeh of Van, dated 856. Sassanid influence was expected logically. Hence, numerous signs of Sassanian art. Returning to Ani, mention should be made of the statue of King Gagik, discovered in the ruins of that city. The precious relic was destroyed by the Turks in 1920. The king was clothed in a tunic with a turban

355

on the head, and held the model of St. Gregory Church, constructed by him. Queen Khosrovanush, the founder of the Church of Haghpat in 991, placed the statues of her two sons showing to them the model of the church. Other dignitaries followed the example.

On Metals

Metal sculpture became the fashion in Cilicia, during the thirteenth century. The silver-gilt Gospel cover, dedicated to Katholikos Constantine I in 1249, is a remarkable specimen. Ivory plates, portraying Christ and Mary with the Baptist, is another type. Reliquaries bearing biblical pictures were in vogue. On several specimens, the Eastern and Byzantine elements are intermixed. On certain relics Moslem art can be easily indicated. As to ornamental designs cut by Armenian artisans, their skill has been acknowledged by authorities. According to archaeologists, sculptural geometric ornaments were known in Armenia long before the Armens settled in the country.

In Foreign Lands

The influence of Byzantium has been traced to Greece and Thessaly, particularly from the ninth century and the period of the emperors of Armenian origin, some of them on khatchkars. The one, in Mistra, Greece, reads — "Joseph, an Armenian, from the Greater Armenia."

Armenian Painting

Pictures and Mosaics

The interior of churches in Armenia were adorned with figures, even some mosaics. Specimens remain in ruins of Zwartnots and in Douin pavements. A fine example of such mosaic is in the beautiful pavement that came to light at the end of the 19th century in Jerusalem. Further still, in Germigny-des-Prés, France, Armenian art came in evidence. In Armenia proper, many of the paintings have been destroyed, but their existence is obvious. Vrtanes Kertogh (the Poet) mentions representations of the Virgin with the Child, St. Gregory as tortured, Ste. Gayaneh, and Ste. Hripsimeh, etc. The Iconoclast movement has had its effect temporarily, also the Paulikian denunciations. The church of Aghtamar was rich in pictures of Gospel miracles, some of them illuminated. Byzantine examples are noticeable in them. A specimen of Syrian and Persian influence is provided by the Gospel (996) of the Walters Art Gallery in Baltimore.

At certain periods, Byzantine touch is seen more than the oriental, especially in miniature decorations. Painting received impetus under Armenian rule in Cilicia. The Hetoumian family, royal or princely, patronized illustrated manuscripts.

They are of Eastern Armenian style. The works of Narek, Shnorhali and Lambronatsi became popular.

Miniature Painting of a Sissouan ms. dated 1330.

Roslin and Pidzak

Among the artists of Cilicia, Thoros Roslin is the most prominent. There are other miniatures whose authors are unknown. An exquisite example is the Gospel ornamented for Prince Vassak, now in the Freer Gallery in Washington. Artists draw attention to the originality of painters of Cilicia, who deal with detail in Gospel episodes, unnoticed until then, Passion week, for instance, and the betrayal by Judas. The most prolific painter of Cilicia was Sarkis Pidzak of the fourteenth century. Among notable artists are Mkrtich Nakashr, Ignatios and Thoros of Taron.

Armenian role

Concluding the treatise, an authority finds that "in painting, as well as in sculpture, these Eastern elements were introduced by Armenian craftsmen."[106]

From Viscount James Bryce, again:—

> "The finest examples of ancient Armenian architecture are to be seen in the ruins of Ani ... while the famous church of the monastery of Etchmiadzin is, though more modern, a perfect and beautiful existing representative of the old type. Etchmiadzin ... is the seat of the Katholikos, or ecclesiastic head of the whole Armenian church." (Introduction, "Armenian Legends and Poems" by Zabelle C. Boyajian, 1916, London.)

---

[106] Sirarpie Der Nersessian, "Armenia and the Byzantine Empire," Harvard University Press, 1945.

Chapter XLV
Armenian Music Secular and Religious

Early Period

Little is known about the first of the two periods of Armenian music. National historians tell us that Pagan Armenians had plenty of singing and played on instruments.

For 150 years after the conversion of the Armenians to Christianity, their music was mostly of Greek and Syrian origin. The national type begins with the invention of the Armenian alphabet in 405. As in all the western countries, so in the Near East, the preachers of the new religion did everything in their power to suppress the old pagan music. Khorenatsi brings forth, almost unwillingly and despisingly, some fragments of the songs of the past — songs of wedding, dancing and rejoicing, as well as songs of a laudatory or funereal nature. There were, even in the lifetime of Khorenatsi, improvisers, mercenary singers and troubadours, the most famous among them those of the district of Goghten (the modern Julfa and Akulis, home of the Zog dialect). Like the Greek rhapsodists up to the fifth century, they went around reciting in songs the great deeds of their ancestors. "The Song of Vahagn" was among the most precious of them. The Cymbal, used by the singers, was a special Armenian instrument of music.

Sharakans

The art of singing attained considerable progress in the 5th century A.D., presenting the same characteristics of the religious chanting of other countries of the time: simplicity and homophony (single voice) and psalmody. In the same period was founded a rich heritage — poetic and musical, collected in the *Sharakan*,[107] the Armenian Hymn-Book by Boghos Taronetsi (Paul of Taron), in the 11th century.

The Sharakan is a thesaurus of sacred songs, partly original and partly translated from Greek liturgy. Some of the hymns, attributed to the Katholikos Sahak the Great, and to Mesrop Mashtots, do not seem to belong to the early Golden Era of the 5th century literature. Among the authentic authors of the Sharakan may be cited the following:

---

[107] The word Sharakan is interpreted in various ways. It may mean a series or string of gems, agn in Armenian being a precious stone. According to Adjarian and Abeghian Sharakan is a compound word, Shar (= row) and the particle akan, meaning pertaining or relating to the row (of hymns), referring to the eight church modes in use in the Armenian Church.

Katholikos Sahak II, 6th century; Katholikos Komitas I, 7th century; Katholikos Hovhannes Otznetsi V, 8th century; Stepan Sewnetsi, 8th century; Katholikos Petros I, 11th century; Katholikos Nerses Shnorhali (the "Graceful"), 12th century; Nerses Lambronatsi, 12th century; Khatchik Taronetsi, 12th century; and Hovhannes Blouz, 13th century. The subjects of these hymns are taken from the life and mysteries of Jesus Christ, of the Virgin Mary, and of the Saints of the Church. Some of its contributors are also the composers of the music of their text. The Sharakan was particularly enriched by the poetry and melodic intonations of Nerses Shnorhali.

The Eight Modes

The eight church modes were adopted by the Armenians, following the Greeks, — some of them as far back as the 5th century, while others were introduced by Stepan of Sewniq, three centuries later. The eight modes are divided in two categories, one half "authentic" and the other half "plagal" (cadenza). These modes have been carefully studied, particularly by Spiridon Melikian, whose book was published in Tiflis, in 1944, but these researches have not yet brought definite results. It is by virtue of the attachment of the Armenians to their tradition that the spirit of the ancient religious chant can still be heard in the music of today.

The neumes, the ancient musical figures (the Khaz), were introduced by the same Khatchatour Vardapet of Taron, who arranged the Sharakan in neumatic notation. The codices of the Sharakan show us neumes in various forms and combinations that are difficult to decipher. They have been studied by European and Armenian experts, the celebrated Komitas among them, but a sure clue has not yet been found. Nevertheless, it was deemed possible, in the 18th century, with the help of antique songs transmitted to us through the human voice, to make an approximate transcription of the liturgical songs in a new notation much like the modern European. The work was accomplished mainly by Papa Hampartzoum Limonjian of Constantinople (1768-1839). His pupils and other artists completed the work. In the imposing volume of the "Adyani Sharakan" (the Altar Song-Book), printed in 1874, are collected the church hymns, with the new notation. Many others followed the above. Despite its advantages for the teaching of the chants, it would seem doubtful whether the Armenian notation can be diffused. The intervals of the Armenian music, unknown in Europe and America (minors of the half-tone), would require a different notation.

Musical Practice

Lazarus of Pharbi (Parbetsi), reports that Katholikos Sahak was "learned in musical signs." The art of singing was intensely cultivated later. The Metropolitan Stepan of Sewniq and his sister Sahakdukht, musician and composer in the 8th century (who taught the choir from behind a curtain), achieved special fame. The monastery of Tadev was also a center of music training in the 9th century. Samuel, the head of the school of Kamrtchatzor, 10th century, was a "master in

Holy Scripture and in the art of singing," says the chronicler Stepanos Vardapet Assoghik.

From a Gospel of Tenth Century in "Parakir" letters, Ornamental

The Arabic Influence

Armenian music was decisively marked by the Arabic influence, prevalent in the Near East during the 8th and 9th centuries. Ashough is a term under which are known the troubadour, the singer, the story-teller, the versifier and the player on instruments.

From the 10th to the 20th centuries, a space of one thousand years, there have been perhaps a thousand Armenian ashoughs, several among them being women and clergymen. The ashoughs dealt in various subjects — the romantic, heroic, religious, moral, descriptive, historic, patriotic, didactic, etc.

The role of the ashough has been of much importance, as indicated by Frédéric Macler. The ashough became a pastor and interpreter, a sort of divine oracle, inspiring good ideas and manners, and higher ambitions.

The Neume (or Sequence)

After the introduction of the neume, the system rapidly spread throughout the Armenian nation, specially in Cilicia, the Monastery of Arkagaghin being a main center. At that time, a number of hymns were composed, full of flourishing notes and rich in sentiment, to which the musicians gave the name of "Manrousmounk" (Little Studies). These hymns are in neumatic notation, of which the codices give seventy different variations, all with different names.

The 13th century produced a number of notable poets and composers, one of them "Badveli (the Reverend) Nerses," the son of King Leon II of Cilician Armenia (1280-1300). Among the principal centers of sacred music in modern times which remained faithful to the ancient tradition, were the monasteries of Etchmiadzin, Jerusalem, Armash, and St. Lazarus in Venice. The Abbot Mekhitar, the founder of the Mekhitarist Congregation, was deeply versed in the singing of the Sharakan, and taught his pupils the traditional tunes of the national hymn-book. Among musical celebrities who resided in European countries were: Father Minas Bzhishkian of Trebizond, who introduced the organ in the Armenian churches of Poland; Archbishop Edward Hurmuz, Father Augustin Kouyoumjian and Abbot Ignatius Kuréghian. The vocal polyphony (plurality of sounds) was introduced into the Armenian community when it was possible to organize professional singers and choruses. Among the masters of such movements are: Tigran Tchukhajian of Constantinople (1836-1898), author of Léblébiji Horhor, Zémiré, Olympia, etc.; Christopher Gara-Murza (1854-1902) of Crimea; Marcar Ekmalian (1854-1902) who wrote the chorals of the Holy Mass, and had an active part in the compilation of the music of the Sharakan of Etchmiadzin, in the modern Armenian notation; Komitas, born in Turkey (1869-1939), who made extensive researches in documents concerning the original Armenian singing. Komitas traveled all over Armenia, exploring even the most obscure corners of the country. He was thereby able to collect a great number of songs of every variety, many of which he published, after harmonizing them. He also organized concerts of choruses for the execution of sacred and popular songs. To his credit may be cited, furthermore, the elimination, to a great extent, of the nasal and monotonous plaintiveness of the church music. Unfortunately, he was compelled to cease his labors, on account of a nervous breakdown, contracted during the horrors of the Armenian Deportations in 1915 and 1916. For almost ten years confined to a hospital, he died in Paris (1935).

Parts of the Armenian Holy Mass chants were published in European notes, by B. Bianchi in Vienna, in 1877. The melodies in three or four voices, by Ekmalian, were also published in Vienna, in 1896.

The Armenian Breviary (Zhamagirq), and the Liturgy were partly or wholly translated into English and published in London and in the U. S. A. The one published by the late Rev. Thoros Thorosian of Fresno deserves special note.

Music in Soviet Armenia

In 1355, even before the invention of the printing press, Grigor Soukiasian of Sourkhat, Crimea, wrote a treatise on Armenian music. It was almost five centuries later that the same subject was, with some hesitation, taken into consideration by Armenian publishers. In the middle of the 19th century, Nigoghos Tigranian developed instrumental music in Tiflis, and his example was followed in Constantinople. However, attempts at using organs or harmoniums in churches raised protests, and the general progress was slow and largely dependent on the preferences or caprices of certain patrons, financing musical publications.

The efficacious and scientific way towards the advancement of Armenian music began with the Soviet régime in the Armenian republic. The progress in that respect within the short space of 25 years, is amazing, indeed. There are now printed hundreds of songs on every phase of life, the major proportion being devoted to labor — in the field and factory, at home and on the hillside. They include such items as plowing, sowing, irrigating, threshing, corn-cracking, wheat-grinding, churning, flock-gathering, dancing, weddings, lullabies, wrestling, and many others, besides the popular festival songs, — those of Vardavar (Transfiguration), of Hambartzoum (Ascension), etc. In short, music now plays an important part in the life of the people in the homeland. The Opera House of Erevan is regarded as one of the most beautiful of its kind in the U. S. S. R. The Conservatory has produced many great musicians. The Philharmonic Orchestra of Erevan gives regular concerts. The Komitas Quartet won the first prize in moscow, in the competition of the year 1939. A. Spentiarian and Aram Khatchatourian have won world-wide reputation as composers.

In the repertoire of national operas, the following are the best known: "Almast," by Spentiarian; "Anoush," by A. Tigranian; "Loussabats," by Haro Stepanian; "Seda," by A. Ghevondian; "Sappho," by A. Mayilian; "Aregnazan," by Grigor Sewny. The last named artist is well known among Armenians in the United States, where he died.

Nor did Soviet Armenia lack in the production ofmartial music. More than 100 war songs were registered to its credit during the great patriotic conflict of the Soviet Nation against Germany.

Chapter XLVI
History of Education among the Armenians

By Prof. Kevork A. Sarafian[108]

The Beginnings

It is almost impossible to fix a definite time at which formal education began to function in Armenia. The chief reason for this uncertainty lies in the fact that Armenian historical records do not go back beyond the date of the introduction of Christianity. Furthermore, such historical records as are available give only meager accounts of the social, educational and cultural conditions of the nation.

The fact that the Armenian language was in full bloom at the time of the introduction of Christianity is a proof that there existed in Armenia intellectual classes, at the courts and in the shrines of paganism, long before the Christian era.

The "weak" King, Artavazd, according to Moses of Khoren, is praised by Plutarch as the author of poems and discourses written in classic Greek. Classic plays were presented not only at Artashat or Tigranocerta, but in the important cities of Armenia, as both Dr. H. Asdourian and Bishop Gulesserian affirm. Father Hatzouni, too, a Mekhitarist scholar, agrees with this belief;—

> The Armenian nation has not had, prior to Christianity, any public education, the result of which is the lack of literary productions. The Armenian was satisfied with the moderate educational training received in the family as well as in military and political circles like the ancient Greeks, who gave such training to their children prior to the glorious development of their culture.

After Introduction of Christianity

When Christianity was formally adopted by King Trdat in 301 A.D. as the official religion of the country, there still existed in Armenia a strong sentiment for the old paganism. It is therefore no wonder that Gregory the Illuminator, after converting King Trdat to Christianity, persuaded him to order the temples of polytheism demolished and in their places new churches constructed. Yet Christianity would not have been able to send its roots into the depths of the Armenian soul without the inauguration of an effective system of education.

---

[108] Prof. K. A. Sarafian, M.A., Ph.D, L.L.D., Holder of Diploma for Distinguished Service to Higher Christian Education.

Agathangelos, the fourth century historian, portrays the details of this educational program:—

> "Trdat, the King, gave orders to gather together Armenian children from different provinces and different locations in the confines of Armenia to train them in the literary arts; he ordered also the appointment of faithful teachers for these children. Furthermore, he ordered the bringing together of some of the foul and pagan priesthood at suitable places in different groups and classes, and financed the education of all by royal subsidies. The plan was to separate them into two major groups, one group to study the Syriac language and literature, the other the Greek. And all at once, in a very short period, the sections of the country in which the people were savage-minded, sluggards and brutish, they all became scholars of the prophets, erudites of the apostles, the heirs of the Gospel, and not at all ignorant of all the Commandments of God."

Agathangelos describes also the establishment of a Royal school, where young princes and even the King himself were educated.

In this campaign for popular education, the Christian church provided the spiritual leadership, and the King's treasury supplied the financial support. However, owing to adverse political conditions, the Armenian state did not enjoy a permanently independent life. Therefore, the responsibility of educating the youth of the nation fell upon the shoulders of the Church. But the Church was able to educate only a limited number of persons for leadership.

The educational progress of Gregory the Illuminator was not native; it was international in character, the teachers were of foreign origin, the chief textbook was the Bible, which at this time had not been translated into Armenian, but was read in the Greek and Syriac languages. Armenia as yet lacked an alphabet of its own.

Second Attempt at Revival

Upon the death of St. Gregory, the momentum of the evangelistic activity and educational endeavors were gradually slackened. Also, the reactionary opposition of the adherents of the pagan worship had begun to reassert itself.

Nerses Partev, the Katholikos, made heroic efforts to revive the educational consciousness of the nation. Nerses was the finished product of the Greek Cappadocian School, having been trained in Caesarea as well as at Byzantium. He called a national council which convened at Ashtishat during 362-363. This famous gathering made, among others, the following decisions of the utmost importance:

a) To open schools at various places to teach Syriac and Greek.

b) To establish at suitable places poorhouses, orphanages, hospices, hospitals, etc., and to support them through the proceeds of agricultural lands belonging to the Holy See.

c) To found monasteries and convents for both sexes. Nerses was the founder of more two thousand such institutions.

The schools established by Nerses were permeated by the international spirit of early Christianity, where foreign languages were taught, and where the Biblical truths were propagated. Nerses himself was a pupil of the Greek father, Basil the Great of Caesarea. He died about 372. The death of Nerses was soon followed by great political upheavals. King Pap confiscated the rich estates attached to the Holy See.

Golden Age

No period in the history of Armenia equals in importance the short space of time which covers the reign of King Vramshapouh (391-414 A.D.) and the pontificate of Sahak Partev (390-439 A.D.). During this period a nation was born — a nation which lived forever after, throughout centuries of persecution, bloodshed and turmoil. It was not, therefore, an idle exercise of the imagination on the part of Korioun, the historian of this age, to say, "At that time the blest and enviable land of the Armenians became unquestionably wonderful."

This Golden Age was a period of feverish activity in the fields of (1) literature, (2) education and (3) evangelization.

The educational program inaugurated by Gregory the Illuminator and Nerses the Great was international in character. The Scriptures were read in the churches, not in the Armenian language, but in Syriac and Greek, of which the great majority of the people could understand nothing. The decrees of the King and all the official records were written in the Greek, Syriac and Persian alphabets. Because of the inefficiency of the native schools, large numbers of students were under the necessity of going abroad for their higher education.

The blessed teacher, Mashtots (Mesrop) worried greatly at seeing the expensive journeys which Armenian students were compelled to take in their wanderings among the schools of Syrian science. For the functions of the church were carried on in Syriac in the monasteries and churches of Armenia, and the masses could hear but not understand anything that was spoken there; they were not familiar with that language.

The Alphabet and Education

Mesrop, who was called the *Teacher of all Armenia,* saw the necessity of a basic intellectual tool, namely, a written language. His great achievement in creating the Armenian alphabet is described in Chapter XLI. With the language reduced to

366

an alphabet, Sahak, Mesrop and all the leading Armenian scholars set themselves to the task of translations, original literary productions and the enrichment of the national literature. Mesrop, actuated by an intense zeal for evangelization, resorted to the most potent means for achieving his end. He and Sahak counselled the King to open schools. Says Moses of Khoren;—

> "When Mesrop arrived and brought with him the alphabet of our tongue, with the order of Vramshapouh, he and Sahak gathered select groups of children who were intelligent, well-bred and sweet-voiced, and established schools in all the provinces, and educated children throughout that portion of Armenia which was under the Persian rule."

Mesrop established two types of schools;—

a) *A School for Leaders.* At Vagharshapat, the capital of Armenia, a central school was founded, offering education to a select group of students who were to be trained as leaders. In this central school the children of the princes were educated also. Especially was this true of the glorious house of the Mamikonians.

b) *Schools for the Common Folk.* Sahak and Mesrop organized also at numerous centers elementary schools where at least the rudiments of reading could be taught the children of the common folk. They "asked and begged from the King, young children to learn the alphabet. And as soon as a great number of them became familiar with it, the latter (Mesrop) ordered the teaching of the alphabet in every place," according to Korioun.

And after the great work of St. Sahak was carried out," says Lazar of Pharb, "schools were established for the education of the common folk, and the classes of literate people were increased, vying with one another."

Hellenism

Tigran the Great had transplanted Greek actors into his newly constructed capital city, where Greek theatres had also been built. Artavazd, another King of the pre-Christian period, wrote Greek tragedies during the days of his captivity at the court of Cleopatra in Egypt. Aside from this fragmentary knowledge, we are in the dark about the Hellenism of the pagan period. Our historians, however, mention several Armenian intellectuals whose genius shone in Hellenic centers.

Tiran Haigazn was a pupil of Dionysius, the grammarian. Lucullus admired his scholarship and personality, and took him to Rome. He was the first man to engage in bookselling as a business, and he organized a library.

Cicero (106-43 B.C.), appreciating the abilities of Tiran, invited him to his house to arrange his books for him. The great Roman statesman and orator organized a school in his home, where Tiran taught grammar and where Roman children came to study the literary arts.

367

Hellenism Becomes Popular

After the introduction of Christianity into Armenia, the Armenians became ardent devotees of Hellenism. Although this type of Greek culture did not exclude the works of Plato, Aristotle and other great philosophers, it was deeply tinged with religious color. It was the Hellenism of the Alexandrian and Neoplatonic Schools. Not only did the Armenians absorb the Hellenism of this period, but they also gave to the world a few outstanding leaders, such as Proeresios, David the Invincible, St. Yeznik of Koghb, Moses of Khoren, Lazar of Pharb, and in later years, Grigor Magistros, Ohan Otznetsi, Nerses of Lambron and others.

Middle Ages

Throughout the Middle Ages and thereafter, education was centered in the monasteries. St. Karapet of Taron owned twelve large burghs with a total population of 22,813. In this way this monastery was equal in its extent and wealth to some of the principalities owned by the nakharars. Even before World War I, there were 216 monasteries in Armenia. It was in these institutions that Armenian culture was preserved during the dark ages; manuscripts were copied, monks were educated and libraries were organized. Even at the present time, some of the monastic centers fill the educational needs of Armenians outside the confines of the Republic of Armenia.

Monastic Activities

The School of Sewniq was the most distinguished center of learning. Orbelian describes it as a fountain-head of knowledge, standing at the head of all Armenian science. "The schools were very far advanced there. They were very rich, and were like the Athenian schools of Greece and Rome."

The School of Sewniq is not mentioned until the commencement of the seventh century. Such famous teachers as Anania of Sewniq, Stepan of Sewniq, Moses the Poet, Ohan Orotnetzi and Grigor of Tadev added luster to the name of this school. The School of Sewniq did for theology and philosophy in Armenia what the University of Paris did for France. Grigor of Tadev (1340-1420) represents in Armenia the peak of the Scholasticism of the Middle Ages. His chief work, *Kirk Hartsmants* (The Book of Inquiries), is the most authoritative essay representing Scholastic learning in Armenia. It is a sort of religious encyclopedia. Besides this, he left two volumes of sermons, entitled *Amaran* and *Dzmeran*, which embody the scholastic thought in religion and morals.

Monastery of Narek

During the tenth century this monastery became prominent as a splendid center of learning. Gregory of Narek (951-1003) made the name of the institution immortal.

Monastery of Sanahin

Another monastery built by the Bagratid Kings which served as their sepulchre, and became a famous seat of learning during the eleventh century, was that of Sanahin.

Some Men of Science

Anania of Shirak was a distinguished mathematician and astronomer of the seventh century. He traveled widely, to satisfy his thirst for scientific learning, and studied under many masters. His work, *A History of the Universe,* in ancient Armenian, served for centuries as the textbook of science in Armenia. He also wrote a book *Measures and Scales,* in imitation of Epiphanus of Cyprus.

Mekhitar Heratsi, in the twelfth century, studied the Arabic works on Medicine and wrote a treatise, *Chermants Kirk,* (Book about Malaria), which became a source-book for Armenian physicians.

Twelfth Century Renaissance

The Bagratid dynasty came to an end with Gagik II. With the fall of Ani in 1046, many Armenians took refuge in the Taurus Mountains and carved out for themselves there the independent Kingdom of Cilicia. Here they established friendly relations with the European peoples. Out of the resulting intercultural contacts, the light of a lesser Renaissance dawned in the new centers of Armenian learning.

Outstanding Leaders

Nerses Shnorhali (1098-1173) was educated by Grigor Vkayaser (the Philomartyr), who is said to have been the translator of Chrysostom's *Life.* Nerses became the Katholikos of all Armenia in 1166. He wrote *Pastoral Letters* for the benefit of monks, bishops and married clergy, and a series of "Instructive Verses," in which he exhorted youth to love virtue, learning and morals. Writing to the married clergy he encouraged them to love learning. "No one among you should love blindness of ignorance in the study of your subjects, as a result of indolence or worldly occupation."

Mekhitar Kosh (died 1213) is another eminent Armenian of the lesser Renaissance, who not only taught many young men in his monastery, Kedig — built by himself — but also enriched Armenian culture through a compilation of the Armenian Code in 1184, at the request of King Vakhtank and Bishop Stepanos.

Monastic Centers

Two of the monasteries of Major Armenia emerged during the thirteenth and fourteenth centuries as centers of education of medieval "university" type. The term Hamalsaran or "university" is used to describe the school located at the monastery of Gailatzor, near Erevan.

Father Hatsouni quotes from a manuscript (IX, 1091), now in the monastery of St. Lazar, Venice, a passage which indicates that in Armenia the licensing of teachers was practiced at this time. Grigor of Datev, giving the rank of vardapet to Thomas, writes to Arjishetsi, "I gave him authority and license to teach, to organize classes and to teach there the laws of God."

We have also information regarding the status of teachers and scientists in Armenia, in the following law;—

> This law exempts from all taxation the medical doctors, vardapets, and all scientists and literary men who live in cities and villages; and no one has the authority to tax them, to dishonor them or to scorn them or to beat them. They can be made trustees for the orphans.

Darkest Age

The period beginning near the end of the fifteenth century may rightly be called the darkest age of Armenian cultural life. While Europe was being flooded with the light of the Renaissance, Armenia was being bathed in bloodshed, as a result of the invasion of the Turks, Tatars and Mongols. Wherever their feet trod, not even an herb was left to tell the story of a living civilization.

Light in the Colonies

The Armenian colonies in Venice, Genoa, Crimea, Moldavia, Valachia, Poland, Amsterdam, Marseilles and even in Madras made their various contributions to the development of Armenian culture. Thus, the first Armenian publication, "Barzadoumar," was printed in Venice in 1512. In the following year four Armenian books were printed. In 1673 Oskan, a bishop, established his printing office in Marseilles. In 1674 Matthew Vanandetsi published in the same city a *Rhetoric* written by Hovhannes Holov.

Besides these activities, Jesuit missionaries made an effort to educate a few young Armenian converts in the College of Propaganda at Rome. Later, they established a Catholic patriarchate in Bzmmar, Lebanon, and in 1852 the seat of the patriarchate was transferred to Constantinople. While the educational influence of these missionaries was not very great, it accomplished beneficial results. It aroused the Armenian leaders from their lethargy and stimulated them to activity.

The Amrdolou Monastery came into prominence during the seventeenth century as a center of awakening. One of the graduates of this monastery, Hovhannes Golod, later Patriarch of Constantinople in 1713, opened a seminary in Scutari (Constantinople). He counteracted the activities of Catholic propagandists, by arming the Armenian clergy with the intellectual weapons of the Latins. "Under Golod, Constantinople was transformed, a literary movement was set in motion which kept up with his school."[109]

Mekhitarists as Factors in Awakening

The influence of the Mekhitarists has been greater than that of the Latin missionaries. The Armenian monks belonging to the order of Mekhitar, although Catholic, were actuated by a yearning desire to educate and enlighten their own nation. Mekhitar, the founder of this monastic order, situated on the island of St. Lazar, Venice, emphasized, among other things, the teaching of Armenian history and language. Later, another branch of this order was established in Vienna. Mekhitarists collected Armenian manuscripts, enriched the Armenian literature, and gave to the nation a host of leaders.

American Missionaries

In the great Renaissance of the Armenian people during the nineteenth century, American missionaries played a very important part. From the first day when Rev. William Goodell settled in Constantinople in 1831 to the end of World War I, the American missionaries made considerable contributions to the education of Armenians. They not only stressed elementary education, but established colleges and other institutions of learning. Notable among these colleges were, The Central Turkey College of Aintab, in 1874; Euphrates College of Harpout in 1878; Anatolia College at Marsovan in 1886; Central Turkey Girls' College at Marash in 1882; St. Paul's Institute at Tarsus, in 1888. Besides these, there were other colleges, such as International College at Smyrna, 1903; American College for Girls at Constantinople, Syrian Protestant College at Beirut — now a University— Robert College at Constantinople, in which institutions many Armenian students received their education.

The chief distinctive contributions of American education have been in the special stress laid on feminine education, liberalization of the curriculum, introduction of physical exercise and popularization of elementary mass education.

Native Seats of Higher Learning

Constantinople was the chief center of the intellectual awakening. Armenian colonists there not only developed a number of elementary schools, but made great efforts to establish colleges as well. Among the colleges, Nubar-

---

[109] *Patriarch Hovhannes Golod,* P. Gulesserian, p93.

Shahnazarian was the most prominent, but was in existence only a short time. The Central College (Getronagan) and the Berberian gave the nation several worthy leaders. Armash, as the center of theological studies, like the ancient monastery of Gailatzor, won great fame during the administration of Patriarchs Malakia Ormanian and Elishé Tourian. Among its alumni are men of great prominence, such as Papken Gulesserian, Adjutant Katholikos of Cilicia at Antilyas, Torgom Koushakian, Patriarch of Jerusalem, Mesrop Naroyan, Patriarch of Constantinople, all deceased, and among the living ones, Archbishop Karekin Khachadourian, long prelate of the Armenians of South Armenia, now Patriarch of Istanbul.

Among the short-lived institutions Sanasarian College at Erzerum, Cilicia Institute of Aintab, Getronagan Varjaran of Mezireh, Harpout, and other secondary schools, such as Sourp Garabet in Caesarea, Yeremian School of Van, and the Senekerimian School of Sebastia, all of high standing, were swept away in the cataclysm of 1915.

The Armenian churches in the provinces financed parochial schools in such towns as offered a quasi-public elementary education. Local private schools also met the needs of children of more prosperous people.

Educational Societies

In addition to the parochial schools, private educational societies maintained a number of elementary schools in the interior provinces. Among these organizations the work of the United Societies has been most fruitful in the past. Azkanouer Hayouhiats and Tebrotsasser Dignants organizations also supported schools for girls. After the extinction of the United Societies, the educational work of this group was taken over by the Armenian General Benevolent Union. This is one of the best Armenian organizations founded by Boghos Nubar Pasha. The ramifications of the A. G. B. Union touch almost every phase of Armenian national life. In the field of education this is the only great lay society that supports elementary schools in the Near East, and the Melkonian Institute, a collegiate foundation on the island of Cyprus, maintained by the Melkonian donation of 500,000 English pounds. This fund is entrusted to the A. G. B. U., and from the proceeds the Union also finances the publication of historical, philological and Armenological works.

The A. G. B. U. at present maintains schools in the Mediterranean Area, and subsidises Armenian classes in Diaspora. Because of their jurisdictional dependence on the Armenian Diocesan authority, the number of Armenian schools in Russia was smaller than those of Turkey. But in Russia the Armenians had developed a more efficient and effective educational system than their compatriots in Turkey. Furthermore, pedagogy as a science grew with such rapid strides in Russian Armenia, under the influence of German education, that before World War I, this portion of Armenia occupied a high standing in this science, even comparable with that of several nations of Europe.

Early Awakening

The awakening of a consciousness for education was stirred by the founding of Nersesian College in Tiflis (1823) and Lazarian College (1816) in the Moscow-Lazarevski Institute. Among the pioneers of the movement was Khachadour Abovian, an alumnus of Nersesian College and the University of Dorpat, Estonia, who became the champion of popular education and the introduction of the vernacular language. Stepan Nazarian was another leader who exerted great influence in the movement of secularization, progress and enlightenment. He too was an alumnus of Nersesian College, and the University of Dorpat (1832), receiving his Ph.D. later from the University of Kazan. Until his death in 1879 he served on the faculty of Lazarian College. Through the newspaper, *Husisapail* (Northern Light), which he began editing in Moscow in 1853, he championed the cause of vernacular Armenian, and fought for its universal adoption.

Mikayel Nalbantian (1829-1866) was another pioneer in the movement towards enlightenment. He especially advocated the education of Armenian girls. Education, according to him, must be free from ecclesiastical influence. Nerses Ashtaraketsi, Katholikos and statesman, was the most brilliant figure in the constellation which illumined the Armenian horizon under the shadow of Ararat in the early decades of the nineteenth century. In 1823 he founded the Nersesian College, where a host of Armenian leaders were trained. Among the schools of higher learning, Kevorkian Jemaran or Seminary of Etchmiadzin, also played a major part in training leaders. It was founded during 1873-74 by Katholikos Kevork (George) IV.

Education in the Republic

In Armenia under the Russian rule, the common school was unknown until the creation of the Republic. In 1913 Katholikos Kevork V reorganized the parochial schools. These schools formerly were restricted by the regulations of Polojenyé, a sort of internal constitution of 1836 for the Armenian community in Russia. However, following World War I, Armenia became independent (1918), and on Nov. 29, 1921 became an autonomous republic, federated with Russia.

Under the new regime, attention was at once given to reorganization of the schools. The result was the creation of a *unified, modern, compulsory* public school system, *secular, supported* and *supervised* by the State. In the heroic efforts to eradicate illiteracy, not only the formal educational institutions but other cultural agencies as well, contributed their share. Throughout the country, cottage reading rooms, clubs and libraries flourished in increasing numbers.

The University of Erevan and other institutions of technology, pedagogy, medicine, agriculture, music and art, offer courses in higher education. The Academy of Science, independent in its organization, is making great contributions to the advancement of technological and scientific discoveries.

The curse of illiteracy having been wiped out in Armenia, a great number of newspapers and periodicals and hundreds of books are being published in the country at the present time.

Education of women has shown notable progress. The head of the Commissariat of Education is a woman. The rector of the Medical Institute is a woman; so is the director of the National Library. There are numerous female doctors, judges, lawyers, engineers and what not. In the University of Erevan, women lecturers — Arishian, Mirzakhanian, etc. — work side by side with men.

The National Library of Armenia is said to be the richest in material in the Soviet Union. It treasures 11,000 valuable manuscripts. These ancient documents are being subjected to a thorough study by historians, linguists and scientists, in search of hitherto undiscovered facts about the cultural and political history of Armenia and its neighboring countries.

Labor and technology have received special emphasis in the education of Armenians. As a result, an essentially agricultural nation has accomplished great results in a technological way and industrialization has advanced rapidly in recent years.

Chapter XLVII
The Armenians Outside of Armenia

Under Darius I Hystaspes

The existence of an important Armenian colony within the empire of Darius, the King of Kings, may be deduced from the cuneiform inscriptions of the Persian monarch. Dadarses, the Armenian general, was commissioned by Darius to suppress the revolt of his fellow-nationals, while he himself was engaged in the siege of Babylon.

Some years after the conquests of Alexander the Great, about the end of the fourth century B.C., Armenian names are found among those of the princes to whom the Seleucidae entrusted the government of Armenia. Later on, during the expansion of the Roman power in the East, in its struggles against the Arsacids of Persia, there existed large Armenian colonies in both capitals, Rome and Ctesiphon.

Armenian Emperors of Byzantium

The partition of the Roman Empire between the two sons of the Emperor Theodosius was soon followed by a predominance of foreign elements in the court of Byzantium, the eastern half of the divided world. The proximity of this capital of the East to Armenia attracted to the shores of the Bosporus a great number of Armenians, and for three centuries they played a distinguished part in the history of the Eastern Empire.

Maurice Emperor (582-602)

The first Armenian who wore the Imperial mantle was Maurice (Moric). Born in Arabissus, Cilicia, in 539, he attained the rank of general, won several victories against the Persians, married Constantia, daughter of the Emperor Tiberius Constantine (578-582), and was crowned Emperor upon the death of his father-in-law. After twenty years of reign, he was dethroned by Phocas and was put to death. His wife and nine children were subjected thereafter to the same fate at various times. Only a daughter, Maria, escaped to Persia and became the wife of King Khosrov II.

Mauricius Tiberius, Constantin and Theodosius

Flavius Heraclius I (610-641)

Heraclius, the patrice and prefect of Africa, a former governor of Armenia and probably a kinsman of Maurice, sent his son, Flavius Heraclius, at the head of a fleet, to Constantinople, to avenge the murder of Maurice. Phocas took flight and young Heraclius assumed the crown. He then led his army against Khosrov II and victoriously entered Armenia in 622. But upon his return to the capital, he neglected military affairs to engage in religious controversies. The Arabs did not fail to take advantage of this. Damascus was captured by Abubekr in 632, and Jerusalem by Omar in 638. With these two strokes the Byzantine Empire had forever lost Mesopotamia, Syria and Palestine. In the reign of Constantine IV ("Pogonat," 668-685), the Arabs laid siege to Constantinople seven times. During the first year of his reign, Constantine found it necessary to suppress an Armenian general, Mazizius (Mzhézh), who had proclaimed himself Emperor in Syracuse, Sicily.

Filepicus Bardanes (711-713)

Tiberius IV, son of Justinian II, was four years old when his father proclaimed him an associate monarch. But in 711, the people in revolt enthroned the Armenian general Philippicus Bardanes (Vardan). His reign, however, lasted only two years. Plotters belonging to the faction of the "Greens," seized and blinded him.

Artavazd (742)

Artavazd, the commander-in-chief of the Armenian army, had married Anna, daughter of the Emperor Leon III. He proclaimed himself Emperor in 742, but was defeated and deposed by his brother-in-law, Constantin V, and his eyes, also those of his two sons were put out.

Leon V, "The Armenian" (813-820)

In 813, Leon V, known in history as "The Armenian," was enthroned by the army, which had just inflicted a severe defeat upon the Bulgarians. The Armenian chroniclers call him Leon Ardzruni. The Greek orthodox church regards him as an iconoclast (image-breaker). Leon had married Theodosia, daughter of the Armenian patrice, Arshavir, and had four sons — Sabatius (Sempad), Basil, Gregory and Theodosius. He was assassinated by Michael the Stammerer, who seized the throne. Upon Leon's death, the Greek Patriarch Nikephorus said, "Religion is saved from a great enemy, but the State has lost a needed prince."

Leo V and Constantin VII

Leo V, the Armenian

Romanus I Lecapenus (919-944)

Romanus Lecapenus, son of Abstactus (Vashtakian), was born in Armenia. He was twenty years old when he ascended the throne of Byzantium. He married Theophanon, who is accused of having poisoned him, as well as her second husband Nikephorus Phocas, who also became Emperor. John Zimiskes, her accomplice in the latter's murder, profiting by the youth of the sons of Phocas, usurped the throne and sent Theophanon into exile. Upon John's death, the two sons of Romanus II jointly came to power.[110]

Coins of Emperor Leo VI The Philosopher (886-912)

Theodora (1041-1056)

---

[110] The Grand-Duchess Vladimir of Russia, whose daughter Anna married Henry I of France, was a granddaughter of Romanus II, says Gibbon in his "*Decline and Fall of the Roman Empire.*"

The following are the princesses of Armenian nationality, who were Byzantine Empresses:—

Marina, wife of Constantine VI (780-797)

Theodosia, wife of Leon V (813-820)

Euphrosina, wife of Michael II, "The Stammerer" (823-830)

Theodora II, wife of Theophilus (830-867)

Helena, wife of Constantine VII, Porphyrogenitus (911-919) (944-959)

Theodora III, wife of John Zimiskes (971-976)

Zoe, wife of Romanus III (1028-1034)

Theodora IV, wife of Constantine X (1041-1056)

Rhita-Maria, wife of Michael IX (1295-1320)

Armenian Functionaries of the Empire

Among the Armenians who have played distinguished roles as State functionaries of the Byzantine Empire, may be cited Narses, the general who crushed the armies of both Goths and Franks, who were overrunning Italy in the 6th century A.D., and returned Rome to Justinian I. From 542 to 568 he governed the reconquered West. Then, from 625 to 643, it was an Armenian, Isaac the Exarch of Ravenna, who presided over the destinies of Italy.

In the Byzantine army, Armenian names are found in striking numbers. The influence of these aliens was felt, not only in military life, but also in other branches of the Government, as well as in the social structure of the Empire. In science, art and business, the Armenians have displayed special aptitudes and made considerable contributions. Samuel of Terjan, King of Bulgaria (989-995), was an Armenian. He and his brother Manuel, together with their warring followers, had stiffened the Bulgarian army. The Greek orthodox church counts many Armenians among its prominent figures. Atticus, the Patriarch of Constantinople in 420, was an Armenian, a native of Sebastia. Bishop Manuel of Adrinople, martyred in 812 by the Bulgarian King Modraz, was another of the same race. So was St. Nikon, a preacher of faith in the island of Crete in 960. Of Theodorus, Patriarch of Constantinople, the Emperor Andronicus I said, "Here is a somber Armenian."

Bagratid Dynasty of Georgia

Among all Transcaucasian countries, the superiority of their southern neighbour, Armenia, had been recognized. From the earliest days, Georgia had been divided into many Eristhawates or princely domains, these being subdivided in their turn into estates of Aznavours or feudatories of the Eristhaws. Under the Sassanid domination, the old system having undergone no change, Georgia had remained without political cohesion until the day when Emperor Maurice, himself of Armenian blood, placed on the throne of that land as sovereign a Bagratid prince named Gouaram, who reigned from 575 to 600 A.D. Since that date, Georgia, Aghouania, Mingrelia and all the small Kartvelian states on the southern slopes of the Caucasus had been governed by Armenian princes. Eréklé II (Heracles) the last King of Georgia, was still of Bagratid blood. Many of these kings were compelled, one after another, to fight against Sassanids, Arabs, Turks, Mongols and Persians. A considerable number of them were forced by the enemy at times to quit their throne in Tiflis or Mtzkhet, unless adequately supported by the Byzantines.

The Georgians, like all other Caucasians, were warriors of the Asiatic type. Their art, inspired by the Byzantines and Armenians, offers, among other things, beautiful examples of Greek and Christian architecture. Among all the Kartvelian races, the Georgians have displayed the highest artistic taste and culture.

Armenians in Iran

The political relationship existing between the Persians and Armenians from the remotest antiquity has been traced in preceding chapters of our history. There are in Persia at present about 80,000 Armenians, constituting two ecclesiastical dioceses — that of the Persian Azerbaijan and that of Irano-India. The first group of communities comprises those of Tabriz and its villages; the Irano-India diocese the communities of Teheran, Ispahan, Hamadan, and other localities, all those of India and Indonesia.

All the numerically strong Armenian communities have schools maintained by themselves, the city of Tabriz leading the rest, with its higher institutions, three for boys, one for girls; next comes New Julfa, near Ispahan. Parochial or private schools in Persia were closed under the last rigidly nationalistic regime, but they were permitted to reopen during the Second World War, in 1942. There was a time when the Armenians of Persia were subjected to persecution by fanatical religious leaders, trying to convert them to the Mohammedan religion. This situation was changed, under the new Persian Constitution, to the establishment of which the Armenian commander, Ephrem Khan, known as Sirdar (Generalissimo) contributed his military genius and efforts, and finally sacrificed his life. The Armenians have also rendered important services to the industrial and commercial progress of Iran.[111]

The Persian Government was represented for a long time in London during Queen Victoria's reign by Malcam (Melcon) Khan, an Armenian. Ohannes Khan Massehian was the Persian minister to Berlin, a scholarly diplomat who translated several plays of Shakespeare into Armenian. Nazar Agha, Persian ambassador to France in the 1880's, was likewise an Armenian. In Iran, as well as in other Moslem countries, many high positions, political and military, have also been held by Armenians turned Moslem. Atabek Azam, the Prime Minister of Nasr-ed-Din (1848-96), was one such apostate.

Ancient Armenian Emigrations

Armenian colonies, already in existence in western Anatolia, centuries before the Christian era, assumed larger proportions, through the facilities offered to commerce by the Roman Empire. They were established in ports on the southern shores of the Pontus-Euxine (Black Sea), such as Trebizond, Cerassus (Kirasson), Amisos, Sinope, Heraclia, and also in various inland centers of mercantile activity. Armenians seem to have been settled at earlier dates in parts of Iberia (Caucasus), in Atropatene, and in Rhaghes. Persepolis, Ecbatana, Babylon, Susa, had formerly been the great commercial centers of the East; they were later on replaced by Pasargada, Ctesiphon, Shouster, Ahwaz and Koweit (the ancient Teredon). To the north, Armenian business men ventured and gradually settled in Astrakhan (southern Russia) and the Crimea.

Mass emigration from Armenia began after the fall of the Bagratid dynasty in 1045. Cilicia and Cappadocia received a great number of Armenians, especially from Ani and the canton of Shirak, following the exile of Gagik II. A considerable part of the emigrants moved towards the North and took refuge in the Crimean peninsula, then mostly inhabited by Tatars. Sections from among them pushed further west towards Moldavia, Galicia, Podolia and Volhynia — countries in the basins of the Vistula and the Dniester Rivers.

Armenians in Poland

A Polish writer, Adolf Novatchinsky, gives us the following sketch of the Armenians of Poland;—

> "Long before the fall of the (Armenian) Kingdom of Cilicia in 1375, the Armenians appeared among us, having been invited here by David, the Prince of Galicia.

> "The first dismemberment of their country brought about a great

---

[111] Sultan Selim I of Turkey (1512-1520), after his victory over the Persians at Tchalderan in 1514, brought from Tabriz to Constantinople a large number of Armenian artisans, in order to improve the industry of his Empire.

emigration. The Armenian emigrants, taking with them a handful of native soil in a piece of cloth, were scattered in southern Russia, into the Caucasus, in the land of the Cossacks, while 40,000 from among them came to us. From then on, new streams of Armenian emigration periodically proceeded from the banks of the Pontus towards the hospitable country of the Sarmatians, and it must be said that these guests, coming from such a distance, proved themselves really 'the salt of the earth,' an exceedingly useful and desirable element. They settled mostly in the cities, and in many places they became the nucleus of the Polish bourgeois class. The city of Lwow (Lemberg), the most patriotic center of Poland, then the theatre of so many historic turmoils, owes its luster in large degree to Armenian immigrants. Kamenetz-Podolsk, that crown of our old fortresses, received its fame from the Armenians who settled there. In Bukowina and in all Galicia, the Armenian element plays a role of the first order in political and social life, in industry and in intellectual movement. Finally, in Poland proper and its capital, Warsaw, the descendants of those who once were the great nation on the Arax, rendered themselves illustrious in all careers. In the battles of Grünwald and Varna, the forebears of the Alexandrovics, the Augustinovics, the Agopsovics and Apakanovics took part. Also from their ranks came forth later renowned Poles, such as the Malowski, Missasowicz, Piramowicz, Pernatowicz, Yakhowicz, Mrozianovsky, Grigorovicz, Barovitch, Theodorovicz, etc."

Through successive immigrations, the Armenians of Poland gradually formed a colony, comprising 200,000. They were welcomed by the Kings of Poland and were granted not only religious liberty, but also political privileges. Casimir III (1333-1370) gave to the Armenians of Kamenetz-Podolsk in 1344 and those of Lwow in 1356 the right of setting up a national council, exclusively Armenian, known as the "Voit." This council, composed of twelve judges, administered Armenian affairs in full independence. All acts and official deliberations were conducted in the Armenian language and in accordance with the laws of that nation. The Armenians of Lwow had built a wooden church in 1183; in 1363 it was replaced by a stone edifice which became the seat of the Armenian prelates of Poland and Moldavia.

In 1516 King Sigismund I authorized the installation in the wealthy and aristocratic center of Lwow an Armenian tribunal called the Ratoushé. Unfortunately, the peaceful life of the colony was troubled by an abbot named Nicol Thorosowitch, who, over the protests of the Polish Romans, was ordained a bishop in 1626 by Melchisedek, the coadjutor-Katholikos of Etchmiadzin. In the ensuing rift between the majority of the Armenian community and a few followers of Nicol, the Jesuit priests took the side of the latter. The dispute grew to such alarming proportions that the Katholikos, Movses III (1629-1632), sent a special legate to Poland, and wrote to the King and the Pope, requesting their protection on behalf of his flock. His intervention was doomed to failure. Nicol, always encouraged by the Jesuits, finally renounced his ancestral faith, became a Roman Catholic and succeeded in confiscating all the properties of the Armenian churches. Even the King, though friendly to the Armenians, feared to resist so

382

powerful a faction. The life of the Armenian community of Lwow was thereby extinguished. Ninety percent of its members, about 45,000 souls, left the city for good, and the remaining 5,000, yielding to the insistence of Vartan Hovnanian, Nicol's successor, embraced the Roman Catholic faith in 1689.

The great colony of the refugees from Ani was thus ruined. Nevertheless, the Armenian origin of many Polish families can be traced even now. They have lost their national church connection and their language, but maintain some traditions. They intermarry among themselves; if they go on religious pilgrimages, they prefer visiting the cathedral of Lwow, built under the inspiration of the churches of Ani. Until recent years, Archbishop Theodorowicz, as the head of the community which, although Catholic, used Armenian Church rites, was a member of the Austrian Senate, together with Latin and Greek colleagues.

A part of the Lwow emigrés, numbering some 10,000, who had settled in Moldavia, moved from there during the Turko-Polish war in 1671, to Bukowina and Transylvania. In Bukowina, they lived in the city of Suczava and vicinity. In Transylvania they founded two new cities, Erszebetvaros (Elisabethstadt) and Szamos-ujvar (Armenierstadt), which, as a special favor, were declared free cities by Charles VI, Emperor of Austria (1711-1740).

Armenians in Western Europe

The next mass emigration was that from Cilician Armenia, three centuries after the fall of Ani. Immensely outnumbered by aggressor forces — Memlouk, Turk, Turkoman, Kurd and others — the Armenians left behind what had become for them a second national home between the Taurus, the Amanus and the blue waters of the Mediterranean, with dwellings, castles, cities and villages, slowly created and become dear to them through the centuries. They sailed westward, seeking refuge in various harbors; in Cyprus, Rhodes, Crete, Smyrna and Constantinople, still under Byzantine rule. Many families went further still, to Venice, Leghorn, Rome, Milan, Naples, Genoa, Pisa and Marseille. Thirty-six Armenian hostelleries, with adjoining chapels, are known to exist in Italy. One of the streets of Marseille still bears the name "Rue des Arméniens."

Armenians in Venice

The oldest Armenian colony in western Europe is the one in Venice, and is also the one which has become the most celebrated as an intellectual, cultural and spiritual center. As related in a precedent chapter the island of St. Lazar has, since 1700, been the home of the religious Congregation of the Mekhitarists, called after the name of its founder, the Abbot Mekhitar. It was in Venice that first printed book in the Armenian language appeared in 1512. The Moorat-Raphael College in Venice has produced a great number of graduates prominent in science, literature, the arts and politics. The Mekhitarists of Vienna have published from their printing press, a great number of books mostly historical and philological, in the original or in translations from classical and modern European languages.

Armenians in India

At the beginning of the 17th century, all commerce with the Orient was conducted by Europeans — English, Portuguese and Dutch — with whom the Moslems could not easily carry on business. Shah Abbas I of Persia, who had transferred thousands of Armenians from Julfa and settled them in the vicinity of his capital Ispahan, encouraged the establishment of Armenian colonies in the important cities of India — in Bombay, Calcutta, Madras also in Ceylon. The Armenians created a vast network of trade, and the hardiest among them ventured to push further east, to Singapore, Java and China. There are records of Armenians in India, dating as far back as 1497. They had in 1690 a center at Calcutta, organized by Job Charnock. The development of that city as a business mart has been credited to Armenians rather than to Europeans.[112] The East India Company issued a charter in 1688, authorizing the Armenian merchants to trade in Indian ports, with certain privileges. Armenians were enlisted in the British army during the 18th and 19th centuries. The Armenians were also conducting flourishing businesses before the Second World War in the Malay Archipelago, in the Philippines, in Siam, Burma, Canton, Nanking, Tientsin and many other places. Some of these communities had their churches. Including the colony of India, they had reached the number of 30,000. The Mardassirakan (Philanthropic) school for boys, and the Sandukhdian for girls, both in Calcutta, have rendered signal service to the diffusion of education for Armenians in the Middle and Far East. The first newspaper in the Armenian language, the *Azdarar* (Monitor), was published in 1794 in Madras by the priest Haroutune Shemavonian, of Shiraz, Persia. Another periodical, the *Azcasser* (Patriot) was launched in Calcutta by Mesrop Taghiatiantz in the year 1844.

Armenians in the Netherlands

During the sixteenth and seventeenth centuries the ports of the Low Countries became great centers of commercial activity. Amsterdam in particular was a rendezvous for myriads of vessels, both Dutch and foreign, and was heaped with merchandise from European and Oriental lands. The city became known as the Empress of Europe. It was in 1594 that the first Dutch vessel entered Constantinople, under the flag of England, with whom Turkey had concluded a treaty in 1580. The maritime importance of Holland had grown to such an extent that the Ottoman Admiral Khalil Pasha, an Armenian by origin, entered into direct negotiation with the Dutch, and made possible, in 1612, the conclusion of a treaty, under which Holland was granted the same mercantile privileges as those enjoyed by the British and the French in Turkish ports.

---

[112] N. and H. Buxton, *Travels and Politics in Armenia,* p194. Mesrovb J. Seth, "*Armenians in India,*" Calcutta, 1937.

As a result of rival intrigues, the Sublime Porte forbade the exportation to Holland of Turkish and Persian products on board any other than Dutch vessels. Armenian merchants, already established in Smyrna, Italy, France and Spain, therefore did their shipping exclusively in Dutch ships, and opened warehouses in Amsterdam, thus contributing towards the further extension of the trade of that city with the Near East. Among the ships sailing under the Netherlands flag there were some owned by Armenian firms.

There is in the archives of The Hague today a letter, dated 1568, addressed to the States-General, concerning some dispute between the Dutch consul of Aleppo and the Armenian merchants of that city. The address is written in Armenian characters, but in the Italian language. The beginning of the letter, the complimentary introduction, is in classic Armenian, but the main body of it is in the dialect of the Persian Armenians.

A contact between Armenian and Dutch merchants took place in East India in 1645. Almost the entire trade of Persia was handled by the Dutch East India Company. Certain Armenians of New Julfa, Persia, had already established flourishing businesses in Amsterdam. They were the successors of their co-nationals who had taken refuge in Holland three centuries before when the Armenian kingdom of Cilicia was invaded by Tatars and Egyptians. Armenians have been mentioned as in the city of Bruges, once a Dutch port, earlier still — in fact, in the twelfth century. Later, in 1345, Armenians had been permitted to sell rugs in front of the church in Bruges. In 1478 the Armenians had their "National Hostelry" in that city, and a priest officiating at the Church of the Carmelites. The city of Gand still honors the memory of St. Macarius, an Armenian thaumaturge (wonder-worker) who died there in the eleventh century.

Somewhere around 1560, Armenian merchants came to Amsterdam to sell pearls and diamonds, and to purchase local products for export. The settlement of Armenians in that country began after 1605, when they had been deported from their homeland by Shah-Abbas, to construct New Julfa in Persia. From Smyrna also, Armenian merchants had come about the same time, in sufficient numbers to give them the legal right to operate in the Stock Exchange. An agreement between a Dutch naval captain, Steen, and six Armenian merchants of Amsterdam stipulated the terms under which the merchandise of the latter was to be delivered in Livorno (Leghorn), in Italy. The document, dated 1627, bears, in lieu of signatures, the name-seals of the merchants — Sarhat, Zakar, Ohan, Marcos, Petros and Hovakim.

The pioneers of the colony, being unacquainted with the Dutch language, had been exploited by alien interpreters. They also made no attempt to correct the Dutch when the latter called them by mistake Persian Christians or Christian Smyrniotes. Even the church built by them was popularly called the Persian Church. The later arrivals, however, were, according to a Dutch historian, "mostly well-bred men who spoke, besides their own language, Italian and French." They soon learned the Dutch language, too, came into close touch with the people and married Dutch girls. They also exhibited a tendency to change their names into

Dutch forms — Serkis Bogos becoming Joris Paulusz, while Eghia di Petros was metamorphosed into Elias Pietersz.

The Armenian business houses of Amsterdam threw off branches into other European cities and countries — Venice, Leghorn, Marseilles, Spain. From the coasts of the Baltic Sea they imported yellow amber, for which there was a great demand in Smyrna. The importation of Persian silk was almost entirely in Armenian hands from 1700 to 1765. As the Mediterranean Sea was infested by pirates during that epoch, their ships were escorted through it by war vessels. Among such sailing ships, one was named *Coopman van Armenien* (Merchant of Armenia). A consular report, dated 1653, states that the *Armenische Coopman*, escorted by the warship *Gelderland*, had reached Smyrna in safety.

The Napoleonic wars put an end to the Armenian life in Holland. The city of Amsterdam was almost depopulated after its occupation by the French. A Dutch writer has said in *De Amsterdammer,* a magazine of the date of August 14th, 1887 that "The story of the Armenian community is a golden page in the history of the city of Amsterdam."

Under the treaty concluded between Turkey and Holland in 1612, these governments mutually guaranteed the religious liberty of their subjects. Armenian Catholic priests could not remain in Holland without special authorization, but the Apostolic Armenians retained the right to have their own priest. In 1713 the city of Amsterdam permitted the Armenian colony to erect a church of their own. After serving its purpose for about a century and a half, this edifice was closed because of the dwindling of its congregation. In 1874, by order of the Katholikos of Etchmiadzin, the building was sold for 10,000 florins, which was transmitted to him.

Armenians in America

In the course of less than a century an important Armenian colony came into being in North America. The estimated number of Armenians living in the United States today is 150,000.

Records show that back in 1623 the first Armenians to go to the New World were two experts in silkworm-breeding, who at the invitation of the Governor of Virginia settled in that English colony.

Very few Armenians landed on the shores of America until the middle of the 19th century. Thereafter began the actual emigration caused by the sufferings of the Armenian people during the Russo-Turkish war of 1876-77. The arrivals in America intended to earn a livelihood and, if possible, save enough money to go back one day to their native land. But few dared to return, as conditions in Turkey not only did not improve but grew worse every day for the Christian minorities. And after the massacres in 1895 and the following years, there was an Armenian exodus on a large scale from Turkey towards the far-off American continent. This immigration swelled by thousands of new refugees in the wake of Turkish atrocities during the First World War.

Another colony has been formed by tens of thousands of Armenians who settled in South America since the last several decades.

Chapter XLVIII
The Armenian Republic
May 28, 1918 to November 29, 1920

I. The Beginning of the Republic

1. The Aftermath of the Russian Revolution

The greatest and most unexpected event of the First World War was the Russian Revolution in February 1917. From that day on the fortunes of the Armenian people were linked with Russia.

During the Provisional Government of Alexander Kerensky, Premier Lvov issued a proclamation putting all the Armenian provinces liberated from Turkey under the protection of Russia. This arrangement was short-lived. On the second day of the following October Revolution which overthrew the Kerensky government, the Bolsheviki issued a call to all the Russian officers and soldiers to return home. This was a great blow to the Armenians to whom the Russian army was a bulwark against the Turks. Thereupon the Turkish hordes overran the entire country and occupied the former Russian districts with all-Armenian population.

Soon after, Lenin and his communist government signed a peace treaty with the Turks (January 1, 1918), which was recognized in the treaty signed at Brest-Litovsk between Germany and Russia. Thus the Bolshevik government began to rule the country.

When finally the Entente Powers defeated Germany and her allies, Czarist soldiers and White Russians under Denikin and Wrangel — with but little outside help — fought the Bolsheviki for many years, but eventually were defeated. Nevertheless, the Bolsheviki were compelled to sign the Treaty of Brest-Litovsk (March 3, 1918) whereby they ceded Kars, Ardahan and Batum to Turkey and permitted Armenia, Azerbaijan and Georgia to fall under Turkish domination. The decree which recognized the right of autonomy for these three countries thus became invalid.

In an effort to maintain their freedom, the three nations united and formed a Council in Tiflis, known as Seym. This Council declared the Trans-Caucasus a Federated Republic, without severing its ties to Bolshevik Russia. The Seym protested against the cession of Kars, Ardahan and Batum to Turkey, but since the Caucasus front was much weakened by the general withdrawal of the Russian forces in November, 1917, the gates were opened for the Turkish invasion. A contributing cause was the disunity among the three nations. The Azerbaijanis were of the same race and religion as the Turks, and desired a Pan-Turanian union with them and the dismemberment of Armenia. The Georgians were unreliable. Thus the Armenians were left standing alone.

2. Armeno-Turkish Relations

The Armenians, foreseeing the future trend of events, promoted a convention in Tiflis in September, 1917. Of the 203 delegates attending it, 103 belonged to the Tashnak party. The convention elected a National Council which, with the consent of the Seym, resolved to assume the defense of the Caucasus against the Turks. The Russian army had left behind a vast quantity of supplies and ammunition. When the Azerbaijani Tatars saw this step taken by the Armenians, they openly sided with the Turks and seized the communication lines, thus cutting off the Armenian National Councils in Baku and Erevan from the National Council in Tiflis.

Meanwhile, both the Ittihad (Unionist) and later the Kemalist Turks moved to win the friendship of the Bolsheviki. Mustafa Kemal sent several delegations to Moscow and the former bitter enemies became close friends — a friendship which proved disastrous for the Armenians.

The signing of the Turco-Russian friendship treaty (January 1, 1918), emboldened the Turks, under Vehib Pasha, to attack the Armenians. They tried to justify this by accusing the Armenians of "crimes" against the Turkish population in the Armenian provinces. Thus a Turko-Armenian war was started. In the name of the Seym, General T. Nazarbekian was appointed commander on the Caucasus front and General Antranig took the command in Turkish Armenia. Under heavy pressure from the combined forces of the Turkish army and the Kurdish irregulars, Armenians were forced to withdraw from Erzingan to Erzerum. After capturing Erzingan, Vehib Pasha also occupied Trebizond, where the Russians had left huge quantities of supplies. Erzerum and Sarikamish were evacuated. Roads were clogged with refugees. Further southeast, in Van, the Armenians resisted the Turkish army until April, 1918, but eventually were forced to evacuate it and withdraw to Persia. Thus all the Turkish districts liberated by the Russians were reoccupied by the Turks. During all these fights, Kurds aided the Turkish army and massacred tens of thousands of Armenians, although the Armenians did not hesitate to retaliate.

3. Treaty of Brest-Litovsk

While these events were taking place in the Caucasus, the Bolsheviks at Brest-Litovsk were signing a treaty with Germany and her allies. The Turks hastening to execute the terms of the treaty, marched upon Batum and crushed the Georgians, April 1, 1918. Under such heavy pressure from the Turks, the Seym was forced on April 9th to declare Trans-Caucasus independent of Russia. Three days later, the president of the Seym, the Georgian Tchkhengeli, without the knowledge of the members, telegraphed General Nazarbekian to surrender Kars to the Turks, who thus reached the heart of Armenia. The three Caucasian nations held a meeting in Batum on April 11th to sign a treaty with the Turks, based on the Treaty of Brest-Litovsk, but the Turkish commander, Khalil Bey, presented demands so severe that they were unacceptable to the Georgians and the Armenians. The war broke out again while the delegates were still negotiating. One Turkish army marched against Tiflis, another against Alexandropol and severed the communication line with Julfa. Cut off from the outside world, the Armenians resisted heroically, routed the Turkish forces near Karakilissé and Sardarabad (May 22-28) and inflicted heavy losses on them.

While the armies were fighting on two fronts, the delegates in Batum were still haggling. Of the three allies, the Azerbaijanis had identified themselves with the Turks, while the Georgians had secretly secured the protection of Germany. Once again the Armenians were left to their fate. On May 26, the Seym declared itself dissolved and the federation of the three Caucasian nations came to an end. On the same day, the Georgians declared their independence; on May 27th the Azerbaijanis followed suit. The Armenians hesitated, since it was extremely dangerous for them to resign from the mighty protection of Russia and be left to the mercy of their traditional enemy and the two unreliable neighbors. But the victorious Turks had demanded that "as a prerequisite to peace the Armenians should declare their independence." (Vratzian, "Armenian Republic," page 132)

Under pressure from the Turks, the Armenians were forced to a declaration of independence on May 28, 1918 in Tiflis. "This independence was not hailed with jubilation and applause. On the contrary, for thousands of Armenians it was a misfortune. The Armenian people was like a mother who had brought a sick child into this world." (Vratzian, "Armenian Republic," page 155)

4. The Treaty of Batum

Seven days after the declaration of independence, on June 4, 1918, a treaty consisting of 14 articles was signed between the Armenian Republic and Ottoman Turkey. Through this treaty the Turks became masters of an important section of Russian Armenia. Armenia was not allowed to have an army, and any force needed for maintaining internal security and order was to be supplied by the Turks, who also retained the right to march through Armenia at any time that "military circumstances" dictated. In eastern Armenia certain cities and provinces were left to the Turks and the Azerbaijanis.

This was the independence of May 28th which the Armenian people had declared "with apprehension." The Turks immediately occupied the delineated boundaries and held positions about 7 kilometers from Erevan and only 10 kilometers from Etchmiadzin. The muzzles of Turkish guns were turned towards the capital of Armenia. Thus the Turks had established direct communication with the Azerbaijan Tatars. They cut off all supplies from coming into Armenia, and famine followed the newly acquired independence.

The Armenian National Council at Tiflis named H. Katchaznouni as Premier, who transferred the cabinet to Erevan on July 17, 1918 with one Turkish and two German lieutenants accompanying them. Fifteen days after the treaty of Batum was signed, the delegates of the three nations were summoned to Constantinople in order to examine and confirm the treaty with the Central Powers. The Armenian delegation consisted of A. Aharonian, A. Khatisian, M. Babachanian and Colonel Ghorghanian. Here a treaty was signed containing 14 articles whereby the Turks recognized the independence of the three Caucasian republics, while the latter assumed the obligation to assist the Turks against the Entente Powers and against Antranig, who was still fighting against the Turkish forces with his Solitary Combat army, because he refused to relinquish the cause of Turkish Armenia and to accept the treaty of Batum.

5. Armenians and Turks Face to Face

The Turks had realized their military objectives. They wanted to avoid having common frontiers with Russia, therefore first they separated Trans-Caucasus from Russia and then the three small peoples from each other. The principal of "divide and conquer" had triumphed.

Despite the peace treaty signed between the new republic and Turkey the fear of massacres was ever present. Therefore, the delegation of Boghos Nubar Pasha in Paris appealed to the Entente Powers to save Armenia from new massacres. This appeal was printed in the European press on January 6, 1919. Allow, while the Brest-Litovsk treaty was being discussed in the German Reichstag it was discovered that the entire Caucasus was left under the influence of Turkey. Lidebuhr, a liberal deputy, protested against the treaty, declaring that it was tantamount to the extermination of the Armenians. The Azerbaijanis and the cases would not permit any food supplies to enter Armenia and the nation was faced with famine. It is reported that from May 28th until December 1919, more than 180,000 Armenians died of starvation and epidemic.

Fortunately this crisis lasted for but a brief period. On October 30, 1918, the victorious Entente Powers forced Turkey to sign a capitulation, and the German surrender followed on November 11th. The Armenian delegates in Constantinople returned to Armenia bringing with them an abundance of gifts and new hope for the future. On November 17th several English warships anchored in the harbor of Batum, and General Stokes came on shore. The Armenians began to breathe freely again.

6. British and American Help

Soon after the defeat of Germany and the signing of a peace treaty, the Turks withdrew from the Caucasus and gathered within the boundaries outlined by the Brest-Litovsk Treaty. The Armenian army reoccupied Karakilssé in November, Alexandropol in December and other communication lines, but the retreating Turks inflicted heavy blows upon the defenseless people and carried away a vast amount of loot. In May, 1919, the Armenians were able with the help of the British to capture Kars, Gaghzouan, Sardarabad and Nakhitchévan. But hunger and epidemics were still reaping large harvests in human lives. Soon the relations between Georgia and Armenia became strained and those between Azerbaijan and Armenia were even worse, as the former were joined by the Turks in furtherance of their scheme of trying to wipe out the Armenian people. Fortunately, through the help of the British the road between Tiflis and Erevan was opened and American help began to arrive through the Near East and European Relief Administration under Herbert Hoover. This committee sent to Armenia 13,000,000 kilos of flour and spent more than $100,000,000. Thereafter, that generous people continued to send food and medical supplies to the famine-stricken nation.

Now let us turn to the events in Baku. Here an Armenian National Council was organized which controlled the city during 1918 and was master of the situation. Armenians had fought courageously against the Turks and Azerbaijanis. This Council refused to recognize the treaty of Batum signed between the Armenians and the Turks, and proclaimed itself the supreme head of the Armenian people. First they joined the Bolsheviki, but when these withdrew from Baku, they called upon the British for help. The British could not defend the city, as their forces were not equal to the combined Turkish and Tatar armies. The Turks received more reinforcements, entered the city and for three days and nights they plundered and massacred 29,000 Armenians. Like the National Council of Baku, General Antranig also did not recognize the treaty of Batum.

7. Two Armenian Delegations in Paris

After the signing of the armistice with Germany, two delegations were organized to plead the Armenian Cause before the Peace Conference in Paris. One represented the Armenian Republic, with A. Aharonian as Chairman; the second was the National Delegation, headed by Boghos Nubar Pasha, to whom General Antranig adhered. In fact, Katholikos Kevork V wrote to Boghos Nubar, entrusting him with the defense of the Armenian Cause, since the Armenian Republic had resigned from that cause, when its representatives signed the treaties of Batum and Constantinople. These delegations did not always agree, but in the spring of 1919 they jointly presented a memorandum to the Paris Conference and demanded an Armenia with an outlet to the Mediterranean Sea.

In those days there was another political party in Armenia known as the Popular Party, which joined Nubar Pasha in suggesting to the Armenian Republic that a special committee be appointed to examine the entire question. In 1919 an All-Armenian Committee was formed for this purpose and after long deliberations rendered important decisions which, however, were never honored. But Aharonian, Armenian President, alone signed the Sèvres Treaty, thus depriving the cause of Turkish Armenia of an official defender.

II. Relation with Neighbors and Great Powers

1. Fights between Two Neighbors

With the victory of the Entente Powers, the Armenian Republic enjoyed a brief

With the victory of the Entente Powers, the Armenian Republic enjoyed a brief breathing spell. As a "little ally," it even began to have high hopes. On the first anniversary of the Republic, May 28, 1919, it declared itself the "Government of United and Independent Armenia."

It soon began fighting with the Georgians, with whom its relations had never been friendly. The Georgians were more fortunate, in that their geographic position was more favorable. A frontier dispute flared into war. The supply line from Batum was cut off and the Armenians in Tiflis were subjected to all manner of persecution. Fortunately through the intervention of the British in Batum a peace was arranged between the two neighbors.

On the other hand, however, the Azerbaijan Republic was never friendly with the Armenians. There was frequent fighting between the two until the bolshevization of Azerbaijan in 1920. Its people were determined to join their co-religionists in Turkey and wanted to eliminate Armenia as a state. In July 1918, the population of Zangezur invited General Antranig to help defend them against Azerbaijani invaders. He accepted the call, drove out the enemy and began to march against Shoushi, capital of Karabagh; but the British halted him. Disgusted and disillusioned, Antranig withdrew to Etchmiadzin, surrendered his army of 4,000 men and all his ammunition and supplies to the Katholikos and left for Europe. Later he came to America.

There are those who believe that by making minor territorial concessions the Republic could have avoided these devastating wars with her two neighbors, especially with Georgia. A remark attributed to Major General Harbord, head of the American delegation sent by President Wilson to study the question of a mandate over Armenia gives significance to this opinion. In his report to President Wilson he said that the Armenian people are endowed with practical qualities, but don't know how to adapt themselves to emergencies; while Hovhannes Katchaznouni, the first Premier of the Republic said in his memoirs that the attitude of the Georgians in these disputes is to be condemned, but our incompetence, political immaturity and unpreparedness for political life have played no small part in them.

2. The British, President Wilson and the Armenians

During the First World War when the Turks were rapidly exterminating Armenians, the Prime Ministers of the Entente Powers — Lloyd George and Balfour in England, Briand and Clemenceau in France and Orlando in Italy — were lavish in their assurances to smaller nations of future "self-determination" and "independence," but none of these governments ever honored their pledges.

In November 1918 the British landed in Batum and in the middle of the following year they withdrew from Trans-Caucasus. During the critical period of the Armenian Republic they did not help our people, but merely sold to the Armenians some rifles and military uniforms. They tried to use the Armenians as tools in their fights against the Bolsheviks. General Stokes, in the name of the

British Foreign Secretary gave the only honest advice to the leaders of the Republic. "England cannot do anything for you," he said, "Try to come to an understanding with the Bolsheviks."

The only country that dealt honestly and sincerely with the Armenians was America. There, both the Republican and Democratic parties desired the Armenians to have independence, but the Republicans opposed an American mandate over Armenia. Many Senators appealed to the President in favor of the Armenians, while President Wilson himself was working to help their cause. Under the joint signatures of Boghos Nubar Pasha and A. Aharonian, an appeal was made to Wilson to take the mandate over Armenia. But one single step taken in good faith by the American President had a disastrous result for our cause. The solution of the Armenian question was tied in with the Versailles Peace Treaty of February, 1919. Wilson asked the Conference that the examination of the Turkish question and the signing of the treaty with them be postponed to a later date. The Versailles Conference agreed to this but unfortunately, the postponement lasted 18 months. All the Great Powers were under the impression that the President wished to have Armenia and all the newly-liberated Near Eastern countries under American mandate. When in April 1919 Boghos Nubar, A. Aharonian and Prof. Der Hagopian met President Wilson in Paris, he expressed willingness to assume the mandate and define Armenia's boundaries with Turkey. In fact, in August of the same year, a mission of 26 Americans headed by Major General Harbord went to Armenia to examine and study the situation with a view to America's taking the Armenian mandate. In the same year Colonel Haskell arrived in Erevan as Commissioner for Armenia, having been appointed by the Allied Powers at the request of President Wilson.

During these inspections and the ensuing delays, time was wasted in Paris. In 1919, a Kemalist movement had started and was spreading far and wide. If the Allies had rendered the verdict on Turkey in February and meanwhile recognized the independence of Armenia, Mustafa Kemal would have neither dared nor been able to do what he accomplished in that and the following year.

On August 10, 1920 the Allied Powers signed the treaty of Sèvres, by which Turkey, among others, recognized the independence of Armenia. A. Aharonian signed on behalf of the Armenian Republic. The question of drawing the boundaries of the new state was left to President Wilson. The state covered 68,500 square kilometers, extending from Russian Armenia to Van, Bitlis and Erzerum. Trebizond was made an Armenian seaport. This map was published on November 22, 1920, just about the day Kars, Ardahan and Alexandropol fell to the Turks. Four days earlier, the Armenian Republic surrendered unconditionally to Kiazim Karabakir, commander-in-chief of the Turkish forces. Seven days later the Armenian Republic collapsed.

3. New Factors Unfavorable to Armenians — 1919-1920

During the 18 months' postponement of the Turkish question, new factors appeared on the political arena of the East, which proved disastrous for the

Armenians in Cilicia as well. First, the victorious Allies allowed the Kemalist forces to establish direct contact with the Bolsheviks. Second, the city of Smyrna was, by the Sèvres Treaty, handed over to the Greeks, who, with the aid of the British, occupied it soon after the Armistice. France, Italy and Bolshevik Russia thought they saw here a British plot to approach the Dardanelles and Constantinople. Motivated by this suspicion the three powers supplied money and munitions to the Turks, theoretically to fight against the Greeks; but the Turks used them against the Armenians in Caucasus and Cilicia. Thirdly, the attitude of the Russians towards Armenia, which had been friendly, now changed. The leaders of the Republic could not come to an understanding with the Russians, but the Turks became close friends with them, because Russia believed that the Kemalists were in opposition to the Imperialist powers of the West. The Bolsheviks steadily grew stronger. They inflicted a crushing defeat on the "White Russian" forces of Denikin and Wrangel, who were notoriously friendly with the Imperialist allies.

It was also during this period that an event took place in America which had serious effect on the entire world, especially for the Armenians. In the Presidential elections in 1920, the opponents of Wilson were the victors. The American Senate now refused to have any part in European or Asiatic affairs, which meant total abandonment of Wilson's plans. The Americans declared that Armenia was Russia's concern; which in turn gave the green light for the Kemalist army to march against Armenia.

Fall of Kars and Alexandropol (Leninakan)

In the middle part of 1920, the Turks were fighting to drive the French out of Cilicia and the Greeks out of Anatolia. The leaders of the Armenian Republic, hoping to take advantage of these circumstances, captured Olti with its coal mines in June 1920, whereupon the Turks left the fight against the Greeks and turned against the Armenians. Shortly thereafter, Karabekir appeared on the Armenian frontier. The Republic was taken unawares; Olti fell, followed by Kars, and other strongholds were threatened. According to arrangements between the British and the Tashnak government, a considerable number of the guns of Kars had been sent to Denikin for use against the Bolsheviks. The Armenian soldiers made no serious effort to defend the city, despite the fact that they had ample war material, including 10,000 rifles supplied by the Greek government. Several commanding officers and about 4,000 soldiers were taken prisoners. The Turks looted and massacred the defenseless population. Karabekir had such an easy conquest of the fortified city that Alexandropol was the next victim. The district of Surmalu had also fallen, and Erevan was in danger.

The Republic reeled under these crushing blows. Khatisian was sent to Tiflis to beg the British for help. But no one was willing to help. The British representative, General Stokes, still insisted that Armenia's only course was to make terms with the Russians.

But the leaders refused to heed his advice. Instead, Prime Minister Ohanchanian sent S. Kulkhantarian, Alexander Khatsian and Colonel Ghorghanian to Karabekir to ask for armistice terms. The Prime Minister, like the Minister of War, was unaware of the situation of the Armenian army and the disposition of the soldiers who wanted the protection of Russia. More tragic still, the leaders were not in harmony as to what steps to take. The capital did not know what was going on at the front. Vratzian in his book says "We did not do anything to avoid this war; on the contrary, we were the immediate cause of it. The most unfavorable point was that we were ignorant of the actual strength of the Turks and we could not evaluate our own forces."

The terms of the armistice imposed by the Turkish army were severe. "To accept them would have been tantamount to ceding more than half of the Armenian territory to the enemy and to disarming our army." However, resorting to arms again would have been suicidal, therefore the government was forced to accept Karabekir's harsh terms. On November 18, 1920, they not only ceded much territory, but also surrendered 2,000 rifles, 20 heavy and 40 light cannon, 4,000 mules, 1,000 cases of shells, 6,000 grenades, two steam locomotives and 50 railroad cars.

While the situation on the Turkish front was so critical there was a second antagonist beyond. This was the Bolshevik movement at the frontier of Azerbaijan, spreading toward the southeast, a serious menace to the tottering Republic. In fact, the Bolsheviks were actually at the northern shore of Lake Sevan. In the districts of Ghazakh and Karavanserai, the Armenian peasants had risen in arms and were playing an important role in the downfall of the government. A mixed Bolshevik army entered Armenia through the mountain passes of Aghstafa, were reinforced in November, and marched into Itchévan, Shamshatin and Dilijan; on the 28th, Karavanserai fell; on the 29th the rebels declared Armenia a Soviet Republic while they had not yet captured Erevan. The news was telegraphed immediately to Lenin. The leaders of the Red Army were Anastas Mikoyan and Kirov; Hovhannes Bagramyan, a young cavalry officer was accompanying them.

The Island and Monastery of Lake Sevan

III. The Final Period

The Last Days of the Republic

There were 203 delegates in the Armenian National Council assembled in Tiflis, of which 103 belonged to the Tashnak party. This group held the reins of the country and the government. The second group was the Popular party, which although not great in numbers included many intellectuals. From the day of independence, May 28th 1918, this group demanded that they be given an equal voice in the government, but they were ignored.

The third party was that of the Bolsheviks, who, noting the victory of the peasants and workers in Russia, wanted a similar regime in Armenia. Many of the leaders of this group were Russian Bolsheviks who did not wish to see Trans-Caucasus separated from Russia. The Bolsheviks were shouting that the Mensheviks in Georgia, the Mussavatists in Azerbaijan and the Tashnaks in Armenia were being used as the tools of the western Imperialist countries and were exploiting the workers.

The first serious Bolshevik movement in Armenia started in May, 1920. Then the rebellion spread to Alexandropol, Kars, Sarikamish and Nor Bayazit. Workers and a great number of the soldiers favored the new order. The Prime Minister Khatisian resigned and Hamo Ohanchanian succeeded him, but the real control of the government was in the Tashnak Bureau, which took over the job of crushing the rebellion. In that month the Armenian Republic sent a delegation to Moscow with Levon Shant as chairman. It was his duty to see Tchicherin, the Foreign Minister, with the aim of establishing friendly relations with the Bolsheviks and to win recognition of the Armenian Republic. These negotiations were long-drawn out and fruitless.

In October, Lenin and Tchicherin sent one LeGrand to Armenia with a delegation consisting of forty high-ranking officials, among them Sahak Der Kalousidan and Ashot Hovhannessian. This delegation continued the negotiations initiated by Levon Shant. LeGrand suggested that Armenians accept the Soviet regime and join the Russians in order to regain the Armenian boundaries of 1914 from Turkey. Boghos Nubar Pasha in Paris was also advising the Armenian government to come to an understanding with the Russians. These suggestions were flatly refused by the ruling clique.

Many days passed and the negotiations with LeGrand finally ended in futility. The Russian communist party was following the events in Armenia with apprehension, as the Turks were spreading havoc and terror all around and were approaching the Armenian capital. Stalin wired Kirov and Mikoyan in Baku to rescue Armenia; "It is urgent to save Armenia at any cost; Armenia should be liberated as promptly as possible," he said. Upon this order, the Bolshevist movement was intensified while the Turks had reached the gates of Erevan.

On November 25th, Ohanchanian and the Tashnak Bureau relinquished their powers and Simeon Vratsian, the chief of the Bureau was elected Premier. To halt the Turkish army, he sent Khatisian to Alexandropol to meet Karabekir and arrange an armistice. In the meanwhile he called an extraordinary council (Nov. 30-Dec. 1) with government and party officials dominating it, to decide whether Armenia should adopt Russian or Turkish orientation. The majority voted for the Russian tie. Immediately following the decision, Vratzian informed LeGrand that Armenia had now become an "Independent Socialist Republic." The next day, December 2nd, 1920 an agreement was signed with LeGrand, according to which Armenia should have a Soviet regime; the Republican army should not be held responsible for its past opposition, the members of the Tashnak party should not be persecuted; on the contrary, two members of the party would be admitted to the ministerial cabinet and Dro, another member, would be appointed military governor of Erevan. Thereupon, Vratsian and his government withdrew from office, after serving only seven days. The Turks remained static for the moment, waiting watchfully. On December 6th, the Revolutionary Committee arrived in Erevan under the presidency of Gassian, to whom Dro surrendered the reins of government.

Treaty of Alexandropol; February Revolution

It was at Alexandropol that the Turks and the Armenian delegation under Khatisian first heard of the bolshevization of Armenia. Karabekir was urging the delegation to sign the armistice the same day. It is rumored that Khatisian telephoned Erevan, asking whether he should sign the armistice, and received an answer, attributed to Vratsian, that he was authorized to do so. It is a known fact that sixteen hours after the bolshevization of Armenia, toward midnight on December 2nd, Khatisian signed the Alexandropol treaty, which can be summarized as follows:

"Turkey recognizes the independence of Armenia; the Armenians yield their rights in the Sèvres Treaty (that is to say the cause of Turkish Armenia); the Akhourian river will be the boundary between the two countries; the Armenian army will not have more than 1,500 soldiers; military service will not be compulsory; the gendarmerie will be responsible for internal security; Turkey will defend Armenia against attack; Sharour and Nakhitchevan will be autonomous territories under Turkish protection," etc.

Scarcely three months later, there occurred a civil war in Armenia known as the February revolt, which claimed thousands of new sacrifices from a bleeding people. The opposing sides have different versions of this ghastly event. The Armenian Bolsheviks accuse the Tashnak party of inciting the people to rebellion, that Vratsian organized a "Liberation Committee" whose sole aim was to overthrow the communist regime. His immediate colleagues were Rupen "Pasha" and commander Nezhteh, who was in Zangezur. On the other hand, the Tashnaks accuse the Bolsheviki of persecuting their members, beating and shooting their former opponents, thus forcing the people to defend themselves.

398

The Tashnak revolt lasted about 45 days — from February 18th to April 2nd, 1921. It is reported that this fratricidal war cost the unhappy nation more than 20,000 lives. Through an unfortunate twist of fate, there was simultaneously a conference in Moscow between the Russians and the Turks, and another in London between British and Turks. To both of these conferences Vratsian who had again become the Armenian Premier, sent telegrams confirming the treaty of Alexandropol. But while Vratsian was dispatching these messages, A. Aharonian, the delegate of the Armenian Republic declared before the Allied Supreme Council on February 26th that he and the government he represented "do absolutely reject the treaty of Alexandropol."

This dissension had a disastrous effect on the cause of Turkish Armenia.

However, when the Bolshevik army reached Erevan, the Tashnak revolt was crushed, and Vratsian fled to the mountains of Sewnik carrying with him the treasury of the Republic. After a futile attempt to set up an independent government in Zangezur, he and his followers moved on to the city of Tabriz in Persia.

Lenin thereupon sent Alexander Miasnikian to pacify Armenia and establish a stable government there, on the Soviet pattern.

Bibliography

Abeghian, M., *History of the Ancient Armenian Literature,* 2 vols., Erevan, 1944, 1946.

— *The Fools of Sassoun,* 2 vols., Erevan, 1936, 1942.

Adontz, N., *Armeniia v Epokhu Iustiniana,* St. Petersburg, 1908.

— *Mashtotz and his Disciples, according to Foreign Sources,* Vienna, 1925.

— *Histoire d'Arménie,* Paris, 1946.

Aidinian, P. A., Fr., *Critical Grammar of Modern Armenian.* Vienna, 1866.

Ajarian, M., *The Armenian Letters of the Alphabet,* Vienna, 1913, 1927.

— *Sources of the History of St. Mesrop and the Invention of the Alphabetic Characters,* Paris, 1907.

Akinian, P. N., Fr., *Classic Armenian and the Mekhitarists of Vienna,* Vienna, 1932.

— *The Vartabed Eghishé and his History,* Vienna, 1932, 1936.

— *The Catholicos Movses III of Etchmiadzin and his Times, 1567-1633,* Vienna, 1935.

Alboyadjian, A., *History of Armenian Schools,* Cairo, 1947.

Alishan, P. L., Fr., *Shnorhali and his Family,* Venice, 1873.

— *Sissouan, or Description of Armenian Cilicia,* Venice, 1885. [*Sissouan ou I'Arméno-Cilicie,* Venice, 1899]

— *Sissakan or Province of Sewniq,* Venice, 1893.

— *Armenian Sophers* (Little pieces), 24 vols., Venice, 1853, 1854, 1861, 1933, 1934.

— *Description of Airarat,* Venice, 1890.

— *Hayapatoum* (Armenian stories), Venice, 1901-1902.

— *The Canton of Shirak,* Venice, 1881.

— *Souvenirs of the Armenian Homeland,* 2 vols., Venice, 1869, 1870.

Arakelian, B. N., Hovhannisian, A. R., *History of Armenia from the Paleolithic Age to the End of the Eighth Century B.C.,* Erevan, 1951.

Arpiarian, A., *History of Literature of Armenians in Turkey in the XIXth Century,* Cairo, 1944.

Aslan, Kevork, *Historic Studies of the Armenian People,* [*Études historiques sur le peuple arménien*] Paris, 1928.

Astourian, P., Fr., *Political Relations between Armenia and Rome, 190 B.C. to 428 A.D.,* Freiburg, 1911.

Balgian, A., Fr., *History of the Catholic Doctrine Among the Armenians and of their Union with the Church of Rome,* Vienna, 1878.

Bedrosian, H., *Bibliography of the Sovietic Esthetic Literature,* Erevan, 1949.

Blackwell, Alice Stone, *Armenian Poems,* Translation, Boston, 1917.

Bodourian, H. M., *The Armenian Press for 15 Years, 1894-1909,* Venice, 1910.

Boré, Eugene, *Letters of a Traveller in the Orient,* 2 vols., Paris, 1840.

Boyajian, Zabelle, *Armenian Legends and Poems,* with an introduction by James Viscount Bryce, and a chapter on "Armenia, its Epics, Folk-Songs and Medieval Poetry" by Aram Raffi, London, 1916.

Brosset, M., *Two Armenian Historians, Kirakos of Gantzac (1200-1272) and Oukhtanes of Ourha, a tenth Century Syrian,* St. Petersburg, 1870-1871.

— *The Historian Thomas Ardzrouni,* St. Petersburg, 1862.

— *The Historian Mekhitar of Airivank,* St. Petersburg, 1865.

— *Collection of Armenian Historians,* St. Petersburg, 1874-76.

Bryce, James, Viscount, *Treatment of Armenians in the Ottoman Empire, 1915-16. Documents presented to Viscount Grey of Fallodon,* London, 1916.

Bugge, S., *On Etymology and Explanation of the Armenian Language,* Christiana, 1889.

Carrière, A., *New Sources of Moses of Khoren; Critical Studies,* Vienna, 1893.

Conybeare, F. C., *The Key of Truth, a Manual of the Paulician Church of Armenia,* Oxford, 1898.

— *A Collection with the Ancient Versions of Greek Text of Aristotle's Categories, and Porphyry's Introduction,* Oxford, 1892.

Dadian, B., *Contemporary Armenian Society.* Extract from *Revue des Deux Mondes,* Paris, 1867.

Daghbashian, H., *Pavstos Puzantatsi and the Falsifiers of his Studies of Sources of Khorenatsi,* Vienna, 1898.

Daschian, H., Fr., *Catalog of Armenian Manuscripts in the Mekhitarist Library of Vienna,* Vienna, 1896.

— *Study of Classic Armenian; Period of Oral Literature,* Vienna, 1920.

Der Nersessian Sirarpie, *Armenia and the Byzantine Empire,* Harvard Univ. Press, 1945.

Dodomiantz, V., *The Role of the Armenians in World Civilization,* Belgrade, 1938.

Dulaurier, Edw., *Collection of the Historians of the Crusaders and Armenian Documents,* Paris, 1869.

— *Political, Religious and Administrative Organizations of the Kingdom of Lesser Armenia during the Crusades,* Paris, 1862.

— *Popular Songs and Traditions of Ancient Armenia,* Paris, 1852.

— *History, Dogma, Traditions and Liturgy of the Armenian Church,* Paris, 1859.

Emin, J. B., *The Armenian Alphabet,* translated from the Russian by E. Prud'homme, Paris, 1865.

Esoff, G. (Esiants), *A Glance at the Study of the Armenian Language in Europe,* Leyden, 1890. (Armenian scholar, assistant to the Minister of Enlightenment in Russia. Discovered history of Jehan Dardel, confessor to the last King of Cilician Armenia.)

Eusebius. Regarded as the father of ecclesiastical history. Attended Council of Nicaea in 325.

Funduklian, K., *Life of Mashtotz, by Korioun,* Jerusalem, 1930.

Garabedian, R., Fr., *Complete List of Armenian Newspapers, 1794-1921*, Vienna, 1924.

Ghazikian, A., Fr., *Armenian Bibliography and Encyclopedia of Armenian Life, 1512-1912*, 2 vols., Venice, 1905, 1912.

Gibbon, Edward, *History of the Decline and Fall of the Roman Empire*, London, 1776-1788.

Goode, A., *A Brief Account of the Mekhitarist Society*, Venice, 1835.

Grousset, René, *History of Armenia from the Beginning to 1071*, Paris, 1947.

Gulesserian, P., Coadjutor-Catholikos of Cilicia, *Historical and Literary Studies of the Patriarch Golod*, Vienna, 1904.

— *Critical Study of Eghishé*, Vienna, 1900.

Gutschmid, A., *Little Writings*, 5 vols., Leipzig, 1899-1894.

— *Agathangelos*, Leipzig, 1877.

— *Moses of Koren*, Leipzig, 1877.

Hatsouni, P. V., Fr., *Education among the Ancient Armenians*, Venice, 1923.

— *Khorenatsi restored to the Vth Century*, Venice, 1935.

Hennig, Hans, *Explorations in Hittite Asia Minor*, Chicago, University, Chicago, 1929.

Hovnanian, P., *Research in the Vulgar Speech of our Ancestors*, 2 vols., Vienna, 1897.

Huebschmann, H., *Armenian Studies*, Leipzig, 1883.

Inglisian, P. V., Fr., *Mekhitar, the Servant of God*, Vienna, 1929.

Injijian, P. Gh., Fr., *Antiquities of Armenia*, Venice, 1835.

Iorga, N. (Prime Minister of Rumania), *The Kingdom of Lesser Armenia from 1080 to 1375*.

Jarian, A., Fr., *History of the Church by Eusebius, explained by New Translations from the Syrian*, Venice, 1877.

Jivanian, N., *Armenian Encyclopedic Dictionary, Historical, Geographical and Mythological, Supplement of Armenian Proper Names,* Constantinople, 1879.

— *Critical History of Eghishé.*

Kalemkiarian, G., Fr., *The More Recent Sources on Eznik of Goghp,* Vienna, 1919.

— *History of Armenian Journalism, 1796-1860,* Vienna, 1893.

Kalousdian, H. Krikor, *Marash or Kermanig and Hero-Zeitoun, Topography and History,* New York, 1934.

Karekin, Bishop of Trebizond, *The Light of the World among the Armenians,* Vol. I, Paris, 1936; Vol. II, Buenos Aires, 1939.

Karst, J., *Historical Grammar of Cilician Armenia,* Strasbourg, 1901.

Khalatiants, B., *Armenian Literature of the XIXth Century,* Heidelberg, 1905.

— *Armenian Popular Epics,* Vienna, 1903.

Khalatiants, G., *Critical Study of the Recent Sources of Moses Khorenatsi,* Vienna, 1896.

— *Zenob of Glak, Comparative Study,* Vienna, 1893.

— *Ghazar Parbetsi and His Works,* Moscow, 1883.

Kheroumian, R., *Introduction to the Anthropology of Caucasus; the Armenians,* Paris, 1943.

Kibarian, G., Fr., *History of Armenian Literature from the Beginning to 1300,* Venice, 1944.

Lacrose, M., Armenian Dictionary, 2 vols., Berlin, about 1735.

Lagarde, P. De, *A Philological Trial,* Berlin, 1854.

— *Armenian Studies,* Göttingen, 1877.

Langlois, V., *Collection of Armenian Historians, Ancient and Modern,* 2 vols., Paris, 1867.

Laurent, J., *Armenia between Byzantine and Islam,* Paris, 1919.

Leo (A. Babakhanian), *Literature of the Armenians of Russia,* Venice, 1904.

Liden, E., *Armenian Studies,* Gottenberg, 1906.

Lynch, H. F. B., *Armenia, Travels and Studies,* 2 vols., London, 1901.

Macler, F., *Stories and Legends of Armenia,* Paris, 1911.

Malkhassian, S., *Study of the History of Pavstos Puzantatsi,* Vienna, 1896. (His Armenian dictionary in 4 vols., 125,000 words, was printed in Erevan, second edition in Beirut.)

Manandian, H., *The Hellenistic School and the Phases of its Development,* Vienna, 1928.

— *The Enigma of Khorenatsi Resolved,* Erevan, 1934.

Mariès, L., *Eznik de Goghp, Literary and Critical Studies,* Paris, 1924.

Marquart, J., *On the Origin of the Armenian Alphabet in Connection with the Biography of St. Mashtotz,* Vienna, 1917.

Marr, N., *Materials for a History of Armenian Literature,* St. Petersburg, 1894, 1899.

Meillet, A., *Armenian Studies,* Paris, 1922.

— *The Armenian Language,* Paris, 1918.

— *Introduction to the Comparative Study of Indo-European Languages,* Paris, 1915.

— *Outline of a Comparative Grammar of Classic Armenia,* Vienna, 1903.

Mekhitarian, K., *A Quarter of a Century of Literature,* Cairo, 1946.

Morgan, Jacques de, *History of the Armenian People from the Earliest Times to our Day,* Paris, 1919.

Nansen, F., *Armenia and the Near-East,* Paris, 1928.

Neumann, C. F., *An Essay of a History of Armenian Literature,* Leipzig, 1836.

Ormanian, M., Patriarch, *Azgapatoum. History of the Armenian Church and Literature,* 3 vols., I and II, Constantinople, 1913, 1914; III, Jerusalem, 1912.

Oshagan, H., *Synoptic Tableau of Western Armenian Literature*, Jerusalem, 1945.

— *The Diaspora and the True Poetry*, Jerusalem, 1945.

Pailakian, A., Fr., *History of the Armenian Church*, Paris, 1942.

Pastamiants, V., Vartabed, *The Law Book of Mekhitar Gosh*, Vagarshapat, 1880.

Patkanian, E., *Researches in the Formation of the Armenian Language*, Paris, 1871.

Portoukal, Pasha Mikael, *Critical Study in the History of Eghishé*, Venice, 1903.

St. Martin, J., *Historical and Geographical Memoirs of Armenia*, 2 vols., Paris, 1818, 1819.

Salmaslian, A., *Bibliography of Armenia*, Paris, 1946.

Sandaljian, J., *Documentary History of Armenia*, 2 vols., Rome, 1917.

Sarkissian, P., Fr., *Two Hundred Years of Activity of the Congregation of Venice*, Venice, 1905.

Sassouni, G., *History of Modern Western Armenians*, 1840-1914, Beirut, 1951.

Sebeos, Bishop, *History of Emperor Heraclius*, published in Constantinople, 1851.

Tchamtchian, M., Fr., *History of Armenia*, 3 vols., Venice, 1781-1786.

Tchirakian, K., Fr., *Armenian Men of Letters of the XIXth Century; Armenian Writers of Russia*, Venice, 1904.

Tchobanian, A., *Armenian Rosary*, Paris, 1918-1929.

— *Armenian Troubadours*, Paris, 1906.

— *Armenian Poems, Ancient and Modern*, Paris, 1902.

Ter-Boghosian, A., *Observations of the History of Pavstos Puzantatsi*, Vienna, 1901, 1919.

Ter-Mikaelian, A., *The Armenian Church in its Relation to the Byzantine from the IVth to the XIIIth Centuries*, Leipzig, 1892.

— *Armenian Studies on its Hymnarium,* Leipzig, 1905.

Ter-Minassian, E., *The Armenian Church in its relationship to the Syrian, up to the XIIIth Century,* Leipzig, 1904.

Thorossian, H., Fr., *Life of Abbot Mekhitar,* Venice, 1901.

Thorossian, H., *History of Armenian Literature,* Paris, 1951.

Torkom, Coushakian, Patriarch of Jerusalem, *The Biography of Patriarch Eghishé Tourian.*

Tournebize, F., *Political and Religious History of Armenia from the beginning to the death of its last King in 1393 in Paris,* [*Histoire politique et religieuse de l'Arménie depuis les origines des Arménies jusqu'à la mort de leur dernier roi (l'an 1393)*] Paris, 1919.

Tourian, Eghishé, Patriarch, *History of Armenian Literature,* Jerusalem, 1933.

Vetter, P., Moses of Koren, N.P., 1893.

— *The Old National Songs of Armenia,* Tübingen, 1894.

Weber S., *The Catholic Church in Armenia,* Freiburg-im-Breisgau, 1903.

Windischmann, F., *The Ground of Aryan Root Language,* Berlin, n.d.

Zarbhanelian, K., Fr., *Literary History of Armenia, Ancient and Modern,* Venice, 1865, 1878, 1886, 1897, 1905, 1932.

www.ingramcontent.com/pod-product-compliance
Lightning Source LLC
Chambersburg PA
CBHW031230090426
42742CB00007B/140